D0560028

The Kennedy Assassination Cover-Up

WITHDRAWN
Monroe Coll. Library

The Kennedy Assassination Cover-Up

Donald Gibson

Nova Science Publishers, Inc.
Huntington, NY

Editorial Production: Susan Boriotti
Office Manager: Annette Hellinger
Graphics: Frank Grucci and Jennifer Lucas
Information Editor: Tatiana Shohov
Book Production: Patrick Davin, Cathy DiGregory, Donna Dennis and Lynette Van Helden
Circulation: Lisa DiGangi and Michael Pazy Mino

Library of Congress Cataloging-in-Publication Data

Gibson, Donald.
The Kennedy Assassination Cover-Up / Donald Gibson.
   p.cm.
Includes bibliographical references (p.) and index.
ISBN 1-56072-727-6.
1. Kennedy, John F. (John Fitzgerald), 1917-1963—Assassination. 2. Conspiracies—United States—History—20th century. I. Title

E842.9 .G53 1999
364.15'24'092—dc21

                    99-042491

Copyright © 2000 by Nova Science Publishers, Inc.
         227 Main Street, Suite 100
         Huntington, New York 11743
         Tele. 631-424-6682   Fax 631-424-4666
         E Mail Novascil@aol.com

All rights reserved. No part of this book may be reproduced, stored in a retrieval system or transmitted in any form or by any means: electronic, electrostatic, magnetic, tape, mechanical photocopying, recording or otherwise without permission from the publishers.

The authors and publisher have taken care in preparation of this book, but make no expressed or implied warranty of any kind and assume no responsibility for any errors or omissions. No liability is assumed for incidental or consequential damages in connection with or arising out of information contained in this book.

This publication is designed to provide accurate and authoritative information with regard to the subject matter covered herein. It is sold with the clear understanding that the publisher is not engaged in rendering legal or any other professional services. If legal or any other expert assistance is required, the services of a competent person should be sought. FROM A DECLARATION OF PARTICIPANTS JOINTLY ADOPTED BY A COMMITTEE OF THE AMERICAN BAR ASSOCIATION AND A COMMITTEE OF PUBLISHERS.

Printed in the United States of America

DEDICATION

I am dedicating this book to all of this country's leaders who lost their lives while they were engaged in an effort to develop themselves and to serve their fellow human beings. Included among those leaders are Alexander Hamilton, Abraham Lincoln, Huey Long, John Kennedy, Malcolm X, Martin Luther King, and Robert Kennedy. They all struggled to promote the general welfare.

CONTENTS

PREFACE   xi

ACKNOWLEDGMENTS   xiii

ABOUT THE AUTHOR   xv

CHAPTER ONE: THE "WARREN REPORT" - AN AMALGAM
    OF IMPROBABILITIES AND IMPOSSIBILITIES   1
    The Official Story   4
    Improbability, Impossibility, and the Warren Commission's
        Conclusion   5

CHAPTER TWO: THE FIRST 72 HOURS   15
    A Real Rush to Judgment: Media Frenzy or Foul Play?   22
    The Media Solves the Case From Afar   27
    Belmont and Hoover   34

CHAPTER THREE: THE CREATION OF THE "WARREN
    COMMISSION   45
    The House Select Committee's Tale   47
    A More Accurate Story   50
    Creating the Warren Commission   54

CHAPTER FOUR: THE MCCLOY-DULLES COMMISSION   89
    The McCloy-Dulles Commission and the Real Pecking Order   90
    Shaping the Investigation   98
    The Commission's Work: Dusting the Evidence   104
    The Magic Bullet   112

Some Other Examples: Dusting On   116
Summary   122

CHAPTER FIVE: THE COVER-UP WAS AN ESTABLISHMENT
PROJECT   **125**
The Network   126

CHAPTER SIX: LONG AND KENNEDY   **139**
Long and His Opposition   148
Assassination   152

CHAPTER SEVEN: FROM HUEY LONG TO CLAY SHAW   **161**
Butler and Ochsner: Establishment Right-Wingers   162
The Higher Powers   165
Freeport Sulphur and the Establishment   168
Boston South   173
Racists and Aristocrats   174
United Fruit and the Drug Trade   176
Shaw's Significance   179

CHAPTER EIGHT: INTERNATIONALISM AND THE
KENNEDY ASSASSINATION   **181**
International House   181
Institute of Pacific Relations, An IH Sister   187
International Trade Mart   192
IPR and Oswald's Cousin   194
Conclusion   202

CHAPTER NINE: ESTABLISHMENT RADICALS AND
KENNEDY: LAMONT, CHOMSKY, AND RUSSELL   **203**
The Ever Curious Corliss   204
Oswald's Lamont Pamphlet   207
Lord Russell   210
Russell and the Kennedy Assassination   214
The British Who Killed Kennedy Committee   216
Rethinking Chomsky   218

CHAPTER TEN: THE INFORMATION AND DISINFORMATION
AGE   **225**
Confused and Not So Confused Critics, Honest and Dishonest   229

CHAPTER ELEVEN: THE BEGINNING   **247**
   Kennedy At War With The Establishment   251
   Kennedy's Stock Plummets on Wall Street   259
   Conclusion and Beginning   266

BIBLIOGRAPHY   **271**
INDEX   **293**

PREFACE

In 1993 I was finishing a book about President Kennedy's conflicts with some of the world's wealthiest and most powerful groups of people. The work that I did for that book over a five year period rekindled my interest in the assassination.

Like most Americans, I thought that the official story was probably false. I had over the years read a few books about the assassination. Once I had systematically reviewed Kennedy's policies, many of which had been given little or no previous attention, I knew there were many reasons for his assassination. I had also gained a much greater appreciation of and respect for Kennedy as a person and a president. The real Kennedy turned out to be better than most of the images of him, even the positive ones.

He actually did try to do, with considerable success, what he had promised to do while campaigning for the presidency. He said he would get the country moving again. Just weeks after taking office he sent a message to Congress entitled "Program to Restore Momentum to the American Economy." This action represented his general intentions and was the first of many initiatives that he undertook as part of his effort to promote economic progress.

Once I understood the significance of his presidency, I also began to see the assassination in a new way. From World War Two to the early-1970s, the U.S. enjoyed an unprecedented level of prosperity. Most people got something out of this prosperity. That long period featured two short but intense periods of improvements in the nation's productive powers. Those occurred during World War Two and in the years 1962 to 1966. Those two short periods were likely the source of much or most of our post-war prosperity.

Since Kennedy's death, we have been sliding into the stagnation and decay of a post-industrial society. Our globally oriented financiers, titans of big business, and upper-class families have decided that our nation's fate will be tied to the semi-free markets that they spend much of their time trying to manipulate. Those interests are not committed to the nation's general welfare nor to the betterment of humankind.

President Kennedy's death brought to an end one battle for economic progress. It is up to each of us to do whatever we can to commence a new battle.

ACKNOWLEDGMENTS

I want to thank the following people for reading part or all of this book at various stages of its development, and for their critical and encouraging comments: Robert Burtt, James DiEugenio, Peggy Gibson, Mark McColloch, Ed Mulready, Lisa Pease, L. Fletcher Prouty, Harold Weisberg. When I turned my attention from Kennedy's presidency to his assassination, it was in the writings of people who had an appreciation of Kennedy's goals that I found leads for the present work. Harold Weisberg's destruction of the Warren Report, L. Fletcher Prouty's arguments about Vietnam policy and the breakdown in Kennedy's security, and James DiEugenio's investigation of events in New Orleans all played a role in stimulating my research for this book.

ABOUT THE AUTHOR

Donald Gibson is Professor of Sociology at the Greensburg campus of the University of Pittsburgh. He earned his Ph.D. in sociology from the University of Delaware and began his teaching career at Oberlin and Middlebury Colleges. He is the author of *Battling Wall Street: The Kennedy Presidency* and his articles have appeared in numerous academic journals.

Professor Gibson was born and raised in the Philadelphia area. He served as a communications analyst in the U.S. Air Force during the 1960s. He is married and lives in western Pennsylvania.

Chapter One

THE "WARREN REPORT" - AN AMALGAM OF IMPROBABILITIES AND IMPOSSIBILITIES

President Kennedy was what his most powerful critics claimed - "the enforcer of progress." In the interest of promoting the general welfare, President Kennedy proposed a multitude of changes. All of the changes were intended to increase the productive powers of the United States as a nation and of people around the world. He undertook this Promethean task aware that there would be opposition; he probably underestimated the depth and intensity of that opposition.

Kennedy made a valiant and partially successful effort to implement policies that would improve the lives of tens of millions of people. He wanted to be President in order to do that. While he was campaigning for the office Kennedy said that:

> The responsibility of the President, therefore, is especially great. He must serve as a catalyst, an energizer, the defender of the public good and the public interest against all the narrow private interests which operate in our society. Only the President can do this, and only a President who recognizes the true nature of this hard challenge can fulfill this historic function.[1]

He believed that the office of President provided the power to achieve the public good. Kennedy said:

[1.] Burns, p. 254.

> I believe that our system of checks and balances, our whole constitutional
> system, can only operate under a strong President. The Constitution is a very
> wise document. It permits the President to assume just about as much power
> as he is capable of handling. If he fails, it is his fault, not the system's. I
> believe that the President should use whatever power is necessary to do the
> job unless it is expressly forbidden by the Constitution.[2]

As we will see in the final chapter, Kennedy did try to use the powers of
the Presidency to defend the public good against those narrow interests. For
now, a very brief description of those efforts will serve as background. In
office, Kennedy proposed a wide range of initiatives and changes which were
intended to energize the U.S. economy. He also attempted to eliminate special
provisions in the tax laws that benefited only the rich or actually encouraged
the rich to invest in ways that undermined the nation's economy.[3] In addition,
he took actions or proposed actions to stimulate progress in a variety of
technical and scientific areas, including the development of nuclear energy
technologies.[4] To support this, he recommended a series of new educational
programs and goals.[5]

President Kennedy also tried to use the federal budget to stimulate
advances in production. This included the allocation and distribution of
resources and overall spending levels. He went beyond Keynesian policies in
his recommendation to incur deficits during a growth period and, more
importantly, in the multitude of specific proposals he was making to influence
investment decisions. Strictly Keynesian policy was much more passive than
Kennedy's program.[6] Also, Kennedy was apparently bypassing the Federal
Reserve System by injecting money into the economy through the Treasury
Department.[7] The Federal Reserve, closely tied to the major banks, usually
controls the introduction of new money into the economy by lending it to the
banks.

[2.] Ibid., p. 255.

[3.] Kennedy, 1961d, pp. 6-9; 1962, pp. 100, 112-13; 1963a, pp. 2-3; 1963b, pp. 16-21.

[4.] Kennedy, 1961a, pp. 11-13; 1961b, pp. 2-6; 1962a, pp. 8-10

[5.] Bernstein, p. 242; Kennedy, 1963, pp. 6-7.

[6.] Heller, pp. 30-31; Kennedy, 1961a, pp. 6-7; 1961d, p. 3; 1962, pp. 90-94, 104-7; 1963,
p. 6; 1964, p. 203; Schlesinger, pp. 1002-3.

[7.] Marrs, p. 275.

In his international policy, President Kennedy proposed a development effort for Latin America, named the Alliance for Progress. In his overall foreign policy, he tried to disengage the United States from the neo-colonialist alliances and commitments supported by his banking and big business opponents in New York and Boston. In practice, neo-colonialism meant that the U.S. government was asked to enforce a policy of keeping countries poor, underdeveloped, and open to outside domination and exploitation. Kennedy refused to use military power or the threat of it to support the foreign economic interests of upper class groups and he rejected neo-colonial goals.[8]

In less than three years Kennedy achieved quite a bit.[9] Among other things, he got his investment tax credit passed, rapidly expanded overall spending for research and development, created a major space program, introduced successful legislation to expand educational institutions and opportunities, and he was reshaping foreign policy. The United States was in the midst of one of the best five year periods (1962 through 1966) in its history.[10]

The assassination of President Kennedy was also the termination of his policies. Most or all of the basic economic policies were changed within about two years of the assassination. Some things changed in just the week following Kennedy's death. Kennedy's budget was scaled back and there were detectable changes in foreign policy, changes that became blatant during the next eighteen months. We will return to these changes at the end of our story.

The official authority on the assassination of President Kennedy was the President's Commission on the Assassination of President Kennedy, usually referred to in a misleading way as the Warren Commission. As we will see, the Commission's Chairman, Supreme Court Chief Justice Earl Warren was far from the most influential member of that Commission. That Commission, with an important contribution from elements of the FBI, did produce the official story, i.e., that Lee Harvey Oswald, acting alone, fired three shots, two of which hit the President. As we will see, the Commission did not originate this story; it was disseminated even before President Johnson could be talked into creating a commission. This official story never was credible or even plausible.

[8] Gibson, 1994, pp. 35-87; Sorensen, p. 602.
[9] Gibson, 1994; Bernstein.
[10] Kendrick.

THE OFFICIAL STORY

Never in history have such crimes been "solved" by such a consistent disregard for truth, honesty and credibility, with so much avoidance of the obvious and such dependence upon the incredible and palpably undependable, with such a prostitution of science, and with so much help from misrepresentation and perjury. (Harold Weisberg)[11]

The Warren Commission developed and presented to the world a most improbable story. In fact, major elements of the story were based on impossibilities. That story, of course, was that Lee Harvey Oswald, acting without accomplices, fired three shots in approximately six seconds from the sixth floor of the Texas School Book Depository. One of the shots hit President Kennedy and Governor John Connally and, after this shot, another one hit the President in the head.[12]

The President's Commission on the Assassination of President Kennedy, was not obligated to establish Oswald's guilt beyond a reasonable doubt; this was not a trial proceeding. They did not establish Oswald's guilt, even though they asserted it, and the Commission's own evidence indicated there was an abundance of reasons to conclude that Oswald could not have done this alone and much evidence that indicated that he had no direct role in the assassination.[13] Within several years of the publication of the Warren Report in 1964, this official story was thoroughly discredited. The Commission's conclusions were shown to be a compilation of plausibilities, implausibilities, improbabilities, and impossibilities.

The destruction of the Warren Commission's story was done in two ways. First, it was shown in a conclusive and overwhelming way that the conclusions of the Commission were inconsistent with the Commission's own presentation of the facts and evidence. Second, it was demonstrated that the Commission ignored, excluded, and suppressed evidence available to it. In the first decade after the assassination, many people contributed to this unpleasant but necessary work.

[11] Weisberg, 1965, p. 7.
[12] Ibid., pp. 167-87.
[13] Fonzi, 1966, p. 38.

The Warren Commission's "conclusion," in the face of some undisclosed internal dissent[14], was that the "shots which killed President Kennedy and wounded Governor Connally were fired by Lee Harvey Oswald."[15] This is an artfully worded statement. There is no use of legal terminology, such as guilty "beyond a reasonable doubt." There are no adjectives, adverbs, or qualifier words. Words like definitely, for certain, beyond a doubt, etc. do not appear. It merely says that a "conclusion" was reached that the shots "were fired by" Oswald. A conclusion can be something like a reasoned judgment or it can be merely a final statement.

What early researchers showed was that this was nothing more than a final statement, a concluding remark. The Commission simply asserted Oswald's guilt. The problem is not that the Commission failed to achieve certainty; this is rare and not even demanded by law in the establishment of guilt. The problem is that the Commission did not even show that there was a probability that its concluding remarks were true. Rather, its own evidence, not to mention the evidence it avoided or suppressed, showed that it was virtually impossible that Oswald did these things.

IMPROBABILITY, IMPOSSIBILITY, AND THE WARREN COMMISSION'S CONCLUSION

If something is probable, it is likely to be true. Our use here of the terms "probability" and "improbability" is not the one familiar to the statistician. In the statistical sense, probability has to do with the likelihood of events in relation to some known or ideal frequencies.[16] That sort of probability, or improbability, had no relevance to most or all of the issues that confronted the Commission. What the Commission was supposed to do, ideally and in conformance with President Johnson's executive order, was to look at all of the relevant facts and evidence and at the relationships between and among those things and render a reasoned judgment, not just concluding remarks, about what most likely happened. This sort of judgment should have flowed directly from answers to certain kinds of questions, questions posed by and

---

[14.] Weisberg, 1995, pp. 226-29, 326.

[15.] President's Commission on the Assassination of President Kennedy, 1964, p. 60.

[16.] Lonergan, 1970, pp. 299-302.

answered satisfactorily by the Commission. Questions like, do our judgments and the account we are constructing make sense in relation to our general stock of knowledge and our experiences? Does the account make sense in relationship to accepted principles in the sciences? In our account, do the events make sense in relationship to each other? Making sense of things, rendering a reasoned judgment, concluding that something probably happened, or could have happened, was dependent on the most careful attention to evidence and on satisfactory answers to those kinds of questions. It is this sort of probability that was or should have been at issue in the Warren Commission's deliberations. Given all the facts, knowledge, and the best reasoning, what probably happened. How did the Commission do?

The Commission concluded that Oswald did it alone, firing the three shots from the Texas School Book Depository. They said there was persuasive evidence that one of the shots caused both Kennedy's neck wound and all of Connally's wounds. In order to arrive at this conclusion, the Commission had to downplay the fact that the time available to Oswald was too short; that the best of marksmen could not do what the not very proficient Oswald allegedly did.[17] The judgment here should have been that it was unlikely, near impossible, that Oswald could have done this.

In order to keep the number of shots down to three, a necessity since the Commission was already stretching things beyond the breaking point in arguing that Oswald had time for the three shots, the Commission had to make a wound in the front of President Kennedy's neck an exit wound. This was also necessary because Oswald was allegedly shooting from behind the President. To keep the number of shots down and to portray the anterior neck wound as one of exit, the Commission simply moved a wound from President Kennedy's back to the back of his neck. This was worse than just an improbable conclusion. The holes in JFK's shirt and suit jacket, the observations by Secret Service and FBI agents at the autopsy, the diagram made at the time of the autopsy by Dr. James Humes, and testimony from another autopsy doctor all put the wound in the back about five or six inches below the neck, where it needed to be in order for the Commission to "conclude" what it did.[18] The Commission could not accept the truth, so they

[17.] Weisberg, 1966, pp. 107, 171; 1995, p. 4.
[18.] Fonzi, 1966, p. 81; Salandria, 1965, pp. 16-22; Weisberg, 1966, pp. 113-14, 119; 1995, pp. 140-49.

did not. They wound up simply asserting that a bullet entered the back of the President's neck and exited the front. The destruction of a first draft of notes for the autopsy report made it easier for the Commission to make such assertions. Dr. Humes burnt those pages.[19]

In the face of strong evidence to the contrary, the Commission now had a bullet going through Kennedy's neck, back to front. This bullet had to do other things. The Commission, a little less emphatic than it sometimes was, said that it was persuaded that this bullet also struck Connally and caused all of his wounds. Even though the Commission did not acknowledge it, this assertion was in fact necessary because there was not enough time for Oswald to have hit Kennedy, when the Commission said he did, and then reload, re-aim and hit Connally. Allen Dulles and John J. McCloy, two of the Commissioners, said that it was they, along with Representative Gerald Ford, who argued that one bullet hit both the President and the Governor. Without this assertion, known later as the single bullet theory, the Commission's entire report was in severe doubt. Three other members of the Commission, Representative Hale Boggs and Senators Cooper and Russell, expressed their doubts about or opposition to this rendition of the events. The final language of the report barely reflected the huge problems in this account and it did not reflect the opposition of three of the Commission's members; it was weighted heavily in favor of the Dulles-McCloy-Ford view.[20]

In order to construct this part of their increasingly improbable story, the Commission had to ignore or downplay the evidence showing that the President and Connally were hit by different bullets. For example, Connally was certain that he heard the shot that hit the President before he was hit. Connally's perceptions were consistent with the photographic evidence, the alignment of the two men relative to the alleged source of the shots, the angles of the wounds in the two men, the fact that the bullet had too little damage done to it for it to have hit both men, and the fact that there seemed to be more fragments in the two men than were missing from this bullet.[21] No problem! The Commission said, anyway, that they were persuaded that one bullet hit both men and caused multiple wounds. In order to get to this point, they had already dismissed the evidence concerning the location of the back wound.

---

19. Weisberg, 1966, pp. 125-26; 1995, pp. 95-109, 165-69.
20. Epstein, 1966, p. 122.
21. Fonzi, 1966, 83; Salandria, 1965, 22-26; Weisberg, 1965, 167-87; 1966, 94-96; 1995, 260-89.

There are still other problems. No whole bullet showed up in either of the two men, or in the car, at least according to the final report. So, where did the bullet that went through both men go? That bullet later designated Commission Exhibit (CE) 399, fortunately turned up elsewhere, back in Parkland Memorial Hospital in Dallas. It allegedly fell out from under a mattress that the Commission arbitrarily decided was the one that Connally had been laying on. This would be the only bullet that could be definitely connected to the rifle allegedly owned and used by Oswald. The evidence for both ownership and use of the gun was very tenuous. It was not and could not be shown that this bullet was fired from the rifle in question on the day of the assassination. This bullet joins the evidence as part of a series of improbabilities and impossibilities, one joined to another.

This would be the bullet which was said to have caused all of the wounds in Connally and at least one in the President. This bullet, found in neither victim, found not at the scene but found after falling from under a mattress, would be the primary evidence linking the shooting to a gun that Oswald may or may not have purchased, may or may not have ever fired, may or may not have taken to the Book Depository.

This bullet allegedly entered the back of the President's neck, not the back where evidence clearly indicated a wound, and came out in the front of the neck. The bullet went on to cause numerous wounds in Connally, leaving all too many fragments in the two men, and somehow got out of Connally's leg and under a mattress.[22] Robert Frazier, the FBI's expert, was surprised to find that there was no trace of blood or tissue on the bullet.[23] All of the improbabilities associated with this bullet must be evaluated in relation to the problems around the location of the wounds and the problems related to the timing and sequence of the shots. The Commission was not only building a house with an extremely weak foundation, or no foundation, but each floor was also constructed out of nothing.

The fortuitous discovery of the (planted?) bullet that could link the gun allegedly owned by Oswald to the assassination and the perhaps convenient destruction of the autopsy notes were not the only unusual events which helped the Commission in making its conclusions. Part of one of the most important pieces of objective evidence considered by the Commission, and much evidence was ignored, was also accidentally destroyed. This accident involved the

---

[22.] Weisberg, 1974, p. 177.
[23.] Fonzi, 1966, p. 84.

destruction of several crucial frames of the film taken of the assassination by Abraham Zapruder. Among the most important frames of this film are those around frame number 210. These frames had an important bearing on when the President was hit and on Oswald's ability to do the shooting. The second issue concerns the fact that Oswald was not able to see clearly or to see at all the President's car until around frame 210 (assuming the camera ran at the speed the Commission assumed it did). When this film was processed by *Life* magazine's photo lab, frames 208 to 211 were destroyed and frame 212 was altered. Although there were copies of the original film, apparently unaltered, in the possession of the FBI and CIA, the Commission used the altered film.[24] If President Kennedy was hit before about frame 210, Oswald could not have been the lone assassin.

Much of the circumstantial evidence indicated that Oswald could not have been on the sixth floor of the Book Depository at the time of the assassination. Harold Weisberg has demonstrated that it would have been extremely difficult, if not impossible, for Oswald to have done the shooting, hidden the rifle where it was later found, and gotten down to the second floor lunchroom where he was seen by Officer Marion Baker immediately after the assassination.[25]

Because there was no eyewitness who could reliably put Oswald on the sixth floor during the minutes immediately preceding the assassination, and the circumstantial evidence suggested that he wasn't, any direct evidence of his whereabouts was obviously important, or should of been important. Amazingly enough there was a photograph taken at about the time of the assassination showing the front of the Depository building. Standing there is someone resembling Oswald and wearing a fairly unusual shirt that looked exactly like the one Oswald happened to be wearing that day. Oswald, with no knowledge of this picture, had claimed while in custody that he had come to the second floor lunchroom, where he encountered Dallas police officer Baker, from the first floor. There was other circumstantial evidence that suggested Oswald came up from the first floor to the second rather than down from the sixth where he allegedly did the shooting.[26] In addition, paraffin tests done on Oswald and tests done later with the rifle indicated that Oswald did not fire a rifle on November

[24.] Weisberg, 1966, pp. 138-9, 215, 219-23; 1976, pp. 20-21, 144; 1995, p. 190.
[25.] Weisberg, 1965, pp. 36-38; 1966, pp. 25, 41-43.
[26.] Weisberg, 1966, pp. 185-94.

22.[27] Like the holes in the President's shirt and suit jacket and the physical evidence relating to the bullet and the shooting itself, this photographic and physical evidence was overridden or ignored.

There were additional problems in the Commission's account of Oswald's behavior and his movements. For example, the Commission claimed that after the assassination and the encounter with officer Baker, Oswald left the Depository and walked seven blocks in a direction away from his destination, his rented room, and then got on a bus headed right back to the Depository building area, which was now a congested area.[28] What he was doing was never explained.

Weisberg demonstrates that if the facts presented in the Commission's volumes are correct, it was impossible for Oswald to get to the scene of Officer Tippit's murder in time to do it.[29] Oswald was seen at another location just before Tippit was shot. The unbelievable speed attributed to Oswald in getting to that murder scene and also from the sixth to the second floor in the Depository building, becomes an unbelievable laggardness in Oswald's trip from the Tippit murder scene to the theater where he would be arrested. Oswald, who was in other parts of the Commission's account a virtual road runner, took thirty minutes to travel the five blocks from the scene of Tippit's murder to the movie theater. Also, in the trip from his rented room to the Tippit murder scene, the Commission again had Oswald initially heading in the wrong direction, waiting briefly for a bus going away from that location.[30] This also was never explained.

Those are some of the significant problems in the Warren Commission's account. There were many others. There were problems in the handling and presentation of medical evidence.[31] The Commission never explained the apparent breakdown in the security arrangements in Dallas on the day of the assassination.[32] Various leads indicating that Oswald had some sort of connection to one or more intelligence organization were not followed up.[33] There were still

---

[27] Weisberg, 1995, pp. 335-37.

[28.] Weisberg, 1965, p. 53.

[29.] Ibid., pp. 52-56; 1966, p. 25.

[30.] Weisberg, 1965, p. 58; 1966, p. 25.

[31.] Wecht, 1972, pp. 28-32; Wecht and Smith, 1974, pp. 105-28.

[32.] Curry; Prouty, 1992, pp. 291-95.

[33.] Garrison, 1988, pp. 48, 66-78.

other areas in which leads were not followed up, the investigation was incomplete, or issues were handled in absurd ways.[34]

The Commission never came close to showing that Oswald, firing three shots from the Depository building, was a lone assassin. Instead, their own evidence, although not their concluding remarks, suggested that it was impossible that this story was true.

If the Commission wanted the truth, they would have deepened and expanded the investigation when confronted with evidence that Oswald could not have done this shooting in six seconds, even if only three shots were fired. They did not. If the Commission wanted the truth, they would have become energetic and determined to clear up the incredible problems in the evidence concerning the wounds and in the evidence suggesting that there were more than three shots fired. They did not. If the Commission was "for real", they would have found these and other problems sufficient to raise serious questions. Most of those involved did not raise those questions. Instead, the Commission bent, ignored, twisted, massaged, misrepresented, and suppressed evidence in order to create their account.

The handling of the evidence relating to wounds, timing, guns and bullets, Oswald, and a host of other things does make sense if the Warren Commission was creating a cover story. Their actions are highly improbable if one assumes or believes that their mission was the construction of a valid account. The Commission, and the FBI, failed to examine seriously and/or to preserve as evidence thousands of frames of film taken at the scene before, during, or after the assassination. As Weisberg points out, this by itself discredits the Commission.[35] The Commission did not even obtain and preserve a direct copy of the original Zapruder film, showing the assassination.[36] The Commission had conflicting information about the speed setting of Zapruder's camera, which had a direct bearing on the timing of the shots, and did not even bother to resolve the conflict.[37]

Neither the Commission nor the FBI followed up information indicating that someone had been passing himself off as Oswald. Information about this from

[34.] Garrison, 1970, pp. 58-65, 101-4, 128-32, 152-56; 1988, pp. 15-21, 54-55, 93-99, 111-12, 196, 209, 216, 244; Meagher, 1967, passim.

[35.] Weisberg, 1976, pp. 30, 42-63, 78-94, 119-20, 136.

[36.] Weisberg, 1966, pp. 212-13.

[37.] Weisberg, 1976, p. 142.

the Dallas police investigators was excluded from the report.[38] Some of the examples of the Commission's mishandling of evidence indicate intent.[39] We will examine some examples of this in Chapter Four. There are examples of work done by individual lawyers wherein the performance is so shoddy that it raises questions about the intent of the lawyers involved or the intent of those giving direction to those lawyers.[40]

The Commission and the FBI failed to investigate a series of relationships that Oswald was involved in while in New Orleans. Since the release of Oliver Stone's movie, *JFK*, a few of these names have become famous. There was information available to the Commission concerning Oswald's connections to David Ferrie and Guy Bannister, and the Commission had information that could have led them to Clay Shaw. These leads were not pursued.[41] The decision not to pursue these areas allowed the Commission to avoid facts and testimony that led to the murky world of government and private intelligence operations.

A variety of explanations have been offered for the Commission's failures, attributing motives to Commission members and subordinates that range from the essentially innocent to the most sinister. In order to decide whether the Commission's failure was a product of conscious intent or the innocent and unintended result of one or more circumstances of its operations, it is necessary to do something that has not been done and, to a considerable extent, could not be done until 1993. We need to examine the way in which the Commission was created and identify the members of the Commission who dominated or influenced its work. If there was an intended cover-up, as Weisberg, Garrison, Prouty, DiEugenio, myself, and others have argued there was, then the creation, makeup, and method of operation of the Commission itself are of the utmost importance.

We need to know who it was that initiated the idea of the Presidential Commission and who it was that shaped its work. If we can establish the identity of the cover-up team with a high level of certainty, we can then examine that team in relationship to John Kennedy's actions and policies and to President Kennedy's known opponents and enemies. Throughout, we will be interested in

---

[38.] Weisberg, 1966, pp. 52-53.
[39.] Weisberg, 1966, pp. 71-87, 99, 121, 132, 218-19; 1974, p. 214; 1976; pp. 301-4; 1995, pp. 138, 242, 384.
[40.] Weisberg, 1965, pp. 36, 56, 173-78; 1966, pp. 94-96, 107-8, 138-40; 1967, pp. 172, 218.
[41.] Garrison, 1970, pp. 102-4; 1988, pp. 56-57; Weisberg, 1967, pp. 64-65, 203-6, 389-94.

evidence that links each stage of the cover-up with the others. Then, we will be in a position to address some of the important questions still unanswered almost forty years after the assassination.

We turn first to the events of the first few days following the assassination. The cover-up began immediately. Even before Oswald was killed and before the effort to create the Commission got under way, people operating within the FBI and particularly the nation's media were already disseminating what would become the official story.

We will turn then to the origin of the "Warren Commission," relying extensively on the now public record of events between November 22 and November 28, 1963. As we will see eventually, this Commission would have been more accurately named the Rostow Commission or the McCloy-Dulles Commission. As we shall also see, this should be thought of more as a blue-blood than a blue-ribbon commission.

Chapter Two

THE FIRST 72 HOURS

Before we examine how the cover story actually developed during the seventy-two hours following the assassination, we need to dispel a myth. The myth is that Dallas officials were primarily responsible for the emergence of the cover-up story. Actually, one Dallas official, the city's mayor, may have contributed to the cover-up. Other officials in Dallas, however, were saying things that were contrary to the emerging official story.

Dallas officials did rush in the first days following the assassination to the conclusion that Oswald was guilty. They are partially responsible for this very serious mistake, but it does appear to be a mistake and not part of a conscious participation in the cover-up. Obviously, the authorities in Dallas were under enormous pressure. The President had been killed in their city; they seemingly failed to protect him. Few people knew that the critical failure in providing security for the President was not theirs. Having failed to keep the President alive, they probably felt strongly that they had to perform in capturing the culprit(s) and solving the crime. There was real circumstantial evidence that made Oswald a suspect (as would be expected whether Oswald was guilty or a skillfully framed patsy). He was an unusual person with a suspicious background. He did work in the general area where the assassination occurred. He did leave that area shortly after the assassination. He should have been a suspect!

Furthermore, after the afternoon of the 22nd, Dallas authorities were being told of significant evidence, direct evidence against Oswald. They were "being told" about this because they had allowed the FBI to take control of most of the "evidence" and much of the investigation. The FBI told Dallas officials, for example, that handwriting evidence definitely linked Oswald to the alleged murder weapon.[1]

With some circumstantial evidence in hand, with strong statements coming from the FBI, with Oswald refusing to discuss some subjects, and, very likely, feeling immense pressure to perform, Dallas authorities wrongly jumped to the conclusion that Oswald was guilty.

However, during the three days immediately following the assassination, they also did something else. They moved tentatively from an early and premature judgement that Oswald acted alone to a stated openness on the question of accomplices. This tendency would have presented a monumental problem to those who wanted to get this case closed. To get this case closed, Oswald had to be quickly "convicted." Just as important, however, was that he had to have acted alone, a real nut case.

Let's briefly review what Dallas Police Chief Jesse Curry, Captain Will Fritz, and District Attorney Henry Wade said during those first few days.

Curry and Wade did most of the talking, in press interviews and press conferences; Fritz was directly involved in the investigation. The Warren Commission criticized Fritz for publicly convicting Oswald on November 23, thereby jeopardizing Oswald's rights.[2] As we will see, the Commission should have criticized elements of the media and the FBI more than local officials in Dallas. On the 24th, Fritz did this again in a press interview. He was less definitive about the possibility that others were involved. Fritz was asked if there "was anyone else connected with Oswald in the matter?" Fritz said, "Well, now, not that I know of."[3]

Chief Curry spoke frequently with the press; he did so at least once on each of those first three days. On the 22nd, he said that they probably had "sufficient evidence" to convict Oswald. He also said "There are still many things that we need to work on." Asked about the possibility of a conspiracy, Curry said "We...there's no one else but him."[4]

---

[1] Weisberg, 1965, pp. 5, 29.

[2] The President's Commission on the Assassination of President John F. Kennedy, 1993, p. 239.

[3] Hearings Before the President's Commission on the Assassination of President Kennedy, 1964, Vol. XXIV, p. 788.

[4] Ibid., p. 751.

His comments on the 23rd were more uncertain. Curry said that he thought they had "the right man," but he also said "we don't have positive proof." Asked if Oswald was the only suspect, Curry said "Yes."[5] Later in the same interview Curry was asked if there was "any evidence that there was anybody else involved in this?" Curry responded: "No, sir, not that we know of." Asked again shortly thereafter about the "possibility of accomplices," Curry said, "We don't believe so at this time."[6]

During the evening of the 23rd, Curry appeared again for press interviews. During one of these, he was asked again if there was any evidence of accomplices. Curry stated that:

> At this time, we don't believe so. We are talking to a man that works in the same building that we have in our subversive files and we are talking to him but he denies any knowledge of it.[7]

Obviously, on the 23rd, the Dallas police were actively interested in the possibility of accomplices. In a different interview that evening, Curry also indicated that there was an ongoing investigation, saying:

> I think our case [against Oswald] was in good shape this morning and it is much stronger tonight. We will continue to work on every possible shred of evidence that comes to our attention.[8]

On the 22nd there was no one else. By the evening of the 23rd, they were looking into a possible accomplice and were continuing the investigation.

On the 24th, before Oswald was murdered, Curry held a press conference. There were several questions raised about accomplices. These questions indicate an ongoing interest on the part of newsmen on the scene in the possibility of a conspiracy. The first exchange follows:

Q: Is there absolutely no doubt now that nobody else is involved as an accomplice?

Curry: I would not make that statement.

[5.] Ibid., p. 753.
[6.] Ibid., p. 756.
[7.] Ibid., p. 765.
[8.] Ibid., p. 783.

Q: Do you have any possible...

Curry: I wouldn't comment on it because I would certainly hate to say we're convinced that nobody else is involved and then have somebody else involved.

A little later. the following:

Q: Could you tell us, sir, if you would, just a little bit about this, the possibility that somebody else might be inter...might be involved in this. We've had statements in the last couple of days saying 'This is the man, and nobody else.' Now...

Curry: This is the man, we are sure, that murdered the patrolman and murdered...and assassinated the President. But to say that there was no other person had any knowledge of what this man might do, I wouldn't make that statement, because there is a possibility that there are people who might have known this man's thoughts and what he might, could do, or what he might do.[9]

In the above exchange, the reporter indicates clearly what is apparent in the record, that is, a shift in view from the 22nd to the 24th in the direction of an increased interest in the possibility of others being involved.

Curry is asked again about the "possibility of other people being involved" and says:

I'll only say this again: we're open-minded regarding this issue, and we will continue to exhaust every effort to explore any possibility that there might have been someone that even was friendly with him that might have known that he even had an idea of trying to harm...[10]

It is true that Curry talks about this in the most cautious of terms, never suggesting that he suspects a conspiracy in the assassination. He, however, did not close the door on this possibility in his public statements.

Later, in a book published in 1969 entitled *JFK Assassination File*, Curry did two things. He pointed out that the role of the Dallas police in providing security

---

[9.] Ibid., pp. 771-772.
[10.] Ibid.

for the President was very limited and that their role in the investigation was also limited. Second, he clearly indicated that he thought there was a conspiracy.

Curry makes it clear that individuals from the Secret Service controlled the security arrangements for President Kennedy's trip and people at the FBI controlled the investigation. According to Curry,[11] Winston G. Lawson of the Washington Secret Service office was the central figure in the planning of security arrangements. Curry emphasizes that the security provided by Lawson was heavy except the "short stretch of Elm Street where the President was shot." Curry notes that the Texas Book Depository was "virtually ignored."

Curry points out that neither the Secret Service nor the FBI asked for any help in locating possible conspirators.[12] The FBI had never shared the information it had on Oswald prior to the assassination. Less than twelve hours after the assassination, Curry transferred the evidence to the FBI, trusting them to do a good job and to return the evidence. They did neither. The Secret Service had already seized the body.[13] Curry says that in the days after the assassination Dallas investigators waited for the release of a detailed autopsy report, complete with photographic evidence.[14] It never came and Curry says that he suspected that some of the material was destroyed.

Curry saw signs of a conspiracy in other aspects of the case as well. For example, Curry points to numerous facts and reports which indicated that the President was hit from the front.[15] He also notes that a picture of the Book Depository shows a man who looks like Oswald standing in front at the time the President was killed. That picture, referred to in Chapter One, is reproduced and discussed in Harold Weisberg's *Whitewash II: The FBI-Secret Service Cover-up.*

Curry criticizes the media and the Warren Commission for distorting eyewitness testimony about whom was in the Book Depository window at the time of the shooting.[16] Curry states that the Dallas police began looking for conspirators immediately after the assassination and continued to do so while the press was focused on Oswald alone.[17]

---

[11] Curry, 1969, pp. 10, 16-17, 21.

[12] Ibid., p. 17.

[13] Ibid., p. 81.

[14] Ibid., p. 122.

[15] Ibid., pp. 30, 32, 34, 100-101, 102, 121-122.

[16] Ibid., 1969, pp. 61-62.

[17] Ibid., 1969, pp. 55, 121.

On November 23rd and 24th, District Attorney Henry Wade stated views
similar to the ones offered by Curry just after the assassination, going a little
further in one instance. Wade held a press conference at 12:30 A.M. on the 23rd.
When asked by two reporters, almost simultaneously, if there were others
involved and if this is "an organized plot," Wade said "There is no one else but
him"[Oswald]. Asked later if authorities were looking for other suspects, Wade
said "we're always looking for other suspects, but we have none at present."
Asked if the assassination is part of a communist conspiracy, Wade said that he
didn't "have any reason to believe either way on it."[18]

Asked again if there was an organized plot against JFK, Wade responded:
"We don't know that answer. He's [Oswald] the only one we have." Later, Wade
is asked if Oswald did this because he was a Communist, because it was part of a
conspiracy, or because he was a "nut." Wade made no comment on conspiracy,
but he did say that he did not think Oswald was a nut,[19] a view stated by other
officials in Dallas[20](the only exception known to the author was Mayor Cabell,
who was sure Oswald was a nut).

On the 24th, after Oswald was killed, Wade held another press conference.
The following exchange took place:

Q: Has your office closed its investigation into the death of President
      Kennedy?
Wade: No sir. The investigation will continue on that with the basis, towards,
      and we have no concrete evidence that anyone assisted him in this. But
      the investigation I'm sure will go on with reference to any possible
      accomplices or...that assisted him in it.
Q: Do you have any suspicion now that there was?
Wade: I have no concrete evidence at present.[21]

After this, Wade affirmed that Oswald did it and was asked if the case was
closed. Wade responded: "As far as Oswald is concerned, yes." Wade was asked
a question, incomplete in the transcript, about a possible Oswald-Ruby
connection. Wade answered by saying, "I think I heard it on radio, or something,

[18.] Hearings Before the President's Commission on the Assassination of President
     Kennedy, 1964, Vol. XXIV, pp. 830, 832-833.
[19.] Ibid., p. 841.
[20.] Ibid., pp. 809, 815.
[21.] Ibid., p. 823.

but I don't know anything about it."[22] Five years later, Wade wrote to Harold Weisberg stating that "I have always felt there was an accomplice or someone else involved in this matter with Oswald..."[23]

As noted above, Dallas officials did leap to conclusions about Oswald and they were creating a prejudice against Oswald, something they were criticized for by the Warren Commission.[24] What they did not do was to conclude that Oswald acted alone and that the case was closed. The only discernible trend from November 22 to 24 is in the opposite direction, one of becoming more open to the possibility of accomplices. Wade's and Curry's suspicions were apparently intensified in the years following the assassination. In the numerous press interviews and press conferences given by Dallas officials, there is no discussion of a communist conspiracy, only the increasing willingness to entertain the possibility of accomplices.

When Waggoner Carr, Attorney General of Texas, testified before the Warren Commission, he remembered only that the idea of a conspiracy was discussed with him during a call from the White House. According to Carr, someone called from the White House around 8:00 or 9:00 P.M. on the 22nd saying that there was a rumor that someone in Texas was going to include the idea of a conspiracy in the indictment against Oswald. Carr informed that caller and the Warren Commission that he was at no time aware that such an idea was to be part of the charges against Oswald. Even though this must have been a significant phone call for Carr and even though he later called this person back, he claimed he could not remember that person's name. Carr also could not recall if the word "communist" was ever used; he did think the term "international conspiracy" was used. The White House caller desired to know and to be reassured that the charges against Oswald would not include a suggestion of conspiracy.[25] It is hard to believe that Carr could not remember the identity of this person.

Compared to what happened elsewhere during the first three days following the assassination, the officials in Dallas were a model of openness and objectivity. Prompted by the FBI's assertions, they did jump to the conclusion

[22] Ibid., pp. 823-824.
[23] Weisberg, 1995, p. 326.
[24] The President's Commission on the Assassination of President John F. Kennedy, 1993, pp. 231-242.
[25] Hearings Before the President's Commission on the Assassination of President Kennedy, 1964, Vol. V, pp. 258-260.

that Oswald was guilty. But they did not close the case, nor conclude that Oswald had no accomplices, nor render a judgment about Oswald's mental health. Others did conclude that he acted alone, that he probably did it because he was a nut, and that the case was closed.

A REAL RUSH TO JUDGMENT:
MEDIA FRENZY OR FOUL PLAY?

Elements in the major media reached a far more comprehensive set of conclusions about the assassination during the first 72 hours than did the police and district attorney in Dallas. The events of the afternoon of November 22 are an important part of the context for this story. We need to briefly review some of those events.

President Kennedy was shot at about 12:30 P.M. Central Standard Time (CST). At 12:45 a description of a suspect was broadcast over police radio. The description was of a very average white male, 5 feet 10 inches tall and weighing 165 pounds, in his early-30s.[26] This description would fit, roughly, tens of thousands of men in the Dallas area. The Commission never determined for certain where this description came from, but it did settle on witness Howard Leslie Brennan as the probable source. Brennan's later comments and his testimony showed him to be a very unreliable person.[27] At the same moment that the first description was broadcast, Officer J.D. Tippit allegedly received over police radio an order to proceed to the central Oak Cliff area of Dallas.

A description of a suspect was broadcast a second time at 12:47, which is also the time J. Edgar Hoover established contact with the FBI's Dallas office, and for a third time at 12:55.[28] At 1:15 P.M., Tippit is killed and at 1:22 a new description of a suspect, based on statements from two witnesses to the Tippit shooting, is broadcast on police radio. This description presents a slightly smaller suspect, 5 feet 8 inches tall, with darker hair, and wearing clothes unlike those

[26] Weisberg, 1965, p. 39.

[27] Ibid., pp. 24, 39-42, 98-99.

[28] Manchester, 1967, p. 321; President's Commission on the Assassination of President Kennedy, 1964, p. 41.

worn by Oswald.[29] A similarity in the descriptions from the scenes of the assassination and the Tippit murder is allegedly noted over police radio at 1:29.[30]

Based on a phone tip about a suspicious person entering the Texas Theater, a large number of police descend on the movie theater where, after a brief scuffle, Oswald is arrested at 1:50. Within minutes Oswald is in a squad car where police inspect his identification and for the first time have Oswald's name and a second name, Alek J. Hidell, from a selective service card in Oswald's possession. Hidell would be the name allegedly used by Oswald to order both the assassination weapon and the revolver he had at the time of his arrest.[31]

Police arrive at headquarters with Oswald at about 2:00 P.M., CST. At about the same time, President Kennedy's body is being removed from Parkland Hospital against the wishes of at least some local authorities and in violation of the law.[32] At about 2:15, Captain Fritz returns to headquarters with the name of Oswald as a possible suspect, only to find him already in custody. Fritz got Oswald's name from Roy Truly, the Texas School Book Depository manager.[33] It is around 2:00 P.M., CST, that Oswald's name is first available as a possible suspect.

Information about Oswald, that he had been in Russia and was pro-Communist, appeared very quickly. J. Edgar Hoover allegedly gave such information to Attorney General Robert Kennedy by about 2:30 P.M., CST.[34] Hoover may have received this information from the FBI files in Washington or from the Dallas FBI office; Dallas police did not have a file on Oswald.[35] The 112th Military Intelligence Group, Fort Sam Houston, also had a file on Oswald and had learned immediately of his arrest.[36] Lt. Col. Robert Jones of the 112th had provided information to the FBI's Gordon Shanklin,[37] apparently sometime

[29] Manchester, 1967, p. 322; President's Commission on the Assassination of President Kennedy, 1964, p. 41.
[30] President's Commission on the Assassination of President Kennedy, 1964, p. 43.
[31] Bishop, 1968, p. 278; Manchester, 1967, p. 323; Weisberg, 1965, p. 139.
[32] Bishop, 1968, 287-289; President's Commission on the Assassination of President Kennedy, 1964, p. 43.
[33] Manchester, 1967, p. 323; The President's Commission on the Assassination of President Kennedy, 1964, p. 45.
[34] Marrs, 1989, p. 355.
[35] Hill, 1963a, p. 1.
[36] Summers, 1989, pp. 60-61.
[37] Ibid.

between 2:00 and 2:30 P.M. At 2:30, after receiving this information, Shanklin called Captain Fritz and asked that the FBI's James Hosty be allowed to participate in the interrogation of Oswald.[38]

At 3:01 P.M., Dallas Chief of Police Jesse E. Curry told Mayor Earle Cabell, brother of the former CIA official Charles Cabell, that the police had a suspect for both the assassination and the murder of Tippit.[39] By 3:23 the television networks were using Oswald's name and at 3:26 they mentioned Oswald's application for Russian citizenship.[40]

Sometime during the early afternoon of the 22nd, a substantial amount of information on Oswald was acquired by the media. This information could have come from the FBI directly or indirectly through the Dallas police. Conceivably, it could have come from some other source that had a file on Oswald, such as the State Department, the 112th Military Intelligence Unit, or the CIA. According to a San Antonio FBI office document, the FBI in that city received information about Oswald from the 112th at 3:15 p.m. CST. Whoever provided the information apparently gave it to a person or persons affiliated with the wire services. By early evening on the 22nd, that information was in print.

One of the, if not the, first newspapers in the world to carry information about Oswald was *The Christchurch Star* in New Zealand. The *Star* hit the streets in the early afternoon of what was November 23 in New Zealand (22nd in Dallas). L. Fletcher Prouty, who was in 1963 the Focal Point or liaison officer between the Pentagon and the CIA and the Director of Special Plans in the office of the Joint Chiefs, was in Christchurch that day. Prouty recalls purchasing the newspaper around 2:30 P.M., New Zealand time. An analysis of the content of the paper (e.g., it contains a report of the arrival of Air Force One at Andrews at 5:00 P.M. CST and it apparently went to press before Oswald was formally charged in Tippit's murder at 7:10 P.M. CST) supports Prouty's recollection.

Taking everything into account, including the time required to get the paper in print and on the streets, it appears that this paper was ready to go to press around 6:00 P.M. CST. As Prouty has pointed out,[41] the information appears to come from an already assembled body of information, such as a file from one of the sources mentioned above.

[38] North, 1991, p. 409.
[39] Bishop, 1968, p. 329.
[40] Manchester, 1967, p. 324.
[41] Prouty, 1992, pp. 306-309.

The story on Oswald appeared on page one of *The Christchurch Star*; Oswald had not been formally charged with anything when this paper was ready for the press. The story includes references to several sources. The Associate Press of America is apparently the primary source, but the story also credits Reuter and the British United Press. There are errors in this story (e.g., that Oswald killed a policeman at the theater were he was arrested) and inconsistencies in other material in the newspaper (e.g., a story describes "Three bursts of gunfire" but quotes a witness reporting three shots). The package of information on Oswald, however, is essentially accurate. Oswald is said to have:

-worked in the building where a rifle was found;
-defected to the Soviet Union in 1959;
-returned to the U.S. in the preceding year;
-a Russian wife and child;
-worked in a Minsk factory while in Russia;
-gone to Russia following his discharge from the Marines;
-become disillusioned with life in the Soviet Union;
-been given an exit permit to leave Russia and return to the U.S.;
-been chairman of a fair play for Cuba committee.

Oswald is also reported to be the "prime suspect in the assassination of the President."[42]

There is a picture of Oswald, dressed in a suit (perhaps a passport photo), and there is a picture of the Book Depository with an arrow pointing to the sixth floor window from which shots were allegedly fired. The caption reads: "An arrow points to the window from which the assassin shot President Kennedy in Dallas today."[43] There are then at least three items in this paper, produced about six hours after the assassination, that make Oswald the focus of attention: the pictures of Oswald and the Book Depository and Oswald's biographical information.

Unfortunately, we do not know who received this information at the wire service(s) and we do not know the source. The background on Oswald may have come from the FBI, but this is only a guess. The photo of Oswald may have come from elsewhere (State Department?) and the photo of the building probably

---

[42.] The Christchurch Star, 1963, p. 1.
[43.] Ibid.

came from a local source, also unknown. As suggested earlier, the 112th Military Intelligence Group may have been a source or the source for both the press and police.

It appears that someone else went beyond just a focus on Oswald during the afternoon of the 22nd. While Air Force One was still in the air, returning from Dallas to Washington, its occupants "learned that there was no conspiracy; learned of the identity of Oswald and his arrest."[44] Air Force One arrived at Washington at 5:00 P.M., CST, 6:00 P.M., EST. Oswald was a suspect by this time, but where would a conclusion that there was no conspiracy have come from? Journalist and author Theodore White says that within an hour of the assassination, President Kennedy's military aide, Major General Chester V. Clifton, had established "contact with the national command center in Washington to find out whether this was indeed coup or conspiracy." By "national command center" White, or his source, seems to mean the White House and the Pentagon.[45] The reference could be to the Situation Room in the White House, a facility under the control of national security advisor McGeorge Bundy.[46]

Why anyone would think that authorities located in Washington would know within a few hours whether or not there was a conspiracy related to an assassination in Dallas is certainly not clear. Apparently, the relevant conversations are either unintelligible on the tapes held by the LBJ Library or those parts of the tape were erased.[47]

People aboard a plane returning to Washington from Hawaii, including much of the President's cabinet, also heard stories about Oswald and his past which were understood to imply that Oswald was the assassin. Although one account vaguely implies that the information was coming from the White House Situation Room,[48] another specifically identifies the source as the wire service machine.[49] Those conversations are also apparently missing from the tapes at the LBJ Library.

In the hours following these events, and still only ten to fifteen hours after the assassination, Oswald became more that just the focus of attention and more

---

[44] White, 1965, p. 48.

[45] Ibid., p. 47.

[46] Salinger, 1966, p. 78.

[47] Air Force One Transcripts, 1995.

[48] Strober and Strober, 1993, pp. 450-451.

[49] Salinger, 1966, p. 10.

than just a suspect. He was convicted as a lone assassin and was quickly declared to be a nut. While Dallas officials were tending in the direction of looking for accomplices, important elements of the media were closing the case.

THE MEDIA SOLVES THE CASE FROM AFAR

The *New York Times* headline on November 23 read, "Kennedy Is Killed By Sniper As He Rides In Car In Dallas; Johnson Sworn In On Plane." The words "By Sniper" implied a lone assassin. Those words could have been left out of the headline and they should have been. Among the page one stories was a lengthy piece by Tom Wicker. The sub-heading for Wicker's story read, "President Is Struck Down by a Rifle Shot From Building on Motorcade Route."[50] The phrase "a Rifle Shot" suggests one assassin. The evidence surfacing in Dallas, even that being reported by the *New York Times,* indicated that the source of some or all of the shots was unsettled. Nevertheless, the *Times* was certain the shot that killed the President came from a building.

This story began with Wicker saying that JFK was killed by "an assassin." Further on he wrote that "The killer fired the rifle from a building just off the motorcade route." According to Wicker, Kennedy succumbed to "an assassin's wounds." Wicker was in Dallas but was on a press bus and saw nothing of the assassination.

In this coverage, the assassination is attributed to a single person in five separate instances. Nowhere does this story explicitly indicate any other possibility. This story does mention, without attribution, that the President's anterior neck wound was reported as a wound of entry, that the President may have suffered two shots to the head, and that the President had a "massive, gaping wound" in the back of the head. Even general and vague knowledge of the shooting should have raised immediate questions about the number and placement of the assassins. There is certainly no reason for the repeated assertion that one person did this. Didn't Wicker recognize this as he was filing his story? Was any of the wording in the story changed before it went to press?

A second page one story, entitled "Why America Weeps," which was written by James Reston, Tom Wicker's superior, began by not only deciding the number of assassins involved, but also provided an explanation for the assassination. In

---

[50.] Talese, 1971, pp. 36, 139; Wicker, 1963, pp. 1,2.

the first paragraph, Reston,[51] who was in North Carolina at the time of the assassination, attributed the shooting to "the assassin" and then offered his own instant analysis. Without, apparently, knowing much of anything, Reston offered that the cause of this murder was "some strain of madness and violence" which plagues the nation as a whole. The sub-heading of the article had already established this theme, reading "Kennedy Victim of Violent Streak He Sought to Curb in the Nation." Reston's story goes beyond the, perhaps, merely hasty and careless conclusions in Wicker's story. Reston not only has it down to one person, but he is already offering up a diagnosis of what was wrong with this individual. This is truly impressive, especially since those in Dallas close to the investigation were saying explicitly that they thought Oswald was quite sane. This performance did not seem to hurt Reston's career. He was promoted to associate editor in 1964 and then to executive editor in 1968. Reston brought Tom Wicker to New York as associate editor.[52]

A page five story, submitted to the Times by Associated Press reporter Jack Bell,[53] who was in Dallas, stated that "the assassin took his stand" in Dealy Plaza and that "His three well-aimed shots plunged America and the world into grief." Many witnesses thought there were more than three shots. As noted above, *The Christchurch Star* reported three bursts of gun fire. Whatever Bell or anyone thought they heard there, he was jumping to the same conclusions reached by Wicker and, particularly, Reston. (The AP-Jack Bell account did include a couple of things which, if valid, would be inconsistent with the story's conclusions and with the Warren Report. The third shot was said to have come "almost immediately on top of the second" and that President Kennedy had a wound in the left temple. The first implies shots fired too quickly for the alleged murder weapon and the second a wound location inconsistent with the Commission's account.)

Another of the page one stories on the 23rd carried the heading "Leftist Accused."[54] This story reported that "Oswald was employed in the Texas School Book Depository, the warehouse from which the fatal shots were fired at the President's car." The location was not known with certainty and the words "fatal shots" were based on early and tentative reports. The words "fatal shots" were

---

[51.] Reston, 1963, p. 1; 1991, p. 295.
[52.] Reston, 1991; Talese, 1971, pp. 615-18.
[53.] New York Times, 1963, p. 5.
[54.] Hill, 1963, p. 1.

consistent with statements referred to above that suggested that the President may have been hit in the head by two bullets.

This article presents two kinds of information that were common in early news accounts: premature conclusions and contradictory or ambiguous facts reported from the scene. Chief Curry is quoted as saying that their case was at that time based mainly on physical evidence. Later in the same story, it is noted that ballistics experts thus far had reached no conclusions concerning the alleged assassination weapon. Consistent with our previous discussion of the attitudes of Dallas officials, the story reported that there were "various lines" of investigation being pursued.[55] Captain Fritz is quoted as having said that there was information linking Oswald to both left- and right-wing political groups, and that Oswald was apparently politically erratic.

On the following two days, the *Times* carried front page stories which seemed intended to lay the dust, a goal more explicitly stated, as we will see, by Commission member John J. McCloy and by the FBI's Alan Belmont. On the 24th appeared a story entitled "Evidence Against Oswald Described as Conclusive."[56] Captain Fritz is quoted as saying that "the case is cinched" and D.A. Wade saying that they had "enough evidence to convict him now." As was noted earlier, there was this rush to judgment about Oswald's guilt. The tendency by Dallas officials to become more open to the possibility of accomplices during the first three days is not discussed in these reports. Even a hint of this would seem to be newsworthy.

In this same edition of the *Times*, there are reports from the doctors in Dallas that one of the bullets had entered in the front of Kennedy's neck and that a bullet had exited the back of his head.[57] Were either of these observations correct, then there was no possibility that Oswald was a lone assassin.

On the 25th, the *Times* carried a story by reporter Foster Hailey entitled, "Lone Assassin the Rule in U.S.; Plotting More Prevalent Abroad."[58] The theme of this story is set forth at the beginning:

> There is one clear distinction between most of the attempts to kill Government figures in other countries and those in the United States.

[55.] Ibid.

[56.] Hill, 1963a, p. 1.

[57.] Ibid.

[58.] Hailey, 1963, p. 9.

In Russia and in Japan the assassinations generally were the culmination of detailed plans made by well-organized groups, usually involving high Government figures. The motivations were political, or nationalistic.

In the United States, in all except two cases [Lincoln and Truman], the attempts were made by a single person, often with little advanced planning and often without any real grievance against the personage attacked.

That seems to have been the case with Lee H. Oswald, the killer of President Kennedy who was himself slain yesterday.[59]

On the 24th, Dallas officials were more open to the possibility of accomplices than on the 22nd. On the 25th, a day after Oswald's murder, when a host of new questions might be asked, Hailey and the *Times* were closing down the discussion and putting their conclusions into their own historical perspective.

With a multitude of unanswered questions about the assassination, about Tippit's death, and now about the startling murder of Oswald only hours before, the *Times* seemingly knew enough to begin offering conclusions about the event and even the nature of the alleged assassin's motives.

Other elements of the media were wrapping up the case with conclusions very similar to those of the *Times*. For example, the *New York Herald Tribune* provided conclusions and a perspective on the assassination on the day after, the 23rd. In a story entitled "Shame of a Nation - History of Assassinations," the *Tribune*, sounding like the *Times*, stated that:

Historically, assassination has been a weapon in the struggle for political power in countries around the world, but attempts on American Presidents have not followed this pattern.

In a book on Presidential assassinations, 'The Assassins,' Robert J. Donovan, former Washington bureau chief of the New York Herald Tribune and now of the Los Angeles Times points out:

'They involved neither organized attempts to shift political power from one group to another, nor to perpetuate a particular man or party in office, nor to alter the policy of the government, nor to resolve ideological conflicts. With one exception [Truman], no terroristic or secret society planned these assaults on our Presidents or was in any way involved.[60]

Shortly after this, Allen Dulles would be pushing these views on his fellow Warren Commission members, referring to and promoting Donovan's book.

[59] Ibid.
[60] New York Herald Tribune, 1963, p. 4.

Donovan, who was with the Herald Tribune from 1937 to 1963,[61] would also later write the introduction to the Popular Library edition of the Warren Commission Report.

On the same day, the 23rd, the *Tribune* would also offer its conclusions about the assassination in its editorial statements. Part of it read as follows:

> Americans take consolation from the fact that the assassins of their Presidents have, in nearly every case, been crazed individuals, representing nothing but their own wild imaginings. There is, however, a climate that encourages the growth of such homicidal fantasies - the passions of the Civil War stirred John Wilkes Booth; and intra-party squabble was Charles J. Guiteau's excuse for killing President Garfield; McKinley was shot down by a professed anarchist, Leon F. Czolgosz.
>
> The heat of normal politics has its reflex on the lunatic fringe. And the `hate sheets,' the rumor-mongering, the unbalanced charges of the lunatic fringe affects the real lunatics, the killers.[62]

There you have it. There was no need for an investigation. In well under 24 hours, the essential nature of the assassination of President Kennedy was laid bare. There was no need for a Dupin or even a Lt. Columbo or Perry Mason. Not only did a nut do it and do it alone, but he did it because he was a nut. That is it in a nutshell.

John Hay Whitney was the fabulously wealthy editor-in-chief and publisher of the *Tribune* from 1961 to 1966. He was a member of the Council on Foreign Relations and the Business Council and received special recognition from the British crown. He was appointed Commander in the Order of the British Empire and was an Associate Knight of the Grand Priory in the British Realm of the Most Venerable Order of the Hospital of St. John of Jerusalem. The latter was an honor also bestowed on an associate of Clay Shaw, Mortimer Bloomfield. Whitney became Ambassador to Great Britain in 1956, replacing former Chase Manhattan board chairman Winthrop W. Aldrich. Whitney was also a trustee of the New York Racing Association and of the Museum of Modern Art.[63]

Whitney may be directly responsible for what appeared in the *Tribune* immediately after the assassination. An October, 1964, *Fortune* magazine article about Whitney contains a brief discussion of Whitney's responsibility for the pro-

[61.] Marquis Who's Who, 1978-79.
[62.] New York Herald Tribune, 1963a, p. 14.
[63.] Burch, 1980, pp. 140-141; Marquis Who's Who, 1978-79.

LBJ editorial policy adopted after Kennedy was gone. Therein the following comment is made:

> Yet Whitney is willing to use the power of the Tribune to push energetically the editorial views he holds in local and national politics.

This suggests that Whitney exercised close supervision of the Tribune's editorial statements.

In what is an official and friendly biography of Whitney, entitled *Jock: The Life and Times of John Hay Whitney*, the author, E. J. Kahn, Jr., says the following:

> On November 22, President Kennedy was killed. Whitney ...was pressed into emergency service that tumultuous night as a copy reader ...[64]

It is not likely that the fabulously wealthy owner of the paper was "pressed" into anything. It does appear that he had a direct hand in deciding what to say about the assassination.

The *Herald Tribune* was not alone in having the ability to solve the crime in less than twenty four hours. Mayor Earle Cabell of Dallas also reached an immediate conclusion. In two separate places in the November 23 edition of *The Dallas Morning News*, Cabell is quoted as saying that the assassination was the act of a maniac, it was "the irrational act of a single man" and that it "could only be the act of a deranged mind."[65] Cabell, the brother of former Deputy Director of CIA, Gen. Charles P. Cabell, may have been the first official to assert the essence of what happened.

Two days later, November 25, the *Wall Street Journal*, one of JFK's most vitriolic critics, not impressed by nor intrigued by the murder of Oswald, contributed its conclusions to the opinion shaping process.

> The dangers of high office, he [JFK] certainly knew were enormous. His sense of history would have told him that they cannot be escaped even in our land of liberty. Idiots we have always amongst us, and if they have coloration at all it is more likely to be the black of night of the individual soul than the political shades of red or white.

---

[64] Kahn, 1981, p. 285.
[65] Dallas Morning News, 1963, p. 14; Raffeto, 1963, p. 4.

His sense of history would have told him that all such murders were the work of individual hysteria, just as was the murder of the assassin, not the working of the historical process. We have had assassinations before, but they are not, as in many other countries, the normal means of political change.[66]

The *Wall Street Journal*, like the *Herald Tribune* and people at the *Times*, was impressive in its ability to judge the facts and reach a conclusion. From afar, they sized up the events and within three days they knew that Oswald acted alone, Oswald's killer Jack Ruby acted alone, neither had any connection to any political group ("red or white"), and both were mentally unbalanced. Oswald and Ruby were hysterics, and idiots to boot.

A week or so later all of the country's three main news magazines did similar things. None of them reported the doubts voiced in Dallas. All three contributed to the then widely repeated rendition, although not always in a consistent way. In its coverage, *U.S. News and World Report* indicated at least three separate times that only one person was involved.[67] They even implied that Lincoln was killed by an assassin acting as an isolated individual.

Time did *U.S. News* one better. They simply stated that Lincoln was killed by a "lonely psychopath." This was meant to help us understand Lee Harvey Oswald against whom, asserted *Time*, the evidence was "overwhelming".[68] *Newsweek*, a little less certain of Oswald's guilt, was sure that there was only one assassin and sure of the reason. The assassin, apparently Oswald, had "cancer of the psyche."[69]

The police and the district attorney in Dallas had some direct knowledge of the events. It was in their city that the President had been killed. They probably felt the pressure to resolve this case and appear to be on top of things. Officials in Dallas were being told by the FBI that the evidence pointed to Oswald. Nevertheless, in the three days following the assassination, they became more, not less, open to the possibility of accomplices and their judgment of Oswald was that he did not appear to be insane.[70]

[66.] Wall Street Journal, 1963, p. 8.
[67.] U.S. News and World Report, 1963, pp. 6, 32, 35.
[68.] Time, 1963, p. 28.
[69.] Newsweek, 1963, p. 27.
[70.] Hearings Before the President's Commission on the Assassination of President Kennedy, 1964, Vol. XXIV, pp. 809-833; Weisberg, 1995, p. 326.

There was no good or understandable reason for people at the wire services, the *New York Times*, *New York Herald Tribune*, or *Wall Street Journal* to jump to these conclusions. No one looked to them to solve the crime. They felt none of the pressures probably felt by officials in Dallas. They conceivably could have been victims of the rumors and the assurances from the FBI that the evidence against Oswald was solid. What is not explainable is their apparent ability to see that Oswald acted alone, that Ruby acted alone, and that Oswald acted because of mental or emotional instability and that alone. This is clear evidence of a desire to dispense with this case as quickly as possible. Some high officials of the FBI were not far behind them.

BELMONT AND HOOVER

As all serious students of the assassination know, individuals within the FBI participated in various ways in the cover-up process. This author has no doubt that J. Edgar Hoover was complicit in this activity and that his complicity was necessary for the cover-up to be effective. However, Hoover does not appear to be the leading figure within the FBI in these events. Accounts such as that provided by Mark North, *Act of Treason*, are particularly misleading. North not only makes Hoover primary in the FBI's complicity in the cover-up, a fairly common mistake, but also attempts to implicate Hoover in events leading up to the assassination. There is no direct evidence to link Hoover to the planning or carrying out of the assassination.

The review of the facts that follows shows that Alan Belmont, the number three man in the formal hierarchy of the FBI, was the primary official in charge of FBI activities following the assassination. It is Belmont, not Hoover, who ran the FBI cover-up.

Alan Harnden Belmont was born in 1907 in New York City, apparently no relation to the famous financier August Belmont. He spent three years at San Diego State College but he received his degree from Stanford in 1931. Belmont worked as an accountant (employer not known) for about five years and then joined the FBI.[71] After brief assignments in Birmingham, Alabama, and in Chicago, Belmont spent several years at FBI headquarters in Washington, DC. He then had three brief assignments in New York, Chicago, and Cincinnati

---

[71.] Marquis Who's Who, 1964-65.

between 1941 and 1943. From 1944 to 1950, Belmont was back in New York as an assistant to the Special Agent in Charge. During at least part of this time, he was in charge of all security work in New York. Early in 1950, Belmont was transferred to Washington and put in charge of the domestic intelligence division (Division Five). He held that position until June 1961, when he became assistant to the director, in charge of all investigative work, a position he held until his retirement at the end of 1965.[72] After leaving the FBI in 1965, Belmont became assistant to the director of the Hoover Institution on War, Revolution and Peace, an ultra-conservative, upper-class think tank. Belmont's boss at Hoover, Canadian born Wesley G. Campbell, was also an important figure at the American Enterprise Institute and the Center for Strategic and International Studies and was a member of the elitist Mont Pelerin Society.[73]

In his last FBI position, Belmont was in charge of all investigative matters, including general criminal matters, organized crime, and those related to domestic intelligence. Testifying before the Warren Commission in May of 1964, Belmont described in general terms his involvement in the investigation of the assassination. Belmont testified that he was involved in the investigation from the time of the assassination. Belmont recounted that even before President Johnson requested it, "we" went into action. Immediately after the assassination, the FBI began working with the Dallas police and they sent men to participate in the interview of Oswald. Belmont stated that he also "participated in or supervised the preparation of reports and other correspondence to the Commission."[74]

In attendance for Belmont's testimony were the following: Chief Justice Earl Warren; Rep. Gerald Ford (part of the time); John J. McCloy; Allen Dulles; J. Lee Rankin, General Counsel; David Belin, assistant counsel; Norman Redlich, assistant counsel; Samuel A. Stern, assistant counsel; Charles Murray, observer from the American Bar Association. None of the three Commissioners who ended up having some problems with the final report were present.

Much of the time was spent on FBI knowledge of Oswald prior to the assassination, on the FBI's working relationship with the Secret Service, and general procedural matters. No one asked Belmont to comment on any of the

[72] Hearings Before the President's Commission on the Assassination of President Kennedy, 1964, Vol. V, pp. 1-33; New York Times, 1965, p. 26.
[73] Dickson, 1979, pp. 303-308; Marquis Who's Who, 1977; 1978-79.
[74] Hearings Before the President's Commission on the Assassination of President Kennedy, 1964, Vol. V, pp. 2, 4, 6, 25.

known problems in the investigation (e.g., discrepancies about the location of wounds; the difficulty of the shooting if it was done by a lone assassin using the alleged murder weapon; the FBI's own conclusions about the sequence and timing of the shots, which was not in accordance with the Commission's eventual conclusions). Even though Belmont had served in Chicago, no one asked him if he had any knowledge of Jack Ruby, who was in Chicago around the time that Belmont was there. McCloy did go out of his way to solicit from Belmont an opinion that Oswald was the lone assassin and that there was "no evidence" to suggest a conspiracy.[75]

There is not much of interest in this testimony beyond what was not discussed. There is one exception. Belmont clearly indicates that from the time of the assassination, it was he, not Hoover, who was directing things. Belmont's statements in this regard are supported by the available documentary evidence. J. Edgar Hoover, unquestionably complicit in the cover-up, played second fiddle in this orchestra. He was not the first fiddle, nor the conductor, nor the owner of the orchestra.

On November 22, 1963, at 2:21 P.M., Eastern Standard Time (EST), Hoover prepared a memo informing top officials of the FBI (Deputy Director Clyde Tolson, Assistant Director Allan Belmont, and six others) of his conversation with James J. Rowley, Chief of Secret Service. Less than one hour after the assassination, Hoover apparently had no significant information. He informs his subordinates that he and Rowley discussed possible elements behind the assassination, Rowley talking about Mexico and Cuba, Hoover about the Klu Klux Klan.[76] It is clear that both men were open to the possibility of a conspiracy in this first hour.

Later in the afternoon, Hoover produced another memo which was ready at 4:01 P.M., but sent out with the previous memo at 5:00 P.M. This was also an internal memo addressed to the same list of FBI officials, including Tolson and Belmont. This memo reports Hoover's conversation with Attorney General Robert Kennedy and the information Hoover had received concerning Oswald.[77] Hoover said in the memo that he had told RFK that he "thought we had the man who killed the President down in Dallas at the present time." Hoover provided the following information on the man: his name is Lee Harvey Oswald; he

---

[75]. Ibid., p. 27.
[76]. Hoover, 1963.
[77]. Hoover, 1963a.

worked in the building from which shots were fired; he was involved in the Fair Play for Cuba Committee; he has communist leanings but is apparently not a member of the Communist Party; he went to Russia and stayed three years; he returned to the U.S. in June, 1963 [1962]; he went to Cuba several times and would not explain those trips.

The final item was apparently not true of Oswald, but was true of the man, Jack Ruby, who would kill Oswald less than 48 hours later. It is a strange error and coincidence. Hoover also noted in this memo, and apparently told RFK, that the FBI had received a couple of tips suggesting that other people may have been involved in the assassination. Finally, Hoover stated that he had instructed the FBI in Dallas to go to police headquarters and participate in the interrogation of Oswald.

A third memo from Hoover to Tolson, Belmont, et al., was written at 5:15 P.M. on the 22nd; it summarized a telephone call from Assistant Attorney General Norbert A. Schlei, Office of Legal Counsel, to Hoover.[78] Hoover reports that Schlei wanted to know "what kind of people murdered the President," asking if they were "madmen" or "segregationist madmen." Hoover wrote that he had told Schlei that "very probably we had in custody the man who killed the President in Dallas but this had not definitely been established." Hoover then recounts in the memo the information he provided to Schlei about Oswald. It appears that Hoover, Belmont, or someone else in the FBI, perhaps Shanklin, provided information similar to this and to that in the 4:01 memo to someone affiliated with the Associated Press or one of the other wire services during the afternoon of the 22nd. The information Hoover gave to Schlei included the following:

Oswald:-spent years in Russia;
      -tried to renounce his U.S. citizenship;
      -returned to the U.S.;
      -came to the attention of FBI when arrested in New Orleans while handing out Fair Play for Cuba leaflets;
      -apparently shot a policeman a block or two from the building from which assassination shots had been fired;
      -a rifle and three shells were found in that building.

[78.] Hoover, 1963b.

Hoover went on to state that Oswald "would be in the category of a nut and the extremist pro-Castro crowd." It is not clear where Hoover got the idea that Oswald was "a nut." Perhaps someone said this to him; perhaps that is merely the way that Hoover talked about radicals or leftists. Hoover is of course mistaken on the location of the shooting of the policeman.

Hoover has already said that Oswald's guilt has "not definitely been established." He mentions that the only two attacks on Presidents about which he was knowledgeable were the Puerto Rican group's attempt on Truman and the assassination of McKinley by a man affiliated with Emma Goldman. For both there is some implication of conspiracy. Hoover had earlier brought up the possibility of Klan involvement. Hoover went on to say that if Oswald "were the man", he would be "in the category of being an extreme radical of the left", and that he was a member but not a leader of the Fair Play for Cuba Committee. Hoover added that Oswald "made several trips to Cuba; upon his return each time we questioned him about what he went to Cuba for and he answered that it was none of our business." Hoover concluded that even though the FBI was getting other leads, he "would think Oswald would be the one" and that Oswald was "the Principal suspect in the case."[79]

As noted above, this author is not aware of any substantial evidence that Oswald made trips to Cuba. That Ruby had gone to Cuba is quite certain[80] and this coincidence is bizarre. Obviously there was no legitimate reason for anyone to be mistakenly referring to Jack Ruby prior to his attack on Oswald. Perhaps this is an honest mistake having to do with some report to Hoover that Oswald had talked of going to Cuba and had that as one of his goals during his alleged trip to Mexico. If there is no such innocent explanation, it then appears that Hoover has mixed up information on two people, one of which, Ruby, should not have been on anyone's mind. If there were real reports of Oswald going to Cuba, and interviews with Oswald, these should have become parts of Oswald's official history.

The final November 22 Hoover memo was completed and sent out to top FBI officials at 5:42 P.M. This memo outlined the actions that Hoover had taken. According to the memo, Hoover had heard the newsflash on the assassination, had called Robert Kennedy to notify him, and he had received a call from Dallas SAC Shanklin, all within twenty minutes of the assassination. Hoover reports

[79] Ibid.
[80] Kantor, 1978, pp. 35-36, 255-56.

that when he told Shanklin "to get in touch with the Secret Service and offer assistance," Shanklin informed Hoover that he had already done this. Did Shanklin do this on his own or was he instructed to do so by Belmont, who later said that he was involved immediately after the assassination? Hoover also said that he instructed Shanklin "to establish liaison with the local police." There is no indication in the memo that Shanklin had done this already, but also no explicit statement that he had not done so at the time he initiated contact with the Secret Service, a few minutes after the assassination.[81] According to a memo written on November 25 by Dallas FBI agent Manning C. Clements, Clements was told to establish liaison with the Dallas police "immediately upon receipt" of news of the assassination. This suggests that the order to establish contact with the Dallas police came at the same time as the instruction to establish liaison with the Secret Service.[82] If so, these were both instructions from Belmont.

The Hoover memo continues with an account of a 2:17 P.M., EST, call from Shanklin wherein Hoover told Shanklin "to go all out on this and find out who did it." Shanklin reports that President Kennedy has died and he provides information which turns out to be false, or so it appears (e.g., that the President was shot with a Winchester rifle and that a Secret Service agent had been killed).[83]

Sometime on the 22nd, an FBI memo was prepared for President Johnson. No time or author is indicated on this memo. The memo reported an August, 1962, Oswald visit to the Soviet embassy in Washington and reported that there was an interview of Oswald by the FBI concerning this visit. It also alleged that Oswald was arrested in August, 1963, while handing out Fair Play for Cuba leaflets and that this was also followed by a FBI interview. The memo states that Oswald had been arrested in connection with the killing of a Dallas policeman and that there was "No direct link with assassination." It also notes that Oswald was "refusing" to answer questions.[84]

As we have seen, there were media accounts which had Oswald identified as the lone assassin within about 15 hours of the assassination; it was implied in the *Christchurch Star's* wire service reports within about six hours. Although there was a definite focus on Oswald within the FBI on the afternoon of the 22nd,

---

[81] Hoover, 1963c.

[82] Hearings Before the President's Commission on the Assassination of President Kennedy, 1964, Vol. XXIV, p. 11.

[83] Ibid., Vol. XXIV, p. 11.

[84] Federal Bureau of Investigations, 1963.

Hoover would continue to qualify his remarks about Oswald into the morning of the 23rd. It is also apparent that Hoover was receiving a stream of inaccurate information or that he was not capable of digesting and/or reporting this information in a reliable way.

At 10:01 A.M. on the 23rd, Hoover called President Johnson and provided something of a briefing on the events.[85] In his report to the President, Hoover mistakenly told LBJ that:

> -a gun used by Oswald had been shipped to a Dallas P.O. box belonging to a *woman* named A. Heidel;
> -officials were in possession of a bullet that fell out of the President when his heart was being massaged;
> -that there were latent fingerprints on the gun;
> -Oswald lived with his mother;
> -the rifle had been wrapped in a blanket in his mother's home;
> -shots were fired from a fifth floor;
> -Oswald engaged in a gun battle with police at the theater.

All of this was wrong. Hoover also referred, in bizarre fashion, to the assassination as "this incident."

Hoover twice indicates to LBJ that there was not yet enough evidence against Oswald. Hoover first said that the evidence against Oswald "at the present time is not very, very strong" and later said that "The case as it stands now isn't strong enough to be able to get a conviction."[86] Although these remarks understate the problems in the case against Oswald, they do show that almost 24 hours after the assassination, Hoover is not the leader of the Oswald-did-it-alone school of thought. James Reston and John Hay Whitney's *Herald Tribune* were way out in front of Hoover.

Less than 30 hours later, Hoover reportedly had been convinced that Oswald was the man. Hoover's views on Oswald and the assassination are reported in a memo from Walter Jenkins, an assistant to President Johnson, to LBJ, dated 4:00 P.M., November 24. Jenkins's memo reports a phone conversation between

---

[85.] Hoover, 1963d.
[86.] Ibid.

Jenkins and Hoover.[87] According to Jenkins, Hoover was upset by events in Dallas. The FBI claimed that as a result of a tip received by them late on the 23rd, they had warned, to no avail, Dallas Police Chief Curry that an attempt would be made on Oswald's life. Hoover was also disturbed by what he viewed as excessive and inappropriate public comments by Dallas police officials. There is no identification of the specific comments that bothered Hoover. Hoover reportedly thought that the Dallas police had no case against Oswald until the FBI had provided them with evidence on the weapon, Oswald's fingerprints on a bag found at the scene, and Oswald's handwriting. This is probably an accurate statement and it reflects, of course, the extent to which the Dallas authorities became dependent on the investigation being run by the FBI. Jenkins related that Hoover said that he, Hoover, and Katzenbach wanted to have "something issued so we convince the public that Oswald is the real assassin." As we will see, Katzenbach was not acting alone in this area.

Close to the time of the Jenkins memo to LBJ, Alan Belmont was preparing a memo for FBI Deputy Director Clyde Tolson. This memo, produced sometime after 4:15 P.M. on November 24, provides the first detailed, emphatic and conclusive FBI statement that Lee Harvey Oswald was the lone assassin.[88] The memo is also notable because some the language suggests something different from a real investigation. It also comes from the man, Alan Belmont, who appears to have been active and in charge of the FBI's activities beginning immediately after the assassination and continuing throughout the FBI's work with the Warren Commission.

In this November 24 memo, and in another on the following day, Belmont indicates that the investigation is essentially over. The caution and uncertainty sometimes expressed by Hoover on the preceding day do not appear in any way in Belmont's memo. Within hours of the murder of Oswald, an event that should have suggested new questions to a real investigator, Belmont has wrapped up the case.

This memo was addressed to Deputy Director Tolson, which meant in FBI communications practices that it was intended also for Hoover. The November 24 memo began as follows:

[87.] Hearings Before the Select Committee On Assassinations of the United States House of Representatives, 1979, Vol. III, pp. 466-73.

[88.] Ibid., Vol. III, pp. 666-67.

> This afternoon I [Belmont] advised SAC Shanklin in Dallas that we are
> sending down Supervisors Rogge and Thompson for the purpose of going
> carefully over the written interview and investigative findings of our agents
> in the Oswald matter so that we can prepare a memorandum to the Attorney
> General, attaching exhibits such as photographs, et cetera, to set out the
> evidence showing that Oswald is responsible for the shooting that killed the
> President. We will show that Oswald was an avowed Marxist, a former
> defector to the Soviet Union and an active member of the FPCC, which has
> been financed by Castro. We will then show the background of Oswald,
> when and where he was born, et cetera, and then the story of what happened
> when the President was shot and subsequently until Oswald was picked up in
> the theatre. We will set forth the items of evidence which make it clear that
> Oswald is the man who killed the President.[89]

Coming from the man in charge of all investigative procedures and a man who
for a decade was in charge of the domestic intelligence division, Division Five,
this is an extraordinary memo.

The murder of the accused assassin obviously would indicate the need to
investigate the possible relationship between that murder and the assassination.
Any conclusions already arrived at about the assassination, conclusions that were
premature, would have to be reviewed in light of the new development. Instead,
on the day when a potentially major new lead develops, Belmont closes the case!
Officials in Dallas were not doing this. In this memo, Belmont lists some of
Oswald's connections to leftist groups. This apparently is of no interest to
Belmont. Also, as noted above, the FBI had been given a tip that Oswald would
be murdered; even this was apparently of no interest to Belmont.

As we will see when we look at the work of the Warren Commission, there
is a similarity between Belmont's proposed memorandum demonstrating or
asserting Oswald's guilt and an outline prepared about seven weeks later by J.
Lee Rankin, General Counsel for the Warren Commission, to provide structure
for the Commission's work. Both set forth an assumption of Oswald's guilt.

On the following day, November 25, Belmont sent a memo to FBI Assistant
Director William Sullivan indicating again that conclusions on the assassination
had already been arrived at, and that the primary problem was one of convincing
others of their validity.[90] Belmont begins this memo by saying that the Director
[Hoover] had been talking to Katzenbach, who in turn had been speaking with
"the White House." Katzenbach reportedly felt that the FBI's report should

---

[89.] Ibid.
[90.] Ibid., pp. 668-69.

include everything which may raise a question in the mind of the public or the press regarding this matter, including information on Oswald's military record, his return from Russia, and his trip to Mexico.

Belmont went on to state that "In other words, this report is to settle the dust in so far as Oswald and his activities are concerned, both from the standpoint that he is the man who assassinated the President, and relative to Oswald himself and his activities and background, et cetera." As we will see in Chapter Four, John J. McCloy would state that the purpose of the Warren Commission should be to "lay the dust." Obviously, any real investigation would not have as its central purpose the laying or settling of dust.

Belmont went on in his memo to state that the Director wants the report as soon as possible, but that providing all the information will require some additional time. Belmont states that Division Six will deal with the assassination itself and "the evidence gathered to show that Oswald is responsible" and that Division Five will handle Oswald's "background, associations, etc." Belmont ends the memo by saying that "This is a difficult report to prepare, but we will have to concentrate our full attention on it in order to produce the desired results."

As in the Belmont memo of the 24th, it is obvious that the FBI's efforts are to back up a conclusion reached sometime prior to the end of the day on the 24th. The phrase "produce the desired results" is not consistent with any idea of real investigation. Full attention is apparently to be focused on the "difficult report," not the difficult investigation. This is consistent with Belmont's lack of interest in Oswald's political connections, in the possible connections between the assassination and Oswald's death, or in much of anything for that matter. He was interested in settling dust.

Belmont was on the 24th and 25th burying all questions and doubts, doubts that should have been greatly intensified by the murder of Oswald on the 24th. A week later, Belmont stated in a memo to Tolson that he was rejecting a request to have an FBI representative at the first executive session of the Warren Commission. Belmont reported that he had told Katzenbach that "there is nothing that we can contribute at this time."[91] This makes no sense. How can Belmont be certain on November 24 and 25 that Oswald alone killed JFK and that the murder of Oswald held no significance and then have "nothing" to contribute ten days later?

91. Ibid., pp. 672-73.

Belmont ends this memo recounting information received from Katzenbach concerning Commission Chairman Earl Warren's intention to select Warren Olney to be chief counsel for the Commission. Belmont stated that Katzenbach was opposed to Olney and that he, Belmont, had told Katzenbach he was also opposed to Olney. As we will see later, John J. McCloy, Belmont's partner in dust control, would lead a successful effort to block the appointment of Olney.

Late on the day of November 24, Belmont committed the FBI to at least major parts of the cover story, i.e., Oswald did it and did it alone. Some hours before Belmont established this as the FBI's mission, another very important effort was getting underway. That was the effort to get President Johnson to agree to the creation of a presidential commission to report on the assassination. It is the next stage of the cover-up process.

Chapter Three

THE CREATION OF THE
"WARREN COMMISSION

There are conflicting accounts of the origins of the President's Commission on the Assassination of President Kennedy, known generally as the Warren Commission. The proposal of such a commission has been attributed variously to President Johnson, Deputy Attorney General Nicholas Katzenbach, LBJ advisor Abe Fortas, or, in one long overlooked account, Eugene Rostow, Dean of the Yale Law School. Due in part to the 1993 release of White House telephone transcripts, it is now possible to resolve the conflicts and to identify most or all of the significant figures involved directly in this important development.

The Warren Commission was officially created by Lyndon Johnson with Executive Order No. 11130 on November 29, 1963. There is nothing of significance in this document about the events leading up to the creation of the Commission. The Foreword to the report of the President's Commission provided more information, but not much more. It mentioned only the obvious events and then went on to identify conspiracy rumors and a desire to avoid multiple investigations as reasons for creating the Commission.[1]

This account reads as follows:

The events of these 2 days were witnessed with shock and disbelief by a Nation grieving the loss of its young leader. Throughout the world, reports on these events were disseminated in massive detail. Theories and

---

[1.] President's Commission on the Assassination of President Kennedy, 1964, p. 15.

speculation mounted regarding the assassination. In many instances, the intense public demand for facts was met by partial and frequently conflicting reports from Dallas and elsewhere. After Oswald's arrest and his denial of all guilt, public attention focused both on the extent of the evidence against him and the possibility of a conspiracy, domestic or foreign. His subsequent death heightened public interest and stimulated additional suspicions and rumors.

The Commission goes on to say that:

> After Lee Harvey Oswald was shot by Jack Ruby, it was no longer possible to arrive at the complete story of the assassination through normal judicial procedures during a trial of the alleged assassin. Alternative means for instituting a complete investigation were widely discussed. Federal and State officials conferred on the possibility of initiating a court of inquiry before a State magistrate in Texas. An investigation by the grand jury of Dallas County also was considered. As speculation about the existence of a foreign or domestic conspiracy became widespread, committees in both Houses of Congress weighed the desirability of congressional hearings to discover all the facts relating to the assassination.
>
> By his order of November 29 establishing the Commission, President Johnson sought to avoid parallel investigations and to concentrate fact-finding in a body having the broadest national mandate.[2]

This description is as vague as it is brief. The source or sources of the "massive detail" are not identified. The source of the contradictions is "Dallas and elsewhere." Even before Oswald was killed on the 24th, there were suspicions of conspiracy. The source of the suspicions is not identified and the suspicions are not elaborated.

There is in this short recapitulation a significant jump from Oswald's death on the 24th to the creation of the Commission on the 29th. In this account, the killing of Oswald precluded discovery of the truth through trial proceedings and there followed a wide discussion of alternatives. It is implied that this discussion involved local, state, and federal officials. This is inaccurate.

This story also indicates that the idea of a commission originated with President Johnson. This is true in a technical sense; President Johnson did sign the executive order which created the Commission. However, the President was pressured into taking this action, and the pressure came from people who did not occupy government positions at that time.

---

[2] Ibid., p. 16.

The first extensive and official description of the events leading to the creation of the Warren Commission appeared in the 1979 account from the Select Committee on Assassinations of the House of Representatives. Some of the earlier misrepresentations were corrected in this account; others were left standing.

THE HOUSE SELECT COMMITTEE'S TALE

Two stories emerge from the Hearings Before the Select Committee on Assassinations. One is the Committee's description of the events; the other is in the testimony from Nicholas Katzanbach, Deputy Attorney General at the time of the assassination. The two accounts are not identical even though the first is ostensibly dependent on the second.

The Select Committee's report contains a section entitled "Creation of the Warren Commission," which begins by saying that on November 22, "President Johnson was immediately faced with the problem of investigating the assassination."[3] This is misleading. As long as Oswald was alive, there wasn't any real question about the investigation; it would be conducted in Dallas during a trial of Oswald. Second, as the evidence will show, President Johnson was confronted with a problem after Oswald was killed, not immediately after the assassination. The problem for LBJ was not just one of investigating the assassination, but was also a problem presented to him by people attempting to shape the investigatory process.

The Committee's rendition of events goes on to say that on November 23, 1963, J. Edgar Hoover "forwarded the results of the FBI's preliminary investigation to him [LBJ]. This report detailed the evidence that indicated Lee Harvey Oswald's guilt." In fact, Hoover told LBJ on the morning of the 23rd that the case against Oswald was not then very good.[4] The Committee's account goes on to say that on the 24th, Hoover called LBJ aide Walter Jenkins and said that Katzenbach had told him that the President might appoint a commission. (As the record will show, Katzenbach was not speaking for the President, who was on

---

[3.] Hearings Before the Select Committee on Assassinations of the United States House of Representatives, 1979, Vol. XI, pp. 3-9.

[4.] Telephone call from J. Edgar Hoover to President Johnson, 10:01 A.M., November 23, 1963. Transcript from LBJ Library.

the 24th opposed to the idea of a commission.) Hoover expressed his opposition
to the creation of a commission, suggesting that the FBI handle the investigation
and submit a report to the Attorney General. Hoover made a vague reference to
problems a commission might cause for U.S. foreign relations. He also
mentioned that he and Katzenbach were anxious to have "something issued so
we can convince the public that Oswald is the real assassin."[5]

The Committee's report then summarizes parts of Katzenbach's testimony to
the Committee, stating that Katzenbach was very concerned about the multitude
of conspiracy theories which had already emerged. Consequently, he wrote a
memo on November 25 to LBJ aide Bill Moyers which emphasized the need to
quiet these rumors. The Katzenbach memo recommends that a statement be
issued immediately indicating that the evidence shows Oswald did it and that
there were no conspirators. The memo suggests that the FBI would be the
primary investigating body. Katzenbach then weakly suggested the formation of
a Presidential Commission.

> The only other step would be the appointment of a Presidential Commission
> of unimpeachable personnel to review and examine the evidence and
> announce its conclusions. This has both advantages and disadvantages. It [I]
> think it can await publication of the FBI report and public reaction to it here
> and abroad.

The wishy-washy nature of this recommendation is significant in understanding
Katzenbach's role in the creation of the Commission. The memo went on to say
that there is a need for "something to head off public speculations or
congressional hearings of the wrong sort." Katzenbach did also claim in his
testimony that he always wanted to know the truth, including the facts
concerning possible conspiracy.[6]

The Committee's description continues, stating that on November 25,
President Johnson ordered the FBI and the Department of Justice, run at this time
by Katzenbach instead of the distraught Robert Kennedy, to investigate the
assassination and the murder of Oswald. By November 27, Senator Everett M.
Dirksen had proposed a Senate Judiciary Committee investigation and
Representative Charles E. Goodell had proposed a joint Senate-House

---

[5.] Hearings Before the Select Committee on Assassinations of the United States House of
Representatives, 1979, Vol. XI, pp. 3-9.
[6.] Ibid.

investigation. Also, Texas Attorney General Waggoner Carr had announced that a state court of inquiry would be established. The Committee cited a statement by Leon Jaworski, who worked for the offices of both the Texas Attorney General and the U.S. Attorney General, indicating that LBJ told him on November 25 that he (LBJ) was encouraging Carr to proceed with the Texas court of inquiry.[7] Jaworski would later serve as the Watergate Special Prosecutor.

This Select Committee account then skips to a November 29 memo from Walter Jenkins to LBJ which stated that:

> Abe [Fortas] has talked with Katzenbach and Katzenbach has talked with the Attorney General. They recommend a seven man commission - two Senators, two Congressmen, the Chief Justice, Allen Dulles, and a retired military man (general or admiral). Katzenbach is preparing a description of how the Commission would function.[8]

This memo and some of Katzenbach's statements before the Committee imply that Katzenbach and perhaps Abe Fortas, and even Robert Kennedy, were the source of the idea for the Commission. Also, there is an implication that this November 29 memo was critical in LBJ's decision making. It was not. LBJ had agreed to the Commission idea not later than November 28.

The Select Committee's story goes on to briefly describe LBJ's efforts on November 29 to convince Chief Justice Earl Warren to serve as head of the Commission. This included LBJ's argument to Warren that if the speculation and rumors about the assassination continued and were to be intensified by the existence of a series of highly publicized and competing investigations, this could ultimately lead to a nuclear war and the immediate loss of 40 million American lives. Warren accepted the job.[9]

This account ends up by referring to a later meeting which included Katzenbach, Fortas, Jaworski, Solicitor General Archie Cox, Waggoner Carr, and Chief Justice Warren. Like Jaworski, Cox would later play an important role in the unfolding of events related to Watergate and the resignation of President Nixon. One result of this meeting was Carr's agreement to change his plan for a

---

[7] Ibid.
[8] Ibid.
[9] Ibid.

Texas court of inquiry.[10] It was transformed into a passive body, cooperating with the Warren Commission.

A MORE ACCURATE STORY

This 1979 House Select Committee rendition is certainly more elaborate than the official story circulated in 1964. The problem is that it substitutes one misleading story for another. The original suggested that LBJ initiated the process; the latter implies that Katzenbach is the most important figure.

Katzenbach's own 1978 testimony before the Select Committee was part of the basis for the Committee's account of the creation of the Warren Commission. Much of his testimony and deposition is consistent with that account. Some of it, however, is not consistent. Also, there were times when Katzenbach hinted at important undisclosed facts and the Committee staff simply did not bother to ask the additional questions. Katzenbach did imply that there was more to the story; the release in 1993 of the White House telephone transcripts shows that this is clearly true.

Katzenbach had testified before the Select Committee in September of 1978; his deposition was taken orally on August 4 of 1978. The Select Committee also included a number of relevant memos with the statements from Katzenbach.[11]

Katzenbach was asked to explain why he was "exerting tremendous pressure right after the assassination to get the FBI report out and to get a report in front of the American people." A November 25, 1963, memo from Katzenbach to Bill Moyers is referenced as evidence of Katzenbach's activities. Katzenbach explained that his concern was to quiet rumors and speculation about conspiracy. Katzenbach then added that his activities were related to the idea of creating a commission "such as the Warren Commission" and that he did not view the FBI investigation as the final or only investigation.[12]

[10] Ibid.

[11] Hearings Before the Select Committee on Assassinations of the United States House of Representatives, Vol. III, pp. 642-750.

[12] Ibid., pp. 643-44.

In his testimony Katzenbach represents the commission idea as his own several times. He also says, "I was never opposed to it."[13] This, of course, suggests that it was not his idea.

Katzenbach was asked whether there was pressure from the State Department to get something out. Katzenbach referred vaguely to concerns of other nations about what had happened and about possible changes in U.S. foreign policy resulting from the assassination.[14]

Later in the questioning, Katzenbach mentioned that by November 25 he was aware of Oswald's stay in Russia and his visit to Mexico. He says he was also then aware that the FBI had concluded that there was no conspiracy.[15] It is obvious that such a conclusion was completely unfounded just three days after the assassination and one day after the murder of Oswald. There is no way that the FBI could have eliminated the possibility that Oswald, even if guilty, could have had assistance or direction from others. As we have seen, officials in Dallas thought this was possible. It seems almost equally impossible that even if someone in the FBI maintained such a view, that there would be no disagreement about such a rapid conclusion. A series of memos reproduced by the Committee and presented in conjunction with Katzenbach's testimony indicate that there were divisions within the FBI about whether Oswald's role had been established.

An internal FBI memo from Alan Belmont to Associate Director Clyde Tolson suggested that the FBI would be able to show that Oswald is an "avowed Marxist, a former defector to the Soviet Union and an active member of the FPCC, which has been financed by Castro" and that "Oswald is the man who killed the President."[16] On the face of it, this is a very strange reaction from the FBI. On one hand they are ready to brand Oswald a communist and to convict him within two days of the assassination. On the other hand, they will display no interest in the possibility of a conspiracy even though Oswald is being associated with a variety of left-wing groups. This means that they are passing up an opportunity to investigate and pursue the very sort of people that Hoover and others had been obsessed with for four decades.

The Select Committee also reproduced in this context an undated memo with no identified author. Based on its content, it appears to be from November 24 or

---

[13.] Ibid., p. 644.
[14.] Ibid., pp. 645-46.
[15.] Ibid., p. 653.
[16.] Ibid., p. 666.

25. It indicates that Cartha DeLoach, head of the Crime Records division, was opposed to Katzenbach's suggestion that the FBI put out a statement saying that the FBI "was now persuaded that Oswald killed the President" but that the investigation was continuing.[17] This memo shows a lack of agreement, at least on what the FBI should be saying at that early date.

As discussed in the previous chapter, Alan Belmont wrote a memo on November 25 stating that the purpose of the FBI's report should be to "settle the dust."[18]

A week later, December 3, Belmont sent a memo to Clyde Tolson informing him that Katzenbach thinks it would be good if either Hoover or Belmont attended the first meeting of the Warren Commission. Belmont tells Tolson that he does not think this makes sense since the FBI was not ready to contribute anything.[19] This seems a little unusual since Belmont had written on the 24th that the FBI was already able to show that Oswald killed Kennedy.

The intertwining of Katzenbach's actions and those of Belmont is indicated in a comment by Katzenbach in his oral deposition. A December 9, 1963, letter to Chief Justice Warren suggested that either the Commission or the Justice Department release a statement saying that the FBI had established "beyond a reasonable doubt" that Oswald killed Kennedy and that the investigation had so far uncovered no information suggesting a conspiracy.[20] Katzenbach had signed this letter, but in his deposition he said that this letter was probably drafted by the FBI.[21] The fact that the Deputy Attorney General is signing his name to something this important that he didn't write suggests how closely interconnected his actions were with those of Belmont and, perhaps, others in the FBI. In this oral deposition Katzenbach also revealed, in contradiction to his testimony, that he was not acting on his own when he proposed a commission to investigate the assassination.

In that deposition Katzenbach mentioned that as of the afternoon of the assassination, he and others at the Department of Justice recognized that "primary jurisdiction" for the investigation was obviously in Texas.[22] Although he did not say so, this was only changed by the murder of Oswald two days later.

[17.] Ibid., p. 657.
[18.] Ibid., p. 668.
[19.] Ibid., p. 672.
[20.] Ibid., pp. 674-76.
[21.] Ibid., p. 725.
[22.] Ibid., pp. 685-86.

In his deposition Katzenbach said that he "felt very early" that some sort of commission would be useful as a way of satisfying people in other countries that the truth was being told and that a commission might act to direct any and all investigations.[23] He was not asked to specify what he meant by "very early".

When asked why he thought that "external review" would be necessary, he mentioned that a commission would be a way of dealing with the conflicting stories coming out of Texas and the general problem of conspiracy rumors.[24] Katzenbach went on to say that he thought that representation on the Commission from the Senate and House would be needed to prevent the development of a "separate House or Senate investigation."[25]

Katzenbach told the Committee that Hoover opposed the creation of a Commission and that President Johnson "neither rejected nor accepted the idea. He did not embrace it. I thought there was a period of time when he thought that it might be unnecessary to do."[26] This definitely understated Johnson's initial opposition. There was then an important set of statements by Katzenbach that should have been followed by specific questions from the House staff; they were not followed up.

Katzenbach was asked who else (presumably beyond the President and Hoover) he talked to during the time he was arriving at the idea of a commission. Katzenbach said that he believed he "recommended it to Bill Moyers" and raised the issue with Walter Jenkins and President Johnson. Katzenbach was then asked about "people outside the President's immediate circle" and he responded that he did talk to such people mentioning Dean Rusk and Alexis Johnson as two people he may have talked to.[27]

Katzenbach then said:

> I am sure I talked about it with people outside the government entirely who called me and suggested old friends or former colleagues.[28]

Katzenbach does not identify and he is not asked to identify those people "outside the government entirely." There is no question asked about the phrase,

---

23. Ibid., p. 689.
24. Ibid., pp. 690-92.
25. Ibid., p. 692.
26. Ibid., p. 693.
27. Ibid., p. 694.
28. Ibid.

"suggested old friends or former colleagues." Instead, the questioning shifted to the views of Rusk and others already mentioned by Katzenbach. Given an opportunity to actually find out how the Warren Commission came into being, the House Committee's staff decided to go on to other things. Because of the release of the White House telephone transcripts, we will now be able to identify some or most of those people who were "outside the government entirely".

A few other comments by Katzenbach are worth noting before we turn to a reconstruction of the events leading to the creation of the Commission that would produce the cover-up story. Katzenbach was asked about possible connections between Oswald and agencies of the government. While acknowledging that the CIA should have told the Commission about the CIA-Mafia operations against Castro, he asserted that there was no evidence connecting Oswald to the CIA or any other government agency.[29] He also said that it was necessary immediately after the assassination "to follow up all that information" relating to the possibility of a foreign conspiracy.[30] As the record will show, tracking down conspiracies, domestic or foreign, seemed to be the last thing on anyone's mind, including those outside the government who got the ball rolling.

CREATING THE WARREN COMMISSION

The release of the White House telephone transcripts, thirty years after the assassination, make it possible to now construct a much more complete account of the Warren Commission's origins. Those transcripts tell the story that Katzenbach hinted at in his 1978 testimony, a story LBJ had also hinted at in 1971. Had the appropriate questions been asked of Katzenbach in 1978, it is at least possible that Katzenbach himself would have filled in some of the gaps left in the record for over three decades.

It appears that the idea of a Presidential commission to report on the assassination of President Kennedy was first suggested by Eugene Rostow, Dean of the Yale Law School, in a telephone call to LBJ aide William Moyers during the afternoon of November 24, 1963. Although the time of this call is missing from the White House daily diary, it is possible to identify the period during which the call was made. Rostow refers to the killing of Oswald, so the call had

---

[29] Ibid., pp. 697-98.
[30] Ibid., p. 718.

to be after 2:07 P.M. Eastern Standard Time, the time Oswald was pronounced dead. The call appears in the White House daily diary prior to a conversation at 4:40 P.M. between President Johnson and Governor Pat Brown of California.[31] There is a memorandum which clearly indicates that Rostow called the White House well before 4:00 p.m., EST.

Rostow told Moyers that he was calling to make a suggestion that a "Presidential commission be appointed of very distinguished citizens in the very near future." Rostow recommended that such a commission be

> Bi-partisan and above politics -- no Supreme Court justices but people like Tom Dewey and Bill Story from Texas and so on. A commission of seven or nine people, maybe Nixon, I don't know, to look into the whole affair of the murder of the President because world opinion and American opinion is just now so shaken by the behavior of the Dallas Police that they're not believing anything.[32]

Rostow does not explain how he has determined the nature of world or American opinion within minutes or an hour or so of the murder of Oswald. As we saw in the preceding chapter, the Dallas police were a model of objectivity and open mindedness compared to Alan Belmont of the FBI and at least much of the major media.

Rostow also said that he had already spoken "about three times" that day to Nick Katzenbach but he was making his suggestion directly to Moyers because of his uncertainty that Katzenbach would pass it on. Rostow explains that Katzenbach "sounded too groggy so I thought I'd pass this thought along to you".[33]

It is highly probable that it was Rostow's call(s) that Katzenbach was referring to in his 1978 testimony when he said that he was "sure" that he had talked to "people outside the government entirely who called me."

Apparently Rostow was making his suggestion in the context of discussions with at least one other person. He said to Moyers:

[31.] White House Daily Diary and telephone logs for November 24. Provided by LBJ Library.

[32.] Telephone call from Eugene Rostow to William Moyers, November 24, 1963. Transcript provided by LBJ Library.

[33.] Ibid.

Now, I've got a party here. I've [or We've] been pursuing the policy, you know, that people need to come together at this time.[34]

Rostow does not identify the individual or individuals with whom he has been talking.

Moyers briefly interrupted this line of discussion by stating his concern that recent events were undermining the credibility of U.S. institutions. He then returned to Rostow's suggestion, saying:

All right. Now, your suggestion is that he [President Johnson] appoint a Special Commission of distinguished Americans, primarily in the field of law, I presume to look into the whole question of the assassination.

Rostow says "That's right and a report on it" and then the conversation ended with Moyers assuring Rostow that he will discuss this with President Johnson.[35] Rostow acted very quickly on what was a momentous decision and he did so even though he had no obligation or responsibility to do anything.

In Volume III of the Hearings of the House Select Committee on Assassinations, there is a copy of a memo written by LBJ aide Walter Jenkins to the President which reports on a phone conversation that Jenkins apparently had with J. Edgar Hoover.[36] According to the memo, Hoover said over the phone that:

The thing I am concerned about, and so is Mr. Katzenbach, is having something issued so we can convince the public that Oswald is the real assassin. Mr. Katzenbach thinks that the President might appoint a Presidential Commission of three outstanding citizens to make a determination.[37]

Hoover goes on to state misgivings about the idea of a commission. It is, of course, of interest that Hoover and, apparently, Katzenbach already have Oswald as the assassin. Did Rostow discuss this with the "groggy" and insufficiently active Katzenbach? The timing of this memo is of immediate interest.

[34.] Ibid.

[35.] Ibid.

[36.] Hearings Before the Select Committee on Assassinations of the United States House of Representatives, 1979, Vol. III, pp. 466, 468-73.

[37.] Ibid., pp. 469, 472.

The time on the memo is 4:00 P.M., November 24. Hoover has already spoken with Katzenbach and received from him information concerning the idea of a commission. Apparently, Hoover spoke with Katzenbach prior to 4:00 P.M. We now have a considerably shorter time frame.

Oswald died at 2:07 Eastern Standard Time. Before 4:00 Katzenbach had spoken with Hoover about a commission. Katzenbach was acting as a result of his conversation(s) with Rostow. We are now down to something well under one hour and fifty-three minutes for Rostow to hear of Oswald's death, consider all the factors, discuss it with at least one other person, and begin to act. The entire time span for Rostow's actions is almost certainly less than ninety minutes, allowing only twenty or so additional minutes for him to talk to Katzenbach and for Katzenbach to talk to Hoover. We don't know who was with Rostow at the time of Oswald's death. Did Rostow act as an individual or was he representing a collective decision when he moved so rapidly to have a Presidential commission established? This probably cannot be answered in a definite way without a candid statement from Rostow and, perhaps, others. There are, however, indications in the events of November 25 to 29 that Rostow and then Katzenbach were acting on behalf of a group of people.

As we have seen, the idea of a commission was suggested to at least two people close to LBJ, Bill Moyers and Walter Jenkins, on the afternoon of the 24th. The suggestion was relayed to LBJ by someone before 10:30 A.M. the next day, November 25. This is clear from the transcript of Johnson's phone conversation with J. Edgar Hoover at 10:30.

President Johnson immediately mentioned the idea of a commission and stated his opposition to it. Johnson:

> Two things. Apparently some lawyer in Justice is lobbying with the Post because that's where the suggestion came from for this Presidential Commission which we think would be very bad and put it right in the White House. Now we can't be checking up on every shooting scrape in the country, but they've gone to the Post now to get them an editorial, and the Post is calling up and saying they're going to run an editorial if we don't do things.[38]

We won't stop to dwell on the incredible and bizarre reference to the assassination as one of many shooting scrapes. Johnson's account is a little

---

[38.] Telephone call from President Johnson to J. Edgar Hoover, 10:30 A.M., November 25, 1963. Transcript provided by LBJ Library.

vague. When he referred to "some lawyer in Justice", did he mean Deputy Attorney General Katzenbach? Perhaps he was confused or poorly informed and the reference was to Rostow. Whatever the case may be, it is clear that LBJ was against the creation of a Presidential commission. LBJ went on to say that he favored an FBI report which would be provided to the Attorney General of the United States, and he expressed support for a Texas court of inquiry, suggesting to Hoover that the FBI and Texas inquiries be coordinated.[39]

It appears that someone of significance at the Washington Post was ready to promote the idea of a commission and to pressure LBJ to accept the idea. The names of the commission supporters do not appear in this conversation, but, as we will see below. they do show up in an FBI memo. The fact that the Post was on board less than 24 hours after Oswald's death suggests some direct connection to Rostow, Katzenbach, or some other promoter of the commission. Before this conversation ends, Hoover told LBJ that in his view, the Post was in the same category as the Communist Party's Daily Worker. One doubts that Hoover is completely serious with this comment; it is indicative of Hoover's brand of conservative politics. Perhaps this comment reflected the mood set by LBJ's reference to the assassination of President Kennedy as a shooting scrape.

As this account will show, various people continued to pressure LBJ to embrace the commission proposal on November 25. As of the 25th, Johnson was opposed to it. As our account will also show, LBJ has changed his mind, or had his mind changed, by the afternoon of the 28th. The available record, as far as this author is aware, is not helpful for the 26th and 27th. Something probably happened on one or both of those days, but those events are not currently accessible. What happened on the 25th, however, is suggestive of both how and why LBJ shifted from anti- to pro-commission. The events of the 25th also seem to represent a continuation of the efforts initiated by Eugene Rostow on the 24th.

Immediately after LBJ's conversation with Hoover, wherein LBJ expressed definite opposition to a Presidential commission, the President received a phone call from Joseph Alsop. This call was made at 10:40 A.M. on the 25th and it was still less than 24 hours since Oswald was killed. Alsop was one of the country's best known columnists and one of the most important promoters of Establishment policies. We will return to this in Chapter Five.

After opening pleasantries, LBJ immediately informed Alsop that there was going to be a state court of inquiry in Texas headed by the Attorney General and

---

[39.] Ibid.

also including one or two outstanding jurists, naming Leon Jaworski and Dean Story as possible participants. Alsop asked if there will be "somebody from outside Texas."[40] The following exchange then transpires.

> LBJ: No, they're going to have FBI from outside Texas, but this is under Texas law and they take all the involvements and we don't send in a bunch of carpet-baggers...that's the worse thing he could do right now...

> JA: You think so...

> LBJ: I know...well, we've got the FBI doing anything that...if there's any question about Texas operations they've got an FBI that's going to the bottom of it and direct with the Attorney General...but paralleling that is the blue ribbon state board of inquiry headed by the brilliant Attorney General and associated with him somebody like John Garwood, Will Clayton's son-in-law, who was a brilliant Supreme Court Justice that's retired...somebody like Roberts did at Pearl Harbor...and that's what the Attorney General is doing...now, if we have another Commission, hell, you're gonna have people running over each other and everybody agreed...now I know that some of the lawyers...they thought of the blue ribbon commission first, the Justice, and we just can't have them lobbying them against the President, when he makes these decisions. We decided that the best thing to do, number one to put the FBI in full force, number two to put the State in full force...

> JA: Nobody...nobody...Mr. President, is lobbying me, I lay awake all night...

> LBJ: They're not lobbying you, they're lobbying me....last night. I spent the day on it...I had to leave Mrs. Kennedy's side at the White House and call and ask the Secret Service and FBI

40. Telephone call from Joseph Alsop to President Johnson, 10:40 A.M., November 25, 1963. Transcript provided by LBJ Library.

to proceed immediately...I spent most of my day on this thing, yesterday. I had the Attorney General from Texas fly in here...I spent an hour and a half with him yesterday evening...I talked to the Justice Department lawyers and to the FBI and the FBI is of the opinion that the wisest, quickest, ablest, most effective way to go about it is for them to thoroughly study it and bring in a written report to the Attorney General at the earliest possible date which they've been working on since 12:30 yesterday. Number one...and they have information that is available to no one...that has not been presented thus far and so forth...Number two...to parallel that, we're having a blue ribbon court of inquiry...

JA: In Texas?

LBJ: In Texas...where this thing occurred..

JA: Mr. President, just let me give you my political judgment on the thing. I think you've done everything that could probably be done...

LBJ: We just don't want to be in a position...I'll make this one more statement and then I'm through...I want to hear you...we don't want to be in the position of saying that we have come into a state other than the FBI...that they pretty well accept...but some outsiders have told them that their integrity is no good and that we're going to have some carpetbag trials...we can't haul off people from New York and try them in Jackson, Mississippi...and we can't haul off people from Dallas and try them in New York.

JA: I see that, Mr. President...but let me...

LBJ: It is their constitutional right...go ahead...now..

JA: Let me make one suggestion because I think this covers...I think this bridges the gap which I believe and Dean Acheson believes still exists...being...and Bill Moyers is the only person I've talked to about it...and Friendly is going to come out tomorrow morning with a big thing about a blue ribbon commission which he thought of independently...it isn't Justice Department lawyers who are carrying on this...it's just things happened thought of by a lot people and you thought of more than...more details than anyone else...and I'm sure you're right except there's one missing piece...I suggest that you announce that as you do not want the Attorney General to have the clean, full, responsibility of reporting on his own brother's assassination, that you have authorized the three jurists and I would suggest the Texas jurists and two non-Texas jurists to review all the evidence by the FBI and produce a report to the nation for the nation...and after the investigation is completed...so that the country will have the story judicially reviewed, outside Texas and if you tell Bill Moyers to call up Friendly and if you'll get out a special announcement this afternoon, you're going to make a marvelous...well, you've already made a marvelous start...you haven't put a damned foot one-quarter of an inch wrong...and I've never seen anything like it, you've been simply marvelous in the most painful circumstances but I do feel that there is that much of a gap and I'm sure that if Moyers calls Friendly, you have a terrific support from the Washington Post and from the whole of the rest of the press instantly...

LBJ: I'll ruin both procedures we've got, though...

JA: No you won't...no you won't just use the procedures you've got and add to those procedures a statement saying that when the FBI has completed its work, when it has completed its work...as you do not wish to inflict on the Attorney General, the painful task of reviewing the evidence concerning his own brother's assassination...you have asked two or three, including I would include the best judge on the Texas bench...American jurists beyond, or individuals, Dean Acheson, for example, two or three individuals beyond any possible suspicion as to their

independence and impartiality, to draw up a written report
giving to the public everything of the FBI that is relevant and
then you will have this written report...not Texas, which tells
the whole story which is based on the FBI evidence...it doesn't
need to use the things that the FBI says can't be used...and yet
will carry absolute conviction and will just be that little extra
added to the admirable machinery that you've already got that
will carry complete conviction...

LBJ: My lawyers, though, Joe, tell me that the White House
must not...the President...must not inject himself into local
killings...and...

JA: I agree with that...but in this case it does happen to be the
killing of the President...and the thing is...I am not suggesting
issue...

LBJ: I know that...

JA: Mind you, mind you, Mr. President, I'm not talking about
an investigative body, I am talking about a body which will
take all the evidence the FBI has amassed when they have
completed their inquiry and produce a public report on the
death of the President. That, I think, you see, that is not an
interference in Texas...

LBJ: No, but its...

JA: Wait a second, now...that is a way to transmit to the public,
without breach of confidence...and in a way that will carry
absolute conviction of that the FBI has turned up...

LBJ: Why can't the FBI transmit it?

JA: Because no one...again…on the left they won't believe the
FBI...and the FBI doesn't write well...

LBJ: You mean Nick Katzenbach?

JA: Well, I just wouldn't put it on Bobby and Nick Katzenbach...I'd have it outside...I think it's unfair to put it on Bobby...it is his own brother's death...

LBJ: Not going to touch it on Bobby...we're putting it on the finest jurists in the land...former head of the American Bar Association...that's number one that we're putting it on...then we're putting it on the top investigative agency and asking them to write a report...

JA: I'm not...I'm not suggesting that you appoint an additional investigating commission...I'm just suggesting that if you want to carry absolute convictions...this very small addition to the admirable machinery that you've already have...will help you and I believe that it will...the imagination of the country and be a very useful, happy thing...and the man asks if you have two seconds...this afternoon for example...ask Dean Acheson...he's the man to ask...I see all the arguments you make and you're dead right and I'm not...my conception is completely wrong...but I do think that this additional feature is needed..

LBJ: I talked to...I guess, after midnight last night...

JA: Well, I know how you must have been concerned...

LBJ: the ablest, the truest civil liberties lawyer in this town in my judgment...the man that's made the best arguments before the Supreme Court and it was his judgment the worst mistake we could make...getting trapped..

JA: And, I now see exactly how right you are and how wrong I was about this idea of a blue ribbon commission...

LBJ: Now, you see, Katzenbach suggested that and that provoked it...the lawyers and the council just hit the ceiling...said , my God almighty..

JA: I see...I see...I see that you're right and he was wrong...what I do..

LBJ: Then I called back to Katzenbach and I thought he accepted...

JA: Well, I don't know anything about Katzenbach...I haven't talked to him for three weeks...but what I am suggesting is not at all what Katzenbach suggested...I am suggesting simply a device...

LBJ: Well, let me talk to Acheson and...

JA: for summing up the result of the FBI inquiry in a way that will be completely coherent, detailed, and will carry unchallengeable convictions and this carrying conviction is just as important as carrying the on the investigation...in the right way...and I worry about this Post editorial...I'd like you to get ahead of them...

LBJ: And I worry about the Post, period, ..but..

JA: Well, I do too...but I'd like you to get ahead of them and if you have...if you make this decision and have Moyers call Friendly or Kay instead of being...well, you know…this is what we ought to do...this is what ought to be done and then what you do being denounced as inadequate, they'll be put so hard and will do you a tremendous piece and I'm sure you will have the strongest possible support...it will be thought that everything has been done that needs doing and...but I do think…my own judgment is that there is that little missing piece...and, Dean, may disagree and you talk to him...

LBJ: I'll talk to him and..

JA: And, I hate to interfere, sir...I only dare to do so because I care so much about you..

LBJ: I know that, Joe..

JA: And I have the deepest faith in you and I think you've been right and I've been wrong...as to the general conception..

LBJ: It's not a question...it's not really my thinking...I'm not enough experienced..

JA: I'm really...what I'm really honestly giving you is public relation advice and not legal advice..

LBJ: Well...I'm not bounded...I don't have a definite civil liberties picture that some of the folks that have worked on this with me...I had a lawyer left my house around midnight...and spent, I guess, three or four hours going over this thing from A to Z...after the Attorney General was called in here yesterday afternoon ..and after the FBI was put on it...after we told Secret Service to make available everything they had...and, we thought, that this was the best way to handle it...

JA: Well, Mr. President...I repeat...I must not keep you because you'll be late getting into your trousers...but I repeat...I think your decisions have been 200% right and I was wrong...from the public relations standpoint and from the standpoint of carrying conviction...there is that missing key which is easy to supply without infringing upon Texas feelings or sovereignty..

LBJ: Thank you, my friend, Bye..

JA: Goodbye...[41]

---

41. Ibid.

At the outset of this conversation, LBJ emphatically asserted that the investigation would be the responsibility of Texas authorities, but with a significant role played by the FBI. LBJ referred to efforts of unidentified lawyers, implying they were in the Justice Department, to get a commission established and he stated that this would not happen. He was probably referring to Katzenbach, perhaps only Katzenbach. The investigation, he said, would be handled by the FBI and the State of Texas.

Alsop then launched an effort to change LBJ's mind, employing a mixture of tactics, including self-deprecation, praise for LBJ, giving advice, argumentation, and manipulation. He also employed the names of other people to buttress his position and to convince Johnson that this commission idea was going to have support from significant people. Along the way he told Johnson that "it isn't Justice Department lawyers who are carrying on this." That observation is consistent with Katzenbach's 1978 testimony that the idea for a commission came from people outside the government. Alsop's assertion also fits with what we have already seen in the intercession by Eugene Rostow.

It is also of interest that Alsop says he has already spoken with Bill Moyers about the commission idea. That means that in less than 24 hours following Oswald's death, both Rostow and Alsop have decided to intervene and they both have chosen Moyers as a channel to the President. Is this a coincidence or were Rostow and Alsop acting as part of a coordinated effort? Their suggestions on the make-up of the commission are different, but neither is definite on this issue.

Alsop indicated that one of the people he has discussed this with was former Secretary of State Dean Acheson. He did not say when he talked with Acheson; it had to be less than 22 hours after Oswald's death. Was Acheson's involvement independent of Rostow's? Alsop's use of Acheson's name seems to be a way of impressing upon Johnson that this idea came from or with the endorsement of heavy-hitters. Alsop also told LBJ that [Alfred] Friendly of the Washington Post had come to the same idea on his own and that the Post will promote the idea. An internal FBI memo from C. D. DeLoach to John P. Mohr, dated November 25, 1963, shows that Washington Post editor James Russell Wiggins was actually the individual pushing for a commission. The memo also mentions, correctly, that James Reston had suggested the creation of a Presidential Commission in the *New York Times* on November 25. (A copy of this memo was provided to the author by Harold Weisberg).

When LBJ stated that such a commission would ruin the proposed Texas-FBI procedures, Alsop interrupted the President to argue that a commission would add to those efforts. It is clear that Alsop, and perhaps others for whom he was speaking, had no intention of excluding the FBI from the investigation. He assured LBJ that such a commission could cooperate with the FBI in not using "the things that the FBI says can't be used." This is being said less than 72 hours after the assassination, less than 24 hours after the killing of Oswald. What is Alsop referring to here? How does he know at this time that there are things the FBI will prefer to keep out of the record? On the face of it, this is curious. LBJ, for whatever reason, did not even ask Alsop what he was talking about. Perhaps LBJ did not really hear this; perhaps he already was getting the feeling that he should not ask. Alsop again mentioned Dean Acheson, this time as a possible commission member.

Alsop suggested that the FBI will gather information and the commission will then produce the report. The final role of the FBI will be close to the one Alsop was suggesting. When LBJ asked why the FBI couldn't issue the report, Alsop told him that people on the left would not believe the FBI and that the FBI didn't write well. Whether either of them laughed about this silly explanation is not discernible in the transcripts.

Alsop engaged in some double talk to the effect that he was and was not proposing something new. He again introduced Acheson's name, saying "ask Dean Acheson...he's the man to ask." He also tries to distance himself from the Katzenbach proposal, but does not specify any differences between his proposal and the one made by Katzenbach.

Alsop recommended that LBJ get out in front of the Washington Post and have Moyers discuss things with Friendly or Kay [Katherine Meyer Graham]. For the fourth time, Acheson is mentioned as Alsop again pressures LBJ to talk to him. LBJ says that he will do so.

Alsop ended by saying that LBJ's decisions were 200 percent correct, but that LBJ still needed to change his mind on the commission. LBJ seemed unconvinced, but no longer as certain about his own judgment. Alsop has been partially successful.

Within three days, LBJ will have reversed himself, becoming a supporter of a commission and, legally speaking, its creator. Douglas Brinkley, an Acheson biographer, says that Johnson phoned Acheson "a few days after assuming the Presidency" and discussed the commission idea. LBJ also apparently sent Abe Fortas to talk to Acheson about this. In Brinkley's account, Acheson was recommending a group of state judges as members of a commission.[42] In Alsop's statements Acheson was represented as an important figure in the emergence of a commission proposal. Acheson's role has been obscured in an edited version of Alsop's call to LBJ which is presented in a 1997 book, *Taking Charge,* edited by Michael R. Beschloss. The Alsop call itself is misrepresented as an effort by President Johnson to get Alsop to pressure colleagues at the Washington Post to oppose the creation of the commission. Also, Rostow's call is excluded entirely from this collection of White House tape transcripts.

There is also the November 25 memo from Katzenbach to Moyers. Katzenbach, apparently not as "groggy" as he was the day before when Rostow talked to him, addresses a number of important issues in this memo, including a Presidential commission. We quoted above one paragraph from this memo. It was sent to Moyers during the morning of the 25th and Katzenbach also hand delivered a copy to Alan Belmont of the FBI. It follows, in its entirety.

November 25, 1963

MEMORANDUM FOR MR. MOYERS

It is important that all of the facts surrounding President Kennedy's Assassination be made public in a way which will satisfy people in the United States and abroad that all of the facts have been told and that a statement to this effect be made now.

1. The public must be satisfied that Oswald was the assassin; that he did not have confederates who are still at large; and that the evidence was such that he would have been convicted at trial.

2. Speculation about Oswald's motivation ought to be cut off, and we should have some basis for rebutting thought that this was a Communist conspiracy or (as the Iron Curtain press is saying) a right-wing conspiracy to blame it on the Communists. Unfortunately the facts on Oswald seem about too pat--too obvious (Marxist, Cuba, Russian wife, etc.). The Dallas police

---

[42.] Brinkley, 1992, p. 206.

have put out statements on the Communist conspiracy theory, and it was they who were in charge when he was shot and thus silenced.

3. The matter has been handled thus far with neither dignity nor conviction. Facts have been mixed with rumor and speculation. We can scarcely let the world see us totally in the image of the Dallas police when our President is murdered.

I think this objective may be satisfied by making public as soon as possible a complete and thorough FBI report on Oswald and the assassination. This may run into the difficulty of pointing to inconsistencies between this report and statements by Dallas police officials. But the reputation of the Bureau is such that it may do the whole job.

The only other step would be the appointment of a Presidential Commission of unimpeachable personnel to review and examine the evidence and announce its conclusions. This has both advantages and disadvantages. I think it can await publication of the FBI report and public reaction to it here and abroad.

I think, however, that a statement that all the facts will be made public property in an orderly and responsible way should be made now. We need something to head off public speculation or Congressional hearings of the wrong sort.

Nicholas deB. Katzenbach
Deputy Attorney General[43]

Katzenbach had still not developed a full-blown commitment to the idea of a commission. Certainly, Alsop and Rostow had delivered more energetic arguments for it. It is brought up late in the memo and Katzenbach observes that a commission would have its advantages and disadvantages.

[43.] Hearings Before the Select Committee on Assassinations of the United States House of Representatives, 1979, Vol. III, pp. 566-68.

The rest of the memo can be read in at least two ways. On one hand, Katzenbach does say twice that all of the facts must be presented. On the other hand, before any investigation has been completed, he has indicted and convicted Oswald as a lone assassin. He mentions some facts, or alleged facts, concerning Oswald's life which could suggest or be used to suggest a Communist conspiracy, but for some reason Katzenbach has already concluded that there was no conspiracy, Communist or otherwise. Hoover, the great pursuer of communists, also passed up these appetizing morsels within hours or days of the assassination.

Between November 25th and the 28th LBJ was transformed from opponent of to promoter of a commission. It is clear that a number of people acted to bring about this change. Eugene Rostow brought up the idea initially, to both Bill Moyers and Katzenbach. Rostow discussed this with at least one unidentified person in the minutes immediately following Oswald's death. Joseph Alsop applied pressure to LBJ less than 24 hours later. If Alsop is to be believed, and there is no reason to doubt this, Dean Acheson was also involved in developing and promoting the idea. Other immediate supporters appear to include both Alfred Friendly and Katherine Graham, and, as noted before, particularly Russell Wiggins.

During the afternoon of the 28th, at 3:21, LBJ called Senator James O. Eastland, Democrat from Mississippi, to get his cooperation in shutting down a proposal for a Senate committee hearing which would produce a record of the facts surrounding the assassination. Eastland reported that Senator Wayne Morse, Democrat form Oregon, and a "great number" of other Senators were requesting that Eastland's committee hold such hearings.[44]

The following exchange then transpires:

> LBJ: And, my thought would be this, if we could do it. We might get two members from each body...you see we're going to have three inquiries running as it is..
>
> JE: Well, I wouldn't want that...that wouldn't do..

44. Telephone call from President Johnson to Senator James Eastland, 3:21 P.M., November 28, 1963. Transcript provided by LBJ Library.

> LBJ: And if we could have two Congressmen and two Senators…and maybe a Justice of the Supreme Court to take the FBI report and review it and write a report…and do anything they felt needed to be done…I think it would…this is a very explosive thing and it could be a very dangerous thing for the country.. and a little publicity could just fan the flames. What would you think about…if we could work it out of getting somebody from the Court and somebody from the House and somebody from the Senate and have a real high-level judiciary study of all the facts.[45]

President Johnson indicated that he expected that there would be three inquiries. This apparently referred to inquiries by the FBI, the commission that he was then supporting, and, still, the Texas board of inquiry. The proposed commission would include two Senators, two Representatives, and a Justice of the Supreme Court.

Eastland was immediately responsive to LBJ's concerns and implicitly supportive of the proposal for a commission. The conversation ended with LBJ indicating that he was confident that Eastland would be able to prevent his Senate committee from holding hearings.

LBJ had now become a or the leading proponent of the commission idea. The morning after the call to Senator Eastland, at 11:10 A.M. on the 29th, LBJ called Senator Mike Mansfield, to promote the idea of a high-level commission. Secretary of State Dean Rusk was with LBJ and he got on the phone to support the proposal.

> LBJ:…several investigations in education. Secretary of State is here with me now and he's quite concerned about it…we have given a good deal of thought…at least I have…on the suggestion of Katzenbach over at Justice…to having a high-level commission…try to get someone from each side…House and Senate…and let them review the investigation that has been made by the Court of Inquiry and the thorough one by the FBI and let them staff it. Now I talked to McCormack and he said that would be agreeable to him…I have talked to Eastland, who started the

---

[45] Ibid.

investigation...and he said that that would agreeable to him. I thought I'd better talk to you and anybody else you suggested...see what your reaction to it might be and maybe I ought to talk to some other people...I haven't talked to any of the Justices or anything like that yet...but we think that is the best way to avoid a lot of television show and I'd like for the Secretary of State to spend a minute with you, telling you some of his concern.

MM: Well, first, Mr. President, I think it is a good idea....O.K. with me and then you ought to talk to Dixon...

LBJ: Go ahead Mike...here is the Secretary..

DR: ...possible implications of this that if the rumors were to leak out as fact and if there were anything in this that had not been fully substantiated it would cause a tremendous storm...and it is very important that we work on the basis of the highest possible information on this situation...meanwhile trying to get it...the absolute truth on it...so I think this is very much in my mind...this has already been commented on and picked up all around the world and if we're not careful here we could really blow up quite a storm.

MM: That's right.[46]

LBJ attributed the idea of a commission to Katzenbach. As the record shows, the idea did not originate with Katzenbach and he was not successful in his early efforts on its behalf. Eugene Rostow, Joe Alsop, and, apparently, Dean Acheson were far more important. Johnson knew that it was not Katzenbach's suggestion that got the ball rolling. LBJ had dismissed the suggestion when it came from Katzenbach. There seems to be no way of knowing why LBJ was attributing this to Katzenbach. Perhaps Rostow and others wanted to be anonymous or maybe

---

[46.] Telephone call from President Johnson and Secretary of State Dean Rusk to Senator Mike Mansfield, 11:10 A.M., November 29, 1963. Transcript provided by LBJ Library.

Johnson could see that there would be fewer questions asked if the idea was attributed to a government source, particularly an official of the Justice Department.

Dean Rusk's comments to Mansfield are vague. In stating his support for a commission, he only refers generally to concern that rumors about the assassination could "blow up quite a storm." Rusk's wording is a little strange, perhaps significant. He seems to draw a distinction between "the highest possible information on this situation" on one hand and "the absolute truth on it" on the other hand. Is he implying that there is some difference between the two? What does he mean by the "highest" information? Maybe Rusk is simply not very articulate. Certainly it has no concrete reference, i.e., to altitude, height, ladders, etc. Does it refer to what is going to be handed down as the official story?

Twenty minutes after he called Mansfield, LBJ called Congressman Hale Boggs to discuss the creation of the commission. Boggs was already familiar with and supportive of the idea, and was apparently involved already in producing a resolution calling for such a group. There is nothing in the conversation to explain why Boggs was already an active supporter. LBJ suggested that Boggs wait on the resolution, implying that it will not be needed. At one point, LBJ said "their thought was to have a Presidential commission." He does not identify who the word "their" referred to. Boggs suggested that LBJ might add "two from the public" making a commission of eight people. Boggs is under the impression that there will be two each from the Judiciary, the Senate, and the House.[47]

This 11:30 A.M. call to Boggs was followed by an 11:40 A.M. call, still on November 29, to Senator Everett Dirksen. LBJ continued his effort to line up support for the commission proposal and for efforts to stop hearings in the Senate and House. Dirksen seemed to be agreeable.[48] (In this conversation LBJ referred to the assassination as "this Dallas affair"; in the preceding call to Boggs it had been "the Dallas thing".)

At 1:15 P.M. on the 29th, LBJ called Abe Fortas, long associated with LBJ as a lawyer and friend, to ask Fortas to see to it that Supreme Court Justice Earl Warren quickly agreed to serve on the Commission. It is not clear who first

[47] Telephone call from President Johnson to Representative Hale Boggs, 11:30 A.M., November 29, 1963. Transcript provided by LBJ Library.

[48] Telephone call from President Johnson to Senator Everett Dirksen, 11:40 A.M., November 29, 1963. Transcript provided by LBJ Library.

suggested Warren. Johnson was concerned because the Commission was being openly discussed in the House and Senate before the members and its leader have been chosen and have agreed to serve.

In this discussion with Fortas, LBJ appeared as both an active participant in the development of the Commission and as passive recipient of others' advice. LBJ told Fortas that Earl Warren must be contacted immediately. Fortas informed Johnson that he has asked Nick (Katzenbach) and the Solicitor General (presumably the current office holder Archibald Cox, later of Watergate fame) to go see Warren.[49] Then the following exchange occurred:

> LBJ: All right. How many men on the Commission are we going to have?
>
> AF: Well, if you had Dulles and the General, and two from the House, two from the Senate, then the Chief Justice...
>
> LBJ: Who do you think of as the General?
>
> AF: Only one I can think of and I don't know many of those fellows...is Norstadt...[Note: Gen. Lauris Norstad]
>
> LBJ: ...if I had any idea who we wanted...
>
> AF: So I thought we'd probably have to take Eastland and the ranking minority member of the Judiciary Committee and similarly on the House but maybe not...it wouldn't necessarily be Judiciary Committee...
>
> LBJ: Yes, but Seller...God I hate to...what would you think about John McCoy [McCloy] instead of General Norstadt?
>
> AF: I think that'd be great...he's a wonderful man...and a very dear friend of mine...I'm devoted to him.

[49.] Telephone call from President Johnson to Abe Fortas, 1:15 P.M., November 29, 1963. Transcript provided by LBJ Library.

LBJ: Let's think along that line...now, we can do this by Executive Order.

AF: Yes sir.[50]

Although LBJ was now fully committed to the creation of the Commission, he acted as if part of the decision making was in other hands. He asked how many people would be on this Commission. Fortas suggested seven, the Chief Justice, Allen Dulles, the General, and two each from the House and Senate. Fortas wasn't even sure who the General was supposed to be.

It is clear that Fortas was carrying water for someone. That is consistent with Bruce Murphy's claim that Fortas was not the source of the idea of a commission and was in fact opposed to it, a view he allegedly conveyed to Dean Acheson.[51] As we saw earlier in the conversation between LBJ and Alsop, Alsop recommended to LBJ that he talk about the idea of a commission with Dean Acheson; LBJ promised he would do so. Acheson biographer Douglas Brinkley says that LBJ did call Acheson a "few days" after November 22 and that he talked to Acheson about the commission idea. Brinkley also says that LBJ sent Fortas to talk to Acheson about the proposal.[52] The conversation continued and LBJ suggested Senators Russell and Cooper and Representative Gerry Ford; Fortas suggested Boggs. Eastland, who could have been suggested by Fortas, Acheson, or someone else, was dropped. We don't know if Boggs was selected by Fortas, Acheson, or someone else. LBJ then summarized, identifying what would be the members of the Commission: Earl Warren, John J. McCloy, Allen Dulles, Senator Richard Russell, Senator John Cooper, Representative Hale Boggs, and Representative Gerald Ford.[53]

Shortly after talking to Fortas, Johnson spoke on the phone to J. Edgar Hoover. This call, at 1:40 P.M. on the 29th, apparently came from Hoover. The conversation begins with the following:

LBJ: Are you familiar with this proposed group that they're trying to put together on this study of your report and other

---

[50.] Ibid.

[51.] Murphy, 1988, pp. 116-17, 166-67.

[52.] Brinkley, 1992, pp. 206, 369.

[53.] Telephone call from President Johnson to Abe Fortas, 1:15 P.M., November 29, 1963. Transcript provided by LBJ Library.

things...two from the House...two from the Senate...somebody
from the Court...a couple of outsiders?

JEH: I haven't heard of that. I've seen the reports on the Senate
Investigating Committee that they've been talking about...

LBJ: Well, we think if we don't have...I want to get by just with
your file and your report...

JEH: I think it would be very very bad to have a rash of
investigations...on this thing.

LBJ: Well, the only way we can stop them is probably to appoint
a high-level one to evaluate your report and put somebody that's
pretty good on it...that I can select, out of the Government...and
tell the House and Senate not to go ahead with their
investigations...because they'll get a lot of television going and I
think it would be bad...

JEH: That's right...it would be a three-ring circus.[54]

Even though he was now on board with the Commission idea, LBJ still referred,
correctly, to "they" as the source of the idea. President Johnson, who had already
discussed this with Fortas, appeared here to be intentionally vague and cagey
about the make-up of the Commission, acting like the selection of its members is
still uncertain. Perhaps LBJ had a specific reason for this caginess; maybe that is
just the way he and everyone else talked to Hoover, i.e., carefully. Johnson sells
the idea to Hoover by telling him it will stop other investigations and that the
Commission will rely on the FBI's report.

Hoover's response to LBJ's opening reference to a "proposed group" which
would study the assassination was to say that he had not "heard of that". As we
saw earlier, in the Walter Jenkins memo to President Johnson, Hoover was aware
of a proposal for a commission on the afternoon of November 24 and had
apparently discussed it with Katzenbach. There are a number of possible

---

[54.] Telephone call from J. Edgar Hoover to President Johnson, 1:40 P.M., November 29,
1963. Transcript provided by LBJ Library.

explanations for this. One, stress and/or Hoover's opposition to a commission have produced a lapse of memory. Two, LBJ is suggesting a group of about seven people and this initially hits Hoover as a different proposal from the one made by Katzenbach. Three, Hoover adopted a posture of ignorance for some reason, playing his cards close to his vest. Whatever the reason for his stated lack of knowledge, Hoover did quickly agree that something should be done to prevent investigations in the House and Senate. Hoover did seem to find the idea of a special commission to be less disturbing than congressional hearings or investigations.

After the exchange quoted above, LBJ ran through a list of possible Commission members. Hoover was agreeable, but expressed some preference for General Norstad over John J. McCloy, whom Hoover viewed as a publicity seeker.[55]

Hoover went on to assure LBJ that the FBI was close to wrapping up its investigation, although there were some unresolved issues relating to Oswald's trip to Mexico City. The FBI had apparently made great progress since November 23 when, as was noted earlier, Hoover said the case against Oswald was not very good. After some general discussion of this Mexico trip, Hoover talked about Ruby, Ruby's shooting of Oswald, and Oswald's ties to the American Civil Liberties Union and to the Cuba Fair Play Committee (actually Fair Play for Cuba Committee), characterized by Hoover as communist dominated and as financed partly by Castro's government.

In the days, months, and years after the assassination, Hoover repeatedly and consistently failed in the case of the Kennedy assassination to live up to his reputation as a red hunter and tireless investigator of communist and left-wing conspiracy. This lack of interest in Oswald's alleged connections to political organizations running from "pink" to "red" appeared right after the assassination and was inexplicable in relation to his public image, his professed views, his history, and what has usually been said about him. This makes sense if one assumes that Hoover had decided to focus or had been ordered to focus all efforts on proving that Oswald did it and did it alone. Hoover and Alan Belmont did act to prevent consideration of any kind of conspiracy, red or any other color.

This conversation took place one week after the assassination. Hoover was either surprisingly ignorant of the events and of the emerging official line or was incapable at this time of coherent and detailed recall. He had the bullet situation

---

55. Ibid.

confused. Not only was he insisting that Kennedy and Connally were hit by separate bullets (a line the FBI would continue to maintain even though it was critically inconsistent with the eventual conclusions of the Warren Commission), but he seemed unaware of which bullet was found under the hospital stretcher.[56] He suggested it was the one that hit JFK in the head. This was obviously impossible and, as far as the author is aware, never suggested by anyone other than Hoover.

Hoover also asserted that there were three shots and that they were fired in three seconds. (Maybe he meant in intervals of three seconds; maybe he meant exactly what he said.) He says that the FBI had proven this is possible. That was not true. Some of his report to the President of the United States was wildly inaccurate. In response to a question from LBJ, Hoover asserted that Kennedy would have been hit by the second shot were it not that Connally was in the way. He repeats this later in the conversation.[57] Since Connally was sitting in front of President Kennedy and Oswald was alleged to have fired from behind, something the FBI was agreeing to, Hoover's rendition was physically impossible.

Hoover had the alleged assassination weapon being found on the fifth rather than the sixth floor of the Book Depository. He presented a similarly sloppy account of Oswald's alleged movements after the assassination. In spite of Hoover's impressive lack of command of the facts, in spite of the short time that has passed, in spite of the tantalizing even if weak leads to political groups Hoover had hated and pursued over four decades, he was sure of the ultimate conclusion. He said to President Johnson that "there is no question but he [Oswald] is the man".[58]

Hoover's inept report to President Johnson is probably a reflection of the fact that at the upper levels of the FBI it was not Hoover who was supervising the FBI investigation, but, rather it was Alan Belmont, Assistant Director of the FBI. The public record, as discussed in the preceding chapter, clearly indicates that Belmont assumed responsibility for the investigation within minutes of the

---

[56.] Ibid.
[57.] Ibid.
[58.] Ibid.

assassination and he continued to oversee the FBI's work throughout the time that the Warren Commission was in existence.[59]

Later on the 29th, at 4:55 P.M., LBJ talked to Speaker of the House John McCormack, Democrat of Massachusetts, about the proposed commission. In this conversation, Johnson referred to Dean Rusk's desire to get the announcement about the Commission out as quickly as possible. LBJ also referred to the need to get Senator Eastland to call off the Senate investigation and he then ran through the proposed list of Commission members. Following a brief discussion of the Commission members (and it is the final seven), LBJ got McCormack's assurance that he would do all he could to stop any investigation in the House of Representatives. LBJ raised the danger that would be created if someone publicly accused Krushchev or the Soviets of killing Kennedy. Other topics were then discussed.[60]

During a call to Dean Rusk at 6:30 P.M. on the 29th, President Johnson briefly discussed an apparently unrelated negotiation with the Soviets and then said he wanted to tell Rusk about "this Presidential Commission". Rusk had already been involved in this, as described earlier, and is clearly familiar with it. The extent and timing of his involvement was not clear. LBJ reviewed the list of commissioners and Rusk immediately concurred, describing them as "absolutely first class".[61]

Immediately before or after his conversation with Rusk, both calls are listed for 6:30, LBJ called Congressman Charles Halleck about the Commission and the need to prevent hearings in the House and Senate. In this conversation, LBJ alluded to the dangers of war which would be created by rumors of Soviet or Cuban involvement in the assassination. Johnson also made vague references to CIA matters which might be brought up or exposed if there were multiple investigations and television coverage. The conversation, in part, went as follows.

[59.] Hearings Before the President's Commission on the Assassination of President Kennedy, 1964, Vol. V, pp. 1-33, Vol. XXIV, p. 11; Hearings Before the Select Committee on Assassinations, Vol. III, pp. 668-9.

[60.] Telephone call from President Johnson to Representative Mike McCormack, 4:55 P.M., November 29, 1963. Transcript provided by LBJ Library.

[61.] Telephone call from President Johnson to Secretary of State Dean Rusk, 6:30 P.M., November 29, 1963. Transcript provided by LBJ Library.

LBJ: Charlie...I hate to bother you but all you damned fellows advocate...I talked to Les Arends and told him I was going to keep trying to reach you till 6:30...I've got to appoint a Commission and issue an Executive Order tonight on investigation of the assassination of the President because this thing is getting pretty serious and our folks are worried about it...it has some foreign complications...CIA and other things...and I'm going to try to get the Chief Justice to go on it...he declined earlier in the day but I think I'm going to try to get him to head it...I'm to try to John McCloy...

CH: Chief Justice Warren?

LBJ: Yes..

CH: I think that's a mistake...

LBJ: I'd be glad to hear you but I want to talk to you about...he thought it was a mistake till I told him everything we knew and we just can't House and Senate and FBI and other people going around testifying Krushchev killed Kennedy or Castro killed him...we've got to have the facts...and you don't have a President assassinated once every 50 years...and this thing is so touchy from an international standpoint that every man we've got over there is concerned about it and we think we've got to have somebody that can not only be judicious and a sure American but somebody that has had some experience with these CIA matters and other things...we we're going to try to get John McCloy from an international standpoint...Allen Dulles...we want to get Gerry Ford from Appropriations Committee...we want to get Dick Russell from the Armed Service Committee...we want to get John Sherman Cooper because he's had some international background and Ambassador with experience...and Allen Dulles and John McCloy...and we want to ask the Chief Justice to preside...we hope...that we talked to the leadership in both houses...and asked them to cooperate with the Commission..

CH: I'll cooperate my friend, I'll tell you one thing...Lyndon...Mr. President.. I think that to call on Supreme Court guys to do jobs is kind of a mistake...

LBJ: It is on all these other things...I agree with you on Pearl Harbor and I agree with you on the Railroad Strike ..but this is a question that could involve our losing 39 million people...this is a judicial question...

CH: I...of course...don't want that to happen. Of course, I was a little disappointed in the Chief Justice...I'll talk to you real plainly...he's jumped at the gun...and of course...I don't know whether the right wing was in this or not...and you've been very discreet...you have mentioned the left and the right...and I am for that...well look Gerry Ford is a top-drawer guy on my part..[62]

Johnson did not explain the connections among the subjects he has raised - the assassination, the danger of war with the Soviet Union, and the "CIA matters and other things." Halleck did not ask for clarification. Perhaps Halleck was already familiar with these problems and issues. Perhaps he either didn't want to know anything about it or felt it was inappropriate to ask for additional information. These were not things that LBJ, as far as the record shows, displayed great concern over in the first three days following the assassination. Halleck, even if not completely happy with the make-up of the Commission, implied that he would go along with it and with the effort to prevent investigations in the House and Senate.

About thirty minutes later, at 7:00 P.M., LBJ calls Joseph Alsop and reviewed with Alsop the announcement he was making on the establishment of a commission. The announcement indicated that the Commission would rely heavily on the FBI and other federal agencies. LBJ was still assuming that a Texas Court of Inquiry convened by the Attorney General of Texas was going forward. Alsop was very positive about the Commission, particularly the

[62] Telephone call from President Johnson to Representative Charles Halleck, 6:30 P.M., November 29, 1963. Transcript provided by LBJ Library.

participation of Dulles, McCloy, and Warren, and the fact that the make-up of the Commission would not be exclusively congressional.[63]

The fact that LBJ called Alsop in the midst of the calls to Secretary of State Rusk and to selected Senators and Representatives is an additional indicator of the important role played in these developments by Alsop.

Immediately after his call to Alsop, LBJ continues to organize support for the Presidential Commission, calling Senator Eastland to inform him that he will be announcing the creation of the Commission to study "the facts and circumstances relating to the assassination." Although not enthusiastic about Earl Warren, Eastland agreed to support the idea by helping LBJ in the Senate.[64]

Some minutes later, at 7:15 P.M., LBJ called Senator Dodd of Connecticut to tell him that he is about to announce the formation of a Commission "to study this assassination thing." Dodd told LBJ that he was a "Johnson man" and that he would do anything he could to be of assistance to LBJ.[65]

Early in the evening of the 29th the creation of the Commission was announced by the White House. By the next day, copies of Executive Order No. 11130, establishing and charging the Commission, were released by the office of the White House Press Secretary. It is quite short, reading as follows:

THE WHITE HOUSE
EXECUTIVE ORDER
NO.11130

Pursuant to the authority vested in me as President of the United States, I hereby appoint a Commission to ascertain, evaluate and report upon the facts relating to the assassination of the late President John F. Kennedy and the subsequent violent death of the man charged with the assassination. The Commission shall consist of --

The Chief Justice of the United States, Chairman;

[63.] Telephone call from President Johnson to Joseph Alsop, 7:00 P.M., November 29, 1963. Transcript provided by LBJ Library.

[64.] Telephone call from President Johnson to Senator James Eastland, 7:03 P.M., November 29, 1963. Transcript provided by LBJ Library.

[65.] Telephone call from President Johnson to Senator Thomas Dodd, 7:15 P.M., November 29, 1963. Transcript provided by LBJ Library.

Senator Richard B. Russell;
Senator John Sherman Cooper;
Congressman Hale Boggs;
Congressman Gerald R. Ford;
The Honorable Allen W. Dulles;
The Honorable John J. McCloy.

The purposes of the Commission are to examine the evidence developed by the Federal Bureau of Investigation and any additional evidence that may hereafter come to light or be uncovered by federal or state authorities; to make such further investigation as the Commission finds desirable; to evaluate all the facts and circumstances surrounding such assassination, including the subsequent violent death of the man charged with the assassination, and to report to me its findings and conclusions.

The Commission is empowered to prescribe its own procedures and to employ such assistants as it deems necessary.

Necessary expenses of the Commission may be paid from the "Emergency Fund for the President".

All Executive departments and agencies are directed to furnish the Commission with such facilities, services and cooperation as it may request from time to time.

Lyndon B. Johnson

THE WIIITE HOUSE
November 29, 1963

President Johnson gave the Commission extensive powers. They would need to go to Congress for the power to subpoena witnesses; they got that power with no difficulty. There were no formal limits put on the Commission. They could do as good or as bad a job as they saw fit to do. They would do far worse than just a bad job.

On the following day, the New York Times reported that "One purpose of the Presidential inquiry is to head off competing investigations" in the House and Senate. Had the Commission looked for the truth, this would not have been destructive; they did not seek the truth. The Times story went on to say that leaders in the House and Senate were cooperating with the White House to prevent Congressional inquiries.[66]

After the White House announcement on the evening of the 29th, LBJ called Senator Richard Russell, who was named to the Commission without his concurrence. Russell stated his dislike of Warren and his opposition to serving on the Commission. LBJ proceeded to arm-twist Russell, as he also had to do with Warren, by telling him that it had already been announced, that a badly conducted investigation could lead to suspicion of Russian or Cuban involvement and to a war in which 40 million Americans would die in an hour, that it was Russell's patriotic duty, and that it was part of Russell's personal obligation to LBJ. After Russell capitulated, LBJ told him that Hoover had informed him of an incident in Mexico City which could lead to suspicion of Russian or Cuban involvement and to war. LBJ was apparently so focused on convincing Russell to serve that he did not even comment on Russell's own suggestion during the conversation that there might have been Cuban involvement.[67]

Senator Russell would later be the most emphatic dissenter from the Commission's conclusions. Senator Cooper and Representative Boggs would also express disagreements with the report. As Harold Weisberg has shown, these dissenting viewpoints were suppressed when the final report was issued.[68]

The first part of the story is almost complete. The possibility of a presidential commission did not really exist until Oswald was killed on the 24th. On the 24th and 25th President Johnson had no inclination to create such a commission and he rejected or resisted early proposals to do so. By the 28th he had been turned around and became fully active on its behalf.

One remaining event is worth noting. On December 4, 1963, LBJ called Dean Acheson to ask him to come to the White House for a visit. After the

---

[66] Morris, 1963, pp. 1, 12.

[67] Telephone call from President Johnson to Senator Richard Russell, 8:55 P.M., November 29, 1963. Transcript provided by LBJ Library.

[68] Weisberg, 1995, pp. 221-29, 326. (Note: Weisberg emphasizes Katzenbach's role beyond what now seems accurate. Many of the documents used to correct the present account were not available when Weisberg was finishing his book.)

exchange of salutations, Acheson immediately praised Johnson, saying "That was the greatest thing...appointing that Commission.." LBJ responded by saying that "Well...we did the best we could and I think we've got Hoover pretty well in line.."[69]

What President Johnson meant by getting Hoover "in line" is not clear. Perhaps he meant getting Hoover to agree to cooperate with the Commission. Perhaps he was referring to getting Hoover to be cautious in areas that might expose CIA or other operations. What is clear is Dean Acheson's enthusiastic approval of President Johnson's decision to create the Commission. This is consistent with the discussion earlier of Acheson's probable role in getting President Johnson's agreement to do so.

In summary, the idea of a presidential commission did not come from President Johnson or from Abe Fortas. Katzenbach was involved in this in a significant way, but at the behest of others and not always with enthusiasm. Eugene Rostow was either the originator of the idea or he was the first active promoter, or both. We don't know the identity of the individual or individuals with whom he was discussing this on the afternoon of November 24. Joseph Alsop is an important figure in these developments. This judgment is based on both his extensive jaw-boning with LBJ and the fact that he was one of the few people informed by LBJ about the announcement. Dean Acheson almost certainly played a role in this, perhaps a major one. It appears that Alsop acted on behalf of Acheson. The record also indicates that Rusk was a relatively early supporter and that people at the Washington Post, Alfred Friendly, Katherine Graham, and particularly Russell Wiggins, were early advocates for a presidential commission. This is all consistent with and fills in the gaps in Katzenbach's statements. It is not, of course, consistent with the representation of Katzenbach's role in the House Committee's analysis of the creation of the Warren Commission.

Some potentially important gaps remain. Perhaps most important is the identification of the person or persons with whom Rostow was conversing on the 24th. The precise timing and nature of Acheson's involvement is still uncertain. Nevertheless, thanks to the 1993 release of White House telephone transcripts, we have been able to construct a more complete account than anything available up to now.

[69.] Telephone call from President Johnson to Dean Acheson, 9:57 A.M., December 4, 1963. Transcript provided by LBJ Library.

It is clear now that some of the early accounts of these events and some of the most recent have been wrong or misleading. It may surprise some that LBJ's relatively early but brief statement about these events was fairly accurate.

One of the early stories was provided by Rowland Evans and Robert Novak. Their 1966 book suggested that LBJ, "assisted by Abe Fortas and other counselors," came up with the idea for a blue-ribbon commission in order to deal with the rumors and to "exorcise the demons of conspiracy." The record shows now that LBJ did not come up with the idea and that Abe Fortas played, at most, a secondary role in these events, and probably did not support the idea initially. Other "counselors" could refer to anyone and is the only possibly correct part of this description.[70]

Very early, 1971, Lyndon Johnson himself provided important parts of the truth. His statement was closer to an accurate account than what was provided by House Committee six years later. The Committee totally ignored LBJ's account and, as far as the author is aware, so did everyone else for over twenty years. In his book, *The Vantage Point*, Johnson said that Eugene Rostow called the White House on November 24th and suggested a commission, and that Joe Alsop and Dean Rusk also recommended a commission.[71]

This account, although brief and incomplete, was closer to the truth than anything said about this between 1963 and 1993. It is more accurate than the selective presentation of telephone transcripts in the Michael Beschloss book referred to earlier. Perhaps it is a tribute to LBJ's lack of credibility that no one paid any attention to this for over twenty years (including the author). Perhaps this was overlooked also because LBJ vaguely implied that he immediately saw a need for something like a commission. That is not true, but it may have diluted the significance of his comments about Rostow, Alsop, and Rusk. Also, some may have found his account unlikely because he claimed that Robert Kennedy suggested that Allen Dulles and John J. McCloy be appointed to the Commission.[72] There is no evidence to support this.

More recently, the creation of the Warren Commission was discussed by Kai Bird in his 1992 biography of John J. McCloy. Bird observes that Rostow, Fortas, Alsop, and Rusk all advised LBJ to establish a commission. He also implies that LBJ had the same view at about the same time. That is clearly

---

[70.] Evans and Novak, 1966, p. 337.

[71.] Johnson, 1971, p. 26.

[72.] Ibid., p. 27.

untrue. There is no hint in Bird's account that LBJ had to be pressured into accepting the idea and there is no reference to the possibility that others were involved. Bird is almost certainly wrong about Fortas. Bird discusses the memo written on the 24th which reports Hoover's phone call to the White House. Bird quotes the memo's quote of Hoover to the effect that Hoover was concerned that something be issued to "convince the public that Oswald is the real assassin".[73] Bird eliminates five words in his quoting of that memo; they are "and so is Mr. Katzenbach." By doing so, he incorrectly represents Hoover as acting on his own rather than reacting to Katzenbach (who was in turn following the lead of Rostow). Instead of checking the then available record, Bird mistakenly or conveniently relies in part on the misleading account of Henry Hurt.[74] In spite of the accurate noting of Rostow and Alsop, Bird's rendition is also very misleading.

In a 1994 biography of Allen Dulles, Peter Grose correctly identifies Rostow as the person who first suggested a commission to the White House and correctly reports that LBJ opposed the idea. However, Grose vaguely attributes LBJ's change of heart to increasing "public pressure" during the November 25th to 29th period.[75] This is not accurate unless the public is defined as Rostow, Alsop, and Acheson.

An incorrect and illogical rendition of events is set forth in Gerald Posner's 1993 book on the assassination, *Case Closed*. Posner authoritatively presents Katzenbach as the moving force behind the creation of the Warren Commission, saying that Katzenbach "worked feverishly behind the scenes to change LBJ's mind and return control of the investigation to Washington."[76] Besides being wrong on the role played by Katzenbach, the statement is not clear. That is, what does "return control" to Washington mean here? Was it in Washington earlier?

Posner goes on to say that the Commission "members and their mandate were so prestigious that other proposed state and federal investigations promptly gave way to the presidential panel."[77] This description is not remotely close to the actual process, which involved various efforts by LBJ to line up support to kill off those investigations. Posner's discussion of the creation of the Warren Commission is similar to the rest of his book - sloppy, incomplete, misleading.

[73.] Bird, 1992, pp. 548, 553-54.
[74.] Ibid.; Hurt, 1985.
[75.] Grose, 1994, p. 541.
[76.] Posner, 1993, p. 405.
[77.] Ibid., p. 406.

We are finished with the second part of the story of the cover-up, the creation of the Warren Commission. If the group of people who intervened in this situation during the five days following Oswald's death were to be categorized in terms of their social status and political connections, what terms would be appropriate and accurate. What label is right for Eugene Rostow, Joseph Alsop, Dean Rusk, Dean Acheson, and perhaps the upper-levels of the Washington Post? As we will see later, there is no question about the correct label. All of these people are clearly part of the upper-class Establishment. Since our story is still far from complete, it does not make sense to detail this here. As we turn to the make-up of the Commission and its operations, we will add to this list of Establishment figures. The list will then include Allen Dulles and John J. McCloy.

Chapter Four

THE MCCLOY-DULLES COMMISSION

As shown in the previous chapter, the members of the President's Commission on the Assassination of President Kennedy had been identified in the November 29 phone conversation between President Johnson and Abe Fortas. In that conversation, neither the President nor Abe Fortas spoke as if they were in charge of this process. Each suggested names of Commission members but both talked to some extent as if they were passive figures in this process.

It is not clear from that conversation how Earl Warren had been chosen as Chairman of the Commission. Both LBJ and Fortas talked as if this had been settled. Fortas brings up the names of Dulles and Boggs. We do not know how Fortas came up with these names. In his biography of Allen Dulles, Peter Grose implies that Dean Rusk suggested Allen Dulles as a commissioner.[1] Unfortunately, Grose is somewhat vague on this and no source for this information is identified. Johnson raised the names of McCloy, Russell, Cooper, and Ford. It is not clear from the conversation whether LBJ chose these men or they were suggested to him by others. Suggestions could have come from anyone Johnson spoke with, on the phone or in person, between November 26 and 29. That would include Dean Rusk, perhaps Dean Acheson, or others such as McGeorge Bundy.

Regardless of the source of these suggestions, it is clear that two of these men would directly and indirectly dominate much of what the Commission did. The two were John J. McCloy and Allen Dulles. As we will see later, these two

---

[1] Grose, 1994, pp. 541-42.

men had numerous and close associations with the men who initiated the effort to have the Commission created.

THE MCCLOY-DULLES COMMISSION
AND THE REAL PECKING ORDER

Earl Warren was the official chairman of the Commission. He would forever defend the Commission's work. For these two reasons, Earl Warren should be viewed as an important figure in these events and he should be held personally responsible for what the Commission did and did not do. However, the standard and almost universal use of Warren's name to identify this Commission is misleading. Warren, of course, had nothing to do with the proposal to create the Commission. Apparently, he was not anxious to be involved in it and he was pressured into this service. More importantly, the record to be reviewed here shows that within the Commission, McCloy and Dulles exercised more authority than did the Commission's official head. This is not to suggest that there were continuous conflicts between the Dulles-McCloy duo and Earl Warren. For the most part, the relationships among these men appears to have been cooperative. A major difference did develop between Warren and McCloy at the very outset and McCloy prevailed. In this conflict and in subsequent events it is clear that the authority and status of McCloy and Dulles was superior to that of the Chief Justice of the Supreme Court and the Commission's formal chairman.

One of the first and most important decisions to be made by the Commission was the selection of the Commission's general counsel. If Earl Warren had any thoughts that his position and status would give him the power to shape the Commission, he quickly found out that this would not be so. A description of what transpired during the selection of the general counsel will demonstrate the real pecking-order within the Commission and this description will correct the misleading account produced by Edward Jay Epstein in his book on the Warren Commission, *Inquest: The Warren Commission and the Establishment of Truth.*

In that book, Epstein misled all who relied on him about the selection of J. Lee Rankin as general counsel for the Commission. In that account, Epstein said that Warren selected Rankin. He also stated that another person was suggested first but was rejected as "too controversial." Epstein relied on John J. McCloy for this account.[2] McCloy misled Epstein. Warren did not suggest Rankin; he did suggest the controversial person who was rejected. This transpired in the early executive sessions of the Commission, the first of these occurring less than one week after LBJ officially created the Commission.

The Commission met for the first time on December 5, 1963. All of its members were present. A number of issues were discussed, including the Commission's relationship to the Texas inquiry and the need to request from Congress the power to subpoena witnesses. There were also remarks made about the purpose of the Commission which will be discussed further on. A good deal of the discussion related to the need for and the selection of a chief or general counsel.

The need for a general counsel was raised first by John J. McCloy, who observed that the Commission needed someone in that position to establish its authority and to achieve efficient operation.[3] Earl Warren immediately agreed with this and after some further discussion about getting subpoena power, Warren brought the Commission back to the selection of a general counsel.

Warren stated that his choice for general counsel was Warren Olney, Director of the Administrative Office of the Federal Court System.[4] Warren went on to make a lengthy and strong argument on behalf of Olney. Warren's case for Olney included Warren's long-term relationship with and in-depth knowledge about Olney, Olney's family background, Olney's diverse and extensive legal experience, his military service, his familiarity with FBI and Secret Service operations, and Warren's high praise for Olney's ability and integrity. This was not a casual recommendation; Warren clearly wanted Olney. Senator Russell was agreeable and Boggs, who knew and respected Olney, immediately expressed definite support.

Gerald Ford was the first to state an objection, saying:

I look upon this group just as Mr. McCloy does, with a very major responsibility, and I want it to have the finest aura or atmosphere. And when the report is written I certainly hope it can be unanimous, it can be the full

[2.] Epstein, 1966, pp. 7, 178.
[3.] President's Commission on the Assassination of President Kennedy, 1963-64, Executive Sessions, December 5, 1963, p. 39.
[4.] Ibid., pp. 43-46.

judgment of all of us. I don't want the Commission to be divided. I don't want
it to be your Commission or the Commission of half of us or otherwise.[5]

Ford did not explain why he was concerned about the danger of a divided
Commission. He mentioned consensus and a fine aura but not the discovery of
the truth. He went on to emphasize that if someone, like Olney, with a long
association with Warren were appointed, it would lead people to view the work
of the Commission and its report as Warrren's rather than the group's.[6]

Ford framed his objection in the context of concerns he shared with McCloy.
McCloy immediately added his objection to Ford's, arguing that the Commission
should give consideration to a number of people. McCloy had his own list of
candidates, which he said were people "of my experience." Warren quickly
asserted that he had proposed Olney because Olney was someone of his own
experience. Warren was ignored by McCloy.[7] Among the names on McCloy's
list were Leon Jaworski and Tom Dewey.[8]

The discussion continued with Boggs supporting Warren. Cooper offered a
compromise that was first supported by and then modified by Boggs. The
compromise was to pick a different chief counsel, but allow Warren to bring
Olney in as a chief of staff.[9] Russell later gave some support to Warren by
suggesting that Olney could be brought in immediately as an "Executive
Officer." After this, Warren again spoke for Olney and Russell again supported
him.[10]

Russell then introduced the idea of appointing a subcommittee to consider
the selection of a chief counsel. Ford supported this proposal and, before the
session ended, a subcommittee of Warren, Dulles, McCloy, and Ford was given
the job of coming up with a recommendation.[11] Warren made an additional,
strong plea for Olney.[12]

The men who later expressed some misgivings about the Commission's
report, Russell, Boggs, and Cooper, all gave some support to Warren. McCloy

[5] Ibid., p. 46.
[6] Ibid., p. 47.
[7] Ibid., p. 48.
[8] Ibid., pp. 48-49.
[9] Ibid., p. 50.
[10] Ibid., pp. 52-53.
[11] Ibid., p. 54.
[12] Ibid., p. 55.

and Ford, who had expressed his concern with reference to views shared with McCloy, opposed Olney. Interestingly, and perhaps significantly, McCloy and Ford were not the first people to express an opposition to the Chief Justice's choice. Two days earlier, on December 3, Alan Belmont, the man running the FBI's investigation, raised this issue at the end of a memo to Clyde Tolson, assistant to J. Edgar Hoover. Belmont's memo stated that:

> Katzenbach said that he had been talking to Chief Justice Warren, and Warren had indicated to him that the chief counsel for the President's Commission will be Warren Olney. Katzenbach thought that this would be most undesirable. Katzenbach said that, as we probably knew, Chief Justice Warren thinks that Olney can do no wrong, and he (the Chief Justice) had made the point that Olney is conversant with the FBI's procedures and thus would be operating in a familiar field. Katzenbach said if we have any ideas as to how Olney can by blocked as chief counsel, he would like to have them. I told him, as far as I was concerned, Olney was an undesirable choice, and if we had any thoughts we would get them to him.[13]

Here we have one of the participants in the first stage of the cover-up, Alan Belmont, trying to figure out a way to influence an important decision in a later stage. Whether Katzenbach was expressing his own views or, as in other instances, the views of others cannot be determined. It is possible that one of these two, or someone associated with one of them, communicated directly or indirectly with McCloy or Ford, or both. That might explain the manner in which objections to Olney were first expressed, i.e., Ford referencing McCloy and McCloy immediately joining with Ford in opposition to Olney. That suggests that Belmont shared his info with McCloy, allowing McCloy to prepare his case against Olney.

The Commission re-convened during the afternoon of December 6 and the discussion of a general counsel resumed. Warren reported on the meeting of the sub-committee, saying that McCloy, Dulles, and Ford all had reservations about Olney. Given this lack of confidence in Olney, Warren had withdrawn Olney's nomination as general counsel. Warren then turned the discussion of this over to McCloy and Dulles. McCloy suggested that the Commission give first consideration to Lee Rankin, former Solicitor General for the United States. Warren voiced his support for McCloy's preference. Dulles, before he left to

---

[13.] Hearings Before the Select Committee on Assassinations of the United States House of Representatives, 1979, Vol. III, pp. 672-73.

catch a plane, stated his support for the selection of Rankin.[14] Dulles then suggested several other names to be considered if the Commission decided to reject Rankin.

After Dulles left the meeting, Boggs raised some other possible candidates to fill the position, but McCloy, Warren, Cooper, and Russell all indicated that Rankin would be acceptable.[15]

Although Warren gave definite support to the selection of Rankin, he also showed through his comments that he knew very little about Rankin. Warren said:

> He [Rankin] is a very personable fellow and he's not political in any sense. I doubt if he ever was in politics before he went in as a lawyer in the administration. He might have had a little background in Nebraska. If he did I never heard of it.[16]

As we will see later, Rankin was a prominent figure in Republican national politics when he was in Nebraska and it was these party activities that apparently led to his appointment in the Eisenhower administration. Warren had come out of the subcommittee's meeting as a willing backer of Rankin, but he did not know that much about him.

Shortly thereafter, the discussion turned to the Texas Court of Inquiry that was being organized by Texas Attorney General Waggoner Carr and to the Commission's efforts to influence that inquiry. Warren read to the others a letter from Katzenbach to Carr, sent with Warren's concurrence. Katzenbach's letter to Carr suggested that the Texas inquiry be postponed and that Carr or Carr's Special Counsel should participate in and work with the Commission. Warren then reported that Katzenbach had been told by someone representing the Texas Court of Inquiry that if they received a letter such as this one, they would agree not to conduct their inquiry while the Commission was in operation.[17] Carr did agree to cooperate with the Commission. As noted earlier, the potential inquiry in Texas never seemed to worry anyone as much as did the congressional hearings.

---

[14] President's Commission on the Assassination of President Kennedy, 1963-64, Executive Sessions, December 6, 1963, pp. 4-6.

[15] Ibid., pp. 8-10.

[16] Ibid., p. 10.

[17] Ibid., pp. 13-16.

Later in this session, Warren again returned to the issue of the general counsel, remarking that this needed to be settled so that the Commission could get itself organized. Warren noted that he "did not propose" Rankin, but that Rankin was fine with him, and that the Commission should move quickly to settle this. Others agreed that this should be taken care of quickly.[18]

Warren did argue enthusiastically and repeatedly for Olney on December 5 and he did try one last time on December 6 to bring Olney on board, this time to serve under Rankin. McCloy intervened again and opposed what would have been a concession to the Chief Justice and Commission Chairman. McCloy reacted to Warren by saying:

> The thing that scared me off more than anything else was the report I got that he [Olney] was at swordpoint with J. Edgar Hoover, and also that he sort of has a disposition, apparently, which makes it difficult for him to get along with people, and I would not think that we ought to commit ourselves. I don't say we should not do it, I think we ought to see if we can get Rankin, let Rankin have a choice.[19]

On the previous day, McCloy had objected to Olney because he had been associated with the Justice Department and, therefore, indirectly associated with the FBI. Now McCloy objects on the grounds that Olney does not get along with people in general and with Hoover in particular. The concessions made by the Chairman of the Commission are of no help to him. McCloy was not going to allow Warren to involve Olney in the Commission's work in any capacity.

When the Commission met again on December 16, Rankin was in place as general counsel and was present at the meeting. The process of selecting assistant counsel had begun. Unfortunately, most of the activity around the selection of assistant counsel takes place outside of the executive sessions. Two lawyers were discussed at that December 16 meeting and both did become assistant counsel for the Commission. Rankin proposed Francis Adams and McCloy supported this, saying that Adams had been on his list and that he came well recommended. Adams, who would leave the Commission well before it finished its work, had earlier worked for the Justice Department, was briefly police commissioner of

---

18. Ibid., pp. 18-19.
19. Ibid., pp. 20-21.

New York City (1954-55), and had recently been associated with the law firm of
Saterlee, Warfield & Stephens.[20]

Warren then said that Albert Jenner of Chicago had been suggested. Warren
did not identify the source of the suggestion. Jenner was with the law firm of
Raymond, Mayer, Jenner & Block and had been previously a law professor at
Northwestern University. He had also been involved with a number of state and
national groups working on legal issues.[21] Warren said that he had checked on
Jenner with a number of people and they all recommended him. Two of Jenner's
references were mentioned by name. Tom Clark, former Attorney General of the
U.S. and active supporter in the Truman years of J. Edgar Hoover's anti-
subversion efforts, knew Jenner through their common participation on the
Judiciary Committee of the American Bar Association.[22] The other named
supporter of Jenner was Dean Acheson, who had worked with Jenner on
Acheson's Committee on Civil Rules. Jenner came to the Commission then with
recommendations from and past connections to one of the people involved in
creating the Commission and someone who at one time, at least, was close to
Hoover.

Unfortunately, there is very little additional information on the selection of
counsel and organization of the Commission in the Executive Session transcripts.
We will have to rely to a considerable degree on Edward Epstein. As we have
noted, Epstein was misled by McCloy concerning the selection of Rankin.
Epstein did not rely on McCloy, or Ford or Dulles, for his information
concerning the selection of assistant counsel and the general organization of the
Commission. As far as it goes, its appears to be accurate.

Epstein indicates that Rankin picked the men who were initially thought of
as the "senior counsel." These were generally the older and more experienced
lawyers. There were seven of them and also seven "junior counsel." These
distinctions between senior and junior counsel did not last very long. According
to Epstein, Rankin picked Francis W. H. Adams, Joseph A. Ball, William T.
Coleman, Jr., Leon D. Hubert, Jr., and Albert E. Jenner, Jr.[23] Jenner, as noted

[20.] President's Commission on the Assassination of President Kennedy, 1963-64,
Executive Sessions, December 16, 1963, p. 23.
[21.] President' Commission on the Assassination of president John F. Kennedy, 1993, p.
478.
[22.] Isaacson and Thomas, pp. 426-27; President's Commission on the Assassination of
President Kennedy, 1963-64, Executive Sessions, December 16, p. 25.
[23.] Epstein, 1966, p. 10.

above, came with the recommendation of Dean Acheson. Rankin also picked Norman Redlich as his own assistant and Redlich, in turn, nominated Melvin A. Eisenberg. That is seven of the fourteen assistant counsel. Howard P. Willens was selected by Katzenbach to act as liaison between the Justice Department and the Commission and was then quickly named as one of the assistant counsel.[24] Willens, like several other counsel, was a graduate of the Yale Law School and he had been editor of the Yale Law Journal. It is possible that Willens was suggested to Katzenbach by Rostow, who was Dean of the Yale Law School and the man who prodded Katzenbach to initiate efforts to have the Commission created.

Epstein says that Willens then selected Samuel A. Stern and Burt W. Griffin (Yale Law School). Epstein implies that Willens also selected Arlen Specter (Yale Law School). Epstein says that David W. Belin and W. David Slawson were recommended to the Commission, but he does not identify their supporters. Finally, Epstein says that Wesley J. Liebler was "recommended to Willens by the Dean of the University of Chicago Law School."[25]

Rankin apparently picked six of the fourteen and his assistant picked an additional member. The Commission's selection of and approval of all fourteen counsel was based on information provided to the Commission by Rankin.[26] Rankin would act as the middle-man or gate-keeper between the Commission and the Commission's assistant counsel and staff. He supervised the investigation and the writing of the report. The two primary writers, among thirty contributors, were, according to Epstein, Redlich and a staff person, Alfred Goldberg. Goldberg and Redlich worked directly for Rankin. At the request of Rankin and other Commissioners, much of the report went through numerous changes and re-writes. Some chapters were rewritten as many as twenty times.[27] Rankin examined most of the important witnesses who did appear before the Commission.[28] Rankin was the liaison between the Commission and a number of government agencies. He apparently dealt with at least one outside figure who was pressuring the Commission to get the report done quickly, i.e., national security advisor McGeorge Bundy.[29]

---

24. Ibid., pp. 9, 11.
25. Ibid., 20.
26. Ibid., p. 12.
27. Ibid., pp. 3, 18, 23-24, 107.
28. Ibid., p. 8.
29. Ibid., p. 24.

Although the "junior counsel" did most of the direct work, they had little influence on the overall direction of the Commission's work, were generally not kept well informed, and were not consulted.[30] Some of the lawyers decided that this meant that the Commission was out of touch with the investigation, but Rankin observed that the assistant counsel did not "understand how a government inquiry worked" and did not understand that the Commission was giving direction and focus to the investigation.[31] If by "the Commission" Rankin meant McCloy, Dulles, and himself, he was correct. They did provide the direction and focus.

SHAPING THE INVESTIGATION

John J. McCloy, who installed Rankin as general counsel against the initial wishes of Earl Warren, suggested guidelines and a purpose for the Commission at that first executive session on December 5, 1963. In a discussion of some of the problems facing the Commission, McCloy argued that the Commission should acquire the right to subpoena witnesses and documents, and not rely completely on reports from government agencies like the FBI and Secret Service. He suggested that such agencies may not always be totally candid because they were concerned with their reputations.[32] McCloy may have had real concerns that there were going to be conflicts over some specific aspects of the assassination or he may have been using this as a way to push the other Commissioners to support more Commission control over the process, or both.

During this discussion, McCloy gave his opinion on the basic purpose of the President's Commission.

This Commission is set up to lay the dust, dust not only in the United States but all over the world.[33]

A moment later, McCloy added in the context of his expressed concern about the Ruby trial in Texas that:

[30.] Ibid., pp. 8, 17, 20.
[31.] Ibid., p. 20.
[32.] Lifton, 1968, pp. 38-39.
[33.] Ibid., 1968, pp. 38-39.

...everybody is looking for it [the Commission] to come forward promptly, unfortunately, with an objective comprehensive report which will lay all the dust...[34]

As noted in a previous chapter, Alan Belmont, who may have warned McCloy against Olney, stated in his November 25 memo that the objective of the FBI's report would be "to settle the dust", i.e., to show that Oswald did it and did it alone.

The common interest in particulate matter may or may not be just a coincidence. What is clear is McCloy's general attitude about the Commission's primary mission - it was to shut down suspicions, rumors, and questions. This was a goal he shared with Belmont. A somewhat recent account of these events presented by Kai Bird in his biography of McCloy is misleading. Bird says that McCloy was the Commission member most inclined "to look for the threads of a conspiracy", but that McCloy, feeling pressured to quickly complete the investigation, early on muttered something "about how the Commission was established "to lay the dust."[35] Bird is wrong. McCloy never pressed or initiated any area of investigation; he frequently acted to prevent the discovery of the truth. Also, McCloy did not just "mutter something" about laying the dust. He stated twice in a clear manner that that was, in his view, the Commission's purpose.

While McCloy was emphasizing the goal of laying the dust, Dulles was offering a conclusion for the Commission' investigation before it had even started. The conclusion was that Oswald did it, did it alone, and did it because he was a nut. Warren had raised the psychiatric issue first, but he was citing what was in the press and he did not dwell on this.[36] It was Dulles who attempted to impose the lone-nut idea on the Commission as a virtual premise for its investigation.

As was noted earlier, James Reston had suggested, less than 24 hours after the assassination, that this act was committed by one person and that the act reflected a "strain of madness" in the country.[37] The *New York Herald Tribune* had editorialized on November 23 that assassins in the United States are typically

---

[34.] Ibid., 1968, p. 39.

[35.] Bird, 1992, pp. 549, 562.

[36.] President's Commission on the Assassination of President Kennedy, 1963-64, Executive Sessions, December 5, 1963, p. 43.

[37.] Reston, 1963, p. 1.

"crazed individuals" and are "real lunatics."[38] On November 25, the *Wall Street Journal* asserted that assassins are "idiots" and suffering with "hysteria."[39] Also, in Dallas, Mayor Earle Cabell was quoted in the November 23 *Dallas Morning News* describing the assassination as the work of a maniac, as an "irrational act" of a "deranged mind."[40] As documented earlier, this was not the view of police officials or the district attorney.

Allen Dulles was the former head of the Central Intelligence Agency. He had decades of experience in intelligence work and in international affairs. He was one of the most sophisticated men in the world. Later, we will discuss the relationship between Dulles and the other early sources of the lone-nut theory. This man probably was not just repeating something he had seen in the newspapers, unless what was appearing in the media immediately after the assassination and what he tried to impose on the Commission had a common source.

On December 5, Warren briefly mentioned the mental illness issue. Dulles then also brought this up and he began but did not get to finish a description of books he had been reading which focused on "the psychiatric angle."[41]

On December 16, Dulles was far more aggressive in his promotion of this "angle." Dulles was handing out copies of a book which analyzed seven previous attempts on the lives of U.S. Presidents. Dulles was giving this book to members of the Commission and to the Commission's lawyers.[42] As indicated by Dulles, the theme of the book was that such attempts were typically the acts of lone individuals, usually individuals with mental disorders. The book that Dulles was pushing was *The Assassins* by Robert J. Donovan. Although Dulles did not identify it, Donovan's book was published in the year mentioned by Dulles as the publication year and Donovan's book contains a statement that is almost identical to something said by Dulles.

In response to a comment from McCloy that there was a plot in the Lincoln assassination, Dulles noted that that was true "but one man was so dominant that it almost wasn't a plot." In his book, Donovan, who was in 1963 the New York

---

[38.] New York Herald Tribune, 1963a, p. 4.

[39.] Wall Street Journal, 1963, p. 8.

[40.] Dallas Morning News, 1963, p. 14; Raffeto, 1963, p. 4.

[41.] President's Commission on the Assassination of President Kennedy, 1963-64, Executive Sessions, December 5, 1963, p. 43.

[42.] Lifton, 1968, pp. 89-90.

Herald Tribune's Washington bureau chief, argued that in the U.S., assassinations are the work of individuals and he went on to say:

> This was true even in the Lincoln assassination in which, though other conspirators were involved, Booth was the moving spirit and dominated his accomplices to such an extent that the plot was the product of one man's will.[43]

The implication of this is that if conspiracies have leaders, they aren't conspiracies! Donovan's analysis contained another ingredient that was important in Dulles's proffered conclusions about the assassination, i.e., that the assassins were usually crazy. Donovan's conclusion:

> By and large the true story behind the assassinations and attempted assassinations of American Presidents is that the assassins not only were lone operators, but were, most of them, men suffering from mental disease, who pulled the trigger in the grip of delusion.[44]

When Donovan later wrote the introduction to the Popular Library Edition of The Warren Commission Report on the Assassination of President John F. Kennedy, he applied his generalizations to the Kennedy assassination:

> For the murder of President Kennedy was so horrifying, so senseless and heart-rending that the act was difficult to comprehend in terms of the average person's experience. To anyone who happened to know the history of the assassinations of American Presidents, Lee Harvey Oswald conformed remarkably to the pattern of obscure misfits, loners, fanatics, cranks and mentally deranged and deluded men who committed these historic crimes. Indeed he even bore a vague physical resemblance to them.
>
> To millions everywhere, however, the crime in Dallas was too momentous in all its implications to be accepted as the pitifully simple thing it was, the solitary act of a deranged and deteriorating wanderer, taking his revenge on the world by destroying one of its finest living figures. Surely, it seemed to many-- especially to many abroad--there *must* be a further explanation, a more complex cause, a plot, a conspiracy.[45]

[43.] Donovan, 1952.

[44.] Ibid.

[45.] President's Commission on the Assassination of President Kennedy, 1964, p. 7.

Donovan uses about eight different terms to suggest that Oswald was a lone nut. The official line that developed during the hours immediately following the assassination had not changed, it was restated with even greater emphasis by Donovan.

Commission member Gerald Ford offered what was but a slight variation on the lone-nut theory in his 1965 book *Portrait of the Assassin*. Ford explained the assassination in psychological terms. Oswald was described as a man who had "deep-rooted resentment of all authority" and as a man with a capacity for violence and desire for a place in history. Ford claimed that Oswald was unable to form meaningful relationships and that Oswald had an "addled head." Ford deviated to a degree from the lone-nut theory by asserting that Oswald was committed to Marxism and communism. This idea did not lead Ford to any examination of Oswald's politics or connections. Ford noted Oswald's politics only to suggest that they alienated Oswald from U.S. society.[46] Ford's performance is entirely consistent with what happened immediately following the assassination. Oswald's unusual history and his apparent political interests were ignored by people in the media and at the FBI in the rush to conclude that he acted alone. Ford's references to Oswald's alleged communist sympathies are similar to those made by J. Edgar Hoover. These references in both cases led directly to conclusions about Oswald's character, mental status, and guilt rather than to any questions about the assassination or Oswald's relationships to other people.

In the hours, days, and weeks following the assassination, there were three specific assertions made: Oswald did it; he did it alone; he was a nut. During the first few days after the assassination, the Dallas police and the District attorney consistently and emphatically supported only the first assertion, and they did this in part because of what the Belmont supervised FBI investigators were telling them. They never declared Oswald a nut and an opposing view of him was given several times. The only other discernible tendency on the part of most Dallas officials was to become more open to the idea that others may have been involved in some way. The Oswald did-it-alone conclusion was reached immediately in the media and was put in writing by Alan Belmont on November 25, just hours after Oswald was murdered. That murder should have raised new questions but, instead, it allowed a premature conclusion.

[46.] Ford and Stiles, 1965.

The explanation for Oswald's actions was produced within hours by Mayor Cabell and by parts of the media. It was soon thereafter pushed by Allen Dulles and later restated by Ford and Donovan. The goal of laying or settling dust and the assumption that Oswald did it and did it alone were both expressed in outlines of the Commission's task which were prepared during the time that the Commission was being organized.

According to Epstein,[47] Howard Willens, the assistant counsel apparently recommended by Katzenbach, prepared a memo on December 28, 1963, which suggested four areas of investigation: (1) the basic facts of the assassination; (2) identification of the assassin: (3) Oswald's background and motives; (4) the possibility that Oswald conspired with others. This outline contained a premature conclusion about Oswald and it prematurely narrowed any consideration that might be given to a conspiracy.

The Commission had already received a December 9, 1963, Summary Report from the FBI. That report, prepared under the supervision of Alan Belmont, had also come to the emphatic conclusion that Oswald had killed President Kennedy and officer J. D. Tippit. The organization of the investigation proposed by Willens in the December 28 memo is very similar to this earlier report from the FBI. The FBI report contained three parts: Part I covered the assassination and the shooting of Tippit; Parts II and III dealt with Oswald.[48] This report formalized the conclusions about Oswald that were already reached by Alan Belmont in his November 25 memo.

By January 11, 1964, Rankin had prepared a "Tentative Outline" for the Commission's work; it was distributed by Warren to the other Commission members. This outline[49] contained three parts. Part I had four subsections and was devoted to a description of the assassination and some of the subsequent events. Parts II and III were focused on Oswald. Part II had eight subsections. The first seven dealt exclusively with Oswald. The eighth supposedly focused on the possibility of a conspiracy, but the outline named Oswald there again and the last part of it was labeled "Refutation of Allegations" concerning conspiracy. Part III had three subsections, all of which related to Oswald's personal history. This is entirely consistent with the goal set earlier by McCloy, i.e., laying the dust.

---

[47] Epstein, 1966, p. 12.
[48] Ibid., 1966, pp. 129-52.
[49] Roffman, 1975, pp. 256-62.

This outline, prepared by the General Counsel who was brought to the Commission by McCloy, organized the Commission's work with the "presumption that Oswald was guilty."[50] As Howard Roffman has pointed out, "The Commission outlined its work and concluded that Oswald was guilty before it did any investigation or took any testimony."[51]

THE COMMISSION'S WORK: DUSTING THE EVIDENCE

As was pointed out in Chapter One, the Commission report contained a multitude of assertions and claims which ranged from the implausible and improbable to the clearly impossible. We will not "reinvent the wheel" here by going back over all of the errors, misrepresentations, and lies in the Warren Commission report. We will look at a few examples that indicate that laying dust was indeed the purpose of some members of the Commission. At a later point, we will connect what is being established here to past research on the assassination, some of which is useful and significant, some of it misleading and worse.

As was noted earlier, officials in Dallas became more open in the days following the assassination to the possibility that people other than Oswald had knowledge about the assassination before it occurred and they implicitly left open the possibility of a conspiracy. The testimony of these officials before the Commission also gives us some clear indicators of the intentions of McCloy, Dulles, and Rankin.

The testimony of Chief Curry and Captain Fritz is lengthy, almost one hundred pages. Neither of them was ever asked to discuss their own perceptions during those first hours and days after the assassination. Neither was ever asked if they changed their views during that time period; neither was asked to explain any of the comments made in Dallas which did suggest that they suspected others could have been involved in some way. McCloy and Dulles were present along with Warren, Ford, and Cooper. Russell and Boggs were not there. Also present were Rankin, who questioned Curry; Waggoner Carr, Attorney General of Texas; and five assistant counsel - Joseph Ball, David Belin, Melvin

---

[50.] Ibid., p. 80.
[51.] Ibid., p. 88.

Eisenberg, Leon Hubert, and Norman Redlich. Ball conducted most of the interrogation of Captain Fritz.

Warren left shortly after Chief Curry's testimony began; he left Allen Dulles in charge. Rankin asked Curry about the selection of the motorcade route. Because there were questions about how and when Oswald might have learned of the intended route and because the route chosen was the only one which both slowed down the motorcade and brought it through Dealy Plaza, this selection was important.

Curry twice indicated that the choice was made by the Secret Service, but he also stated that the choice was left "entirely up to the host committee and to the Secret Service."[52] Dulles and McCloy were participating in the questioning of Curry. Neither they nor Rankin made any attempt to arrive at a definite identification of the person or persons who made the motorcade route decision. No one asked for the names of the members of the Dallas host committee; no one made a concerted effort to identify the relevant Secret Service officials. They allow Curry to finish his discussion saying vaguely that "They chose" the route. When the Commission's report was published, the review of the selection of the motorcade route is about why the route was chosen and not about who chose it.[53]

As was noted earlier, Chief of Police Curry said in his 1969 book that Winston G. Lawson of the Washington Secret Service office was responsible for the lack of security provided for "the short stretch of Elm Street where the President was shot." Curry had tried to tell the Commission about this, but Rankin, McCloy, and Dulles were having no parts of that.

When Curry testified in April of 1964[54] he said that the choice of the Trade Mart for the President's luncheon appearance pretty much dictated that the motorcade would use Houston and Elm Streets and go by the Book Depository. That decision, Curry said, was made by the Secret Service. Curry was correct. The Trade Mart had been selected by the Secret Service in Washington based on the recommendation of Winston Lawson.[55]

[52]. Hearings Before the President's Commission on the Assassination of President Kennedy, Vol. IV, pp. 169-70.

[53]. President's Commission on the Assassination of President John F. Kennedy, 1993, pp. 31-40.

[54]. Hearings Before the President's Commission on the Assassination of President Kennedy, Vol. IV, p. 169.

[55]. Hearings Before the Select Committee on Assassinations of the United States House of Representatives, 1979, Vol. XI, p. 517.

In his testimony Curry made one of the most significant remarks ever made about the assassination by an official with first hand knowledge, attempting to tell the Commission about the critical lack of security where the President was killed. The Dallas Police Chief was discussing security arrangements in situations where there are tall buildings when the following exchange occurred.

> Rankin: Do you know of any effort that was made to search any of the buildings?
>
> Curry: Not to my knowledge. We did put some extra men from the special service bureau in the downtown area to work in midblocks to watch the crowd and they were not specifically told to watch buildings but they were told to watch everything.
>
> Rankin: Where were they located?
>
> Curry: On the route down Main Street. We didn't have any between Elm Street and the railroad yard.
>
> Rankin: But you say in midblock?
>
> Curry: Yes Sir; especially midblock along the route through the downtown area.
>
> Rankin: Where would the downtown area be?
> Curry: It would be from Harwood Street down to Houston Street.
>
> Rankin: Chief Curry, do you know whether Officers Fostor and White were on the underpass?
>
> Curry: I would have to look at the assignment sheet to determine that, sir.

McCloy: May I ask at this point, unless I may be interfering with your examination, but was it usual for the representatives of the news media to attend showups in the police headquarters apart from this incident?[56]

From this point on, McCloy, Ford, Rankin, and Dulles asked about all sorts of relatively unimportant things and no one ever asked Curry to explain what he meant when he said that there was no security between "Elm Street and the railroad yard." Curry, as we saw earlier, noted in his 1969 book that Lawson was responsible for that lack of security in the area in which the assassination took place. The Commission never asked Lawson about this security breakdown unless it was off the record.

In his Commission testimony Curry also noted that the Dallas police had planned to have Captain Fritz and several homicide detectives in a car immediately behind the President's car. They would have high powered rifles and submachine guns and would be ready to act immediately. Curry said that they had done this in the past for Presidential visits but that Lawson and Secret Service agent Sellers vetoed this plan.

The performance of Rankin, McCloy, Dulles, and Ford in this session is worse than just bad. It is consistent with what they did during the interrogation of other critical witnesses. It smacks of intent to cover-up.

When Curry reported, in response to questions from Rankin, that he thought, based on his own observations, that the first two shots were fired in rapid succession, neither Rankin nor anyone else asks the Police Chief if he thought Oswald could have fired those two shots that quickly using the alleged murder weapon.[57]

Further on, Rankin and Dulles asked some questions about the handling of the evidence and the interaction between the Dallas police and the FBI. Curry indicated that he and other officials in Dallas were concerned that the evidence, requested by and given to the FBI late on the 22nd, would not be available when needed for presentation in court in Dallas. Curry then said:

We got several calls insisting we send this, and nobody would tell me exactly who it was insisting, 'just say I got a call from Washington, and they wanted this evidence up there,' insinuating it was someone in high authority that was

---

[56.] Hearings Before the President's Commission on the Assassination of President Kennedy, Vol. IV, pp. 174-75.

[57.] Ibid., p. 172.

requesting this, and we finally agreed as a matter of trying to cooperate with them actually.[58]

Neither Rankin nor Dulles, nor anyone else, asked any follow-up questions. No one asked him to identify who it was that told him about these calls. They apparently did not want to pursue this or clear it up. It was important. Given that the Commission was fully aware that allegations had been made that Oswald worked for the FBI,[59] you would think that they would have wanted to clear this up so that potential questions about interference in the investigation by federal authorities would be answered. No one asked if Curry suspected then or learned later the identity of the "someone in high authority." No one asked him if he had any sense of whether this someone was in the FBI or from some other part of the government. No one asked him if he thought this was unusual or improper. The actors and decision-makers in this important event were left unidentified, just as they had been in the selection of the motorcade route.

At one point, the question of accomplices is brought up, but it is raised only briefly and in a narrow way. Curry is asked if any attempts were made to determine if there were others involved. Curry replies that inquiries were made and that no evidence was discovered.[60] Neither Rankin nor Dulles, nor anyone else, asked Curry to explain the comments or thinking of Dallas officials, including Curry, on the second and third days following the assassination. No one asked Curry for any general judgment on the possibility of others being involved.

Those kinds of questions were not asked of Captain Fritz either. This was a man with over thirty years of experience supervising and conducting homicide investigations. No one asked him to comment on the things said about accomplices, primarily by Curry and Wade, on the 23rd and 24th of November. No one asked him to provide his best judgment on the probability or possibility of accomplices. As with Curry, some potentially important matters were not followed up.

The plan for the motorcade had included a provision that Fritz and other officers would be in a car following directly behind the Vice-President's car. On the night before, Fritz was told that he should be, instead, at the Trade Mart.

[58.] Ibid., p. 195.

[59.] Weisberg, 1974, pp. 37-52.

[60.] Hearings Before the President's Commission on the Assassination of President Kennedy, Vol. IV, p. 191.

According to Fritz, there was nothing for him to do there. According to Fritz, he was told of that change by [Deputy] Chief Stevenson, but no one sought to identify the person who had made the decision.[61] Lawson made most of these decisions.

Later, Fritz was asked questions about his interrogation of Oswald. Oswald, according to Fritz, readily admitted that he had gone to Russia and he just as readily discussed his Fair Play for Cuba Committee activity, but he vehemently denied having been in Mexico City.[62] No one asked Fritz, who had forty years of experience as a police officer, for his views on when Oswald was telling the truth or if he had any idea why Oswald would immediately acknowledge two controversial political associations, but become very upset about a trip to Mexico City.

Fritz did offer later, as had other officials in Dallas, his judgement that Oswald was not a nut.

Dallas District Attorney Henry Wade appeared before the Commission about six weeks after the appearance of Curry and Fritz. Present for Wade's testimony were Commissioners Warren, Cooper, and Dulles. Also there were Rankin, assistant counsel Norman Redlich, Waggoner Carr, and Alfred Goldberg.

Without being asked about it, Wade mentioned that he had heard on the radio late on the 22nd that the idea of an international conspiracy was going to be included in charges filed against Oswald. Wade said that he thought he had talked about this to Barefoot Sanders that same night. Wade had no idea where such an idea might have come from and he explained that there never was a possibility that such a charge would be made because being a part of an international conspiracy was not defined as a crime anywhere in Texas law.[63]

In different ways, Wade implied that he thought there had been a conspiracy. Discussing the press interview he had participated in around midnight, the night of the 22nd, Wade remembered that he was asked about Oswald's connection to communism and he recollected that he had responded with the following:

> ...well, now, I don't know about that but they found some literature, I understand, some literature dealing with Free Cuba Movement. Following this - and so I looked up and Jack Ruby is in the audience and he said, no, it

[61.] Ibid., p. 203.

[62.] Ibid., pp. 210, 224.

[63.] Hearings Before the President's Commission on the Assassination of President Kennedy, Vol. V, pp. 218-20.

is the Fair Play for Cuba Committee. Well, he corrected me, you see, to show you why I got attracted to his attention, why someone in the audience would speak up and answer a question.[64]

Rankin had been asking the questions, but Dulles intervened at this moment. Dulles did not ask Wade what he thought of this event, did not ask if Wade found this to be suspicious in light of later events. He merely asked if Wade had known Ruby before this time. Rankin, similarly, did not ask for Wade's interpretation of this odd event, but, instead, asked a totally irrelevant question about whether any of Wade's assistants were present at the showup, i.e., a lineup for Oswald.

Senator Cooper later raised a direct question about the possibility of conspiracy and Wade said that he knew of no evidence, but that there were many items of evidence he had not seen.[65] Rankin, shortly thereafter, asked Wade if he "ever had any evidence that Oswald was involved with anyone else in actually shooting the president?" Wade answered:

Well, I will answer that the same way, I have absolutely no evidence myself. Now, of course, I might have some type of opinion or some connection with reference to the Fair Play for Cuba and these letters that they told me about. If that was so there may have been some connection or may not, but I have no evidence myself on it.[66]

Rankin did not ask Wade for his opinion nor did he ask who the "they" was that told him about the letters nor did he ask what Wade meant by "some connection." Instead, Rankin shifted to what Wade knew about Jack Ruby.

It was Senator Cooper, who had raised the issue initially, who brought the discussion back to the issue of conspiracy, asking Wade if he had ever been told that someone else was involved in the assassination. During this exchange, Wade said that:

From what I picked up it appeared to me there was no question that he [Oswald] received his inspiration on this and maybe other help from somewhere.

Wade also said:

---

[64]. Ibid., p. 223.
[65]. Ibid., p. 231.
[66]. Ibid., p. 232.

I mean he planned the thing. He practiced shooting [no evidence was developed for this], and he had his inspiration from somebody else. Whether he had a - was working with someone, I don't know. I never did know, it was rumored all over town that they had an airplane there to carry him out of town. I am sure you all have checked into that but I never know whether they did or not.

There seemed to have been something misfired in the thing if there was anybody tried to get it. I don't think there was anybody with him in the shooting but you [Senator Cooper] are getting at is if there was anyone back of him.

I always felt that the minimum was an inspiration from some cause, and the maximum was actual pay, but like you for evidence, I don't have any.[67]

Since the FBI and the Commission had taken over almost immediately, there was, of course, little chance that evidence would have been developed in Dallas. After an additional exchange between Cooper and Wade concerning rumors about a getaway plane, Dulles shifted the discussion to allegations that Oswald was acquainted with Ruby. None of this discussion about conspiracy would likely have occurred if Senator Cooper had not asked Wade to discuss it. Neither Rankin nor Dulles pursued this; no one asked Wade if he could identify anyone who might know something about this. No one asked Wade if his views on this had changed at any time. No one asked Wade if he had any reaction to the early stories in the media which concluded that Oswald acted alone.

A little later, Rankin did ask Wade if any official had ever asked Wade not to discuss involvement of a foreign government. Wade replied:

Your FBI man may have. I don't know. I talked to him two or three times. I wish I could think of his name because I don't think I ever met him. He was an inspector out of Washington.[68]

Dulles interrupted Wade. Dulles did not do this to express concern that someone in the FBI may have improperly pressured Wade nor did he ask questions that might have helped Wade to recall who this was. Instead, he interrupted to point out to Wade that the FBI man did not work for the Commission. Wade went on to say that the calls from the FBI were primarily made to express FBI concerns that there was too much public disclosure of information.

[67.] Ibid., p. 235.
[68.] Ibid., p. 236.

When the Director of the FBI testified before the Commission in May of 1964, he was asked about very little and he offered very little. Present that day were Warren, Dulles, Ford, Cooper, Boggs, and, among others, Rankin.

Hoover did offer, based on the FBI reports he had read, his opinion of what happened. Hoover opined that: Oswald did it; he did it alone; he was a dedicated communist; he had a "twisted mentality." Hoover did not always speak with certainty. He acknowledged that he had no evidence for the twisted mentality assertion and he said that he was not sure whether Oswald was trying to kill the President or Governor Connally.[69]

Dulles attempted to get from Hoover as strong a statement as possible to the effect that there was no conspiracy. Hoover offered that view, unsolicited, by declaring that the FBI's report indicated that Oswald "was not connected with any conspiracy of any kind, nature or description." A moment later, Hoover said that he was convinced that there was no connection between Oswald and Ruby. Dulles, apparently wanting as much of this on the record as possible, interjected asking Hoover if he would go so far as to say that he was convinced that Oswald was not associated with "anybody else." Hoover agreed to this, but he also said that there was "suspicion at first this might be a Castro act."[70] Hoover explained that the FBI had information from another intelligence agency that Oswald was seen receiving money from someone at the Cuban Consulate in Mexico. Hoover said that the FBI investigated this "very thoroughly." Hoover went on to say that the possibility of an Oswald-Ruby connection was thoroughly investigated. Obviously, these two thorough investigations could not have been completed when Alan Belmont wrapped up the case on November 25, 1963.

THE MAGIC BULLET

As all students of the assassination know, the circumstances of the assassination were such that one key element of the cover story, that Oswald did it alone, was dependent on a demonstration that one bullet caused, or could have caused, two wounds (entrance and exit)in President Kennedy and all of the wounds suffered by Governor Connally. As noted in Chapter One, the alleged bullet, Commission Exhibit 399, was not found at the scene nor was it discovered

---

[69.] Ibid., Vol. V, pp. 103-5.
[70.] Ibid., p. 103.

in either victim. Instead it was found on a stretcher at Parkland Hospital. This bullet, as many researchers have demonstrated,[71] had characteristics clearly indicating that it could not have done what the Commission asserted that it did. For example, its shape was virtually unchanged and it did not look like a bullet that had caused all the damage it supposedly did, especially damage to bones in Governor Connally. The evidence indicated that there were more fragments in the two victims than were missing from the bullet. There were no traces of blood or tissue on the bullet. When these kinds of facts are viewed in conjunction with the mysterious appearance of this bullet, the correct conclusion should have been obvious. The bullet probably was not fired in Dealy Plaza at the time of the assassination and it appeared to have had nothing to do with the wounds in either man. The Commission's leaders, however, needed to conclude otherwise, and they did so.

The Commission did take the testimony of the autopsy doctors. The doctors did not give the Commission all that it needed. This has been examined extensively by other people, particularly Harold Weisberg. This constitutes a critical test for the argument being presented here and we will examine it in that light. That is, if I am right, then there should be evidence that either Dulles or McCloy, or Rankin, or all three, acted to preserve the cover story and that this happened in way that only makes sense if it is part of a cover-up.

Commander James J. Humes, U.S. Navy, was the physician directly in charge of the autopsy, although not the highest ranking officer in the room. He was certified in anatomic pathology and clinical pathology and was Director of Laboratories of the Naval Medical Center at Bethesda. During the autopsy, he was assisted by Commander J. Thornton Boswell, Chief of Pathology at the Naval Medical School, and by Lt. Col. Pierre Finck from the wound ballistics section of the Armed Forces Institute of Pathology.

Assistant counsel Arlen Specter conducted the primary questioning of Commander Humes.[72] Specter tried to take care of one of the Commission's other problems before he got to the problem of the "magic bullet." That is, there were holes in the President's shirt and suit jacket that were about six inches below the collar and slightly to the right of the middle of the President's back. This location corresponded with the placement of the wound in the original autopsy chart and

---

[71.] Fonzi, 1966, pp. 83-86; Wecht, 1972, pp. 29-30; Weisberg, 1995, pp. 162-3.

[72.] Hearings Before the President's Commission on the Assassination of President Kennedy, Vol. II, pp. 348-84.

in an early FBI report.[73] This location was, however, inconsistent with the assertion that one bullet caused the wounds in the President and Governor Connally and therefore inconsistent with, and clear evidence against, the Commission's reconstruction of the shooting. That reconstruction was critical, for numerous reasons, in the claim that Oswald did the shooting alone.

Specter handled this problem, with support from McCloy and Dulles implied by their silence, by eliciting from Humes the opinion that the wound was actually in the back of the neck and that the discrepancy with the holes in the clothing could be explained away by arbitrarily asserting that the shirt and suit jacket were, because the President was a "muscular young man," pushed high up on the back.[74] The assertion was ludicrous in itself and inconsistent with the autopsy diagram. The Commission had to override the evidence of the early autopsy diagram and the clothing in order to have the bullet come from behind and above, where Oswald allegedly was, and to have it pass through the President in such a way that it had even a tiny chance of going through Connally.

At a certain point in the questioning, McCloy intervened and the following exchange occurred.

> McCloy: Quite apart from the President's clothing, now directing your attention to the flight of the bullet, quite apart from the evidence given by the President's clothing, you, I believe, indicated that the flight of the bullet was from the back, from above and behind. It took roughly the line which is shown on your Exhibit 385. [A later drawing vaguely consistent with the Commission's eventual conclusions.]
>
> Humes: Yes, sir.
>
> McCloy: I am not clear what induced you to come to that conclusion if you couldn't find the actual exit wound by reason of the tracheotomy. [Performed in Dallas and allegedly concealing the bullet wound from the doctors at Bethesda during the autopsy.]

[73.] Weisberg, 1965, pp. 195-97.

[74.] Hearings Before the President's Commission on the Assassination of President Kennedy, Vol. II, pp. 365-66.

Humes: The report which we have submitted, sir, represents our thinking within 24-48 hours of the death of the President, all facts taken into account of the situation. The wound in the anterior portion of the lower neck is physically lower than the point of entrance posteriorly, sir.

McCloy: That is what I wanted to bring out.[75]

In asking the question, McCloy twice emphasized that he wanted Humes to ignore evidence of the shirt and jacket. He seeks a mere assertion to back up a diagram made at a later time, not during the autopsy. He did not ask Humes to explain what he meant by "all facts taken into account." McCloy made it clear that he was not trying to ascertain facts, but was instead trying to "bring out" a particular conclusion. This conclusion was needed so that they could say that a bullet was fired from the Book Depository and went through both Kennedy and Connally. The conclusion was inconsistent with original diagrams of the wound, with the holes in the clothing, and the condition of the bullet. Even when they were done with all of this, they were still going to have problems with the angles involved in the two men's wounds.

All of this should have created more than just doubts in the minds of Dulles and McCloy, two of the most sophisticated and experienced men from the upper echelons of American society. Instead, they pushed forward, settling as much dust as they could on this very dry and windy range.

Later in the testimony, McCloy and Dulles would sit quietly while Humes and Lt. Col. Finck offered explicit testimony which was in conflict with the assertions supported by McCloy and Dulles. Those conflicting views were also supported implicitly by Commander Boswell. Looking at CE 399, Humes offered the opinion that it was "most unlikely" that that bullet could have caused the wound in Governor Connally's wrist.[76] Faced with this testimony that the story supported by them was not plausible, McCloy and Dulles remained completely silent.

Humes went on in fact to say not only that there were too many fragments in Connally's wrist for that wound to have been caused by the intact 399, but also that there were too many fragments in the thigh wound. McCloy, who had

---

[75.] Ibid., pp. 368-69.
[76.] Ibid., 374.

intervened to elicit from Humes an arbitrary opinion about the neck (back) wound, said nothing.

Commander Boswell's brief testimony followed Humes. He had been present while Humes was testifying and he stated that he agreed with everything Humes had said. McCloy and Dulles said nothing.[77]

Colonel Finck, also present for Humes's testimony, came next. He also stated, twice, that he agreed with everything that Humes said. Specter did ask Finck specifically if he thought that the CE 399 bullet could have caused the wound in the Governor's wrist. Finck answered clearly that it could not have done so and he also explained that there were too many fragments in the Governor's wrist and too little material missing from the bullet.[78] Again, neither McCloy nor Dulles asked any questions. Neither suggested that this or any other fact presented any problem for the story that they were creating.

All of the issues raised by diagrams, clothing, angles, and the bullet could have been reviewed in relationship to the photographs and x-rays taken during the autopsy. Those could have been presented during the testimony of the doctors or examined before hand. They were not reviewed for the record.[79]

The performance of McCloy and Dulles in this critical area could be viewed as an oddity, that is, not explained at all. The explanation for it, however, is obvious. The two of them had from the beginning set out to lay dust and show that a lone nut did this. Given this purpose, the evidence was often not much more to them than an irritant.

SOME OTHER EXAMPLES: DUSTING ON

Secretary of State Dean Rusk was asked to appear before the Commission. At the outset of Rusk's testimony, Warren instructed Rankin to advise Rusk of the areas that the Commission wanted to cover. Rankin informed Rusk that the Commission was interested in whether the Secretary had knowledge of "any foreign political interest in the assassination of President Kennedy."[80] Since

---

[77.] Ibid., pp. 376-77.

[78.] Ibid., pp. 381-83.

[79.] Weisberg, 1965, pp. 181-86.

[80.] Hearings Before the President's Commission on the Assassination of President Kennedy, Vol. V, p. 363.

President Kennedy had profound differences with leading interests in Great Britain and the Netherlands, as well as with the U.S. foreign policy establishment,[81] this was a possibly useful area of inquiry.

Almost immediately, Dulles interrupted and the discussion went off the record. When the Commission came back on the record, the questioning began with a focus exclusively on the possible involvement of the Soviet Union and Cuba. It is not possible to determine if that was where Warren and Rankin were headed anyway or if that was the focus suggested by Dulles. As a member of the foreign policy establishment, Dulles knew that there were other questions that should have been raised. He had every reason not to raise them.

Much of the Rusk testimony is about the improbability of Soviet or Cuban involvement. Rusk was, as noted in Chapter Three, involved in the establishment of the Warren Commission, perhaps in only a minor way. Rusk was well acquainted with the people who got the ball rolling and with Dulles and McCloy. Rusk may have had a clear understanding that the idea was to arrive at conclusions, not raise questions or do an investigation.

Rankin asked Rusk if he could see any possibility that a "distant wing" of the Soviet Communist party might have an interest in Kennedy's assassination. Rusk answered that he could not imagine any rational purpose for such an involvement. He added that:

> If these dissident elements were aiming to change the present Government of the Soviet Union or its leadership or to return to an early range of policy by the elimination of present leadership or seizure of control, I don't quite see how the elimination of the President of the United States could contribute to that purpose.[82]

Any significant change in the relationship between the U.S. and the Soviet Union could have major effects on groups within each nation. This would be true across a wide range of issues, from aid and trade to military spending. Changes could have a bearing on global economic trends and could have a big impact on the relationships between underdeveloped countries and both the United States and the Soviet Union. Any change of U.S. President that also is a change in policy toward the Soviet Union is a change that would likely effect things all over the

---

[81.] Gibson, 1994, pp. 35-101.

[82.] Hearings Before the President's Commission on the Assassination of President Kennedy, Vol. V, p. 365.

world. It is absurd for Rusk to say that he could not imagine any element in the
Soviet Union having an interest in a change of U.S. leadership. Rusk did have a
problem here. Had he acknowledged that there might have been such elements in
the Soviet Union, he would have found it difficult to deny that they might exist in
the United States.

A little later, Rankin asked Rusk if he was in communication after the
assassination with Thomas Mann, who was then Ambassador to Mexico. No one
mentioned here that Mann's foreign policy views were very different from those
of the dead President.[83] Rusk said that they had "a number of exchanges"
concerning Oswald's visit to Mexico and that there were daily consultations
about this matter, which also involved Deputy Under Secretary of State for
Political Affairs U. Alexis Johnson. Rusk said there was intense interest in the
possibility that "another government," apparently meaning Mexico, was in some
way implicated, but that nothing came of this.[84] For some reason, the logic
applied to potential interest in a leadership change on the part of Soviet elements
did not seem to apply in this instance.

Rankin, Dulles, and McCloy were asking most of the questions. None of
them asked Rusk to identify the government and the matter was dropped. Mann
was involved in actions that represented a change in foreign policy following
Kennedy's death. Mann played a role in the 1964 military coup in Brazil (a coup
supported by and supervised by McCloy), in the decision to invade the
Dominican Republic in 1965, and in the dumping of Kennedy's Alliance for
Progress policies.[85] His role in those discussions of Oswald's activities in Mexico
is, for that reason, intriguing. No one asked the necessary questions.

Rusk was asked if he was aware that there was a rumor on the evening of
November 22 that authorities in Dallas were going to include the issue of an
international conspiracy in their indictment of Oswald. As described earlier, this
issue came up during the testimony of Waggoner Carr, Attorney General for
Texas. Carr said someone called from the White House with a concern about
this. He could not remember who it was.[86]

[83.] Gibson, 1994, pp. 78-80.
[84.] Hearings Before the President's Commission on the Assassination of President
Kennedy, Vol. V, p. 366.
[85.] Gibson, 1994, pp. 78-80.
[86.] Hearings Before the President's Commission on the Assassination of President
Kennedy, Vol. V, pp. 259-60.

Rusk said that he was not aware of it. At this point, Abram Chayes, the legal advisor for the State Department who apparently accompanied Rusk, interjected that Katzenbach had told him about this on the phone late on the 22nd. Chayes recalled that Katzenbach was concerned about this and was seeking the cooperation of Barefoot Sanders, U.S. Attorney in Dallas, in an attempt to keep references to such a conspiracy out of the indictment.[87] Perhaps Katzenbach had someone call Carr; it seems unlikely, however, that Carr would have forgotten Katzenbach's name.

At the end of Rusk's testimony, Rankin asked him if he knew of any evidence showing or indicating any conspiracy, domestic or foreign. Rusk said he had no such evidence. No one questioned Rusk about his knowledge of Oswald's stay in the Soviet Union or his return to the United States.

During the testimony of Alan Belmont, referred to briefly in Chapter Two, an issue was discussed in a way that indicated that Dulles was cooperating with McCloy and Belmont in their efforts at dust control. Near the end of Belmont's testimony, Dulles mentions that he has gotten a copy of a book not yet published which is entitled *Who Killed Kennedy?* Earl Warren reacts by saying to Belmont that "If you find any factual matters in there that contradict your findings, we would expect you to call it to our attention." Dulles says to Belmont that "if there are allegations there, any evidence you can factually deny, that would be helpful to have it."[88] Warren is interested in what might be learned from the book while Dulles thinks in terms of refuting it.

There are other examples of the failures of the Dulles-McCloy-Rankin trio which indicate that their objective was to produce a report supporting the pre-ordained conclusion. These have been noted in the work of Harold Weisberg and Sylvia Meagher.

As noted in Chapter One, it was necessary for the Commission's conclusion that Oswald was a lone assassin to also conclude that only three shots were fired. There were only three shells found where Oswald allegedly did the shooting and there was not enough time in the Commission's reconstruction of events for Oswald to have fired those three, more less four or more shots. In order to keep the number at three, the Commission had to conclude that one shot went through both Kennedy and Connally. As noted earlier, there were huge problems in this

---

[87] Ibid., 368-69.

[88] Hearings Before the President's Commission on the Assassination of President Kennedy, Vol. V, p. 30.

assertion. Two of those were the lack of damage done to the bullet, the famous Commission Exhibit 399, and the fact that there were more fragments in the victims than were missing from this bullet. There was also the problem that the film taken at the time of the assassination by Abraham Zapruder showed a delay between the time the President was hit and the time Connally appeared to have been hit.

When the doctor who treated Connally appeared before the Commission, McCloy demonstrated some of that dust settling intention. McCloy tried to get from Dr. Robert Shaw a statement that there might have been a delayed reaction by Connally to his wounds. McCloy tried three separate times to get Shaw to agree that Connally may not have known immediately that he was hit. Shaw would not agree to this; he said that the damage to the rib would have been felt immediately by Connally.[89] McCloy then tried to get Shaw to speculate that the bullet caused flesh to expand and the expanding flesh, not the bullet, caused the damage to Connally's rib, something that Connally might not have felt immediately. Doctor Shaw rejected that possibility.[90]

Other "laxities" are evident. Harold Weisberg has shown that Rankin cooperated with J. Edgar Hoover to deny the Commission the opportunity to view film taken by amateur photographers in Dealy Plaza around the time of the assassination. Rankin also failed to acquire film taken at the scene on the 22nd by the television networks.[91]

Rankin was responsible for withholding from the record Senator Russell's objections to the single-bullet theory and suppressing the objections of Senator Cooper and Representative Boggs.[92]

Meagher concludes that Rankin knowingly caused the Commission to accept testimony from Oswald's wife, Marina, that was contradicted by FBI and Secret Service reports.[93]

According to Weisberg, Dulles cooperated as a member of the Commission with people at the CIA to withhold information from the Commission that related to the possibility that Oswald was acting as an agent of some intelligence organization while he was in the Soviet Union.[94] During the executive session of

[89] Meagher, 1967, p. 30.
[90] Weisberg, 1965, pp. 174-75; 1975, p. 97.
[91] Weisberg, 1976, pp. 101-3, 113.
[92] Weisberg, 1995, pp. 222, 326.
[93] Meagher, 1967, p. 240.
[94] Weisberg, 1976, pp. 306-9.

January 22, 1964, the Commissioners were discussing allegations that Oswald had worked in some capacity for the FBI. Dulles proposed that the record of this session be destroyed. Rankin twice emphasized that this rumor must be refuted.[95]

In 1967, McCloy misrepresented the failure of the Commission to examine the autopsy pictures by falsely claiming that the pictures were in the hands of the Kennedy family and not available to the Commission.[96] Also in 1967, McCloy helped to shape a CBS documentary that supported the final assertions of the Warren Commission.[97]

One other example needs to be mentioned even though it does not directly involve McCloy, Dulles, or Rankin. As was shown earlier, Mayor Earle Cabell was one of the first public officials, perhaps the first official, to offer the mental illness explanation for the assassination. Mayor Cabell was the brother of former assistant director of the CIA General Charles Cabell, who served under Allen Dulles. Cabell and Dulles were fired by President Kennedy shortly after the Bay of Pigs fiasco. Kennedy felt that Dulles and others at the CIA had misled him.[98] Cabell's testimony was taken in Dallas by assistant counsel Leon Hubert in July of 1964.

During this interview the following exchange occurs:

> Hubert: Now there is some information, Mr. Cabell, that Jack Ruby was around the hospital some place, either near the entrance or near the pressroom, or something of that sort. And, of course, I take it that you now know what he looks like, from pictures in the press?
>
> Cabell: Well, I knew him by sight.
>
> Hubert: You knew him by sight prior to this?
>
> Cabell: Yes.
>
> Hubert: How long had you known him?

---

95. Weisberg, 1974; 1975, p. 406.
96. Weisberg, 1975, pp. 300, 553; 1995, p. 179.
97. Hennelly and Policoff, 1992.
98. Gibson, 1994, p. 44; Sorensen, p. 332.

Cabell: I would say for several years.

Hubert: Did you see him around the hospital then at any time?[99]

Hubert, perhaps stunned by Cabell's comments, never asks Cabell why or how he had known Ruby. Cabell's relationship to Ruby may not have been significant, but he was the brother of Allen Dulles's former assistant and he was perhaps the first official to publicly offer a version of the lone-nut explanation. Apparently neither Dulles nor Rankin ever had any interest in clarifying this matter, and Rankin certainly read the transcript of this interview.

SUMMARY

We have seen in this chapter that McCloy and Dulles attempted to control the Commission and its work from the beginning. McCloy, with support from Ford, and apparently, Dulles, acted to prevent Warren from selecting Olney as the Commission's general counsel and he successfully opposed Warren's effort to appoint Olney to some other position with the Commission. At least two days before McCloy challenged Warren on this, Alan Belmont and Katzenbach had discussed Warren's desire to pick Olney and they had agreed that the appointment of Olney should be prevented.

McCloy's choice, J. Lee Rankin, was appointed as general counsel. Rankin would play a major role in the selection of the Commission's assistant counsel and he controlled or influenced most of the Commission's work.

At the first executive session, McCloy set the tone by stating that the Commission's task was to lay the dust. This echoed Alan Belmont's memo, written about ten days earlier, which stated that the FBI's report was intended to settle the dust.

Before the Commission began its work, Dulles set forth the conclusion that Oswald did it, did it alone, and did it because he was a nut. Dulles was introducing a pre-ordained conclusion that already had been suggested by Mayor Cabell, James Reston of the *New York Times*, and the editors of both the *New York Herald Tribune* and the *Wall Street Journal*. Those conclusions were stated

[99.] Hearings Before the President's Commission on the Assassination of President Kennedy, Vol. VII, p. 480.

within 72 hours of the assassination; in a couple of instances it was within a few hours. Ford would later provide a slight variation of this conclusion, one similar to that coming from J. Edgar Hoover. That was the communist-lone-nut theory. For forty years Hoover had almost always thought in terms of groups and conspiracies when he thought about communism. The communist-lone-nut idea was then a bit of an oddity for Hoover. At a later point, we will provide an explanation for this oddity. The Commission and the FBI, led by Belmont and Hoover, did structure its work with the presumption that Oswald did it.

During the testimony of witnesses before the Commission, Dulles, McCloy, and Rankin repeatedly acted as if settling dust and reaching pre-established conclusions were their primary goals. On issues related to the questions about security, to wounds and the infamous CE399 bullet, to the question of conspiracy, and to numerous other matters, the trio of McCloy, Dulles, and Rankin repeatedly behaved as if cover-up was their real purpose. They were joined in this by others, including Alan Belmont, Gerald Ford, and Arlen Specter.

We have established two groups of people, along with various support figures, that played crucial roles in the cover-up. The Rostow-Acheson-Alsop group instigated the creation of the Commission. Alan Belmont surfaces as a key figure in the FBI's role in the "investigation." J. Edgar Hoover also quickly becomes complicit. Nicholas Katzenbach and individuals such as Dean Rusk act in what were apparently support roles. Mayor Cabell and elements of the media made significant contributions to the cover-up. In some areas, media figures took the lead. The contributions of McCloy, Dulles, and Rankin were critical.

We need to examine the relationships among these people and begin to identify the social forces for whom they acted.

Chapter Five

THE COVER-UP WAS AN ESTABLISHMENT PROJECT

Participants in a criminal conspiracy do not have to be fully knowledgeable of all of the relevant events nor of the overall aims of the conspiracy. They can be more or less witting, be involved prior to or following a criminal action, be directly or only indirectly active in support of the conspiracy, and be minor or major contributors. In this chapter we will examine the relationships among the individuals who participated, wittingly or unwittingly, in the cover-up. Those who did not know what they were involved in should have known. These individuals made up the three groups that we have been discussing: those in the media who created the cover story in the hours immediately following the assassination; the group that persuaded President Johnson to create the Warren Commission; the group that controlled the operations of the Warren Commission. A fourth group, discussed later, turned Lee Oswald into a patsy. The framing of Oswald was part of the cover-up.

All of these men played important roles in the cover-up. There is no direct evidence that any of them had knowledge of the assassination before it occurred. I have no direct evidence that any of them knew who it was that ordered the assassination. Their participation in the cover-up may have been on a no-questions-asked basis. Their roles may have been limited to specific tasks, like getting the Commission created or blaming the assassination on Oswald. It is possible that none of them had any direct, factual knowledge concerning the assassination.

Whether conspirators or co-conspirators, whether the involvement was before or only after the fact, regardless of how witting was their participation, these men did oversee important stages in the cover-up. The cover-up was in a couple of ways like a relay race. Each phase of the race was run by a group, not an individual. The cover-up was conducted in a series of stages and the early stages had to be executed with sufficient speed to prevent any other account of the events from becoming influential enough to force an honest investigation.

The official cover story, that Oswald did it alone and did it because he was a nut, or a communist nut, had to be immediately disseminated. As we have seen, this was done through the media. The patsy in this intentionally confusing mess also had to be eliminated to prevent him from talking and to prevent a serious investigation. After the initial dissemination of the cover story and the elimination of the patsy, the next two stages were the creation of and the control of the official investigation. The first of these two stages, as described earlier, was carried out directly by Eugene Rostow, Joseph Alsop, and Dean Acheson. The second stage was supervised by key participants in the investigation. Someone orchestrated the overall investigatory process and it was not, with one exception, the Warren Commission counsel and staff. Most of the counsel and staff had no authority over the general direction that was taken by the Commission. The obvious supervisors of this stage of the cover-up were Allen Dulles, John J. McCloy, Alan Belmont, and the lawyer who was installed as chief counsel by McCloy, J. Lee Rankin. These men, with support from Gerald Ford and the compliance of Earl Warren, supervised this stage of the cover-up. They constituted one team in a relay of teams. They were connected to the Rostow-Alsop-Acheson team, from whom they took the baton. All of these men had at least one close relationship with someone else involved in the process. Usually there were multiple relationships.

THE NETWORK

Among these men there was probably no one who had performed a greater variety of important services for the Establishment than John J. McCloy. In fact, there may have been no one in the country who had handled so many difficult and important tasks on behalf of the higher circles. McCloy was the utility player par excellence for the inner core of the upper-class Establishment. At the time of the assassination, McCloy's resume included the following: partner in the

Morgan related law firm of Cravath, de Gersdorff, Swaine and Wood from 1929 to 1940; assistant Secretary of War, 1941-1945; President of the World Bank, 1947-1949; high commissioner to Germany, 1949-1952; Chairman of the Board of what was initially Chase National and then Chase Manhattan Bank, 1953-1961; trustee of the Rockefeller Foundation and Chairman of the Ford Foundation; Chairman of the Council on Foreign Relations since 1953; director of United Fruit, Union Pacific Railroad, Allied Chemical, AT&T, Metropolitan Life.[1]

In the 1950s, McCloy became the representative of and trouble-shooter for the major oil companies and the bankers who financed those companies.[2] He would continue in that capacity into the 1970s. McCloy handled some of the personal affairs for the Rockefeller family and he worked with Robert Lovett and Averill Harriman on behalf of the Union Pacific Railroad.[3] McCloy was involved in controversial matters such as the decision to place Japanese Americans in internment camps during World War Two and the decision to protect and use high level Nazis after the war.[4] McCloy was related by marriage to Lewis Douglas, an heir to Phelps Dodge money, who was president of Mutual Life Insurance Co. and a trustee of the Rockefeller Foundation and to John S. Zinsser, a long-time director of J. P. Morgan & Company.[5] Within the Establishment, McCloy was one of the Establishment's most versatile, experienced, sophisticated, and trusted agents.

No less trusted and sophisticated was Allen Dulles. Like McCloy, Dulles had longstanding connections to both Morgan and Rockefeller interests.[6] Dulles came from a family with a long history of involvement in the upper levels of public and private power (e.g., his grandfather was Secretary of State in the Harrison administration and an uncle was the chief foreign policy advisor to President Wilson).[7] In the years prior to World War Two, Dulles had various government jobs related to foreign policy and practiced law with Sullivan & Cromwell.[8] By 1935, at age 42, he had become sufficiently important to be the representative of

[1.] Burch, 1980; Marquis Who's Who, 1962-63.
[2.] Isaacson and Thomas, 1986, p. 572.
[3.] Ibid., pp. 69, 120.
[4.] O'Neill, 1993, pp. 230-32.
[5.] Burch, 1980.
[6.] Collier and Horowitz, 1976, pp. 270, 412; Quigley, 1966, p. 952.
[7.] Mosley, 1966, pp. 30, 46-47.
[8.] Marquis Who's Who, 1962-63.

the Council on Foreign Relations at a high level conference in London. Dulles chaired the study meetings and gave one of the opening speeches.[9] Dulles's service with the Office of Strategic Services during World War Two led to his later appointment as Director of Central Intelligence, serving as Director from 1953 to 1961 when he was fired by President Kennedy. Before the Warren Report was published, President Kwame Nkrumah of Ghana was shown a copy of the report. When he saw Dulles' name, he immediately said that that confirmed his suspicion that the report was a cover-up.[10]

Eugene Rostow graduated from Yale in 1933, went as a student to King's College, Cambridge, the next year and then returned to the Yale Law School. Rostow became the Dean of the Yale Law School in 1955. He spent an additional year at King's College, 1959-60, as Pitt Professor.[11] Rostow worked at the State Department from 1942 to 1944 as an assistant to Dean Acheson, then Assistant Secretary of State. Later, 1966 to 1969, Rostow was Under-Secretary of State for Political Affairs.[12] Rostow was a member of the influential American Law Institute, a group funded by the Rockefeller Foundation to promote or develop legal policies for the country.[13] McCloy, of course, was a trustee of the Foundation.

Joseph Alsop was in the early-1960s one of most prominent journalists in the United States and he was among a few journalists with high level connections to the intelligence community. During World War Two, Alsop worked as speech writer and public relations man for General Claire Lee Chennault when Chennault was in China.[14] After the war, Alsop became deeply connected to the CIA, maintaining close personal relationships with people such as Richard Helms, Frank Wisner, and Ed Lansdale.[15] Lansdale used Alsop as an outlet for propaganda about the situation in Vietnam.[16] There is a claim that Lansdale was in Dealey Plaza when Kennedy was killed.[17] The Alsop family was part of what

---

[9] Quigley, 1981, p. 195.
[10] DiEugenio, 1999, p. 25; Mahoney, 1968, pp. 249-50.
[11] Marquis Who's Who, 1962-63.
[12] Whitworth, 1970, p. 16.
[13] Reisman, 1998, pp. 187, 190, 267.
[14] Davis, 1991, pp. 166-67.
[15] Powers, 1979, pp. 92, 350; Valentine, 1990.
[16] Valentine, 1990, p. 339.
[17] Stone and Sklar, 1992, pp. 182-83.

Stephen Birmingham has called "America's Secret Aristocracy."[18] Alsop came from a long line of Anglophiles. One of his ancestors, John Alsop, was a committed Tory who actively opposed the American Revolution. Joseph's mother was Teddy Roosevelt's niece.[19]

Dean Gooderham Acheson, Secretary of State under Truman, was born and raised in the United States, but his parents were Canadian. Acheson's family, like Alsop's, were Anglophiles. His mother, a member of the wealthy Gooderham family, was educated in England and she probably contributed to Acheson's life long Anglophilia and his great admiration of the British Empire.[20] Acheson, a graduate of Groton and Yale, viewed the majority of human beings as a "vulgar mass."[21] He reportedly thought little of JFK and spoke of Joseph Kennedy as the "social-climbing" bootlegger. Acheson backed Symington for the Democratic presidential nomination in 1960 with hopes of stopping JFK.[22] Acheson served briefly as Under Secretary of the Treasury in FDR's administration, but left because of a policy dispute. This is similar to McCloy's brief service as arms control advisor under JFK. When Acheson was being considered for that Treasury job, Senator James Couzens, Republican from Michigan, accused Acheson of being as much an agent of the House of Morgan "as anybody we could possibly put in the Treasury."[23] Acheson was a partner for three decades in the Rockefeller-Schroder related law firm of Covington, Burling, Rublee, Acheson and Shorb. He also served for eight years as vice-chairman of the Brookings Institution and he was involved during the World War Two period in planning post-war international policy, including the creation of the International Monetary Fund.[24]

These five men shared much in common. They were all men of influence, status, and wealth. Three of them, Dulles, Alsop, and Acheson, were members of the exclusive Metropolitan Club in Washington. McCloy and Alsop belonged to the Links and to the Brooks Clubs in New York. McCloy and Acheson belonged to the Century Club in New York. All of these are among the elite social clubs in

[18.] Birmingham, 1987, p. 62.
[19.] Yoder, 1995, pp. 33, 37.
[20.] Burch, 1980, p. 114; Isaacson and Thomas, 1986, pp. 51, 55, 136; McLellan, 1976, pp. 1-2.
[21.] Isaacson and Thomas, 1986, p. 56.
[22.] Isaacson and Thomas, 1986, pp. 590-91, 612.
[23.] Isaacson and Thomas, 1986, p. 134.
[24.] Burch, 1980, pp. 57, 82, 164, 418; Isaacson and Thomas, 1986, p. 233.

the United States.[25] Four of them, Alsop excepted, were members of the Council on Foreign Relations. Two of them, McCloy and Dulles, were directors and officers of that high level policy making organization.[26] The CFR was a significant organization because its members and particularly its leaders were bound together through a multitude of personal relationships.[27] These men knew each other and several of them had long-standing close ties to each other.

James DiEugenio, Harold Weisberg, and a few other researchers have correctly portrayed McCloy and Dulles as controlling figures within the Warren Commission. We have looked at some examples of their misbehavior. Even Peter Grose's all-too-kind biography of Dulles, *Gentleman Spy: The Life of Allen Dulles*, states that Dulles tried to shape the investigation and that he prevented the exploration of some areas.[28] As of 1964, Dulles and McCloy had been very close friends for over three decades.[29] McCloy's Council on Foreign Relations study group recommended the intervention in Guatemala that was shortly thereafter carried out by fellow CFR officer Allen Dulles.[30] While McCloy was at the Ford Foundation in the 1950s, he helped Dulles to get Foundation funding for CIA activities.[31] While he was Chairman of the Chase Manhattan Bank, 1955-1961, McCloy allowed the CIA to use that bank for its operations.[32]

McCloy, with support from Dulles, or Ford, or both, imposed J. Lee Rankin on the Commission. Dulles and McCloy imposed their views on the Commission, giving the Commission a goal, settling dust, and a conclusion to work toward, Oswald was the lone nut who did it. These two men had multiple connections to the group that imposed the Commission on LBJ to begin with, connections beyond membership in the Council on Foreign Relations. They and the creators of the Warren Commission also had numerous connections to those in the media who initiated the cover-up.

For example, Dulles's relationship with Alsop went back at least to 1940 when the two, along with Dean Acheson and Whitney H. Shepardson, were

[25] Domhoff, 1983, pp. 46-47; Marquis Who's Who, 1962-63.
[26] Council on Foreign Relations, 1963.
[27] Donovan, 1974, p. 267; Lucas, 1971, p. 34.
[28] Grose, 1994, p. 532.
[29] Bird, 1992, pp. 76, 411-12, 485; Fischer and Fischer, 1994, pp. 122, 241; Grose, 1994, p. 249.
[30] Bird, 1992, p. 435.
[31] Ibid., p. 428.
[32] Ibid., p. 485.

members of an Establishment group, the "Century Group," formed to promote aid to Great Britain.[33] Alsop was among a few high level journalists who were among Dulles's "steady social contacts" in the 1950s.[34] At the time that Alsop, Dulles, and Acheson were part of the Century Group, Dulles was a director of J. Henry Schroder Banking Corporation which had close ties to Acheson's law firm. Stewart Alsop once identified Dulles, Acheson, McCloy, and Lovett as examples of the Anglo-Saxon Elite friends of himself and his brother Joe.[35]

McCloy was probably even closer than Dulles to Acheson. McCloy was for thirty years one of Acheson's closest friends and someone with whom he frequently worked.[36] Like Dulles, McCloy worked with Acheson during the 1940s in the effort to promote assistance to Great Britain.[37] McCloy supported Acheson when he came to the defense of accused traitor Alger Hiss.[38] Acheson recommended McCloy as one of the high commissioners in Germany after World War Two and he recommended McCloy to JFK as Secretary of State.[39] When Acheson's daughter married William Bundy, brother of national security advisor McGeorge Bundy, the wedding breakfast was held at McCloy's home.[40] William Bundy worked under Allen Dulles at the CIA in the 1950s.

McCloy and Acheson worked together on a variety of other projects. The two were part of a five man group appointed after World War Two to formulate a policy for the international control of atomic energy.[41] They worked together on post-war policy toward Japan[42] and they, along with Lovett, were offering advice to JFK during the missile crisis.[43] They both supported escalation of the war in Vietnam after JFK's assassination.[44] They were, with Dean Rusk, among the most vocal critics of Charles de Gaulle in 1967.[45] According to Isaacson and

---

[33.] Bird, 1992, pp. 111-12; Burch, 1980, p. 111.

[34.] Grose, 1994, p. 387.

[35.] Merry, 1996, p. 447.

[36.] Isaacson and Thomas, 1986, pp. 493, 515.

[37.] Acheson, 1969, p. 28; Isaacson and Thomas, 1986, pp. 135-36.

[38.] Ibid., pp. 493, 515.

[39.] Ibid., pp. 515, 592.

[40.] Ibid., p. 193.

[41.] Bundy, 1988.

[42.] Acheson, 1969, pp. 426-27.

[43.] Isaacson and Thomas, 1986, p. 621.

[44.] Brinkley, 1992, p. 254.

[45.] Brinkley, 1992, pp. 230-31.

Thomas (*The Wise Men*), McCloy and Acheson shared an elitist disdain for democratic processes.[46] Acheson and McCloy had a close personal relationship and Acheson thought highly of McCloy.[47]

Both McCloy and Acheson, like Dulles, were closely acquainted with Joseph Alsop. McCloy's friendship with Alsop went back to at least the early-1940s.[48] Acheson knew Alsop at least as early as the 1930s and they became close friends, socializing with and writing to each other and working together with Dulles as members of the Century Group.[49] The families of Alsop and Acheson had been close to each other for at least a generation.[50]

Acheson and Eugene Rostow knew each other and were a two man mutual admiration society. Rostow worked for Acheson in the 1942-44 period when Acheson was Assistant Secretary of State. In his book, *Peace In The Balance*, Rostow described Acheson as "an authentically great man."[51] Acheson, in *Present at the Creation*, said that he considered Rostow one of his most important colleagues in that period.[52] Acheson was a Fellow of the Yale Corporation and Rostow the Dean of the Yale Law School.[53] Acheson supported the choice of Rostow to be Dean in 1955.[54] Rostow and Acheson, of course, got the ball rolling in the creation of the Warren Commission.

One or more of these five men was close to or associated with other figures who played prominent roles in the development of the cover-up story. As head of the domestic intelligence division of the FBI from 1951 to 1962 Alan Belmont must have had numerous contacts with CIA director Allen Dulles.[55] In 1960 Belmont and Dulles were among the ten men serving as members of the United States Intelligence Board, an organization which provided intelligence estimates

[46] Isaacson and Thomas, 1986, p. 186.
[47] Acheson, 1959, pp. 22, 37-38, 51, 173; Fischer and Fischer, 1994, pp. 54, 121, 143-144, 159, 167, 177, 195-196, 241.
[48] Bird, 1992, p. 125; Fischer and Fischer, 1994, pp. 160, 169, 172, 226; Merry, 1996, pp. 88, 179, 447.
[49] Almquist, 1993, pp. 61, 72; Bird, 1992, pp. 111-12; Isaacson and Thomas, 1986, pp. 431, 581; Merry, 1996, pp. 181, 355, 367, 447.
[50] Merry, 1996, p. 87.
[51] Rostow, 1972, p. 130.
[52] Acheson, 1969, p. 91.
[53] Marquis Who's Who, 1962-63.
[54] Chace, 1998, p. 371.
[55] Marquis Who's Who, 1964-65.

for the President and Congress. (A list of the members was published in the February 17, 1960, edition of the *New York Times*, p. 11.) Mayor Earle Cabell of Dallas, perhaps the first person to offer the lone-nut theory, was also connected to Allen Dulles. Earle's brother, Charles Cabell, was Dulles' assistant.

James Reston, one of the first and most important people in the media to label Oswald the lone assassin and to imply that he was insane just hours after the assassination, was close to Dean Acheson.[56] In fact, according to Acheson biographer James Chace, Reston was someone with whom Acheson could plant stories.[57] Reston was also close to McCloy. McCloy lived across the street from Reston in the 1940s and became an unidentified source for some of Reston's stories.[58]

Joe Alsop briefly worked for John Hay ("Jock") Whitney, owner of the Herald Tribune, and the two were well acquainted.[59] Whitney was a millionaire publisher with all the right credentials. His education included Exeter, Yale, and Oxford. Whitney's father and grandfather were members of Yale's secret and elitist society Skull and Bones.[60] Commenting on George Bush's association with Skull and Bones, James Reston referred to the "noble tradition of Skull and Bones."[61] As noted in chapter two, Whitney was a knight of St. John of Jerusalem and honorary commander of the Order of the British Empire. He was a member of the Council on Foreign Relations and the Business Council.[62]

Whitney's granduncle was Oliver Payne, a partner with John D. and William Rockefeller in Standard Oil.[63] For over sixty years the Whitneys were close allies of both Morgan and Rockefeller interests.[64] Jock Whitney was a friend of the Rockefeller family.[65] Around 1930 the board of the Morgan controlled Guaranty Trust Company featured Harry Payne Whitney, Cornelius Vanderbilt Whitney,

[56] Reston, 1991, pp. 140-156.
[57] Chace, 1998, pp. 178, 199; Isaacson and Thomas, 1986, p. 409.
[58] Bird, 1992, pp. 125, 313; Fischer and Fischer, 1994, pp. 160, 241; Reston, 1991, p. 163.
[59] Hersh, 1992, pp. 308, 324; Merry, 1996, pp. 337-38, 371-73.
[60] Kahn, 1981, pp. 10, 18.
[61] Reston, 1991, p. 264.
[62] Council on Foreign Relations, 1963; Marquis Who's Who, 1978-79.
[63] Fortune, 1964, p. 119; Myers, 1910, Vol. II, p. 210.
[64] Quigley, 1966, p. 530.
[65] Collier and Horowitz, 1976, p. 226.

W. A. Harriman, and Morgan partners Thomas W. Lamont and Grayson M-P Murphy.[66]

In the late-1930s, the Whitneys were also among a group of major stockholders controlling *Newsweek* magazine. That group included Paul Mellon, the Harrimans, and the Astors.[67] The Whitneys were related through marriage to the Harrimans and the Vanderbilts as well as to William Paley of CBS.[68] Jock Whitney's cousin, Senator Stuart Symington, was, as indicated earlier, something of a great-blue-hope in 1960, i.e., a non-campaigning candidate that many blue-bloods hoped could steal the nomination from Kennedy at the 1960 convention.[69]

Eugene Rostow, apparently the first person to act to get the Warren Commission established, served with Jock's brother-in-law, Charles Payson, on the board of directors of the Texstar Corporation in 1962.[70]

Across the upper levels of the media there were many other secondary or indirect connections and associations. On the New York Herald Tribune board of directors with Whitney was Samuel C. Parker, Jr. An assistant to Whitney, Parker earlier in his life had spent seven years with J.P. Morgan & Co. and in 1963 he was a member with Alsop and McCloy of the Links Club.[71] Another member of the Links Club who was on the board and who served as president of Whitney Communications was Walter N. Thayer. Thayer was a director of the Morgan controlled Bankers Trust and had worked for the law firm of Donovan, Leisure, Newton & Lumbard.[72] "Donovan" was William Donovan, World War Two head of the Office of Strategic Services, the forerunner of the CIA. Donovan worked for the Morgan group early in his career.[73] Whitney himself cooperated with the CIA in money transactions and there were personal connections to such high level CIA officials as Frank Wisner and C. Tracey Barnes.[74] Also on the board was Whitelaw Reid. Reid was, like Whitney, a member of the Council on Foreign Relations (CFR) and he belonged to the Metropolitan Club with Dulles, Alsop, and Acheson. He was also a member,

---

[66.] Lundberg, 1937, pp. 222-23.

[67.] Ibid., p. 259.

[68.] Kahn, 1981, p. 60; Lundberg, 1937, pp. 11-12, 15.

[69.] Kahn, 1981, pp. 92, 224.

[70.] Burch, 1980, pp. 198, 224.

[71.] Marquis Who's Who, 1962-63.

[72.] Marquis Who's Who, 1962-63.

[73.] Chernow, 1990, p. 211.

[74.] Hersh 1992, pp. 308, 324; Kahn, 1981, p. 146.

with Dulles and Rostow, of the Century Association. All of these Herald Tribune men (Reid, Park, Thayer, Whitney) had been students at Yale.

There were many similar associations at the other media institutions. For example, the publisher and a director of the New York Times, Arthur H. Sulzberger, was a member of the CFR, Metropolitan Club, and Century Association. He was also a trustee of the Rockefeller Foundation. Five of the Times' ten directors were members of the Sulzberger family; another was married to a Sulzberger. Among the other directors was Eugene Black who was an executive for fourteen years with the Rockefellers' Chase National Bank and went on to head the World Bank.[75] Black also served as a trustee of the Population Council, an organization created by John D. Rockefeller 3rd in 1952.[76] Another Times director, Amory H. Bradford, was a member of the CFR and Century Association and a trustee of the Carnegie Institution. Bradford's wife was Carol Warburg Rothschild Bradford.[77] The Warburgs and Rothschilds are two of the world's most famous banking families. Director Orvil Dryfoos was married to one of Arthur Sulzberger's daughters. He was a member of the executive committee of the Rockefeller Foundation.[78]

There were also extensive links between Morgan-Rockefeller interests and the other media mentioned here, i.e., Dow Jones (Wall Street Journal), Time, Inc., and *Newsweek*.[79] McCloy, Dulles, and Acheson were themselves personally close to the Morgan-Rockefeller interests.[80]

The cover-up was very much a private, not a government, affair. Even though Belmont of the FBI was involved early on, the Oswald did it alone story was first promoted by the media. Rostow and Acheson intervened to get the Commission created and, in the process, prevented Senate-House investigations. McCloy and Dulles dominated the Commission. This was essentially an Establishment cover-up. Only an Establishment network could do all of these

[75] Marquis Who's Who, 1962-63.

[76] Collier and Horowitz, 1976, p. 287.

[77] Marquis Who's Who, 1962-63.

[78] Marquis Who's Who, 1962-63.

[79] Bird, 1992; Chernow, 1990, pp. 312-13, 417, 420-21, 480-85; Collier and Horowitz, 1976, p. 91; Davis 1991, p. 173; Gibson, 1994, pp. 68-73; Isaacson and Thomas, 1986, pp. 120-22; Kotz, 1976, p. 163; Lundberg, 1937, pp. 37, 257-59, 289, 308; Marquis Who's Who, 1962-63; Moody's Investor Service, 1963-64.

[80] Bird, 1992; Collier and Horowitz, 1976, p. 412; Gibson, 1994, pp. 70-73; Quigley, 1966, p. 937, 952.

things. Only they could reach into the media, the CIA, the FBI, the military (control of the autopsy), and other areas of government.

Most of the men contributing to the cover-up operated at the upper levels of the Establishment; all worked on behalf of that Establishment. People like Whitney and Acheson were probably at a higher level in the pecking order than a James Reston or Alan Belmont. This Establishment combines old money with not so old big money; it is an amalgamation of Boston Brahmins and New York financial powers. Its power and influence is rooted in the control of strategic assets. The Establishment owns banks, oil companies, and media, as well as an assortment of other corporations. Associated law firms protect its interests and it uses foundations and think tanks to develop and promote parts of its agenda. Establishment families use all of their resources, but particularly money and media, to affect the electoral and political processes. Although they make deals with and have alliances with groups in dozens of countries, their primary international connection is to similarly situated factions of the British upper class. Anyone wishing to gain an understanding of these interests in the decades leading up to the Kennedy presidency, or today, would be well advised to begin with Ferdinand Lundberg's *60 Families* , George Seldes' *One Thousand Americans*, and Carroll Quigley's *Tragedy and Hope* and *The Anglo-American Establishment*, perhaps supplemented by G. William Domhoff's *Higher Circles* and David Kotz's *Bank Control of Large Corporations in the United States*.

Given the role of these Establishment members (Acheson, Dulles, McCloy, Whitney, Alsop, and Rostow) and agents of the Establishment (Rankin, Belmont, Reston) in the cover-up, any connections between these individuals or other clearly related Establishment interests and the events leading up to the assassination are of obvious importance. There is only one individual that we know with certainty was significant in the period leading up to November 22. That person is the patsy Lee Harvey Oswald. We do not know the names of the men who made the decision to have Kennedy killed. We do not know the names of the men who did the shooting. However, we do now know the names of the men who conducted the cover-up. Any connections between them and Oswald, especially in the period just prior to the assassination, are significant. In fact, setting Oswald up as a patsy would itself be part of the cover-up.

Much of Lee Harvey Oswald's life was strange. There is probably no way to determine how much of that unusual history is directly relevant to his role as a patsy in the assassination. It may be much of his life and it may be only the months immediately preceding the assassination. We will consider only those months.

Oswald lived in two places during those months - New Orleans and Dallas. He moved to Dallas, for his second period of residence there, only seven weeks or so before the assassination. He moved to Dallas from New Orleans where he spent the previous five months, that following his first stay in Dallas which lasted about six and a half months.

Oswald 's time in New Orleans has been examined in relation to organized crime (through his connection to David Ferrie or through his uncle Charles Murret), to anti-Castro Cubans, and to various intelligence agencies. Only in a few instances has anyone bothered to look at New Orleans in relation to the national upper class and particularly the New York-Boston Establishment. In the next chapter we will enter a history of intrigue and machination in Louisiana through a door that can be opened with a surprising key - the 1935 assassination of Senator Huey Pierce Long.

We will look at Long and his death because his life and his death bear similarities to the life and death of JFK, because Long's opponents and enemies were much the same as Kennedy's, and because there are a variety of direct and indirect connections between the two men, the two eras, and the two deaths.

Chapter Six

LONG AND KENNEDY

Long and Kennedy had very similar ideas about the uses of government and they also had very similar enemies, even in some cases identical enemies. Like earlier leaders such as Lincoln and Alexander Hamilton, both viewed the government as one of the nation's most useful instruments to achieve economic and social progress. In this view the state is not to be celebrated, romanticized, or exaggerated in its importance, but it is also not to be forgotten that government is the only available form of organization to accomplish many necessary and worthwhile goals. In the late twentieth century it is also the only organized force that can counter the vast influence of international banks and corporations, of banking and raw materials cartels, and of the many other private organizations which attempt to influence almost all aspects of life.

The Long-Kennedy view of government rejects the idea that the state should own and manage all or nearly all elements of the economy. It is opposed to communism. It also rejects the other extreme which is variously known as English liberalism, economic conservatism, laissez faire, or "free enterprise." The free enterprise idea of government in practice means that government submits to or cooperates with powerful private interests even if those interests are destroying the economy. The Long-Kennedy approach recognizes that economies can be undermined or destroyed by the forces of the market itself and by combinations of interests which exploit or abuse less powerful sectors of the economy. It is also recognizes that class interests and political and social objectives have an impact on the economy. Both Kennedy and Long believed that there were things the government had to do and things only it could do, and they believed that the government had to use its powers to maintain or create a generally positive direction for the economy.

Kennedy used the tax system to reward companies for making useful investments in the domestic economy, the investment tax credit. He proposed many changes in the tax code, most of which never received enough support in congress. For example, he proposed changes in the tax policy to discourage speculation and to prevent the use of foreign tax havens to avoid taxes. He proposed changes that would have discouraged corporations from moving production and investments to Canada and Europe. Kennedy was an opponent of the kind of globalization that was coming in the decades after his death. Those and other tax measures were meant to stimulate useful investments in the production of real wealth in the U. S. and in poorer nations. In education, Kennedy's proposals led to the growth of enrollments in community colleges and four year schools through grants and loans. His policies stimulated interest in and education in the natural sciences and he was responsible, of course, for a vast expansion of the space program. Kennedy made constant efforts to ensure that interest rates did not go up and that there was credit available for investment, production, and consumption. He sought expanded powers for the President so that action could be taken to soften or prevent economic downturns. Kennedy initiated the Alliance for Progress and other changes in foreign policy which were intended to move the United States away from neo-colonial or imperialist policies. He circumvented existing international institutions such as the World Bank and International Monetary Fund and attempted to deal directly with leaders of foreign nations on matters of aid and trade. He resisted the use of U.S. military power for the protection of private economic interests. In these and in other ways, Kennedy began, with considerable success, to move the country forward, making it more prosperous and capable and giving it worthwhile purposes in the reduction of poverty, the exploration of space, and doing many other things. In the process he incurred the anger of Rockefellers, of the Morgan interests, and of other leaders of the aristo-finance elite.[1]

Long, of course, was never president. Certain powers were never available to him. However, his policies as governor along with his record as a senator, and his statements as a potential presidential candidate give us three sources on his thinking and intentions with respect to the nation's direction.

[1.] Gibson, 1994.

Huey Long was for seven years, 1928 to 1935, the dominant political figure of the state of Louisiana. He was governor and then senator and unofficial governor; the man replacing Long as governor in 1932, O. K. Allen, was handpicked by Long. Over two-thirds of the voters supported the candidate for governor in 1936 who claimed to be Long's successor, indicating that not only the vast majority of the poor, but other people from all social circumstances supported Long. It was the judgment of Louisiana's people on the almost eight years of Long's leadership. Why that positive judgment? Because Long got things done for people and he was willing to publicly oppose the most powerful interests in Louisiana and the country.

Huey Long may be better known for what he proposed than for what he did and only one of his proposals has received a great deal of attention. That is his share-the-wealth program. That program actually evolved over time and never became a clear and detailed set of proposals.[2] The general idea was to limit annual income to a few million a year and to limit the size of accumulated fortunes. All amounts above the limits would be taken through taxation or other measures. While in the Senate, Long said that the money taken from the rich would be spent for education, infrastructure, veterans, and other programs.[3] Aspects of the program were left unexplained or were unworkable as presented (e.g., Long never explained how non-monetary assets taken from the wealthy would be disposed of or used by the federal government).

If one focuses on Long's simplistic statements about the redistribution of wealth and treats them as if they represent Long's thinking on the economy, it is easy to portray Long as a fool and a liar.[4] A more objective evaluation of Long's ideas, however, shows that the redistribution of wealth was one element in a much broader economic program and that the simplistic statements were not much more than polemical devices.

Long thought the concentration of wealth was a longstanding problem[5] which was related to questions of economic policy, social justice, and power, and he thought about it in relation to the depression. Beside his oft repeated opinion that it was wrong for a few people to have more money than they could ever use while many had little or nothing, Long also argued that the great fortunes had

---

[2] Williams, 1969, pp. 663-4, 726, 729.
[3] Ibid., 1969, pp. 663-4.
[4] For example, see Hair, 1991, p. 271; Jeansonne, 1993, pp. 123-4.
[5] Long, 1985, pp. 103-4.

been accumulated "from manipulated finance, control of government, rigging of markets, the spider webs that have grabbed all businesses."[6] Long's view, backed up by people such as Matthew Josephson, Gustavus Meyers, and Ida Tarbell,[7] was far more accurate than either the mythology of meritocracy or the myth that these titans were in any positive way the fittest. Once these huge fortunes were passed on to the next generation, these flimsy myths were completely irrelevant. Huey Long was addressing real issues of social justice and he was pointing out the obvious, that is, in some segments of the society there was (and is) no connection between work and rewards.

Long thought, with good reason, that the accumulation of massive private wealth led to a concentration of power.[8] The huge fortunes were allowing a very small group of people to dominate the affairs of the nation. Long thought that these interests were preventing the adoption of policies to end the depression. The redistribution of wealth was a way to break this concentrated power.

Long's idea of taxing wealth to pay for government programs or to directly transfer money to low income people was also part of his assessment of the causes of the continuation of the depression. Long argued that the lack of mass purchasing power was a major cause of that continuation.[9] Long had already used deficit spending in Louisiana during the 1929 to 1933 period to raise purchasing power in order to counter the impact of the depression.[10] The tools available to the federal government would have given a President Long much greater flexibility. Long's focus on the lack of consumption as a primary problem put him ahead of most public figures of his time.

It is apparent to this reader that Long was using the share-the-wealth issue also as a polemical tool or symbolic issue. He thought it was a major issue and he intended to do things about it. He also emphasized it because it had instant appeal to a fairly large number of people. The polemics got people involved in a way that lent direct support to Long's challenge to the interests, to big wealth.

Long was frequently a leader in efforts to make changes that were beneficial to the nation. Long was a defender of labor, small business, and the person of average or less than average means. Long's voting record as a Senator was

[6] Ibid., p. 125.
[7] Josephson, 1934; Myers, 1917; Tarbell, 1925.
[8] Long, 1985, pp. 126-7.
[9] Ibid., 1985, p. 106.
[10] Williams, 1969, pp. 580, 586.

consistently pro-labor.[11] He was one of the first Senators to publicly support federal government guarantees on bank deposits and he got the smaller banks included in legislation that otherwise would have benefited only big banks. Also, Long successfully opposed an effort to give big banks greater freedom in establishing branch operations, thus protecting local banking.[12] Long was one of the Roosevelt administration's leading supporters in the effort to provide regulation of utility holding companies. Long went so far as to suggest in 1935 that public ownership might be necessary.[13] Long played an important role in the passage of a law which helped many indebted farmers hold on to their land by allowing them to declare bankruptcy and then pay the assessed value of the land to the creditors over a five year period.[14]

In the area of tax policy Long favored, of course, a steeply graduated federal income tax rate and increases in the inheritance tax,[15] ideas embraced by FDR. Long proposed that a tax be imposed on transactions of the stock exchange and the cotton exchange.[16] This tax, a type of transfer tax, was apparently aimed at raising revenue while it simultaneously lowered the profits on speculative activity. In Louisiana, Long had reduced property taxes and abolished the poll tax.[17] He had used taxes as part of a carrot-and-stick strategy in his conflicts with Standard Oil. He succeeded over Standard's opposition in getting a tax enacted on each barrel of oil refined in Louisiana and then suspended eighty percent of the tax in return for Standard's agreement to expand its production and refining operations in Louisiana.[18]

Given the depressed economy, Long was more interested in spending than in taxing, except with the super-rich of course. In Louisiana that spending had been partly on infrastructure. Long's program added about 2,500 miles of paved roads and 6,000 miles of gravel roads and built over 40 bridges, at a time when most states drastically reduced such investments.[19]

[11.] Ibid., 1969, p. 669.
[12.] Ibid., pp. 654, 659-60.
[13.] Ibid., p. 879.
[14.] Long, 1985, p. 50.
[15.] Ibid., pp. 5, 20-21, 65.
[16.] Ibid., p. 7.
[17.] Howard, 1957, p. 130; Williams, 1969, p. 899.
[18.] Sindler, 1956, pp. 94-5; Williams, 1969, pp. 782-3.
[19.] Howard, 1957, p. 130; Williams in Long, 1935, p. xvii.

In Louisiana that kind of spending required borrowing. It is not clear whether Huey intended to finance his proposed federal program differently, but it is clear that he was planning something big. In February of 1935 Senator Long proposed that the Federal government spend 2.5 billion dollars on highway construction. The year that Long suggested this, the total budget of the government was 6.5 billion dollars. Long argued that this would stimulate the economy and at the same time improve the country's transportation system. Long criticized FDR for increasing the federal debt while failing to bring the country out of depression. Long also thought that road construction was more meaningful work than the make-work projects that had been implemented.[20]

When Long talked of what he would do as President, he said he would spend over ten billion dollars on big projects such as flood control, irrigation, and water power. Long noted that such projects provide employment and increase the country's ability to produce wealth.[21] In principle this is how the country was finally pulled out of the depression. Unfortunately, the great project was World War Two. What Long was suggesting was competent and thoughtful economic policy. Had something like this been done in 1931 or 1933 the depression might have ended for the U.S. much earlier. A return to prosperity for the U.S. would have affected the whole world, perhaps making the rantings of Adolph Hitler appear to everyone for what they were.

Long had come to believe that the growing debt was unpayable. He proposed in Louisiana and considered for the country a debt moratorium, arguing that this had been done before (which it had) and that this had support in the Bible.[22]

As indicated above, Long was very interested in banking, playing a prominent role in the reforms enacted by FDR. He had bigger changes in mind. Long indicated in 1934 that he wanted to do something about the problem of centralized economic and political power and that one way to attack this problem was to do something about control over credit.[23] One of the things he had in mind was the creation of a new central bank, an idea that posed a direct threat to the private banking power exercised through bank cartels and the privately dominated Federal Reserve. Long was open to ideas about how to structure the

[20] New York Times, 1935, p. 2.
[21] Long, 1935, pp. 26, 31-2.
[22] Long, 1985, p. 37; Williams, 1969, p. 776.
[23] Ibid., pp. 44-5.

proposed bank. Tentatively, he thought it should be administered by directors elected in general elections. Long thought that if each presidential administration appointed the directors, the polices would change too easily. He criticized private systems because they were prone to restrict credit too much and also because the control over credit gave too much power to private bankers.[24]

Long often proposed reforms or policies which would at once improve the economy and reduce the power of big money interests. Political and economic objectives were intertwined. This is apparent above in the central bank proposal and it is obvious in his redistribution ideas. Years earlier, when he was Chairman of Louisiana's Public Services Commission, he had initiated a rule to reduce the cost of transporting oil by rail. While intended to lower prices, it also aimed at breaking up the control over the movement of oil held by oil pipeline companies.[25] Long tried to use reform measures to reduce the power of Standard Oil in Louisiana and he publicly attacked the Morgan and Rockefeller interests in order to gain support for reforms at the national level.[26]

Long did or tried to do many other things. Even if he had not, his initiatives in the areas of infrastructure, redistribution of wealth, and banking and credit would make him a significant figure, nothing remotely like the buffoon or fascist he has been portrayed as by some.

Long was opposed to the use of military force except in defense of the country. Senator Norris, the man Huey was closest to in the Senate, was one of only six Senators to represent the majority of Americans and vote against entry into World War One.[27] Huey's apparent respect for the anti-imperialist views of General Smedley Butler and his opposition to the deployment of U.S. forces to protect the foreign holdings of companies such as United Fruit[28] indicate that Long did have a developed viewpoint on these issues. One account has it that Long had people in Central America trying to organize boycotts against United Fruit and Standard Oil.[29]

Long held other views which were inconsistent with the increasingly internationalist aims of interests such as United Fruit, J.P. Morgan & Co., and Standard Oil. For example, he favored the use of government measures such as

---

[24] Long, 1935, pp. 35-37.

[25] Long, 1933, p. 85.

[26] Ibid., p. 61; 1985, pp. 7, 10.

[27] Karp, 1979, pp. 262, 270, 308, 322-3.

[28] Beals, 1935/1971; Williams 1969, p. 747.

[29] Williams, 1969, pp. 747.

tariffs[30] to promote the national economy while his opposition on Wall Street was thinking more and more in terms of global "free trade."

At both the state and national level, Long was very interested in educational policy. In Louisiana Long was responsible, solely or in part, for the following: providing over 500,000 free textbooks; establishing free night schools at which over 100,000 adults learned to read and write; a general increase in spending on schools; increase in public school enrollment by 20 percent; the development of the Louisiana State University school of medicine; expansion of LSU from 1500 to 5000 students.[31] Long proposed building thousands of colleges throughout the country and he suggested that college and vocational education be publicly financed.[32] Nothing close to this would happen until the 1945 to 1970 period, when the G.I. Bill, rising income, and measures like the ones taken by Kennedy at least made such education more attainable.

In Louisiana Long expanded hospitals and increased services for the poor (i.e., majority of people in Louisiana) and achieved some improvements in the mental hospitals.[33] Long had a new state capitol built.[34] In 1935, he launched an attack on gambling interests in New Orleans.[35] Long publicly denounced the Ku Klux Klan and he rejected the policy of making all civil servants, teachers, and professors sign loyalty oaths.[36]

Long was one of the earlier and most vocal supporters of the creation of an old age pension system.[37] He discussed the possibility of new legislation to reduce the work week.[38] Long argued in 1935, revising an earlier view, that the problem in agriculture was not, as some said at the time, one of overproduction, but was instead a problem of underproduction and underconsumption. Long argued, based on expert recommendations for a good diet, that even before the depression the country was not producing enough food.[39]

---

[30] Ibid.
[31] Christman in Long, 1985, pp. vii-viii; Howard, 1957, p. 130; Williams in Long, 1933, p. xvii; Williams, 1969, pp. 551, 899.
[32] Long, 1985, p. 52.
[33] Howard, 1957, p. 130; Williams, 1969, p. 899.
[34] Howard, 1957, p. 130.
[35] Beals, 1935/1971, p. 320.
[36] Christman in Long, 1985, p. xiii.
[37] Long, 1985, pp. 32, 53, 109.
[38] Howard, 1957, p. 129; Long, 1985, p. 32.
[39] Long, 1985, pp., 122-3.

In all probability, Long achieved some other important things that were less tangible than schoolbooks, roads, and hospital beds. In the view of some, it was Huey Long who forced the Roosevelt administration to expand the scope of the New Deal and to seek change faster than they otherwise would have.[40]

According to T. Harry Williams, "the new, significant issues that Long introduced aroused popular interest in politics to a degree unmatched in any other southern state."[41] In that context, Williams went on to say that Long "inspired thousands of poor white people all over the South to a vision of a better life" and "introduced into all of Southern politics, which had been pervasively romantic, a saving element of economic realism."[42]

It might be added that Long brought to Southern and national politics an element of political sophistication. In the following description of a meeting in Shreveport Long displays a high level of awareness of the differences between ordinary businessmen, the small oil companies or "independent group," and the representatives of cartels and high finance, the "Standard Oil group."

> The faces of the Standard Oil group bore expressions of self-content. About these men there was that undefinable something that betokens freedom from money cares and anxiety as to the future. But the faces of the men in the independent group told a different story. Care, and in some cases, desperation, was written in every line.[43]

Long understood that the men of Standard Oil represented a business and finance aristocracy, men whose economic power and political connections placed them in a different category than the businessmen subject to the forces of the market and to the force of that concentrated power.

Long offered an extensive program of change and reform, much of it major. To say that Long had no practical program, as has Jeansonne in a recent Long biography,[44] is ludicrous. Also ridiculous is the claim that Long merely exploited issues and had no commitment to anything but himself.[45] Long offered a coherent program of change, going further in some areas than the program offered by President Kennedy, but very similar in its purposes and similar in the means to

---

[40.] Christman in Long, 1985, p. xiii.

[41.] Williams in Long, 1933, p. xviii.

[42.] Ibid.

[43.] Long, 1933, p. 42.

[44.] Jeansonne, 1993, p. 189.

[45.] For example, Sindler, 1956, pp. 60-61.

be used. Kennedy's economic program was opposed by powerful private interests; Long had similar enemies.

LONG AND HIS OPPOSITION

Many of Long's enemies were in state and local politics or they were part of the Louisiana economic and social elite. There were a number of factions in the state and Long sometimes aligned himself with one of those factions. In order to win elections or to get things done, Long sometimes embraced people that he had earlier been against and Long and those allies often split after a common goal had been achieved.[46]

When these alliances ended, Long frequently absorbed some of his former ally's people into his organization.[47] Some of those people probably were not committed to Long. Also, Long's rise in Louisiana politics was extremely rapid and his need for people to fill government or political positions also increased rapidly. By necessity, Long had to bring large numbers of people into his political organization and his administration that he had no time to evaluate. This created a situation wherein some of Long's enemies may have been inside his organization.

Long's political organization was itself factionalized. For example, there was a group of businessmen and politicians led by Seymour Weiss that backed Long on some issues but not others. This group did not support Long's goal of reducing the size of big fortunes. There was a country politician group. One of its leaders, Allen Ellender, would end up helping Long's enemies within the Roosevelt administration. There was also the share-the-wealth group led by Gerald K. Smith.[48] These groups were held together by Long and unity did not last long following Huey's death.

Long's opposition within the state was also factionalized. One faction was known as the Old Regulars, Old Ring, or the Choctaws, and in Long's time was led by New Orleans Mayor T. Semmes Walmsley. A distinct faction within the Old Regulars was led by Louisiana politician Jared Y. Sanders, Jr. The Old Regulars were tied to the New Orleans business elite and to outside corporate

---

[46] Beals, 1935/1971, pp. 94, 200.

[47] Ibid., p. 367.

[48] Ibid., p. 413.

and financial interests. Another faction, the New Regulars, was led by John P. Sullivan and had connections to vice and gambling. A third group, the Square Dealers, was linked to Standard Oil and the Ku Klux Klan.[49] A number of significant political figures shifted their positions over time, usually ending up in the anti-Long camp. Two major figures in the state followed this path; Senators Joseph E. Ransdell and Edwin S. Broussard, both at one time supported by Long, went over to Long's opposition after 1931.[50]

Most of Long's important enemies in Louisiana had connections to interests operating at the national and international levels. Some of these were the same as the interests Kennedy would clash with thirty years later. Long's strength in fact was based partly on his ability to mobilize and weld together all of the groups in Louisiana that had grievances against the state's elitist power structure and the New York and Boston economic interests that operated in the state. Long brought together the poor, city workers, farm and lumber workers, and elements of the middle class and local business community who were tired of the backward policies of the big out-of-state interests and their aristocratic Louisiana allies.[51]

Some of Long's Louisiana opponents, such as Sanders and Sullivan, were close to Standard Oil.[52] Others, such as Senator Joseph Ransdell and his nephew Joseph Montgomery, had connections to Sam Zemurray, first the head of Cuyamel Fruit Company and then an executive of United Fruit. When Long ran against Ransdell for the U.S. Senate, he attacked Ransdell as a "Wall Street tool." He criticized Ransdell for supporting the deployment of troops to Central America, charging that this was to protect interests such as United Fruit and not the interests of the United States. Long accused Zemurray of financing revolutions in Central America and of using mercenaries such as General Lee Christmas and Guy Maloney to protect private interests.[53]

One of Long's primary local opponents was the New Orleans lawyer Esmond Phelps. Long charged that Phelps and a group of New York bankers controlled the Times-Picayune company and that it was they who were behind the newspaper's efforts to have Long impeached in 1929. Phelps was also attorney for the Western Union Telegraph Company, later Clay Shaw's

[49.] Ibid., p. 412; Swindler, 1956, pp. 22-6.
[50.] Long, 1933, pp. 211, 253.
[51.] Howard, 1957, pp. 123-30.
[52.] Beals, 1935/1971, p. 375; Long, 1933, p. 157; Sindler, 1956, pp. 60-61.
[53.] Beals, 1935/1971, p. 191; Long, 1933, pp. 213-19.

employer, and for the Texas and Pacific Railroad. In addition, Phelps was head of the Board of Supervisors of Tulane University, where he worked with the Rockefeller Foundation, a source of financial support for the University.[54] Finally, Phelps was the President of the very elitist Boston Club. This New Orleans club will be discussed in Chapter Seven. Many of Long's most bitter enemies were members of this exclusive club, including ex-Governor John Parker and Norris C. Williamson, both officers of the anti-Long Constitutional League of Louisiana.[55]

Long's opponents at the national and international level included Standard Oil, the Morgan financial group, the Boston Brahmin dominated United Fruit company, and the Time-Life company. This is very much the same interests with which Kennedy was in conflict in the early-1960s.

Long charged that 90 percent of America's wealth was owned or controlled by 600 families, led by the Morgans, Rockefellers, Mellons, Baruchs, Bakers, Astors, and Vanderbilts.[56] Long's conflict with Standard Oil interests is probably the one that is best known and most often mentioned by both Long and his biographers.[57] Long mentions Standard Oil repeatedly in his 1933 book *Every Man A King* and he also mentions that the biggest financial backer of the generally hostile Tulane University was the Rockefeller Foundation.[58]

In that book Long also identified J. P. Morgan & Co. and Morgan partner Thomas W. Lamont as important antagonists. At the 1932 Democratic convention Long played a major role in breaking the Morgan group's influence.[59] There is some evidence that the Morgan interests launched a national press attack on Long in 1933.[60] Long claimed in 1933 that the Morgan interests and financier Eugene Meyer, Katherine Meyer Graham's father, had infiltrated and coopted the Roosevelt administration.[61]

In 1930 Long charged that Senator Ransdell was attempting to have American troops sent to Central America to protect the property and interests of

[54] Beals, 1935/1971, pp. 165-6, 203; Williams, 1969, p. 215.
[55] Long, 1933, p. 183.
[56] Long, 1985, p. 90.
[57] Liebling, 1960, p. 42; Sindler, 1956; Zinman, 1993, pp. 35-7.
[58] Long, 1933, pp. 39-49, 61, 63, 124, 140, 153, 157-9, 181, 186, 335.
[59] Beals, 1935/1971, p. 11; Williams, 1969, pp. 608-10.
[60] Williams, 1969, pp. 672-3, 684-6.
[61] Schlesinger, 1960, pp. 54-5.

Sam Zemurray,[62] a major United Fruit stockholder from 1929 onward and Managing Director of the company in 1935. According to Long, Zemurray was financing anti-Long political activity in the early-30s[63]. Williams, Long's fairest biographer, says that in 1934 Guy Maloney was a leading anti-Long activist and that Maloney had been an agent of Zemurray in Central America.

All of these interests were interconnected with the local power structure in numerous ways. The Rockefeller-Standard Oil, Morgan, and United Fruit interests were Long's most powerful enemies. These interests tried a variety of strategies to defeat Long in Louisiana and at the national level. They financed his political opponents, backed the effort to impeach him, and assaulted him in the press. This attack on Long also received support from a few high level people within the Roosevelt administration.

After having aggressively supported Roosevelt for President in 1932, Long became frustrated quickly with what he perceived as too much passivity and too much subservience to the big interests. Relations between the administration and Long turned sour. There were several people within FDR's government who were energetic in their efforts to get Long, particularly Secretary of the Treasury Henry Morgenthau and Postmaster General James A. Farley. The exact role played in all of this by FDR is unclear.

At the beginning of 1934, Morgenthau, who had just been appointed Secretary of the Treasury, resurrected a revenue department investigation of Long that had been started under President Hoover and suspended around the end of 1932.[64] Arthur Schlesinger indicates that Morgenthau himself pushed this investigation.[65] In 1934 several low level Long people were indicted and in December of that year Seymour Weiss, a significant figure in the Long camp, was indicted for income tax evasion. In March of 1935 Joe Fisher became the first Long supporter to be sentenced to prison.[66] Secretary of the Interior Harold Ickes was channeling federal money into New Orleans so as to give support to the anti-Long Walmsley group and Farley was engaged in similar activities.[67]

Long's conflict with Standard Oil and the indictment of Seymour Weiss may be important elements in the last year of Long's life.

[62] Williams, 1969, p. 490.
[63] Long, 1933, 213-6, 335-6.
[64] Williams, 1969, pp. 836-7.
[65] Schlesinger, 1960, p. 57.
[66] Williams, 1969, pp. 838, 860.
[67] Beals, 1935/1971, p. 328; Schlesinger, 1960, p. 242.

ASSASSINATION

In January of 1935 Long charged that Standard Oil and an assortment of local officials (four sheriffs, a district attorney, and a judge) were involved in a plot to kill him. An anti-Long politician that Huey had long charged with being a Standard Oil agent, J. Y. Sanders, Jr., accused Huey of fabricating the story.

In December, 1934, Long had gotten a five cent per barrel tax put on oil refined in Louisiana. Standard Oil laid off some of its workers claiming that this was necessitated by the new tax. A group of mostly white-collar Standard employees met to discuss the situation. Ernest Bourgeois, an alleged Standard Oil strike breaker, emerged as a leader of the group, which called itself the Square Deal Association. In January, 1935, the Association briefly seized the East Baton Rouge courthouse in response to a rumor that one of their own had been arrested and was being forced to talk. Long, acting through Governor Allen, put Baton Rouge and East Baton Rouge under martial law and he called out the national guard. Long said the plot was instigated by Standard Oil and he scheduled a hearing on his charges.

At the hearing, Sidney Songy, a Long spy infiltrated into the Association, testified that a group in the Association was planning to kill Long. Shortly after this, January 22, 1935, Long and Standard Oil came secretly to a compromise. Huey promised to reduce the tax and Standard agreed to use mostly Louisiana oil in its refineries in Louisiana and to fire certain Square Dealers. Huey apparently fooled Standard Oil. They expected a change in the tax law; what he gave them was temporary suspension of 80 percent of the tax. It could be brought back at any time by executive action.[68] Talk of a Standard Oil plot subsided after this deal was struck. The informant Songy would have a most difficult life, more of this later.

In April of 1935 *Time* magazine made its contribution to the atmosphere of violence that surrounded Huey Long. On the April 1 cover, under a picture of Long, *Time* printed the following: "Candidate Long: Give him honor or give him death!" If we stretch things, we can view this as sort of a play on a question allegedly asked of Long by an unidentified reporter about whether Huey would live up to his own statement that the next man in the White House should commit suicide if he fails to carry out his promises. That is a stretch. The reason for the cover story appears to have been Time's perception that Long was gearing

---

[68.] Williams, 1969, pp. 820-32.

up for a run at the presidency.[69] *Life*, *Time*'s sister publication, would later, in 1946, liken Long to Hitler, to a hardened criminal, and to Lucifer. *Life* said that Long became "the most powerful antagonist of democracy this country has ever produced."[70] These statements are made about a politician who acquired his positions only through popular elections, a man whose popularity rose almost continuously throughout his political career. These comments are made in a publication associated with some of the most powerful private interests in the world, including Morgan and Rockefeller interests.[71] The comments are absurd, obviously propagandistic. This is the same media corporation that would describe President Kennedy as a cultist and a reactionary, and discuss his conflict with the Morgan-dominated U.S. Steel in a *Fortune* magazine article entitled "Steel: The Ides of April."[72]

In August, 1935, a new plot to kill Long was alleged. On August 9, 1935, Long announced to other Senators that a plot to kill him was hatched at a meeting at the DeSoto Hotel in New Orleans. The story told by Long indicated that pro-Roosevelt people were involved. This story has been retold many times. There are strange things about this story that have not been examined.

The story implicating pro-Roosevelt people in an assassination plot came from three allegedly pro-Long men. They somehow had learned that a very unusual attack on Long was to be proposed at a meeting to be held in July during the DeSoto Hotel Conference of anti-Long Democrats. One of the three, John De Armond, somehow then secured a job as desk clerk at the DeSoto Hotel and he gave a room adjoining the room of the alleged meeting to the other two allegedly pro-Long men, Herbert Christenberry and B. W. Cason. Cason was secretary of the Louisiana Senate. Herbert Christenberry was an attorney and the brother of Huey Long's secretary, Earle Christenberry. The day after Long was assassinated, Earle would announce that Long's assassin, Carl Weiss, had been at this meeting.[73]

Herbert Christenberry claimed that with the use of a dictograph he was able to overhear the July 22 meeting in the adjoining hotel room and that he took it down in shorthand. A typed version was given to Seymour Weiss, then under

[69.] Time, 1935, pp. 15-17.

[70.] Basso, 1946, pp. 106-21.

[71.] Gibson, 1994, pp. 68-70.

[72.] Gibson, 1994, pp. 16, 57-60.

[73.] Williams, 1969, pp. 675, 881-2; Zinman, 1993, 231-3.

federal indictment, who gave it to Long, who then went public with it.[74] Arthur Schlesinger has asserted that this story was true, supporting Christenberry, but that the incident is not significant because there is no evidence of a conspiracy. I am going to suggest here that the story is either untrue or irrelevant to the assassination but the telling of the story is itself important and is evidence of a conspiracy.

One month after Long had passed on the Christenberry story, he was back in Louisiana to promote some new legislation, including one item that would likely lead to an election defeat for a Judge Pavy, the father-in-law of Dr. Carl Weiss. On the evening of Sunday, September 8, 1935, the 42 year old Long was shot once while in the hallway of the capitol building; he died early on September 10. The generally accepted account is that Dr. Carl Weiss shot Long once and was then killed by Long's bodyguards. It is alleged that Long could have been saved but for an oversight, i.e., the unrepaired kidney damage that killed Long could have been detected with pre-operative examination, but the exam was not done. Long was operated on by a team of doctors led by Dr. Arthur Vidrine, a Rhodes Scholar appointed by Long to be the first dean of the new LSU medical school. Vidrine was not an experienced surgeon. It was apparently Vadrine's fault that the kidney damage was not discovered.[75]

Following the assassination the only thing that was completely clear was Long's popularity. Those campaigning under his name scored huge victories in the 1936 Louisiana elections. Everything else related to his death seemed murky or was made to seem that way. Some speculation focused on the bodyguards, either as assassins or in killing Weiss as part of a cover-up. It seems possible and logical that if the second were true, it would have been part of a double-cross, i.e., Weiss was told that the bodyguards were involved and would protect him. The bodyguards had come from various places, such as the Highway Patrol and the Bureau of Criminal Identification (BCI).[76] The BCI had been created by anti-Long legislators in 1928 and was expanded in the early-30s.[77] These were not, for the most part, men who had close ties to Long. The man who reportedly was the first to grab Carl Weiss after Weiss shot Long had been with Long for only nine months and had been assigned to Long by General Guerre, head of BCI.[78] One of

---

[74.] Williams, 1969, 882-3.

[75.] Williams, 1969, pp. 904-9, 917-20; Zinman, 1993, pp. 146, 150, 170, 175.

[76.] Williams, 1969, p. 339.

[77.] Beals, 1935/1971, pp. 71, 371.

[78.] Zinman, 1993, pp. 202, 212.

Long's earlier bodyguards, Harry "Battling" Bozeman had contributed to the impeachment effort against Long by claiming that Long had hired him to assassinate Jared Y. Sanders.[79] There certainly is no reason to rule out the possibility that one or more of the bodyguards played a role in the assassination.

Dr. Carl Weiss was in some ways an unlikely assassin. He was young, successful, and he had a nice family and many friends. He reportedly liked his work. On the other hand, he was friends with two of Long's important enemies in Louisiana, John M. Parker and Jared Sanders. He did not like Long. Weiss's wife's sister and uncle and a friend all lost jobs as a result of Long's political house cleaning. Carl Weiss's wife's father lost his judgeship due to Long, although he reportedly did not care about this. Weiss's father, Dr. Carl Weiss, Sr., hated Long. One person claimed that Weiss had a connection to the far-right Minute Men and that it was actually a meeting of these men that Weiss attended at the DeSoto Conference, not the meeting Christenberry surveiled.[80] Was there enough motive for Weiss to commit murder? Was there enough motive for him to throw away his life? The latter may not be relevant if he had assurances that the situation would be controlled and that the case could later be fixed in some way.

Investigations were not aggressively carried out and then most of the case material and records disappeared. The bodyguards were not made to give accounts right away, leaving time for their stories to be rehearsed and coordinated. Some of the investigation was carried out by Long's enemies.[81] The district attorney in charge of the investigation had been accused by Long of involvement in the Standard Oil plot to kill Long.[82] When a resolution was passed in the Louisiana House in 1936 to investigate the assassination, then Governor Leche prevented it.[83] According to Williams, Leche was a corporate lawyer who was bought by Long.[84] Perhaps Leche had put himself up for sale again around the time of the assassination. Almost all of the records disappeared for almost sixty years. In 1991 the gun allegedly used to kill Long and a 600 page police report turned up. They had wound up in the private possession of

---

[79] Beals, 1935/1971, pp. 146, 151; Williams, 1969, pp. 338, 373-4, 399.

[80] Sindler, 1956, pp. 96-7; Williams, p. 915; Zinman, 1993, pp. 58-9, 86, 155.

[81] Zinman, 1993, p. 195.

[82] Daniell, 1935, pp. 1, 18.

[83] Zinman, 1993, p. 243.

[84] Williams, 1969, pp. 596-7.

retired Brigadier General Louis Guerre, who headed the state police investigation of Long's death.[85]

A complete reconstruction of the events of the night of the assassination is now impossible. It seems unlikely that Weiss was framed. It also seems unlikely that he acted alone. As we will see, there are indications of conspiracy and there are a variety of connections to the assassination of President Kennedy. There are things about both assassinations we will never know. It makes sense to concentrate on those things we do know or can know.

We know, or can know, that Long's policies and goals were almost identical to Kennedy's. We know that Long's enemies were similar to or identical to Kennedy's. These two things are important, they help us to understand the history of our country, and they are relevant to today's debates over the future of our country. Those two things would be important even if both men had died of natural causes, rather than at the hands of real or alleged assassins who were then shot and killed. The ideas and actions of the two men are what is most important. The nature of their enemies is a close second. Who killed them is third. The three things together are of more significance than any one separately.

Although he never discussed it in public, JFK probably was aware of the similarities between his policies and opposition and those of Long. Kennedy read a great deal of U.S. history and he probably picked up some idea that way of what Long was doing and of who opposed him. In his book *Profiles In Courage*, Kennedy gave separate chapters to eight men, one of whom was Republican Senator George Norris of Nebraska. Norris was the Senator that Huey Long respected above all others; Long and Norris were very close friends.[86] The Democrat that Long was closest to was Burton Wheeler.[87] JFK's father was very close to Wheeler.[88] These associations make sense. The ideas of John Kennedy and Long were similar. In fact, if one looks at Joseph Kennedy's 1936 book, *I'm for Roosevelt*,[89] it is obvious that JFK's father and Long would have agreed on some things. Long's policies were more dramatic and thorough going, but the direction was similar. That is why they both initially supported Roosevelt. There are also direct links between the two assassinations. One of those was through the person of attorney and later federal judge Herbert Christenberry.

[85.] Zinman, 1993, pp. 258-9, 305.
[86.] Christman in Long, 1985, p. ix; Williams, 1969, pp. 588, 602.
[87.] Williams, 1969, 589, 602.
[88.] Whalen, 1964, pp. 73, 121,296, 335, 346.
[89.] Kennedy, 1936.

As noted above, it was Herbert Christenberry who provided the July 1935 account of the pro-Roosevelt Democrats plotting at the DeSoto Hotel to kill Long. He gave that account to Seymour Weiss who passed it on to Long. Weiss (no relation to Dr. Carl Weiss) is always portrayed as a friend and close confidant of Long.[90] There seems to be no reason to doubt that completely. However, Weiss was in a very vulnerable position in 1935 and he could have been pressured to play the limited role of lending credence to Christenberry's DeSoto Conference story. Grounds for that suspicion are as follows. In the Spring of 1935 Weiss was distraught because he was the target of the aforementioned investigation directed by Secretary of the Treasury Morgenthau.[91] Weiss was under indictment and was looking for a way to repair his relations with people in the Roosevelt administration.[92]

After Long was killed, the charges against Weiss were dropped. Weiss then went to the Democratic National Convention as a fully rehabilitated committeeman.[93] Later he would be on the board of the International Trade Mart. We have already seen that Governor Leche prevented an investigation of the assassination in 1936. These kinds of events lend credence to the rumors that deals were made between people in the two camps.[94] It is likely that the dealmakers were only nominally pro-Long and pro-Roosevelt.

Seymour Weiss shared control of Long's political money with Earle Christenberry, Herbert's brother and Long's secretary. That money disappeared and the only account of it is Weiss's claim that Huey had hidden it.[95] Was that money part of a payoff to Weiss or Christenberry or both? There is also a charge that Weiss and Christenberry were using their positions to make money together from buying and selling oil leases.[96] It was Earle Christenberry who claimed the day after the assassination that the name "Doctor Wise" appeared on his brother's transcript of the DeSoto meeting, thus implicating pro-FDR Louisiana Democrats. In the late-1960s, Weiss told T. Harry Williams that he had the transcript but nobody would ever see it. Weiss told someone else that the name

[90] Beals, 1935/1971, pp. 146-7; Williams, 1969, pp. 393-4; Zinman, 1993, p. 141.
[91] Kane, 1941, 181-2; Williams, 1969, p. 838.
[92] Sindler, 1956, p. 118.
[93] Kane, 1941, pp. 182, 185.
[94] Sindler, 1956, p. 126.
[95] Williams, 1969, pp. 795-6, 904.
[96] Kane, 1941, p. 160.

Weiss or Wise was not in the transcript.[97] This is strange behavior for a Long loyalist.

Seymour Weiss was much better off after the assassination. What of the Christenberry brothers? These two men appeared to be Long men. They have certainly been identified this way for over sixty years. As Long men they worked for and supported the man, Huey Long, who was viewed within the Roosevelt administration by Morgenthau and Farley as an opponent, even as an enemy to be destroyed. If they were what they appeared to be, Long supporters, one would expect that such men would get no help from the Roosevelt administration. Surprising things happened following the assassination. After a brief time serving Huey's wife, who was interim Senator, Earle was given a state government job as liaison with the Roosevelt administration.[98] An unusual post for someone who had played a role in implicating supporters of the Roosevelt administration in a political murder.

And what of the man who originated the charge that Louisiana Democrats loyal to Roosevelt were planning to kill Long, the man who tried, with Weiss's complicity, to blame the assassination on Roosevelt people? As an enemy of the Roosevelt Democrats, Herbert Christenberry should have had no chance in the short term for a career with the federal government. He should have been discriminated against. The opposite happened. In 1937 he became U.S. attorney for the Eastern District of Louisiana. In 1942 he was nominated by someone in the administration to be U.S. attorney at New Orleans and he was confirmed by the Senate in January of 1942. Apparently, no one asked him to explain his role in blaming Roosevelt supporters for murder. In 1947 he was elevated to the position of U.S. District Judge. Not bad for a supporter of an alleged extremist. The man who had been a source for the story about Standard Oil earlier in the year did not do so well. Sidney Songy was prosecuted by the Federal Government for bootlegging and for impersonating a federal officer. He was almost beaten to death while he was in prison.[99] It seems that making accusations against Standard Oil was a far more risky activity than was making charges against pro-Roosevelt Democrats.

One explanation for Christenberry's good fortune is obvious. Christenberry and his brother, who was with Long only for a few years, were never seriously

---

[97]. Williams, 1969, pp. 883, 912-5.

[98]. Kane, 1941, pp. 192, 201.

[99]. Zinman, 1993, pp. 230-1.

pro-Long, or perhaps at all pro-Long. What is quite likely is that Herbert was an agent of Long's enemies and that Earle also was or at some point became an agent. Herbert Christenberry's story of the pro-Roosevelt plotters served several purposes. First, it presented a false lead to anyone who did think there was a conspiracy. The false lead would interfere with finding the truth about the assassination itself and, more importantly, would prevent people from understanding the reasons for the assassination. Second, it made pro-Roosevelt forces rather than Standard Oil or other private interests the subject of conspiracy rumors. Third, it would split some Long people from some Roosevelt people, perhaps people who might agree on policies were it not for suspicions about the assassination. Fourth, it had the potential of hurting Roosevelt's popularity. The purpose of the assassination itself, of course, was to eliminate Huey Long and to eliminate the discussion of the policies that Long presented.

In the 1960s Herbert Christenberry was the senior judge of the United States District Court for the Eastern District of Louisiana. In March of 1969 Jim Garrison was preparing to prosecute Clay Shaw for perjury. Shaw had been found not guilty in the murder of President Kennedy, but he had testified falsely that he did not know Oswald associate David Ferrie. The United States District Court prevented Garrison from prosecuting Shaw. It did so by giving an extremely broad interpretation to a law which allowed federal interference in a state court. This situation did not fit the criteria specified for such interference but the District Court intervened anyway. The order to stop Garrison was signed by Christenberry;[100] this probably saved Shaw from a perjury conviction.[101]

Four years later, 1973, the U.S. Justice Department prosecuted Jim Garrison on trumped up corruption charges related to pinball gambling. The senior judge of the District Court set aside a number of more important and complex cases and gave six weeks to Garrison's trial. The judge, of course, was Herbert Christenberry. Fortunately for Garrison, the prosecution had not done a very good job in fabricating a case against him and he was acquitted.[102] The trial probably did cost him re-election as district attorney.[103]

The judge who protected Clay Shaw and then oversaw the trial of Garrison had as a young lawyer played a key role in events just prior to the assassination

---

[100.] Garrison, 1988, pp. 253, 261.

[101.] DiEugenio, 1992, pp. 207, 374.

[102.] Garrison, 1988, pp. 261-5, 271.

[103.] DiEugenio, 1992, p. 269.

of Long. In his books Garrison did not say that he was aware of Christenberry's connection to Huey Long. Garrison was a friend of Huey's son, Senator Russell Long. Long got Garrison started on his investigation of President Kennedy's assassination when he told Garrison that he had no confidence in the Warren Commission's report. Perhaps Russell Long and Garrison talked about these connections.

The Christenberry connection is not the only flesh-and-blood link between the Clay Shaw episode in New Orleans and the events surrounding the assassination of Huey Long. The story of the other connections will bring us to the International House in New Orleans and the affiliated International Trade Mart. It will also bring us to the elitist Boston Club and the upper class interests who opposed Long and Kennedy.

Chapter Seven

FROM HUEY LONG TO CLAY SHAW

One of Huey Long's opponents was a prominent physician by the name of Alton Ochsner. Reportedly, Ochsner was bitterly anti-Long. At one time Ochsner's attacks on Long caused Long to use his influence to have the Doctor's visiting privileges withdrawn at New Orleans's Charity Hospital.[1] In 1929 Governor Long went after another of his opponents. He discovered that the New Orleans Dock Board (Board of Commissioners of the Port of New Orleans) had engaged in deception in the issuance of bonds and he also charged that the Board was setting tariff rates so as to benefit the Texas investments of its chairman, Edward S. Butler.[2] Long launched a successful effort to replace Butler as Chairman and to gain a loyal majority on the five member Board. Ochsner and Butler's grandson and namesake would turn up later as part of a network of people associated with Clay Shaw, the only man ever prosecuted in the Kennedy assassination, and Lee Oswald. Both also had numerous connections to people opposed to Kennedy.

---

[1] Williams, 1969, p. 543.
[2] Beals, 1935/1971, pp. 171-2.

BUTLER AND OCHSNER: ESTABLISHMENT RIGHT-WINGERS

About thirty years after Long had broken Edward Butler's control of the Dock Board, Butler's grandson, also Edward S., appeared on a talk show with Lee Harvey Oswald. Butler presented himself as a staunch anti-Communist, proclaiming his great admiration for Joe McCarthy. This presentation was partially authentic. There is no doubt that Butler was anti-Communist, but he was more the elitist or East Coast Establishment type of anti-Communist than the mid-west, populist, McCarthy type.

Both of Butler's grandfathers had belonged to the most exclusive social club in New Orleans, the Boston Club, and the paternal grandfather, Long's enemy, had also been president of the Cotton Exchange, another target of Long's policies. Much of the later Butler's political work would be supported by the Establishment types who were often accused of communist sympathies or tendencies by McCarthy or his supporters. That political work came to be centered in an organization, the Information Council of the Americas (INCA), founded by Butler in May of 1961, one month after the Bay of Pigs operation failed. Butler started INCA as an anti-Communist, psychological warfare operation. Interestingly, INCA would claim after November, 1963, that Oswald was inspired by communist ideology but that the assassination was not the result of a communist conspiracy.[3] This supported the most important part of the lone nut theory, the "lone" part, that was sprung on the country by the *New York Herald Tribune* and by Mayor Earle Cabell of Dallas within hours of the assassination. The INCA version would point anyone doubting that Oswald acted alone in the direction of a left-wing conspiracy. The lone-commie theory of INCA was essentially the same as the Belmont-Hoover-FBI view, and neither INCA nor the FBI challenged the rendition put forward by the Establishment media immediately after the assassination, i.e., Oswald did it alone and was a nut.

Butler's partner in the creation of INCA was the rabidly anti-Long Alton Ochsner. When Garrison reopened his investigation of the Kennedy assassination both Ochsner and Butler attacked Garrison and both reportedly felt threatened by that investigation. There were rumors that Garrison was considering the possibility of bringing indictments against Ochsner, a member of the Riley

---

[3.] Carpenter, 1989, pp. 120-32.

family (Oswald's onetime employer), and Seymour Weiss, who had done very well indeed after his "friend" Huey Long was murdered.[4]

Like Butler, Ochsner at times identified himself with views that could be thought of as anti-Establishment (e.g., he praised the ostensibly anti-Establishment Birch Society book, *None Dare Call It Treason*[5]). But as with Butler, any image of Ochsner as a red-neck, anti-Establishment, right-wing, populist would be very misleading. He was racist, anti-union, and anti-welfare, but he was associated with and committed to upper-class conservatism.[6]

Ochsner was part of the local aristocracy and he was thoroughly plugged into the national power structure, particularly the "internationalist" parts of it. Any right-wing yahoo looking to Ochsner for leadership would have been shocked to learn that Ochsner was thoroughly connected to the very same old, big moneyed interests that non-upper-class right wingers love to hate, or love to pretend to hate. Ochsner was a leader in the 1960s of both the International House (IH) and the International Trade Mart (ITM), where he worked with Clay Shaw. He was a member of the exclusive Boston Club and was a guest in 1965 at the Bohemian Grove in California, a place where big East Coast money mingles with the wealth of the West and South. Ochsner served as a director of National Airlines and of Florida National Banks of Florida, Inc., the latter position achieved through a friendship with Edward W. Ball of the DuPont interests.[7] The DuPonts had investments in a number of Latin American countries, giving them an interest in common with Ochsner.[8] Everything considered, Ochsner's social world had little in common with small-business and middle-class right wingers.

Ochsner was comfortable with a more sophisticated type of conservative. At Tulane University, where he became Chairman of the medical school's surgery department, Ochsner was involved in efforts to orient the school's programs toward support for the growing U.S. upper class involvement in Latin America. Ochsner had become a supporter of the Somoza regime in Nicaragua. Due in part to the efforts of Ochsner, Tulane became a major center for Latin American study. The University was aided by grants from the Rockefeller Foundation and the Carnegie Corporation, where C. D. Jackson, another expert on right-wing propaganda and the man who acquired the Zapruder film for Time, Inc., was a

[4] Carpenter, 1987, pp. 255-6; 1989, p. 136; Wilds and Harkey, 1990, p. 202.
[5] Carpenter, 1987, pp. 270-1.
[6] Wilds and Harkey, 1990, pp. 34, 61, 64, 217.
[7] Carpenter, 1987, p. 134; 1989, p. 126; Wilds and Harkey, 1990, p. 204.
[8] Zilg, 1974, pp. 405-11.

trustee. Two of Huey Long's United Fruit enemies, Samuel Zemurray and Joseph Montgomery, were trustees of Tulane at that time. Ochsner became president in 1956 of the Cordell Hull Foundation which was established to promote "free enterprise" by providing scholarships to Latin American students for study in the U.S.[9] In this context "free enterprise" means that neither the U.S. government nor the host country's government will interfere with the operations of organized, powerful, private interests. The U.S. government can be called upon to back up those private interests with military power or other government resources.

Ochsner was personally close to the leaders of the New Orleans elite and he was directly connected to many in the national power structure. Among the New Orleans associates was Theodore Brent, who also was personally close to Clay Shaw. Brent was president of the Mississippi Shipping Company and a director of the Hibernia National Bank. He was a founding trustee of the Alton Ochsner Medical Foundation and he helped to finance the Ochsner Foundation Hospital, opened in 1954.[10] Brent was also a director of the ITM affiliated International House.[11] IH was a New Orleans based but nationally connected promoter of "free trade" with Latin America. Brent's Mississippi Shipping apparently subsidized the *Latin American Report*, published in the 1940s and 1950s by William G. Gaudet.[12] Gaudet, who also received support from Ochsner and was associated with Edward Bernays of United Fruit,[13] claimed that he worked for the Central Intelligence Agency. Whatever his true employer, Gaudet turned up as the man who accompanied Lee Oswald (or an Oswald imposter) on the famous trip to Mexico.[14]

Another of the local elite who Ochsner was close to was Brent's friend Rudolph Hecht,[15] Chairman of the Hibernia National Bank of New Orleans. In Long's time Hecht was willing to cooperate with Huey if the situation dictated, i.e., Long held office and his decisions could affect Hecht's bank. Hecht's association with Long appears to have been one of convenience. In the years following Long's death, Hecht became an even more important local figure and, like Brent, he became closely associated with out-of-state powers. For example,

[9] Carpenter, 1987, pp. 133-4, 137-9, 232; 1989, p. 127.
[10] Caldwell, 1965, pp. 21, 39, 69; Carpenter, 1987, pp. 176-7, 188.
[11] Marquis Who's Who, 1947.
[12] Carpenter, 1987, pp. 183-5.
[13] Schlesinger and Kinser, 1982, pp. 79-80.
[14] DiEugenio, 1992, p. 220.
[15] Caldwell, 1965, p. 21.

Hecht had close ties to National City Bank (Citicorp/Citibank today) in New York,[16] linking him to the Stillman-Rockefeller interests.

Hecht provided a non-collateralized loan to Alton Ochsner and four other doctors to establish the Ochsner Clinic, opened in 1941. Brent and New Orleans attorney J. Blanc Monroe also were involved in the creation of the clinic.[17] Hecht and Brent were, with Clay Shaw, members of the governing board of the ITM at the time of its incorporation in 1945. Also on that board was Seymour Weiss, the Long supporter who seems to have been bought off around the time of Long's assassination. The involvement of Ochsner's associates with the ITM was one of his many connections to higher levels of power.

THE HIGHER POWERS

Among Ochsner's friends and supporters were people associated with America's great fortunes and most powerful private institutions. Ochsner had a friendship with Turner Catledge, managing editor of the *New York Times*.[18] Ochsner was personally close to Samuel Zemurray of United Fruit and to Edgar B. and Edith Rosenwald Stern of the Sears Roebuck fortune. United Fruit's southern headquarters was in New Orleans and Sears opened an export office in New Orleans in 1948.[19] Ochsner's foundation and hospital received financial support in the 1950s from Crawford Ellis of United Fruit, from the Ford Foundation, and from three of the wealthiest Texas-based families -Murchison, Richardson, and Bass.[20] The chairman of the Ford Foundation from 1953 to 1965 was John J. McCloy,[21] who spent part of the summer of 1963 with Clint Murchison.[22] McCloy also served as honorary chairman of International House in New York City and he was a director of United Fruit. In the early 1960s, David Rockefeller, a close associate of McCloy and, like McCloy, Kennedy's opponent on many issues,[23] was a trustee and chairman of the executive committee of IH.[24]

[16.] Carpenter, 1987, p. 191.

[17.] Caldwell, 1965, pp. 8, 21; Wilds and Harkey, 1990 ,pp. 144-5, 152.

[18.] DiEugenio, 1992, p. 379.

[19.] Carpenter, 1987, pp. 160, 167.

[20.] Caldwell, 1965, pp. 62, 74-5, 79, 89, 104: Wilds and Harkey, 1990, pp. 156-61.

[21.] Marquis Who's Who, 1978-79.

[22.] Bird, 1992, p. 542.

[23.] Gibson, 1994.

David's interest in IH went back at least to 1946 and his family contributed regularly to IH.

At the 1959 dedication of a new building for the Ochsner hospital, Ochsner introduced as guest speaker Monroe J. Rathbone, President of Standard Oil of New Jersey (Exxon).[25] Rathbone had been an executive of Standard Oil in Louisiana during the time that Standard clashed with Huey Long.[26] In 1962 Ochsner was president of IH; his tenure there probably overlapped with Shaw's time as Managing Director of IH. Shaw's predecessor and one of the creators of IH in New Orleans was an anti-Long journalist who rose to be New Orleans bureau chief of Associated Press, Charles P. Nutter.[27] Nutter was close to Shaw.[28] Around the time of JFK's assassination, the board of Ochsner's hospital featured the son, Ashton Phelps, of one of Huey Long's enemies, Boston Club president Esmond Phelps,[29] and it included Joseph W. Montgomery of United Fruit.[30]

When Ochsner and Butler created the Information Council of the Americas (INCA) a month after the Bay of Pigs failure, they acted not as local right wingers, but as Establishment right wingers. When Butler formed INCA in May of 1961 he was forming his second right-wing group in a year. He had created Free Voice of Latin America in 1960; it was headquartered at the ITM. According to historian Arthur Carpenter, INCA developed from three sources: Edward Butler, Alton Ochsner, and elite anti-communism. In Carpenter's view, the organization was intended to stimulate anti-Communist fears and then to exploit those fears to discredit opponents of the elite and to justify elite policies. Butler had longstanding interests in these kinds of psychological warfare efforts.[31]

A few months after he and Ochsner created INCA, Butler was bragging about his relationship with CIA Deputy Director Charles P. Cabell,[32] who would soon be fired by President Kennedy. As noted earlier, his brother, Dallas Mayor Earle Cabell, would be the first public figure to offer the lone assassin theory, a

---

24. Hoffman, 1971, pp. 105, 114.
25. Caldwell, 1965, p. 92.
26. Marquis Who's Who, 1962-63.
27. Carpenter, 1987, pp. 64-9.
28. Files of Jim Garrison, courtesy of James DiEugenio.
29. Williams, 1969.
30. Caldwell, 1965, p. 110.
31. Carpenter, 1987, pp. 233-5; 1989, p. 118.
32. Carpenter, 1987, p. 235.

view also promoted by INCA. The newly formed INCA had interesting members and supporters.

William B. Reily and H. Eustis Reily of William B. Reily & Company, onetime employers of Lee Oswald, were members of INCA. Apparently, two of Oswalds's cousins also worked for Reily.[33] Percival and Edgar B. Stern of the Sears Roebuck family were also members; they owned the local NBC station WDSU on which Butler and Oswald appeared together.[34] According to James DiEugenio, people at WDSU cooperated with NBC in smearing Garrison in 1967. Other members of INCA included William Zetzmann, president of ITM, George Dinwiddie, president of IH in 1960, Ashton Phelps, son of a Boston Club president, and Joseph Montgomery of United Fruit. Montgomery and Crawford Ellis of United Fruit were, with Ochsner, members of the Boston Club. INCA received financial support from Standard Oil, the Reily Foundation, Mississippi Shipping Company, the Hibernia Bank, and ITM.[35] INCA was a creature of the upper class.

Clay Shaw served for many years as managing director of ITM. He was in 1961 and 1962 managing director of IH. In that capacity, Shaw was linked to Ochsner and to the many interests which were hostile to Kennedy and, earlier, to Long. That would include Morgan interests, Rockefellers, and the Boston-United Fruit group.

The first managing director of IH in New Orleans was Herman C. Brock of the Morgan controlled Guaranty Trust Company. During the early-1930s Shaw had worked for Western Union. According to Lewis Corey, a J. P. Morgan biographer, Western Union came under the control of Morgan around 1910.[36] In the late-1930s Shaw worked for the Lee Keedick Lecture Bureau. Lee Keedick would be a member in the 1950s of the Morgan-Rockefeller linked Foreign Policy Association.[37] One of Clay Shaw's associates was Lucius Morris Beebe, a descendent of James Beebe who was a partner of Junius Spenser Morgan.[38] That company was J.M. Beebe, Morgan & Company.[39] Interestingly, Beebe was

---

[33.] Scott, 1971, IV. p. 10.

[34.] Carpenter, 1987, pp. 239, 246: DiEugenio, 1992, pp. 157, 206.

[35.] Carpenter, 1987, pp. 193, 239-40; 1989, pp. 128-9.

[36.] Corey, 1930, pp. 258, 353.

[37.] Marquis Who's Who in the South and Southwest, 1959-62; Shoup and Minter, 1977, pp. 31, 70-2.

[38.] Marquis Who's Who, 1978-79; Clay Shaw's address book.

[39.] Hoyt, 1966, p. 48.

drama critic at the New York Herald Tribune when Joe Alsop was a reporter there and both Beebe and Alsop hung out at the Artist and Writers Club on West Fortieth Street.[40] Also, Beebe had been a classmate of John Hay Whitney at Yale and they were communicating in the late-1950s.[41]

Herman Brock was replaced at IH by J. Stanton Robbins, Nelson Rockefeller's special assistant in the 1940s at the Office of the Coordinator of Inter-American Affairs. In January of 1944, Rockefeller had helped IH President Zetzmann, who was close to Montgomery, Brent, and Hecht, to announce the formation of IH on the radio.[42] Three years later, the Rockefeller controlled Venezuela Basic Economy Corporation opened its New Orleans office.[43]

People related to United Fruit and Associated Press were also involved with IH. Crawford Ellis was a founding member, vice-president, and director of IH. Zemurray supported IH. Reportedly the idea for IH in New Orleans originated with Shaw's friend, Charles Nutter, ex-Associated Press bureau chief for New Orleans.[44] Nutter, who covered the important Moscow purge trials in the late-1930s, became the first managing director of IH, as Shaw was of ITM.[45]

Clay Shaw, Alton Ochsner, and Edward Butler were thoroughly entrenched in this Establishment network connected to ITM and IH. That network included people associated with the Freeport Sulphur Company.

FREEPORT SULPHUR AND THE ESTABLISHMENT

In his 1975 book, *The Rockefeller Syndrome*, Ferdinand Lundberg observed that Freeport Sulphur was under the control of the Rockefeller, Stillman-Rockefeller, and Whitney families.[46] On the board of directors of Freeport was Augustus Long who was chairman of the giant Texaco oil company and a director of the Rockefeller controlled Chemical Bank. A second director was Jean Mauze who was the third husband of Abby Rockefeller, granddaughter of

---

[40] Merry, 1996, p. 48.
[41] Kahn, 1981, pp. 9, 35.
[42] Carpenter, 1987, pp. 79-84.
[43] Carpenter, 1987, p. 167.
[44] Fortune, 1952, p. 140.
[45] Carpenter, 1987, pp. 85-6.
[46] Lundberg, 1975, p. 55.

John D. Rockefeller. Freeport director Godfrey Rockefeller was the brother of James Stillman Rockefeller. Director Benno C. Schmidt was an original partner at J. H. Whitney & Co. and he owned a ranch in Australia jointly with David Rockefeller. John Hay Whitney himself had been board chairman of Freeport Sulphur from 1949 to 1956 and he was a major stockholder in the 1960s. Director Chauncey Devereux Stillman was a descendent of the William Rockefeller and James Stillman wing of the family. Stillman had been an advisor to the Department of Defense in 1947 and he worked for the National Security Council from 1948 to 1951.[47] This upper-class environmentalist would team up in the late-1960s with J. Lee Rankin, then counsel for New York City, to stop construction of a pumped-storage plant on the Hudson River. The plant was intended to provide power for New York City.[48] Freeport president Robert Chadwick Hills was in 1963 a director of the Chase International Investment Corporation, i.e., Rockefeller. Langbourne Williams was married for 26 years to Elizabeth Goodrich Stillman.

One of the other significant Establishment figures on the Freeport board was Robert Abercrombie Lovett. Robert's father, Robert S. Lovett, married into the Abercrombie family, part of Texas aristocracy, and he rose to be E. H. Harriman's successor as chairman of the Union Pacific Railroad. Robert A., born in 1895, attended Yale, was a member of the secret society Skull and Bones, and married Adele Brown of the Brown Brothers banking family in 1919. Roland and Averill Harriman, Prescott Bush (father of President George Bush), and Knight Wood, all of the Harriman firm, were all Bonesmen as were several partners at Brown Brothers.[49]

In 1926, Robert, only about 31 years of age, became a partner at Brown Brothers and a director of the Union Pacific.[50] In 1930 the Harriman and Brown Brothers firms were merged to form Brown Brothers Harriman and Lovett took over the firm's international transactions.[51] Lovett was later a director of New York Life and a trustee of the Rockefeller Foundation and of the Carnegie Foundation.[52]

---

[47] Marquis Who's Who, 1964-65.

[48] Tucker, 1977, pp. 47-56, 73-80.

[49] Isaacson and Thomas, 1986, pp. 110-111.

[50] Isaacson and Thomas, 1986, pp. 21, 61-63, 93, 108-109.

[51] Isaacson and Thomas, 1986, pp. 111, 117.

[52] Isaacson and Thomas, 1986, 338.

Lovett had many friends among the wealthy and powerful. Among his closest friends was Henry Luce, a major force at the anti-JFK Time-Life-Fortune empire.[53] One of Lovett's longest (over 60 years) and closest friendships was with Warren Commissioner and Morgan-Rockefeller lawyer John J. McCloy.[54] Lovett and McCloy, known as the "Heavenly Twins" at the World War Two War Department, were among Dean Acheson's oldest and closest friends.[55] Lovett was frequently called in by Acheson and Averill Harriman to provide advice to President Harry Truman.[56] Truman went public in 1960 in an effort to prevent JFK from getting the Democratic nomination. Lovett and McCloy, at the request of Dean Rusk, offered "outsider" advice to LBJ on Vietnam in 1965. They, along with Dean Acheson, recommended escalation.[57] Lovett, Acheson, and McCloy all recommended Dean Rusk to JFK as Secretary of State.[58] Kennedy once remarked after being handed a list of potential State Department appointees of which three-fourths were CFR members that "I'd like to have some new faces here, but all I get is the same old names."[59]

Freeport Sulphur's Robert Lovett was then extremely close to one of the men who instigated the creation of the so-called Warren Commission, Dean Acheson, and to one of the overseers of that Commission, John J. McCloy.

Freeport's Chairman and longtime Whitney associate Langbourne Williams, Freeport Vice-Chairman Charles A. Wight, President Robert Hills, Vice-President Peter Black and Chauncey Stillman were all members of the Council on Foreign Relations. Clay Shaw almost certainly knew a few or more of these men.

At least two individuals provided information to Jim Garrison indicating that Clay Shaw was involved with Freeport's Vice-Chairman Charles Wight.[60] It is highly likely that Shaw knew Freeport Vice-President and director Edmund Duane Wingfield.

[53.] Isaacson and Thomas, 1986, p. 193.

[54.] Bird, 1992, p. 105; Isaacson and Thomas, 1986, pp. 120, 194, 734.

[55.] Hersh, 1992, p. 143; Isaacson and Thomas, 1986, pp. 18, 417-418, 462, 493, 539, 581, 716.

[56.] Isaacson and Thomas. 1986, p. 338.

[57.] Brinkley, 1992, pp. 247-248.

[58.] Isaacson and Thomas, 1986, p. 592.

[59.] Lucas, 1971, p. 126.

[60.] Pease, 1996; 1996a.

We return first to suspected Clay Shaw associate, Charles A. Wight. After 17 years with Bankers Trust, including about four years in its London office, Wight moved to Freeport Sulphur as its executive committee chairman and as a board member. Wight also served as a director of two Freeport affiliates, the National Potash Company and the Sulphur Export Corporation.

Bankers Trust was controlled by or at least closely affiliated with the Morgan interests from the beginning of the century to, at least, the 1970s. In fact, the bank was created by two men who became major figures at J. P. Morgan & Co. - Thomas W. Lamont and Harry P. Davison.[61] This suggests that the Morgan interests played some important role at Freeport Sulphur. There is more.

Freeport Sulphur shared ownership of the Sulphur Export Corporation, created in 1958, with Texas Gulf Sulphur. Thomas S. Lamont, the son of Bankers Trust founder and J. P. Morgan partner Thomas W. Lamont, was on the board of Texas Gulf as early as 1927 and was still one of its directors in 1963. F. R. Stettinius, a Morgan partner, helped to reorganize Texas Gulf in the 1920s.[62] The Morgan bank reportedly controlled Texas Gulf Sulphur from the 1930s into the 1960s.[63]

Thomas S. Lamont, following the path of his father, rose to be Vice-Chairman of Morgan Guaranty Trust. As noted above, Lamont, also a director of Phelps Dodge, was in 1964 a leader of the National Independent Committee for President Johnson. Two other leaders, John L. Loeb and Edgar Kaiser, turned up four years later as leaders of the stop RFK-movement. Lamont's father, Thomas W., had been a leading figure in 1932 in the stop-Roosevelt movement. Morgan interests played a significant role in the creation in 1934 of the anti-Roosevelt American Liberty Lobby.[64] According to Jules Archer's 1973 book, *The Plot to Seize the White House*, this Morgan activity, perhaps led by Grayson Mallet-Prevost Murphy, included a possible overthrow of the Roosevelt administration. Allen Dulles's uncle married into the Mallet-Prevost family.

Thomas S. Lamont's brother, Corliss Lamont, turned up in a most curious way in the activities of Oswald. In August, 1963, Oswald handed out a pamphlet in front of Clay Shaw's International Trade Mart. The pamphlet, entitled "The Crime Against Cuba," was written by Corliss Lamont. That pamphlet, like other

---

[61.] Chernow, 1990, pp. 143-153; Kotz, 1978, pp. 70, 88; Marquis Who's Who, 1962-63.
[62.] Forbes, 1974.
[63.] Chernow, 1990, pp. 365-366, 562-563; Sherrill, 1983, p. 242.
[64.] Burch, 1980, pp. 55, 195-196, 230.

of Oswald's handouts, was stamped with the address "544 Camp Street," Guy Bannister's office.[65] We will look at this pamphlet and its author later.

Clay Shaw had to have known Freeport Vice-President Duane Wingfield. Wingfield was also a director of International House, a member and director of the Chamber of Commerce and member of the New Orleans Board of Trade.[66] International House worked closely with Clay Shaw's International Trade Mart to promote global "free trade" and to make New Orleans a free trade zone. In fact Clay Shaw was a member of the World Trade Development Committee of International House and he served as acting manager of International House from May, 1961, to April, 1962.

At the time that Wingfield and Shaw were engaged in these global initiatives there were parallel activities going on in New York City, efforts led by, among others, the Rockefeller interests. The principal speaker for the 1948 opening of Shaw's Trade Mart was William McChesney Martin.[67] Martin later became Chairman of the Federal Reserve Board and then a supervisor of the Rockefeller family's trust fund. During the Kennedy administration he actively opposed Kennedy's low interest rate policies.[68]

The local activities of Shaw, Ochsner, and Butler were related to the programs, policies, and institutions of a series of interconnected upper-class interests based in Boston and New York. What did this group, led by the Morgan-Rockefeller-Boston Brahmin network, want? We get some idea from a New Orleans conference organized in 1955 by ITM, IH, and Time Inc., featuring speakers such as millionaire J. Peter Grace, Time co-founder Henry Luce, and Milton Eisenhower. The conference was intended to promote private enterprise and global "free trade", to discourage government intervention in trade (such as the policies of JFK), and to criticize nationalism and communism.[69] What this group, which opposed Long's and Kennedy's policies, wanted was for the United States to pursue an imperialist or neo-colonialist policy toward Latin America. This would include the need to maintain or create an alliance between big U.S. banking and raw materials interests and the landed oligarchy of Latin America.[70] What would the people of the United States get from that? Nothing. If anything

[65] DiEugenio, 1992, pp. 218-219.
[66] Marquis Who's Who, 1964-65.
[67] Popham, 1948, P. 41; 1948a, p. 43.
[68] Gibson, 1994, p. 74.
[69] Carpenter, 1987, pp. 127-9.
[70] Carpenter, 1987, p. 5

they would lose by not having the benefit of a growing and prosperous hemisphere. What would the majority of people in Latin America get from that? Perpetual backwardness and poverty. Time, Inc. openly attacked President Kennedy because he was pushing a program of economic development that threatened these neo-colonial interests.[71]

The development of Clay Shaw's International Trade Mart and of it sister organization, International House, was part of the role that New Orleans was playing in the neo-colonial relationship between the New York-Boston Establishment and Latin America. The involvement of that Establishment in Louisiana increased throughout this century, as did the involvement in Latin America. However, this connection between the East and Louisiana did not begin in this century; its origins go back to the period before the Civil War, something we can see by looking at the background of New Orleans's elitist Boston Club.

BOSTON SOUTH

The Boston Club connects the pre-Civil War aristocracy to the New Orleans of Huey Long's time and to the 1960s New Orleans of Clay Shaw, Alton Ochsner, and Edward Butler. The Club also reflects and perpetuates a link between the upper class of Louisiana and that of Boston and New York, relationships evident a century after the Club's founding.

The author of the official history of the Boston Club says that the club was named after a card game called "Boston," but he offers no proof that the club's namesake was the game rather than the city. In any event, the game was named after the city. Why would anyone name a club formed in New Orleans after a city that was two thousand miles away? The answer of course is that the elites of the two cities were tied together. For example, there was a New England Society in New Orleans before the Civil War; some of its members belonged to the Boston Club. The Daily Picayune referred to Club members as "Bostonians."[72] This apparently was not a reference to their choice of card games.

The Boston Club, organized in 1841, is one of the three oldest upper-class clubs in the United States and it had connections to one of the other two, the

---

71. Gibson, 1994, p. 59.
72. Landry, 1938, pp. 45, 47, 201.

Union Club of New York. Both clubs were modeled after the English elite club, for which the model is White's of London, and both clubs had Englishmen as members at the time they were founded. Boston and Union had "ties of mutuality" due to numerous individuals belonging to both clubs. In its first two decades the Boston Club, which had two hundred or fewer members, had at least nine members, and probably six additional members, who were also members of the Union Club.[73] Two of these are relevant to our interests - Judah P. Benjamin and John Slidell.

RACISTS AND ARISTOCRATS

Slidell was very close to President James Buchanan, was a U.S. Senator from 1853 to 1861, and was an ambassador to England and France for the Confederacy. His three daughters married European aristocrats and his son was part of the Louisiana elite and was a member of the Boston Club. Slidell's niece, the daughter of his sister and Commodore Perry, married August Belmont, Sr., the famous financier who was an agent for the Rothschilds and worked at times with J. P. Morgan.[74]

One of the young men who studied law in Slidell's office was Judah Benjamin, fresh from several years at Yale University. Benjamin would go on to serve as U.S. Senator and then Secretary of War and Secretary of State for the Confederate President Jefferson Davis. Benjamin, who was an honorary member of the Boston Club and a member of the Union Club, escaped to England at the end of the Civil War and became a major figure in English jurisprudence.[75] The Boston Club linked together the Anglo-Saxons of Boston, New York, and England with the Southern aristocracy.

The connections between the national elite and Louisiana were a continuous part of the history of the Boston Club. It was noted earlier that Alton Ochsner was a 1965 guest at the elitist Bohemian Grove in California. The Grove is part of the San Francisco Bohemian Club which was started in the late-1800s by Horace Fletcher, an early globe trotting business agent who was a member of the

---

[73.] Ibid., pp. xi, 1, 5, 9-12, 19, 205.

[74.] Chernow, 1990, pp. 5, 40; Landry, 1938, pp. 326-7.

[75.] Landry, 1938, pp. 276-80.

Boston Club from 1890 to 1898.[76] In 1916 both Frank A. Vanderlip and James A. Stillman of National City Bank were guests at the Boston Club.[77] Stillman and Vanderlip served on the board of City Bank (Citicorp) with J. P. Morgan, Jr., William Rockefeller, and Robert S. Lovett.[78]

In Huey Long's time Alton Ochsner and Edward Butler could rub shoulders at the Boston Club with Crawford Ellis of United Fruit and with a host of local notables who had ties to the higher circles, virtually all of whom were Long's enemies. Among those were Edwin S. Broussard, T. Semmes Walmsley, Esmond Phelps, Joseph Montgomery, and John Parker. Many of the Boston Club members would be directors of the Trade Mart and of the International House in the 1940s and 1950s. That included Times Picayune president Leonard Nicholson, businessman Kemper Williams, United Fruit executive Montgomery, and banker Dale Graham.[79] Graham came to New Orleans in the early-1930s with George Champion and Oliver Lucas in the Chase Bank's takeover of Canal Bank & Trust, renamed the National Bank of Commerce.[80] Champion would go on to be Chairman of the Chase Manhattan, holding that position in between John J. McCloy and David Rockefeller.

During the twentieth century the local power structure of Louisiana became a junior partner in the neo-colonialist efforts of the East Coast Establishment. Clay Shaw, Alton Ochsner, and Edward Butler played significant roles in the Louisiana part of those operations. In the 1980s Alton Ochsner, Jr., appeared to be continuing that tradition. He was involved with the Nicaraguan Contras, an extension of the Establishment's neo-colonial policy who were also involved with drug trafficking, and he appeared at a press conference with a Contra leader known to be a part of the drug trade.[81] This is actually not surprising. The Boston-New Orleans connection has been important in what is a longstanding involvement of the Establishment in the drug trade.

---

[76]. Ibid., p. 294.

[77]. Ibid., p. 171.

[78]. Lundberg, 1937, p. 103.

[79]. Marquis Who's Who, 1957.

[80]. Carpenter, 1987, p. 60.

[81]. Carpenter , 1987, pp. 344-5; Scott and Marshall, 1991, pp. 105-17.

UNITED FRUIT AND THE DRUG TRADE

United Fruit was incorporated in 1899 in New Jersey but its real base was in Boston. At its formation United Fruit combined a number of existing companies and it would later absorb others, including the Cuyamel Company founded by Samuel Zemurray. One of the companies merged to create United Fruit was owned by the New Orleans based Macheca crime family.[82] The first officers and directors of United Fruit included Andrew Preston, Minor Keith, Lamont Burnham, and T. Jefferson Coolidge, Jr.

There are several clear links to the opium trade. The Coolidge family played an important role in the trade in the mid-1800s.[83] T(homas) Jefferson Coolidge's grandfather, Joseph, was involved with the two most important American firms active in the opium trade at that time. He was a member of Russell & Co. and then was a founder of Augustine Heard and Company.[84] Another Coolidge, Archibald, was the first editor of the Council on Foreign Relation's mouth piece *Foreign Affairs*.[85] The Coolidges were descendents of Thomas Jefferson. Their involvement in the development of the New York-Boston dominated Council on Foreign Relations (CFR) is but one of many instances in which the East Coast Establishment intersects with openly right-wing and racist interests. For example, Laurence Shoup and William Minter make the following comments on the CFR's image and its first president, John W. Davis:

> As the Council on Foreign Relations is identified with the 'liberal' establishment, it is interesting to note that Davis was instrumental in forming the right-wing American Liberty League to oppose the New Deal, and represented South Carolina in defending segregation before the United States Supreme Court.[86]

The Establishment's idea of "liberalism" has much more in common with the elitist English social philosopher John Locke than it does with the ideas FDR or JFK. As Jules Archer shows in his *The Plot to Seize the White House*, Morgan

---

[82] Chandler, 1975, pp. 73-97.

[83] Stelle, 1981, pp. 97-8.

[84] Stelle, 1981, 97-8.

[85] Shoup and Minter, 1977, pp. 198-9.

[86] Shoup and Minter, 1977, p. 105.

and other Establishment interests were extensively involved with the American Liberty League in the 1930s.

In the 1930s, W. Cameron Forbes, the grandson of Ralph Waldo Emerson and a descendent of another opium trading family was a director of United Fruit.[87] Also involved in the opium trade in the 1800s and with United Fruit in the 1900s was the Cabot family.[88] In 1954 when the CIA engineered the coup against the Arbenz government in Guatemala, John Moors Cabot was Assistant Secretary of State for Inter-American Affairs. He had served earlier as President of United Fruit. Henry Cabot Lodge (the Lodges were also United Fruit stockholders) used his influence in the Senate on behalf of United Fruit.[89] Michael Paine, husband of Ruth Paine, Oswalds's hostess in Dallas, was related to both the Forbes and Cabot families. One of Michael's cousins, Thomas Dudley Cabot, served as president of United Fruit. Michael's grandmother was Elise Cabot Forbes. Michael's mother, Ruth Forbes Paine Young, had a friendship with Allen Dulles' lover, Mary Bancroft.[90] Even though she and Michael were separated at the time, Ruth Paine remained personally close to the Forbes family. Marina Oswald lived with Ruth and Ruth helped Lee Oswald to get the job at the Book Depository.[91]

The organizers of the 1954 coup against Jacobo Arbenz Guzma included United Fruit stockholder Allen Dulles, C. D. Jackson, Tracy Barnes, and David Atlee Philips.[92] The Guatemalan intervention had been recommended in 1953 by one of John J. McCloy's Council on Foreign Relations study groups.[93] The Dulles's law firm, Sullivan and Cromwell, represented United Fruit.[94] Dulles, with McCloy, would steer the Warren Commission and C. D. Jackson would be involved in the Time-Life decision to acquire and then suppress the Zapruder film. McCloy was a director of United Fruit.[95] Tracy Barnes, a close friend of Dulles,[96] was involved with a far-right group known as the Cuban Revolutionary

[87.] Marquis Who's Who, 1935; Stelle, 1981, pp. 53, 60, 91.
[88.] Stelle, 1981, p. 28.
[89.] Schlesinger and Kinzer, 1982, pp. 76, 82-3, 103, 106.
[90.] Hewett, Jones, and LaMonica, 1996; Hewett, 1997; LaMonica, 1998.
[91.] Scott, 1971, IV, pp. 2-4.
[92.] Schlesinger and Kinzer, 1982, pp. 108, 114, 155, 178.
[93.] Bird, 1992, p. 435.
[94.] Cooke, 1981, p. 221; Hersh, 1992, p. 336.
[95.] Cooke, 1981, p, 229.
[96.] Grose, 1994, p. 248.

Council. The Council had links to INCA and it had headquarters at Bannister's 544 Camp Street. David Ferrie knew Council leader Sergio Aracha Smith.[97] Harold Weisberg noted the possible significance of Butler's INCA and the Council in his 1967 book *Oswald in New Orleans*.[98] Weisberg also noted that two of the men involved in what looked like an attempt to frame Oswald by having an impersonator display hostility toward JFK were arrested less than a month later on a dangerous drug charge.[99] David Atlee Philips would be identified by Gaeton Fonzi as Oswald's handler "Maurice Bishop."[100] As noted earlier, William Gaudet, a United Fruit propaganda man,[101] accompanied Oswald or an Oswald impersonator to Mexico.

One of the other men brought into the coup operation was William Pawley. Pawley had helped to transform the World War Two China-based Flying Tigers into the CIA's Civil Air Transport.[102] Civil Air Transport became Air America and it was involved in transporting drugs. Thusly, we get from Cabot involvement in the Far East opium trade in 1804[103] to a Cabot related institution involved in the Southeast Asia opium trade in the 1950s and 1960s.[104] Perhaps relevant as historical background is the fact that the Louisiana territory was purchased with financial assistance from a group, the Barings of London, that was connected in the 1800s to the opium trade through their involvement with the East India Company and then the Hong Kong and Shanghai Banking Corporation.[105]

[97] Garrison, 1988, p. 305.

[98] Weisberg, 1967, pp. 51-2, 255, 345.

[99] Meagher, 1976, pp. 376-87; Weisberg, 1967, p. 273.

[100] Fonzi, 1993.

[101] Schlesinger and Kinzer, 1982, p. 82.

[102] Schlesinger and Kinzer, 1982, p. 145.

[103] Stelle, 1981, pp. 12-3.

[104] McCoy, 1972.

[105] Chernow, 1990, pp. 5, 50; Wechsberg, 1968, pp. 79-80, 85, 124.

SHAW'S SIGNIFICANCE

Jim Garrison said in his 1988 book, *On The Trail Of The Assassins*, that Clay Shaw was "only a small part of the overall conspiracy."[106] Shaw's role in the assassination may have been limited to management of Oswald's New Orleans activities. He was involved in that area in a variety of ways. He knew Oswald and was involved with Bannister and Ferrie.[107] He was close to Ochsner who was, in turn, close to the Sterns who owned the station on which Oswald appeared. Ochsner and Butler were active in promoting the lone-commie theory, a variation of the lone-nut theory sponsored by Mayor Earle Cabell, the Whitney family's *Herald Tribune*, the *Wall Street Journal*, James Reston, and the Dulles-McCloy led Warren Commission. Butler appeared on WDSU with Oswald. Butler was close to the Reily family, Oswald's employer.

Shaw, Ochsner, and Butler were deeply involved with the New Orleans elite which has been for over a century a part of the national and international power structure. The local upper class was long integrated as a social subsidiary of the Boston-New York commercial-financial aristocracy. The interests of that aristocracy clashed with the goals of Huey Long and JFK. That aristocracy wanted to and wants to control economic and social policies through its private organizations and networks and it wants to dictate policy to the government. Kennedy and Long thought that government had a useful and necessary role to play, a role independent of Establishment interests. The aristocracy wanted to maintain Latin America in perpetual backwardness. Kennedy sought ways to spur development. That aristocracy thought and thinks that the United States military exists as a police-extension of institutions such as United Fruit, Exxon, and National City Bank. Long thought the proper role for the military was providing for the defense of the nation and Kennedy opposed its use to support neo-colonial interests. Long and Kennedy thought that the government had an important role to play in stimulating the national economy and in protecting the majority from highly organized centers of wealth and power. The aristocracy believes that the government should perform only the tasks they give it.

It is not surprising then that Long and Kennedy are linked in other ways. Linked through the persons of Christenberry and Ochsner and the Butler family. Linked because Huey Long's opponents would fill positions at the International

---

[106] Garrison, 1988, p. 229.
[107] DiEugenio, 1992.

Trade Mart and the International House and would be Clay Shaw's associates. Linked because the Louisiana of Huey Long was dominated by the same New York-Boston interests that appear in the time of Kennedy and Shaw. Their lives were linked to each other and it appears that their deaths were as well. The same networks and interests probably killed both of them.

I think that Garrison was correct when he said that Shaw's role was relatively minor. But he did have a role to play. The role was probably one of orchestrating or assisting in the orchestration of Oswald's time in New Orleans. It is significant that Shaw was connected through his personal relationships and his work with the International Trade Mart and the International House to the networks of people who opposed Kennedy and then controlled events after he was murdered. The history of IH and ITM is deeply tied to the history of internationalism and globalism in the United States. That history is an important part of the history of the Kennedy assassination.

Chapter Eight

INTERNATIONALISM AND THE KENNEDY ASSASSINATION

In 1925 leading interests within the upper class created three private organizations, each of which was designed to serve the interests of an increasingly internationalist financial elite. In the years leading up to the assassination of President Kennedy, two of these organizations and a successor of the third were intertwined with each other and each was connected to Kennedy's enemies and to Clay Shaw or Lee Oswald. During 1925 International House (IH) was created in New York City, the Institute of Pacific Relations (IPR) was formed in Hawaii, and a forerunner of the International Trade Mart (ITM), the International Trade Exhibition, was started in New Orleans.

The organizations are not important in and of themselves. We will focus on them because they are related to the networks of people who opposed Kennedy and they had direct or indirect connections to many of the people who played a role in the cover-up. We begin by looking at each of the three organizations separately.

INTERNATIONAL HOUSE

The first International House opened formally at 500 Riverside Drive, New York City, in 1925. It would become over the succeeding decades host to and refuge for thousands of students, over one-third of which have been from other countries. This has included large numbers of graduate and post-graduate students.[1] It was located near Grant's Tomb and the Union Theological Seminary, co-founded by John D. Rockefeller, Jr.,[2] and was only a block or so from the home of Corliss Lamont, whose father and brother were J.P. Morgan partners.

According to news accounts, the idea of International House was brought to John D. Rockefeller, Jr., by Harry Edmonds, an official of the New York Young Men's Christian Associations (Y.M.C.A.). Rockefeller founded IH in New York City and in at least three other cities, Chicago, Berkeley, and Paris.[3] The Institute of Pacific Relations was also created in 1925 and with Rockefeller money. This transpired at a Y.M.C.A. conference organized by John Mott. According to Peter Collier and David Horowitz, Institute personnel became "the core of the U.S. intelligence network in the Pacific."[4]

Other International Houses were begun in the U.S. and abroad. IH opened in Geneva, Switzerland, in 1937, in Rome in 1951, and in Tokyo in 1955.[5] In the 1950s the managing director of IH in Japan was Shigeharu Matsumoto. IH was started in Japan with money from Japanese interests and from the Rockefeller Foundation. In the late-1930s Matsumoto was closely associated with Hotzumi Ozaki, one of the leading Japanese figures involved with the Institute of Pacific Relations. Ozaki was also a close associate of and collaborator with the famous spy Richard Sorge.[6]

In the U.S. an IH was started in New Orleans in 1943, though not formally dedicated until 1946.[7] In New Orleans IH was thought by some to be a part of the trade initiatives made toward Latin America by Secretary of State Cordell Hull. New Orleans, long one of America's most important port cities, was the only other port beside New York where goods could enter and leave without payment of duties. In the early-1960s New Orleans ranked second, by value of cargo handled, in the U.S., trailing only New York.[8] IH got some unwanted publicity in 1977 when it was charged by many, including a few of its own members, with racism or reactionary politics when its members voted not to allow African

---

[1.] New York Times, 1925h; 1937b; Jones, 1958.

[2.] Collier and Horowitz, 1976, p. 153.

[3.] New York Times, 1927; Samuels, 1960; Smith, 1969.

[4.] Collier and Horowitz, 1976, p. 279.

[5.] New York Times, 1937; 1951; 1954a.

[6.] New York Times, 1954a; Prange, 1984.

[7.] Healy, 1946; New York Times, 1977a.

[8.] New York Times, 1946b; 1963; 1977a.

American Andrew Young to speak. Young had been born in New Orleans and in 1977 was the U.S. delegate to the United Nations. IH subsequently changed its position and invited Young.[9]

In 1947 the International House Association was formed to provide an organization for former IH students. This was followed later, in 1965, by the formation of a worldwide alumni council.[10]

Since 1925 representatives of the wealthiest and most influential families have been involved with IH. The Rockefeller involvement continued. David Rockefeller became chairman of the executive committee of the board of trustees of the New York IH in the 1940's.[11] Also a trustee was David's brother, John D. Rockefeller 3d.[12] In 1964 Nelson Rockefeller, then Governor of New York, received an IH award; he used the occasion to attack Kennedy's Alliance for Progress.[13] David would do the same in an April, 1966, article appearing in the Council on Foreign Relation's *Foreign Affairs*.

The Morgan interests, intertwined with the Rockefeller interests in many areas, were also involved with IH. For example, the first managing director of IH in New Orleans was Herman C. Brock, formerly in charge of the Latin American division of the Morgan controlled Guaranty Trust Company.[14] One of the trustees of the New York IH in the early-1960's was Morgan Guaranty vice president Peter H. Vermilye [15]

The chairman of the board of trustees of New York's IH in the 1950's and 1960's was John J. McCloy.[16] Close to both Morgan and Rockefeller interests, McCloy would play a leading role in the Warren Commission's operations. As chairman of New York's IH for a decade or more, McCloy must have been at least familiar with the name of New Orleans IH and International Trade Mart official Clay Shaw. McCloy may well have known Shaw or Shaw's associate at IH and ITM, Alton Ochsner. McCloy also may have known Ochsner because he was chairman of the Ford Foundation when it gave money to Ochsner's hospital and foundation.

[9.] New York Times, 1977; 1977a; 1977b.

[10.] New York Times, 1947d; 1965.

[11.] New York Times, 1947.

[12.] New York Times, 1949.

[13.] New York Times, 1964.

[14.] New York Times, 1944.

[15.] New York Times, 1961a.

[16.] New York Times, 1955; 1965.

The position of New York IH board chairman had been held earlier by Henry L. Stimson, Secretary of War under Taft and Secretary of State in the Morgan dominated Hoover administration.[17] Stimson was pushed onto the Roosevelt administration by Thomas W. Lamont, who was actively involved with one of our other two organizations, the Institute of Pacific Relations, for over twenty years.[18] As FDR's Secretary of War, Stimson was McCloy's superior and mentor.[19] Collier and Horowitz, in *The Rockefellers: An American Dynasty*, note that

> Stimson was then [World War Two] recognized as the dean of American diplomacy, having served as Secretary of War or State in four Cabinets going back to the Taft administration; he was the guiding eminence of the Council on Foreign Relations, and his office had become a kind of academy for young men like McCloy, Robert Lovett, and others who would shape American policy in the postwar era, the best and brightest of their time and place, but who outside their own elite world, were virtually anonymous.[20]

When Stimson was chairman of IH in the late-1930's, his trustees included John D. Rockefeller 3d, Raymond B. Fosdick, and Frederick Osborn.[21]

Fosdick was a trustee of the Rockefeller Foundation and he had served as a representative of the Rockefeller Bureau of Social Hygiene. He was an expert on police organization.[22] Frederick Osborn was a partner in G.(rayson) M.(allet) P.(revost) Murphy & Company. He was associated with the Rockefeller Institute and with the Carnegie Corporation. He was a commissioner of Palisades Interstate Park Commission and he served as a director of the Population Association of America, of the American Eugenics Society, and of the Association for Research in Human Heredity.[23] Frederick's father was a prominent corporation lawyer and one of his uncles was Cleveland H. Dodge, long an associate of J.P. Morgan and William Rockefeller. Another of Osborn's uncles was eugenicist Henry Fairfield Osborn. Frederick went from Princeton to Wall Street and then to the work of promoting eugenics. In 1947 Frederick was

---

[17.] Lundberg, 1937, pp. 108, 183.
[18.] Lamont, 1956, pp. 65-66.
[19.] Bird, 1992, pp. 110, 119-26.
[20.] Collier and Horowitz, 1976, p. 240.
[21.] New York Times, 1936a.
[22.] A. N. Marquis, 1926.
[23.] A. N. Marquis, 1940.

appointed by Dean Acheson to be one of the U.S. representatives to the United Nations Atomic Energy Commission.[24] Although he tried to distance himself from Nazi eugenics, he promoted the idea after World War Two that there was too much reproduction among inferior lower classes. In 1952 he and John D. Rockefeller 3d established the Population Council and Osborn became a prominent population control activist.[25] As noted earlier, Osborn's business partner, Grayson M-P Murphy, was involved in an attempt in 1933 to organize and manipulate veterans in order to intimidate or even replace FDR. Also implicated in this activity were Thomas W. Lamont and John W. Davis, chief attorney for J. P. Morgan & Co. and Democratic candidate for President in 1924.[26]

Other notables associated with International House have included Secretary of State John Foster Dulles, Sears, Roebuck chairman Robert E. Wood, Rockefeller in-law and Council on Foreign Relations executive director George S. Franklin, George W. Ball of Lehman Brothers, and Henry Kissinger.[27] Among the former students of IH was Ferenc Nagy, onetime premier of Hungry.[28] As Jim DiEugenio has pointed out, Nagy was involved in the creation of Permindex. Permindex was accused of involvement in assassination attempts against Charles de Gaulle and it may have played some role in the Kennedy assassination. Nagy's fellow Permindex directors included Jean DeMenil of Schlumberger Corporation, Paul Raigorodsky, and Clay Shaw. Nagy and Hans Seligman had worked with Clay Shaw in moving Permindex from Basel, Switzerland, to Rome, Italy. Nagy lived in Dallas in 1963. DeMenil's Schlumberger Corporation owned the ammunition dump raided by Oswald-Shaw associate David Ferrie. Raigorodsky, a wealthy oil man involved in the Dallas White Russian Community, was a friend of Oswald's pal George DeMohrenschildt.[29]

What was the purpose of International House? We get some idea from a statement made by Dr. Raymond Fosdick at the founding of IH, Chicago, in 1932. Fosdick, who was chairman of the Rockefeller Foundation's committee on the extension of International Houses, said:

[24.] New York Times, 1947.

[25.] Kevles, 1985, pp. 170, 259; Lundberg, 1937.

[26.] Archer, 1973, pp. 6-11, 15, 184.

[27.] New York Times, 1950; 1950a; 1956; 1974; 1975.

[28.] New York Times, 1974a.

[29.] DiEugenio, 1992, pp. 209-13.

> The knell has sounded for the old concept of political nationalism just as
> much as it has for economic nationalism.
>   Sixty nations cannot span the earth with their ships and airplanes and
> competing systems of commerce and expect the business to run without some
> centralized technique of understanding and supervision.[30]

This is a straightforward statement of outlook and purpose. It is an expression of
the aims of international banking and of transnational or multinational
corporations, before the latter terms were even in use, and of the globally
oriented upper-class groups that control those institutions. The goal was to create
and control a global economy. It indicates a hope that nations and national
governments can be made irrelevant and that new international organizations can
be formed.

Those involved with IH repeatedly stated their desire for a unified, peaceful
world. For example, in 1932 IH students demonstrated in favor of world
disarmament.[31] In 1936 IH students and officials worked with organizations such
as the Foreign Policy Association and the American Friends Service Committee
to promote world peace.[32] When the International House Association was formed
in 1947, it was dedicated to world brotherhood and peace.[33] There is no reason to
doubt the sincerity of their desire for peace, but only the most naive will believe
that they wanted peace on any but their own terms.

International House has been affiliated with a variety of organizations. At its
founding IH worked with the National Council of Christian Associations to
promote the World Court.[34] In New Orleans its work was aided by United Fruit.[35]
Its efforts were often joined with those of the Foreign Policy Association and it
collaborated with the Institute of Pacific Relations.[36] One of the Institutes
controversial leaders, Frederick Field, worked in 1936 with IH to present a
seminar on world problems. Field and, in fact, much of the IPR staff were
accused of communist sympathies. A similar charge was made against
International House in the early-1930s by Ralph M. Easley, chairman of the

---

[30.] New York Times, 1932b.
[31.] New York Times, 1932.
[32.] New York Times, 1936.
[33.] New York Times, 1947c.
[34.] New York Times, 1925f; 1925g.
[35.] New York Times, 1954; 1957.
[36.] New York Times, 1936a; 1937a.

executive committee of the National Civic Federation.[37] Easley characterized IH as a "hotbed of radicalism." This type of attack on IH would be repeated by Joe McCarthy against the IPR two decades later. If Easley and later McCarthy had meant by "radical" only the idea that IH and IPR wished to make fundamental changes in the organization and goals of the United States and other nations, they would have been on firm ground. McCarthy chose to obfuscate matters by using the term communism in a lose and often misleading way.

INSTITUTE OF PACIFIC RELATIONS, AN IH SISTER

We know with certainty that the first conference of the Institute of Pacific Relations (IPR) was held in Honolulu in July of 1925. As noted earlier, one account is that the IPR was born at that conference with leadership provided by Charles F. Loomis and John Mott of the Y.M.C.A. and money from John D. Rockefeller, Jr.[38] A secretary of the American Council, later known as the American IPR, for many years was Edward C. Carter, a veteran of the Y.M.C.A. movement.[39] Carroll Quigley offers a different account in *The Anglo-American Establishment*, saying that IPR was founded late in 1924 at Atlantic City and was part of the network of organizations created by the UK US elite which included the Institute of International Affairs and the Council on Foreign Relations.[40] Newspaper accounts at the time mentioned still other origins, one pointing to the Williamstown Institute of Politics and another mentioning the Pan-Pacific Union of Honolulu.[41]

The role of the Y.M.C.A. officials may seem incongruous. It is an organization known to most for its recreational services and its Christian identity. The organization's history, however, suggests that it may have multiple purposes. It has been supported and led by many of the most influential men in the world. The name, Y.M.C.A., was first used in 1844 by a group in London led by Sir George Williams. The first Y.M.C.A. organizations in North America were begun in 1851 in Montreal and Boston. Early leaders and supporters included

---

[37] New York Times, 1932a.

[38] Collier and Horowitz, 1976, p. 279; Hopkins, 1951.

[39] Thomas, 1974, p. 4.

[40] Quigley, 1981, pp. 192-4.

[41] New York Times, 1925b; 1925d.

J.P. Morgan, Theodore Roosevelt (the first President Roosevelt's father), William E. Dodge, Dwight L. Moody, Cornelius Vanderbilt, John D. Rockefeller Sr. and Jr., Cyrus McCormick, J. Ogden Armour, Julius Rosenwald, William Sloane, Mrs. Russell Sage, and the Swift family.[42]

Within just eleven years, by 1855, 250 associations were formed in locations around the world, and many others were to be created later.[43] In addition to its role as a hospitality and exercise center and as a promoter of its own brand of "muscular Christianity" (it may be a forerunner of today's Promise Keepers), the Y.M.C.A. organizations around the world would be excellent covers for a variety of intelligence activities. They would be useful, at the least, to provide information to the globally oriented millionaires and billionaires who have directed and financed this movement.

Whatever the details of the IPR's founding may be, its general nature is fairly clear. It was backed by figures associated with Morgan and Rockefeller interests and it had close associations with the Milner group within the British establishment. The Institute's leading supporters in 1925 included President Lowell of Harvard, W. Cameron Forbes (a United Fruit director and relative of Oswald's acquaintance Michael Paine), Bernard Beruch, John D. Rockefeller, Jr., Fletcher S. Brockman of the International Y.M.C.A., and Julius Rosenwald.[44] Rosenwald's daughter, Edith Stern, knew Clay Shaw and the Sterns's WDSU-TV station, as noted earlier, presented Oswald.[45]

For years the leading figure of the IPR was Jerome D. Greene. Greene was an official of the Rockefeller Foundation and then of the banking firm of Lee, Higginson and Company. He was also a member of the American Social Hygiene Association and of the General Education Board.[46] According to Quigley:

> Greene 'wrote' the constitution for the IPR in 1926, was for years the chief conduit for Wall Street funds and influence into the organization, was treasurer of the American Council [of the IPR] for three years, and chairman

---

[42.] Eddy, 1944, pp. 20-35, 94, 117; Morse, 1919, pp. 3-15, 70, 75, 86, 227, 258.

[43.] Eddy, 1944, p. 37.

[44.] New York Times, 1925; 1925a; 1925c; 1925d.

[45.] DiEugenio, 1992, pp. 157, 202, 206, 218.

[46.] A.N. Marquis, 1926.

for three more, as well as chairman of the International Council for four years.[47]

Quigley added that Greene linked the financial circles of London, and their leading representative Lionel Curtis, to those of the eastern United States. Those U.S. financial circles provided the money for IPR for three decades after its creation. That money came from the Rockefeller Foundation, the Carnegie Foundation, Standard Oil, ITT, International General Electric, National City Bank (Citicorp) and the Chase National Bank as well as from individuals such as Frederick Vanderbilt Field, Thomas W. Lamont, and Jerome Greene.[48] Lamont was vice-chairman of the IPR's American Council when Greene headed that group. Field later served as secretary of the American Council. Greene and Lamont worked closely with officials of the Council on Foreign Relations, the Foreign Policy Association, and the Carnegie Corporation.[49] Lamont handled the media for the Morgan interests, maintaining close relationships with Henry Luce of Time, Inc., Arthur Hays Sulzberger of the New York Times, and Mrs. Ogden Reid of the New York Herald Tribune.[50]

On the British side, IPR's significant early figures included Lionel Curtis of the Royal Institute of International Affairs, W. P. Kerr (Lord Lothian) of the Rhodes Scholarship, and W. W. Astor.[51] According to Thomas Mahl, Lord Lothian worked with Thomas W. Lamont to secure the Republican nomination for president for Wendell Wilkie in 1940. This effort was backed by the New York Herald Tribune. In this same period, the Establishment group working in the U.S. on behalf of a U.S.-British alliance included Alsop, Dulles, and Acheson.[52]

As was noted above, the IPR came under attack in the years after World War Two from non-Establishment conservatives who believed, or said they believed, that the IPR was serving communist interests. For a time IPR lost its tax exempt status and it relocated its headquarters from New York to Vancouver.[53] Although

---

[47.] Quigley, 1966, p. 956.
[48.] Quigley, 1966, pp. 946-7.
[49.] New York Times, 1929; 1953.
[50.] Lundberg, 1937, pp. 313-14.
[51.] New York Times, 1927a.
[52.] Mahl, 1998, pp. 26-27, 156-57, 175.
[53.] New York Times, 1955a; 1960; 1961.

the IPR was accused at times of promoting the interests of the Soviet Union,[54] which did affiliate with the IPR for a short period in the 1930's, the more substantial accusation was that IPR supported the Chinese Communists against the Nationalist Government of China. For example, Alfred Kohlberg, a member of IPR from 1928 to 1947, accused the IPR in 1953 of instigating a shift in U.S. foreign policy in July of 1943 by initiating a series of attacks on the Nationalist Government. Kohlberg, whose views were described by Thomas Lamont as "silly",[55] also complained that the IPR's trustees refused to remove communists from the IPR after he had made their identity known to the trustees.[56] Another former IPR member, and one-time adviser to General Douglas MacArthur in Tokyo, Kenneth Colegrove, informed a Senate committee investigating tax exempt foundations in 1954 that when the Rockefeller Foundation was informed in 1945 that the IPR was being "captured" by subversives, the Foundation failed to investigate the situation and continued giving money to the IPR.[57] In 1947 Arthur Dean, a J.P. Morgan man,[58] chaired a meeting of IPR officials and supporters which reviewed charges of communist influence within IPR and rejected those charges.[59]

For some reason, conservatives such as Kohlberg and Colegrove found it difficult to formulate the hypothesis that would explain the odd behavior of the IPR's leaders and backers. That hypothesis would be that those leaders and backers were themselves responsible for the change of policy on China and they wanted a certain type of leftist working for IPR because they were useful. This is a very important issue and it merits far more attention than can be given to it here. I think, however, that a sense of it can be gained by looking at a conclusion reached by Ron Chernow in his 1990 book *The House of Morgan*. About the Morgan group's view of government and the economy, Chernow concluded that the "House of Morgan always favored government planning over private competition, but private planning over either."[60]

This observation needs some revision and a little more clarity. The older dominant circles of finance in the U.S. definitely prefer to control events through

---

[54.] New York Times, 1959.
[55.] Thomas, 1974, p. 41.
[56.] Kohlberg, 1953.
[57.] Trussell, 1954.
[58.] Quigley, 1966, p. 952.
[59.] Thomas, 1974, pp. 43-44.
[60.] Chernow, 1990, p. 56.

private organization - that is their first choice. If this is not possible, they will support government action if they feel confident that they can dominate the government agency or the formation of the policy. Domestically, this produces a staunch general opposition to "big government" but it also means a willingness to create or expand government when this is the only way to achieve a goal (as with, for example, the creation of the Interstate Commerce Commission, the Federal Reserve system, and the Central Intelligence Agency).

In the international arena the thing they cannot tolerate is any effort, public or private, which will undermine their power in the world economy. They oppose any type of economic nationalism aimed at economic development, diversification, and independence. This is a policy with roots in the early history of colonialism. It is a policy of keeping other areas of the world poor and backward in order to exploit those areas and to prevent the rise of other centers of economic influence in the world. No one has done this better (or worse) than the British ("the sun never sets on the British empire"; "Britannia rules the waves"; "the white man's burden"; etc.). In the last couple of decades the neo-colonial policy has become mixed with a movement toward a global economy.

Non-Establishment conservatives misread the Establishment's outlook and purposes. Any strong political movement committed to using government to promote economic development, even if it preserves much of a capitalist economy, is intolerable to the Establishment. In the international arena, and in different ways at home as well, the primary enemy is activist government committed to economic progress. Establishment interests would prefer a weak or manipulable leftist regime, or even a communist government, in underdeveloped nations if that government has little or no development ambitions.

In China the U.S. and British establishments were confronted with a difficult choice. Back the Chiang Kai-shek nationalist movement, which included some pro-development, anti-colonialist people, or back the substantially anti-modernist, Maoist communists. Neither option was desirable. The Establishment fragmented over the choice with some important figures continuing to back the Nationalists (e.g., Henry Luce of Time, Inc.), but with the majority assuming positions ranging from unenthusiastic and relatively passive support for Chiang to reluctant tolerance of Mao. People associated with the IPR were in the second category. For example, in a book written just after World War Two, Thomas Lamont continued his long criticism of Chiang Kai-shek, opposed aiding the Nationalists, and questioned whether the communists in China really were communists.[61] Some of the lower level IPR people looked like or in some ways were "left-wing." Unfortunately, that was the only thing that interested many of the conservative critics of IPR.

INTERNATIONAL TRADE MART

In 1947 the International House in New Orleans, the International Trade Mart, and the International Trade Zone were three different but related elements of a drive to make New Orleans a major port for international trade.[62] The recently established Trade Mart, headed by Clay Shaw, was part of the general effort to create a system of international trade, free of government interference when possible. The file on Shaw compiled during the Garrison investigation noted that Shaw testified before the House Ways and Means Committee in 1956 as an expert on foreign trade. Then and at other times Shaw spoke in favor of global "free trade" and he opposed government measures, such as tariffs, to regulate trade.[63] As noted above, the ITM had a forerunner in New Orleans which was created the same year that IH in New York and IPR got under way. That was the International Trade Exhibition established in 1925. One of those involved in this effort was L.S. Rowe, the Director General of the Pan American Union.[64] The Union was almost certainly a sister organization of the Pan-Pacific Union of Honolulu which was involved in the creation of the IPR.

In 1947 IH and ITM were visited by Orin C. Judd, the secretary of the World Trade Corporation, headed by Winthrop Aldrich, chairman of the board of Chase National Bank. The Aldrich family was related to the Morgans, Whitneys, and Rockefellers.[65] Judd wanted to see if anything useful could be learned for similar efforts underway in New York.[66] Serving on the board of the Trade Corporation was Herbert Brownell,[67] who later was Attorney General under Eisenhower and brought with him to Washington his friend from Nebraska J. Lee Rankin. The

[61.] Cohen, 1978.
[62.] New York Times, 1947a.
[63.] Copy provided by James DiEugenio.
[64.] New York Times, 1925e.
[65.] Quigley, 1966, p. 530.
[66.] New York Times, 1947a.
[67.] New York Times, 1946.

year before the Trade Corporation was created, in 1946, Alrich and Allen Dulles gave speeches on world trade to a luncheon gathering in New York. Also addressing the group was John E. Lockwood, then a partner in the law firm of Curtis, Mallet-Prevost, Coit & Mosle. Lockwood, who had numerous connections to the Rockefeller interests, would be in the early-1960s a partner of John J. McCloy at Milbank, Tweed, Hadley & McCloy.[68]

In the same year that the World Trade Corporation was started, 1947, another significant group intensified its actions to promote international trade. This group, the World Commerce Corporation (WCC), started in 1945 as the British American Canadian Corporation. The president of the WCC was Frank T. Ryan of John J. Ryan & Sons. The WCC board included former Secretary of State (1944-45) Edward Stettinius of U.S. Steel, Canadian E.P. Taylor, former O.S.S. director William J. Donovan, and Sir William Stephenson ("Intrepid"), who ran British intelligence operations in the United States during World War Two.[69]

Stephenson worked closely during the war with Lord Halifax, the British ambassador to the United States.[70] In his 1957 book, *Fullness of Days*, Lord Halifax (Edward Frederick Lindley Wood, 1st Earl of Halifax) noted his friendships with Thomas W. Lamont, Dean Acheson, and John J. McCloy.[71] Halifax, then, knew well one of the three men directly responsible for the creation of the Warren Commission (Acheson), one of the two or three most important figures overseeing the operation of the Warren Commission (McCloy), and the father (Thomas Lamont) of the author (Corliss Lamont) of a pamphlet, stamped with the address "544 Camp Street", handed out in New Orleans by Lee Harvey Oswald.

Carroll Quigley, in *Tragedy and Hope*[72] and in *The Anglo-American Establishment*,[73] recounts how Neville Chamberlain, Lord Halifax, and Viscount Runciman acted to support Nazi aggression and virtually forced Czechoslovakia to capitulate to Hitler. Viscount Runciman's son, Sir Steven Runciman, was acquainted with Clay Shaw and knew some of Shaw's friends, including Sir Michael Duff and Peter Montgomery. Montgomery was the lover of Anthony

---

[68.] New York Times, 1946a; 1964a; Marquis Who's Who, 1962-63.

[69.] New York Times, 1947b.

[70.] Hyde, 1962.

[71.] Halifax, 1957, pp. 10, 247, 266, 289.

[72.] Quigley, 1966, pp. 632-5, 653-5.

[73.] Quigley, 1981, pp. 285-6.

Blunt, the famous spy associated with Kim Philby, Guy Burgess, and Donald Maclean.[74]

One of Anthony Blunt's closest associates in the late-1930s was Michael Straight. Michael was the son of J.P. Morgan partner Willard Straight and Dorothy Payne Whitney. The Payne family was a major investor in Standard Oil. Willard Straight was the founder of the *New Republic* and Michael became its editor in 1946. According to Quigley, the *New Republic* was created as a means of influencing the left. This was part of a general strategy of infiltrating all political organizations, conservative, liberal, left-wing, and right-wing. Thomas Lamont handled the left while Grayson Murphy handled the right.[75] As we will see in the next chapter, another Lamont, Corliss, was handling the left around the time of the assassination.

Michael Straight and the alleged spies Anthony Blunt and Guy Burgess were members of the Apostles, an "intellectual brotherhood" established at Cambridge in 1820. Another member was Bertrand Russell, the famous philosopher and activist.[76] We will look at Russell's peculiar involvement in events following the assassination in the next chapter. Before we leave Michael Straight, it is worth noting that he had some sort of affiliation with the Institute of Pacific Relations and he was acquainted with the IPR journalist Mark Julius Gayn.[77]

IPR AND OSWALD'S COUSIN

In light of the many conflicts between JFK and the Morgan-Rockefeller dominated Establishment over foreign and domestic policy, it is important that we recognize the direct connections between this network, or its close allies, and the events surrounding the assassination and cover-up. We have seen that John J. McCloy headed the New York branch of the Rockefeller backed International House while Clay Shaw was an officer of IH and of ITM in New Orleans. A relative of Oswald's "friend" Michael Paine, W. Cameron Forbes, was a founder of IPR. The daughter, Edith Stern, of another IPR supporter, Julius Rosenwald, owned the television station on which Oswald appeared and was, with her

---

[74.] Frewin, 1994, pp. 15, 18, 22, 26.
[75.] Costello, 1990, pp. 127, 203, 232, 357; Quigley, 1966, pp. 938-41, 945.
[76.] Costello, 1990, pp. 130-33, 240-41.
[77.] Costello, 1990, pp. 444-47; Flynn, 1953, pp. 40-42.

husband, friendly with Clay Shaw. These kinds of connections, along with the prominent role played by Rockefeller-Morgan people in the IPR, indicate that we take a new look at an old story about Oswald's cousin Dorothy Murret.

As Michael Canfield and Alan Weberman point out in their 1975 book *Coup d'etat In America*, there were allegations that Dorothy Murret was associated with Harold Isaacs while Isaacs was doing CIA backed work at the Center for International Studies. Isaacs, who for a time paraded as a Totskyist, had earlier written for the *Shanghai Evening Post*, *Newsweek*, and the *Christian Science Monitor*.[78] According to Dick Russell (*The Man Who Knew Too Much*), Isaacs was the house guest of Shigeharu Matsumoto, managing director of International House in Tokyo, at the time Kennedy was killed.[79] Isaacs was close to the mysterious Agnes Smedley, who was affiliated with the IPR and also worked for or with the famous spy Richard Sorge. Isaacs wrote for the IPR's *Pacific Affairs*. Matsumoto had been close to Sorge's collaborator Hotzumi Ozaki.[80] (I think it is important to note that while people affiliated with IPR such as Isaacs, Smedley, Ozaki, and Sorge appear a number of times in Russell's book, he never discusses the IPR or its connections to these people. Instead, he takes his analysis in the direction of people like the Hunt family and General MacArthur's aide General Charles Willoughby. The decision to ignore IPR, which has many more obvious connections to the assassination or cover-up than General Willoughby, seems arbitrary.)

Sorge was a Russian-born German who allegedly gravitated to the German communist party after his service in the German military during World War One.[81] Sorge is one of the most mysterious figures of the twentieth century. A German citizen born in Russia and executed in Japan, Sorge had strong connections to significant people in Germany, Japan, Russia, the United States, and Great Britain. The generally accepted view is that he was a communist spy in the 1930's and 1940's. I think that there are good reasons to question this view. The evidence clearly suggests an alternative hypothesis, i.e., Sorge was a spy for a network of powerful private interests with only limited loyalties to any particular nation. This network included people involved with the Institute of Pacific Relations.

[78.] Canfield and Weberman, 1978, p. 269; Cohen, 1978, p. 298.

[79.] Russell, 1992, p. 123.

[80.] Russell, 1992, pp. 122-3; Thomas, 1974, pp. 15-16, 19; Willoughby, 1952, pp. 206, 209.

[81.] Deakin and Storry, 1966, p. 20.

Among the people arrested and prosecuted in Japan in 1941 and 1942 in connection with the Sorge spy ring was Hotzumi Ozaki, Sorge's chief assistant and an active IPR member. Ozaki was executed with Sorge in November of 1944. Also implicated but not punished was the Oxford educated Prince Kinkazu Saionji, a longtime IPR member.[82] Not arrested, but implicated in Sorge's activities and affiliated with IPR were American Agnes Smedley and the German born Guenther Stein.[83] Stein later turned up at a 1945 IPR conference in Virginia as a member of the British delegation.[84] Like Harold Isaacs, Stein wrote for the Establishment's *Christian Science Monitor*.[85] Also a journalist, Agnes Smedley worked for Sorge's employer, the *Frankfurter Zeitung*, in the 1930's. Smedley left the United States in 1950 just before being ordered to appear before the House Un-American Activities Committee and died suddenly, at age 56, in a London nursing home.[86] Smedley had been close to Harold Isaacs in the 1930's.[87] The IPR apparently infiltrated General Douglas MacArthur's Tokyo headquarters at the end of the war in an attempt to learn about or influence MacArthur's investigation of Sorge.[88]

It is possible that Sorge worked for IPR related groups based in the United States and England with associates in Germany, Japan, and, perhaps, Russia. Some of the important things Sorge is credited with doing for the Soviet Union he may have done for the English establishment or England's friends within the U.S. upper class. For example, one of the most important of Sorge's accomplishments in Japan, where his cover was that of German newspaperman, was to propagandize in favor of a Japanese military strike to the south rather than against Russia.[89] The problem here is that a strike southward meant a strike against the United States. Everyone in England and the U.S. who wanted to bring the U.S. into the war on the side of England had an interest in seeing that happen. So, who were Sorge and his IPR related associates serving in this enterprise?

Sorge was, at any rate, a rather strange communist. He described his brother as having been an "extreme leftist," saying that the brother had "strong anarchist

[82] Prange, 1984, pp. 162-3; Willoughby, 1952, p. 219.
[83] Pringe, 1984; Willoughby, 1952, p. 218.
[84] Willoughby, 1952, p. 218.
[85] Quigley, 1966, p. 953.
[86] Willoughby, 1952, p. 212.
[87] Willoughby, 1952, p. 206.
[88] New York Times, 1951a.
[89] New York Times, 1951a.

leanings rooted in Nietzsche and Stirner".[90] Sorge's concepts of political direction were broad enough to include the ultra-reactionary, nihilist Friedrich Nietzsche as part of the "left."

Sorge's own history is rather unusual. Born in Russia, educated in Germany, he studied under Dr. Kurt Gerlach who had been educated in England. While still in his twenties, Sorge spent time at the Institute for Social Research in Frankfurt in the early 1920s and was at that time close to Alfons Paquet, a Quaker writer. According to F. W. Deakin and G. R. Storry (*The Case of Richard Sorge*), there were indications around 1926 and 1927 that there were two Richard Sorges, one in Germany and one in Russia.[91] It is hard to ignore the parallel with Oswald being seen in the United States while he was in Russia.

Sorge went to Shanghai in 1930 where he began, or renewed, a relationship with Agnes Smedley. The IPR associated Smedley introduced Sorge to the IPR member Hotzumi Ozaki who later would become Sorge's primary link to Japan's premier in the years leading up to World War Two, Prince Fumimaro Konoye.[92] IH managing director Shigeharu Matsumoto was an advisor to Konoye in those years and the IPR's Prince Kinkazu Saionji was close to Konoye.[93]

While in Shanghai in the early-1930's Sorge served on a committee with Harold Isaacs that was formed to defend a member of the Swiss Communist Party arrested in Shanghai in 1931.[94] Back in Germany in 1933 Sorge prepared to go to Tokyo as a correspondent for the *Frankfurter Zeitung*. He got a letter of introduction to use in Japan from Karl Haushofer, the famous Nazi theorist of geopolitics.[95] In 1938 Sorge wrote a two part article that appeared in Haushofer's *Zeitschrift fur Geopolitik*.[96]

Sorge's espionage activities in Japan extended over a period of almost a decade. His performance was at times less than satisfactory in the eyes of his Soviet masters (or dupes). During the time of the Russo-German nonaggression pact, signed in August of 1939, Sorge was severely criticized for the lack of and low quality of intelligence that he was providing.[97] His performance would make

---

[90.] Willoughby, 1952, p. 103.

[91.] Deakin and Storry, 1966, pp. 25-33, 45.

[92.] Deakin and Storry, 1966, pp. 70-76.

[93.] Prange, 1984, pp. 163, 182.

[94.] Deakin and Storry, 1966, p. 88.

[95.] Deakin and Storry, 1966, pp. 100-1.

[96.] Prange, 1984, p. 203.

[97.] Deakin and Storry, 1966, pp. 219-22.

sense if he was working for a London-New York-IPR network. A Russian-German alliance offered nothing very useful to an Anglo-American Establishment which then had an interest in pitting Germany and Russia against each other.[98]

In the 1936-41 period, money for Sorge's group, allegedly coming from Moscow, was funneled through the Stillman-Rockefeller-Morgan controlled National City Bank (today's Citicorp/Citibank) and the American Express company.[99] This is somewhat puzzling if Sorge was an important Soviet spy; it makes complete sense if Sorge's group was part of an IPR related operation.

Ozaki was arrested as a traitor and spy on October 15, 1941. The IPR associated Japanese Prime Minister, Prince Konoye, resigned the next day. Sorge was arrested on October 18. As noted earlier, Sorge and Ozaki were executed in 1944. Fifteen other people were convicted as participants in the Sorge ring. All but one, Sorge's radioman Max Klausen, were Japanese.

The man who oversaw the investigation of this spy ring after the war ended was MacArthur's assistant General Willoughby. Willoughby, who later wrote *The Shanghai Conspiracy*, apparently believed that Sorge was a Soviet spy. Assuming that, he then suspected the IPR people of being communists or the dupes of communists. Given Sorge's associations and history it seems reasonable to reverse that thinking. That is, Sorge worked for those New York-London finance aristocrats and quite naturally had the multiple connections to IPR.

Deakin and Storry end their book about this affair by saying that the roles of Agnes Smedley and Guenther Stein in the Sorge affair are "baffling."[100] Their roles seem extremely odd as long as we hold onto the official story that Richard Sorge was a Soviet agent and that he controlled this spy ring. If either of those two assumptions is wrong, then the participation of Stein and Smedley is no longer odd. If Sorge was a double agent or was himself manipulated by agents of the IPR network (like Smedley or Stein or even the radioman Max Klausen), then the only odd thing to explain is the extent to which the Soviets were deceived.

If Oswald's cousin did know or work for Harold Isaacs, then we have still one more direct link between members of the Anglo-American Establishment and those involved in the events surrounding the murder of the principled thirty-

---

[98.] Quigley, 1981.

[99.] Deakin and Storry, 1966, pp. 212-3.

[100.] Deakin and Storry, 1966, pp. 341-2.

fifth President of the United States. This is not meant to imply that Dorothy Murret knew about or played any role in the assassination. I know of no reason to think she knew anything prior to the assassination. If, however, she was connected to Isaacs it is still one more area in which the Establishment enemies of Kennedy show up. Some other figures, involved in the cover-up, do show up in relation to IPR.

Of the three men who acted to have the Warren Commission created, Joseph Alsop, Eugene Rostow, and Dean Acheson, two played some role in the controversy surrounding IPR. Also, two of the top men at the FBI who directed the FBI's cover-up of the assassination, Alan Belmont and J. Edgar Hoover, participated in key events related to IPR. All of the above mentioned four men acted in ways that were supportive of IPR or its members. Much of this developed around the somewhat mysterious Owen Lattimore.

Oswald's cousin's alleged associate Harold Isaacs and two of Sorge's known IPR associates, Guenther Stein and Agnes Smedley, were acquainted with Owen Lattimore of IPR.[101] The case of Owen Lattimore was the most publicized of a series of instances in which members of the IPR or the organization as a whole were accused of communist ties or sympathies by Senator Patrick A. McCarran's Internal Security Subcommittee and by Senator Joseph McCarthy. McCarthy acted in relation to the McCarran Committee and on his own. As has happened frequently in areas like this, Senators McCarran and McCarthy and others knowingly or unknowingly misrepresented the nature of the problem. Lattimore, rather than being the agent of a communist government, was used as an agent by the higher circles associated with the IPR. One possibility is that McCarran and McCarthy were seeing too much red to be able to systematically investigate that relationship.

One of the people who came to the defense of people associated with Owen Lattimore was Dean Acheson. Acheson did claim that he did not know Lattimore personally; others implied that he did.[102] Acheson's agent in pressuring President Johnson to create the Warren Commission, Joseph Alsop, was more deeply involved, at least in public, in the defense of Lattimore. In September of 1951 Alsop entered the controversy by publicly attacking Senator McCarran and

---

[101.] Newman, 1992, pp. 24, 183.

[102.] Acheson, 1969, pp. 363-4; Flynn, 1953, pp. 74, 92-5; Newman, 1992, p. 24.

defending IPR and Lattimore. This repeated the defense of IPR offered in 1944 by another Establishment luminary, Thomas Lamont of J. P. Morgan & Co.[103]

Alsop tried to put IPR's alleged Chinese communist sympathies in a positive light by pointing to the anti-nationalist and somewhat pro-Mao Tse Tung articles published by *Time*, the *New York Herald Tribune*, and the *New York Times*.[104] Alsop and Lattimore had known each other in the early-1940's when Alsop was an aide to General Claire Chennault.[105] Alsop also played a role in the events surrounding the Sorge spy ring. In 1948 columnist Drew Pearson said that Secretary of Defense James V. Forrestal wanted to give the Army's top secret report on the Sorge spy ring to Joe Alsop.[106]

What we have here is Establishment conservatives coming to the defense of friends under attack by non-Establishment conservatives. The image of poor liberals under assault by right-wing fanatics is substantially an Establishment created image and myth. This myth making was helped by the contentless and inconsistent use of political labels by people such as Joe McCarthy. Toward the end of McCarthy's reckless activities he was going after elements of the U.S. Establishment, but he persisted in talking as if he were chasing commies. Consequently, few people understood why he was turned into a symbol of evil. It was not because he was an unscrupulous red hunter. There were plenty of those around. It was because he chose to hunt on the Establishment's preserve. New York Times writer J. Anthony Lukas was correct when he said that Joe McCarthy's "real target was the Eastern Establishment."[107] It is interesting and it makes sense that John J. McCloy compared McCarthy to those in Congress who attacked the corporate establishment during the New Deal.[108] In saying this, McCloy was implicitly agreeing with what Lukas said about McCarthy.

In some ways, an even more intriguing link between the IPR controversy and the Kennedy assassination is evident in the FBI's response to the non-Establishment conservative's attack on IPR. Although there were people in the FBI anxious to pursue charges against Lattimore and the IPR, J. Edgar Hoover and Alan Belmont, who was the head of the New York office and then the number three man in the FBI, were not interested in doing so. This is virtually

---

[103.] Newman, 1992, pp. 127, 341.
[104.] Newman, 1992, p. 342.
[105.] Newman, 1992, p. 63.
[106.] Willoughby, 1952, p. 9.
[107.] Lukas, 1971, p. 123.
[108.] Brinkley, 1983, p. 42.

identical to their attitude toward Lee Harvey Oswald. That is, the normally enthusiastic red hunters at the top of the FBI had no interest in Oswald's various connections to ostensibly left-wing people because such an interest would have gotten in the way of the single assassin story and real investigation of Oswald would have led to International House and the Institute of Pacific Relations rather than to Fidel Castro. The FBI's determined avoidance of information in the case of the Kennedy assassination had been demonstrated earlier in the Lattimore-IPR episode.

On numerous occasions the FBI refused to cooperate with the conservative critics of IPR and Lattimore. In 1950 the FBI reacted to a State Department investigation of IPR by criticizing the investigation rather than IPR.[109] Part of the State Department report was based on information provided by the former IPR member Alfred Kohlberg. Back in 1947, Belmont, then head of the New York FBI office, had challenged Kohlberg's credibility when Kohlberg had first raised charges against IPR. Belmont later subjected Kohlberg to a very hostile interview. In October of 1950 the FBI simply stopped talking to Kohlberg.[110]

Also in 1950 Hoover sent a memo to Assistant Attorney General Peyton Ford in an attempt to discredit another IPR critic. In September of 1950 the FBI turned down a request from Joe McCarthy to see the FBI's summary analysis of Lattimore. When a former communist, Joseph Kornfeder, charged Lattimore with being a communist, Belmont challenged Kornfeder's veracity.[111]

For about two years, from 1953 to 1955, Lattimore was under indictment and prosecution by the Justice Department. At the outset Belmont refused to cooperate with a Justice Department effort to scare a witness into testifying against Lattimore and throughout the two year period Hoover refused to cooperate in any way with the prosecution of Lattimore.[112]

This behavior is on the surface inconsistent with the FBI's history. There had long been at the top of the FBI a clear enthusiasm for surveilling, harassing, and intimidating a variety of people perceived to be subversive or radical. In the case of Lattimore and IPR, Hoover and Belmont lost their normal obsession with pinkos and radicals. I suggest that this is so because they knew, or came to know, that an investigation would lead to the highest levels of power. Similarly, when it

---

[109.] Newman, 1992, p. 172.
[110.] Newman, 1992, pp. 262-4, 269, 307.
[111.] Newman, 1992, pp. 225-6, 276, 325.
[112.] Newman, 1992, pp. 446, 454, 460-1, 464, 485, 487.

came time to investigate that unusual left-wing figure, Lee Oswald, there was more than just disinterest. Belmont and Hoover acted to prevent any real investigation because they knew, as with Lattimore and IPR, that they could not go where an investigation would lead.

CONCLUSION

The Institute of Pacific Relations, International House, the International Trade Mart as well as Permindex and the World Commerce Corporation were all expressions of the interests of groups of wealthy people based in New York, Boston, and London. They wanted an integrated global economy under their control. Kennedy wanted strong, independent nations cooperating with each other to advance common purposes. They wanted a passive and submissive federal government. Kennedy was an activist President in the tradition of Lincoln and Roosevelt. They wanted the majority of people to submit to whatever economic and social conditions the Establishment offered. Kennedy stimulated a hope for a better future. They thought that much or most of the world's people should remain forever poor. Kennedy sought an effective course of action to stimulate national and global progress. Kennedy, following the Constitution, thought that the Federal Government was obligated to promote the "general welfare." They thought it was supposed to promote their welfare. Kennedy believed in democracy. They did not.

Chapter Nine

ESTABLISHMENT RADICALS AND KENNEDY: LAMONT, CHOMSKY, AND RUSSELL

Leaders are usually killed because some group does not like their ideas and policies. If the ideas and policies survive and continue to guide decision making, then the assassination is a pointless and risky exercise. The ideas and policies must also be "assassinated." In order to cover up the assassination, the assassins must control the investigation. We have seen how this was done. A successful cover-up also requires that the leader's actual ideas and policies are never connected to the assassination. That would lead to the real assassins. The assassination of the ideas is then also part of the cover-up.

It follows that the cover-up of an assassination requires control over the actual investigation, a patsy, and an incorrect image of the dead leader. As we have seen, mainstream or conservative Establishment figures gained control over the investigation and created the official cover story, i.e., the President was killed by a lone nut, one who may have had communist tendencies. Around the time of the assassination and later a group of not so conservative Establishment figures were making their contribution to the cover-up. These Establishment radicals either attacked Kennedy or they suggested others patsies, or both. They contributed to the cover-up by distorting Kennedy's record and by directing suspicions to people who had little or nothing to do with the assassination. We will focus on three such Establishment radicals: Corliss Lamont, Wall Street's man on the left, the internationally renowned linguist Noam Chomsky, and Lord Bertrand Russell, grandson of Prime Minister John Russell, Duke of Bedford.

THE EVER CURIOUS CORLISS

Corliss Lamont's father, Thomas W. Lamont, was a leading figure at J. P. Morgan & Co. for decades. Corliss' brother, Thomas S., followed in his father's footsteps. The Lamonts were part of the East Coast Establishment which was and is elitist and very often Anglophile. Thomas W., like Warren Commission creator Dean Acheson and Warren Commission overseer John J. McCloy, was close to top British establishment figures such as Lord Halifax. The Lamont backed Institute of Pacific Relations, as we have seen, was a joint U.S.-British establishment organization which had several connections to Clay Shaw's International Trade Mart and International House and, perhaps, to Lee Oswald.

It was a pamphlet written by Corliss Lamont, entitled "The Crime Against Cuba," that connected Oswald to Guy Bannister. The pamphlet, which Oswald was handing out in front of Clay Shaw's International Trade Mart, was stamped with Bannister's office address, 544 Camp Street.[1] We will analyze this 1961 pamphlet in some detail later. It bears a striking resemblance to a 1993 book that attacks President Kennedy.

Corliss Lamont has been generally portrayed as a leftist. Certain types of conservatives have viewed him as a communist. Establishment commentators, like the editors of the New York Times, have portrayed him as a leftist or radical, perhaps with socialist or communist leanings or sympathies.

Corliss, like his father, attended one of the most prestigious prep schools, Phillips Exeter Academy, graduating in 1920. He graduated from Harvard in 1924, did graduate work at the New College, Oxford University, in 1924 and 1925, and received a Ph.D. from Columbia in 1932. His first name was his mother's maiden name; she was Florence Haskell Corliss. The Lamonts and Corlisses were also joined in business, in the form of Lamont, Corliss & Company, a distributor of goods produced in Europe, particularly of products from its Swiss subsidiary, the Peter Cailler Kohler Swiss Chocolates Company[2] (discussed briefly in an April 10, 1947, article in the New York Times, "Succeeds to Presidency of Lamont, Corliss & Co.", p. 41). Corliss was for many years a member and a director of the American Civil Liberties Union. In 1951 he

---

[1.] Gibson, 1996.
[2.] A. N. Marquis, 1940.

broke away and formed the Emergency Civil Liberties Committee. He served as chairman of that organization and was its primary source of financial support.[3]

The truth about Corliss Lamont is in the public record. While Senator Joseph McCarthy accused Lamont in 1953 of having communist affiliations and Republican Representative J. Parnell Thomas charged earlier, June of 1946, that Lamont was a propagandist for the Soviet Union,[4] it is pretty obvious that Lamont was always a member in good standing of the East Coast Establishment and there are many reasons to take Lamont at his word when he denied McCarthy's charges. As noted earlier, McCarthy had a habit of talking about communism while he pursued Establishment figures. Lamont said at the time that:

> In general, I prefer to see, not Communist parties, but moderate Socialist or Labor parties, like the British Labor party, put across socialism in Western Europe and elsewhere.

Declaring himself a "naturalistic humanist" similar to John Dewey, Lamont distanced himself from communism, saying that he rejected the idea that "a radical change in the economic system will do away with all social evils."[5]

The Establishment *New York Times* certainly agreed with Lamont's self-characterization. The day after McCarthy threatened to seek a Senate contempt citation against Lamont, the New York Times editorialized on behalf of Mr. Lamont's right to privacy. The *Times* implied that it accepted Lamont's disavowal on the charge of being a communist. It was McCarthy's accusations against people like Lamont and Dean Acheson that got him into trouble with the Establishment and it is this that led the Establishment to make him the symbol of ruthless, anti-Communist fanaticism. There were certainly other candidates for that role.

The *Times'* defense of Lamont and Lamont's own statement indicate that his socialist or labor politics were, "like the British Labor party", politics that did not threaten the upper levels of private Anglo-American wealth and power. That is, Corliss Lamont was a "house leftist" and the house was owned by the Establishment. Like a real upper-class house, it has a great many rooms, a couple

---

[3.] New York Times, 1967.
[4.] New York Times, 1946; 1953a.
[5.] New York Times, 1953b.

of which are devoted to controlling, defining, leading, or influencing what comes to be called acceptable leftist views.

In 1929, at the age of 27, Corliss Lamont joined a group supporting the mayoralty candidacy of socialist Norman Thomas. The *New York Times*, reporting on this in a neutral or favorable way (October 18, p. 10, "Fosdick On New List Of Thomas Backers"), noted that the list of Thomas supporters was headed by Dr. Harry Emerson Fosdick of the Union Theological Seminary. Harry Fosdick and his brother Raymond were both close to the Rockefeller family. In various ways they were involved in stimulating and supporting the increasingly internationalist activities of the Rockefeller interests. The internationalist efforts were part of the Rockefeller involvement with the Council on Foreign Relations (CFR), the Institute of Pacific Relations, and the Foreign Policy Association.[6]

Corliss' father, Thomas W., had been an important figure in the early development of the CFR. In fact, Lamont was a member of the United States Round Table Group which was one of a number of such groups created by Britain's Lord Milner. The CFR emerged from Lamont's Round Table Group.[7] In 1963, Corliss' brother, Thomas S. Lamont of J.P. Morgan & Co., was a member of the CFR. As is indicated on the pamphlet handed out by Oswald, Corliss was himself a member of the Rockefeller-Morgan backed Foreign Policy Association. In a 1940 letter to the *New York Times*, Lamont cited a Foreign Policy Association report as the source of his views on policy toward China.[8]

In December, 1932, the *Times* reported that Lamont gave a speech in New York promoting better U.S.-Soviet relations. Some right-wing Republican might see this as evidence of Corliss' communist inclinations. However, less than seven months later the *Times* was reporting on similar efforts led by Corliss' banker father and people such as Thomas S. Gates, future Secretary of Defense in the Eisenhower administration and one of the architects of the Bay of Pigs operation.[9] That is the kind of leftist that Corliss was. (Note: In June of 1934, Corliss got into some legal difficulties while participating in an ACLU street demonstration. His lawyer in this affair was Abraham Wirin.[10] As Lisa Pease has

[6] Collier and Horowitz, 1976, pp. 150-1.
[7] Shoup and Minter, 1977, pp. 12-13, 105.
[8] New York Times, 1940.
[9] New York Times, 1932c; 1933.
[10] New York Times, 1934; 1934a.

pointed out,[11] Wirin was a defender of the Warren Commission and its report and he was also the first lawyer to come to the aid (?) of Sirhan Sirhan. Some worlds are very small.)

In 1942 Corliss gave an address at a New York luncheon which opened a two-day session of the Congress of American-Soviet Friendship. Corliss was the chairman of the Congress. The honorary chairman also addressed the luncheon. That was Joseph Davies, a lawyer married to the primary owner of General Foods Corporation.[12]

In 1951 the Times reported on a letter written by Lamont to the Senate Subcommittee on Internal Security. Lamont once again, and truthfully, denied being a communist. He accused the Committee of trying to discredit the Institute of Pacific Relations (IPR). Lamont asserted that his own involvement with the IPR was quite limited although his father, he pointed out, was an active member and generous supporter of the IPR for over twenty years. Lamont described the IPR as an "excellent organization" and stated that in its attempt to paint the IPR "Red" the Committee was "concealing the fact that leading bankers and conservatives have been among its chief backers.[13]

Corliss was an Establishment leftist. As a house radical he criticized certain aspects of U.S. policy, particularly foreign policy. In various circumstances he may have done so to maintain his leftist credentials or to express Establishment disagreement with government policy or to promote a faction's viewpoint or to misdirect those who listened to him. He generally worked with or was in harmony with the Anglo-American interests with which his family was long associated. This remained true in the months leading up to the time when Oswald distributed that famous pamphlet stamped 544 Camp Street.

OSWALD'S LAMONT PAMPHLET

In the early-1960s Lamont was visible on a couple of fronts. He was an aggressive critic of U.S. government (i.e., Kennedy administration) policy on nuclear weapons and he was attacking Kennedy for his policy in Vietnam, invoking against Kennedy on more than one occasion the authoritative views of

---

[11.] Pease, 1998.

[12.] Lundberg, 1937, p. 413; New York Times, 1942.

[13.] New York Times, 1951b.

high level Establishment insider Walter Lippman. One of Lamont's attacks on the
Kennedy administration (and by implication Kennedy himself) came just weeks
after a serious rift developed between Kennedy and John J. McCloy over how to
organize and pursue peace and arms negotiations with the Soviets. Lamont took
no note of this conflict in his statements and apparently had no criticisms of
McCloy. (On June 30, 1961, the *Times* published two articles which clearly
display a conflict between Kennedy and McCloy ("Kennedy Urges Congress To
Set Up Peace Agency" and "Kennedy and McCloy Letters Proposing
Disarmament Unit"/pp. 1, 4[14]). These articles are important because some writers
portray Kennedy and McCloy as close collaborators in this process; they were
not.)

Corliss Lamont was also a critic of Vietnam policy. Even here he does not
appear to have wandered to far away from Establishment interests. As late as
1968 Lamont could still work with wealthy individuals such as Stewart Rawlings
Mott, heir to a huge General Motors fortune, and Robert Gimble, heir to
department store wealth, in offering to support Hubert Humphrey against
Nixon.[15] More importantly, when Lamont criticized Vietnam policy he did not
criticize the real forces that created that policy. Instead, he attacked President
Kennedy and President Johnson, referring in 1968 to the war as "Johnson's
war."[16]

In "An Open Letter to President John F. Kennedy," April 11, 1962, Lamont
attacked Vietnam policy. He addressed Kennedy or referred to him at least ten
times in the letter's thirteen pages. He referred critically to President Diem of
South Vietnam five times.[17] Nowhere did Lamont even allude to the major role
played by CFR associates of his father and brother in the formulation of a war
policy for Southeast Asia.[18]

In a May, 1962, statement published in *New World Review* Lamont again
attacked Vietnam policy. Here he does refer critically to John Foster Dulles,
Secretary of State under Eisenhower, three times. The U.S. government is
criticized four times, JFK seven times, and Diem twelve times.[19] Again there is
no mention of the origins of Vietnam policy at Wall Street's Council on Foreign

---

[14.] Also see Lamont, 1961; Waggoner, 1961.
[15.] Knowles, 1968.
[16.] Lamont, 1962; New York Times, 1968.
[17.] Lamont, 1974, pp. 221-24.
[18.] Shoup and Minter, 1977, pp. 223-49.
[19.] Lamont, 1974, pp. 225-31.

Relations and there is no mention of the fact that many of his father's friends and associates were promoters of U.S. intervention. Even with Dulles, Lamont presents him as simply a government official, leaving out his CFR-Wall Street background and connections. Both Kennedy and Diem would be dead in eighteen months. In a 1967 pamphlet Lamont was still saying that it was Kennedy's and Johnson's war.[20]

Some Americans could readily be forgiven for representing Vietnam policy as something originating with JFK and LBJ. In the 1960s most people did not know of Kennedy's inclination to disengage or of the pressure applied to Johnson to expand the war. Most Americans also had no real knowledge of the ways in which the Establishment influenced government policy (although that influence proved insufficient with Kennedy). As a member of one of America's most influential families and as a member of the Foreign Policy Association, Corliss Lamont most certainly did know about this. What Lamont was doing was leading all who disliked the war away from the real culprits. Opponents of the war, under Lamont's influence, were to blame JFK, LBJ, the government, or the United States, never the real actors.

This gets us to the Lamont pamphlet distributed by Oswald in front of Clay Shaw's International Trade Mart.[21] (Incidentally, Clay Shaw's employer in the 1930s, Lee Keedick, was a member from New York of the Foreign Policy Association in the 1950s and, therefore, probably knew Lamont.[22]) This pamphlet, which is reproduced in the Warren Commission's volume XXVI as Commission Exhibit 3120, is about Cuban policy and the Bay of Pigs operation. It is much like Lamont's writing on Vietnam.

In his criticism of the Bay of Pigs operation, which was planned in part at least by his father's associate at J. P. Morgan, Thomas Gates, Lamont does mention the Dulles brothers at the outset, but he has them acting on orders of the "Eisenhower administration" and the "National Security Council." There is no mention of the lifelong association of the Dulles brothers with various centers of private power. There is no analysis of the Security Council. The CIA as a bureaucracy is criticized several times. Lamont, of course, never even alludes to the huge connection between the top levels of the CIA and various elements of the upper class Establishment.

---

[20] Ibid., pp. 233-35.
[21] DiEugenio, 1992, pp. 217-19.
[22] Marquis Who's Who, 1954-55.

The real target of this pamphlet was, of course, Kennedy. JFK was assaulted by name about a dozen times and Lamont attacked the "Kennedy administration" an additional five or so times. The American government is also criticized a couple of times. In other words, as with Lamont's criticism of Vietnam policy, no important private entity, person, or group is focused on. He did mention favorably two of the Establishment's most loyal journalists - Scotty Reston, who was Johnny-on-the-spot declaring Oswald the lone assassin the day after the assassination, and Walter Lippman.

With both issues, the Bay of Pigs and Vietnam, Lamont's mission seems to be to lead "leftist" and "liberal" criticism of policy away from the Establishment and to focus it on political figures and government. Since the Establishment usually wants to limit the powers of government and since they are not keen on popular, elected figures who represent the many, Lamont's type of propaganda helps to create a win-win situation. In effect, the Establishment has it both ways. Go along with government policies they create or help to weaken government by blaming it for everything you don't like.

The people at the CFR and at the headquarters of institutions such as Citicorp, Chase Manhattan, and J. P. Morgan & Co. are happy to have the people hate JFK, LBJ, Nixon, or "the government". They didn't like JFK either and were and are lukewarm about the rest. Corliss Lamont performs, therefore, an important service and he is not alone. One of the century's best known philosophers, Bertrand Russell, performed much the same role. In fact he was Corliss Lamont's idol.

LORD RUSSELL

The last sentence in Lamont's autobiographical book *Voice in the Wilderness* is the following:

My aim is to follow the example of England's famous philosopher Bertrand Russell and keep on fighting for the great human causes until my dying day.[23]

[23.] Lamont, 1974, p. 320.

If we look at Lamont's idol, with whom he did have a personal relationship,[24] we will see what kind of leftists we are dealing with and the sort of thing that Lamont and Russell included in "great human causes."

Lord (or Earl) Bertrand Russell, who was born in 1872 and lived to the very ripe old age of 98, said that his early interest in history was further intensified by the fact that his family had played an important role in the affairs of England since the 1500s. As noted earlier, his grandfather, Lord John Russell, was Prime Minister in the time of Queen Victoria. Russell said that he learned history through the eyes of those who fought to limit the power of the King.[25] The limits sought would have been on behalf of the few, the English upper class and aristocracy, not the many.

Russell had an early attraction to an Hegelian idea that matter is illusory and that the world consists of nothing but mind.[26] (He did become critical of what he viewed as Hegel's glorification of the State.[27]) This may explain why he argued in his famous *Principia Mathematica* (1910) that mathematics is completely a matter of symbols and logic, i.e., it is not to be understood in any relationship to physical reality.[28] Russell's sometimes lack of interest in the material world was probably facilitated by the fact that he never had to concern himself with such matters. He was born to privilege and chose in his early-20s to be a man of leisure, an aristocrat. He then received a six year fellowship at Trinity College, Cambridge, which gave him status, money, and access to facilities but required no work.[29]

This background would provide at least part of the explanation for Russell's life-long lack of interest in achieving economic and material progress. As we will see, this leftist (and those who follow him or think like him) was essentially an aristocrat and certainly would find very little in Kennedy's policies to be pleased about and a great deal to dislike.

Aristocrats typically do not care much for the majority of human beings, a tendency which would provide part of the explanation of Russell's suggestion in the late 1940s that the U.S. launch an atomic strike on the Soviet Union.[30] They

---

[24.] Feinberg and Kasrils, 1983, pp. 77, 135; Lamont, 1974, pp. 71, 314.
[25.] Clark, 1975, pp. 24, 29.
[26.] Ibid., p. 45.
[27.] Russell, 1953, p. 53.
[28.] Clark, 1975, p. 107.
[29.] Ibid., pp. 60-63.
[30.] Feinberg and Kasrils, 1983, p. 10.

see no reason for most people to enjoy material comforts, are not appreciative of applied science and industry, and do not like strong government that is responsive to the many. They prefer weak government or, when necessary, strong government responsive to the few. Russell was at times less hostile to science and industry than some aristocrats, but he was otherwise a thoroughgoing aristocrat and elitist who thought that the world had to be organized under global institutions controlled by the right people.

In Russell's view, man's "collective passions are mainly evil" and when combined with the power of science those passions are a threat to "our civilization." Russell suggested, in 1924, that the "only solid hope seems to lie in the possibility of world-wide domination by one group, say the United States, leading to the gradual formation of an orderly economic and political world government."[31]

According to Russell, economic internationalism will have to develop first if political internationalism is to be successful.[32] Even then, the establishment of the new order will require violence. Russell said that if a single group becomes dominant in this increasingly integrated world, they will have to prove their dominance against resistant groups in the world, but, after suppressing "the first half-dozen revolts" most people will give up and submit to the "victors in the great world-trust."[33] Russell was about 52 years old when he wrote that.

Writing almost thirty years later, Russell said that if either of the major powers becomes dominant, the U.S. or Russia, it can "establish a single Authority over the whole world, and thus make future wars impossible. At first this Authority will, in certain regions, be based on force, but if the Western nations are in control, force will soon as possible give way to consent."[34] This is the man who somehow acquired the reputation of being one of the world's leading advocates for peace.

Russell's ambivalence toward science and technology is readily apparent in his 1953 book *The Impact of Science on Society*. Therein, he frequently acknowledges the positive potential of science,[35] but he also associates science and technology with a variety of evils (war, tyranny, dehumanization) and he indicates his preference for a kind of aristocrat's science, a science geared more

---

[31] Russell, 1924, pp. 62-63.

[32] Russell, 1924, p. 36.

[33] Ibid., p. 41.

[34] Russell, 1953, p. 93.

[35] Russell, 1953, pp. 6, 41-42, 85, 93.

to satisfying idle curiosities and less to production or the solution of practical problems.[36]

Because of Russell's desire for a unified world, he found JFK's interests in arms control to be a plus and he would support any peace initiative that he thought could lead in the direction of his new world order. However, most of Kennedy's program was diametrically opposed to Russell's goals. That would include, among other things, Kennedy's aggressive support for scientific and technical progress, for rapid improvements in standard of living in the U.S. and abroad, for strong and independent nations, and for strong and democratically responsive national government.

Since the arms race heightened the sense of nationalism and because it was part of the East-West tensions that made creation of a world government impossible, Russell was extreme in his criticism of anyone he perceived as contributing to it. This led Russell to charge that Kennedy and Harold Macmillan "are much more wicked than Hitler." He also referred to JFK and Macmillan as "murderers" who were among "the wickedest people that ever lived in the history of man."[37] Russell, of course, never referred to someone like Corliss Lamont's father or brother in this way. Thomas W. Lamont actually was affiliated with people who did support Hitler.

Russell's profound sense of superiority is reflected in a racial remark he once made. While visiting the United States Russell wrote in a letter his impressions of servants. He wrote:

I find the coloured people friendly and nice - they seem to have something of a dog's liking for the white man - the same kind of trust and ungrudging sense of inferiority. I don't feel any racial recoil from them.[38]

This remark was not made by an eighteen year old rich kid still influenced by aristocratic parents and peers. Russell was a sophisticated, world traveled 38 year old when he wrote that.

Russell made many equally horrible comments about other matters. Unlike Kennedy, Russell never argued for economic development as a way to painlessly slow down population growth. Instead, he offered a choice between a Malthusian solution of wars, pestilences, and famines on one hand and a world government

---

[36.] Ibid., pp. 19-20, 25-26, 49-51, 58, 60, 70.

[37.] Russell, 1969, p. 144.

[38.] Clark, 1975, p. 229.

which would impose controls on population growth on the other.[39] Noting that past wars had not been very successful in slowing population growth, Russell looked hopefully to the potential of bacteriological war saying that:

> ...perhaps bacteriological war may prove more effective. If a Black Death could be spread throughout the world once in every generation survivors could procreate freely without making the world too full. There would be nothing in this to offend the consciences of the devout or to restrain the ambitions of nationalists [as would be the case with Russell's world government solution]. The state of affairs might be somewhat unpleasant, but what of that? Really high-minded people are indifferent to happiness, especially other people's.[40]

Aldous Huxley, a co-founder with Russell in the 1930s of the Peace Pledge Union, expressed similar enthusiasm in 1959 for the possibility that a virus might appear that eliminated large numbers of people.[41] These kinds of comments reveal the real Bertie, and Aldous.

Russell wrote that he grew up assuming that the British Empire and British naval superiority would last forever. Therefore, he said, "it is difficult to feel at home in a world of atomic bombs, communism, and American supremacy."[42] World government would put control over those bombs in the hands of never identified Western leaders and reduce or eliminate the power that America, communism, and nations had acquired. Russell never did focus on the question of who would run this world government. He most certainly had in mind men such as himself.

RUSSELL AND THE KENNEDY ASSASSINATION

Lord Russell's life-long work, taken together, indicates that the way to get peace, equality, and freedom is to create a world government controlled by an Anglo-American elite which will impose its will on the world, with violence if necessary. Given this sort of thinking, it should not be surprising that Russell offered to solve the Kennedy assassination by putting together a committee of

[39.] Russell, 1924, pp. 44-48; 1953, p. 111.
[40.] Russell, 1953, pp. 103-4.
[41.] Bedford, 1973, p. 648; Clark, 1968, p. 240.
[42.] Russell, 1953, p. 108.

people drawn from a British elite that despised Kennedy. This group and their followers would then blame everyone and anyone who had little or nothing to do with the assassination.

In his 1969 autobiography, Russell says that he became suspicious of a cover-up in the months after the assassination and that he met Mark Lane in June of 1964. Shortly after this Russell and some associates formed The British Who Killed Kennedy? Committee. Russell pushed the view that the sponsor of the assassination was either in the United States government or it was local right-wingers or both.

Russell said that he suspected that "American Authorities" were responsible for the cover-up and that the problem with the Warren Commission was that all of its members were affiliated with or connected to the "U.S. Government."[43] Elsewhere he charged the Government with suppression of the truth and the United States Government with trying "to hide the murderers of its recent President."[44]

It is technically true that all of the Commissioners did hold or had held government office. But, Allen Dulles and John J. McCloy were first and foremost representatives of Wall Street and old money, not government. The same is true of the men who got the Commission created (Dean Acheson, Joe Alsop, and Eugene Rostow) and the men who managed the media's role in the cover-up. The man who appears to have run the FBI's part of the cover-up operation, Alan Belmont, left the FBI a year later and went to the private and very elitist Hoover Institution on War, Revolution and Peace where he was assistant to the director, Canadian born Wesley Glenn Campbell. We also know that two or three of the government men on the Commission had misgivings about it. In short, Russell is promoting a view which leads people to have vague suspicions about government bureaucracies while overlooking powerful private interests that we know played definite and critical roles in the cover-up.

Russell went to say that

It is known that the strictest and most elaborate security precautions ever taken for a President of the United States were ordered for November 22 in Dallas. The city had a reputation for violence and was the home of some of the most extreme right-wing fanatics in America.[45]

[43.] Russell, 1969, pp. 165, 198.

[44.] Feinberg and Kasrils, 1983, pp. 208-9.

[45.] Russell, 1969, p. 199.

As Fletcher Prouty, Dallas Police Chief Jesse Curry,[46] and others have pointed out, there were real breakdowns in the security arrangements. Maybe Russell knowingly used the word "ordered" rather than "implemented" in this statement.

The "right-wing fanatics" that orchestrated this assassination and cover-up clearly did not have pickup trucks and Texas accents, as is claimed by Russell. Virtually all the evidence available now clearly points to fanatics with Yale and Harvard diplomas and slightly British accents. Even in 1969, Russell, who had written a book on social and political power, had to have known he was misrepresenting the Commission and ignoring the important role played in the cover-up by the Establishment media. This was conscious misdirection.

THE BRITISH WHO KILLED KENNEDY COMMITTEE

Of the fifteen members of the British Committee set up by Russell, fourteen were listed in the British *Who's Who*. Most of them had attended Oxford or Cambridge colleges. They were part of the English Establishment. One of them, Sir John Calder, had worked for many years in various capacities with the Colonial Office, serving from 1948 to 1953 as Senior Crown Agent for the Colonies. Another, Sir Compton Mackenzie, worked for the Secret Intelligence Service (SIS) during World War Two and had at least some additional intelligence background.[47]

Also on the Committee was Hugh Redwald Trevor-Roper, long-time Rugius Professor of Modern History at Oxford. In his book, *Mask of Treachery*, John Costello indicates that Trevor-Roper was for a time a member of MI5, England's rough equivalent to the FBI.[48] At any rate, Trevor-Roper was acquainted with some of the famous or infamous people of the intelligence world. He was pretty close to the infamous Kim Philby and he knew Anthony Blunt[49] (both operating in the netherworld of double and triple agents, or something).

Trevor-Roper was a speaker at the first meeting, in 1950, of the CIA backed Congress for Cultural Freedom. This was part of an effort to organize and control an anti-Soviet left, an effort backed by Kennedy opponent and Warren

[46.] Curry, 1969; Prouty, 1992, pp. 291-95, 316.
[47.] Stevenson 1976, p. 13.
[48.] Costello, 1988, p. 380.
[49.] Ibid., pp. 381, 406-7.

Commission leader John J. McCloy.[50] Also, the CIA and McCloy, who served as a High Commissioner for Germany after the war, supported a magazine published in Germany, entitled *Der Monat*, which featured anti-Soviet leftists, including Bertrand Russell.[51]

Anthony Blunt was not only acquainted with Trevor-Roper, he also knew Lord Russell.[52] This indicates an indirect connection between Russell and Clay Shaw. Peter Montgomery was Anthony Blunt's lover and Montgomery's name was in Clay Shaw's address book. In addition, Sir Michael Duff, who also appeared in Shaw's address book and with whom Shaw reportedly had a sexual relationship, knew Peter Montgomery. Finally, Sir Steven Runcimann, an old friend of Montgomery, was also in the Shaw address book. Sir Steven's father worked closely in the 1930s with the Earl of Halifax, a close friend of Dean Acheson, co-creator of the Warren Commission.[53]

When Lord Russell and Hugh Trevor-Roper offered their advice and assistance to Mark Lane, one of the first critics of the Warren Report, Lane should have been very cautious. Was he? Trevor-Roper wrote an introduction to Lane's *Rush to Judgment* in which he implicates the Dallas police at least eight times in twelve pages while arguing that the Warren Commission made an honest effort. This absurd viewpoint is still being circulated in the 1990s. Was Jim Garrison suspicious when Bertrand Russell and his Secretary, Ralph Schoenmann, offered their support to his investigation? At the very least, he should have understood that he was consorting with people who detested most of what President Kennedy tried to do and most of what he was. Those are not the kind of people who would help solve the case.

Given the background we have reviewed on Russell, it should not be surprising that the man who gave the Russell Lectures at Trinity College, Cambridge, the year after Russell's death also wrote one of the most vitriolic attacks on President Kennedy - that is Noam Chomsky. Chomsky published those lectures as a book entitled *Problems of Knowledge and Freedom: The Russell Lectures* in the same year, 1971.

[50.] Bird, 1992, p. 357.
[51.] Ibid.
[52.] Costello, 1988, pp. 123-24, 129, 131.
[53.] Acheson, 1969, pp. 22, 29-33, 59-60, 68, 70, 125, 166, 659; Costello, 1988; Frewin, 1994, pp. 14-15, 22-23, 26; Quigley, 1966.

RETHINKING CHOMSKY

Noam Chomsky's *Rethinking Camelot: JFK, the Vietnam War, and US Political Culture* (1993) discredits and attacks Kennedy while protecting the private interests that promoted the Vietnam involvement long before Kennedy was President and continued to do so after Kennedy was assassinated. Like Lamont and Russell, Chomsky studiously avoids any mention of the Council on Foreign Relations (CFR) even though the CFR's leadership began planning for U.S. intervention in Southeast Asia in the early-1940s.[54] He never refers to high level figures at the CFR who were active promoters of the Vietnam War. Among the leaders of that group were John J. McCloy, Allen Dulles, David Rockefeller, and Henry M. Wriston.[55]

Since they were part of the Kennedy and Johnson administrations, CFR members McGeorge Bundy and Dean Rusk are mentioned, Bundy about ten times.[56] Their affiliations outside of government, including their CFR memberships, are never discussed, leaving the impression that the most important indicator of who they were is their position in Kennedy's government. Similarly, Averill Harriman, George Ball, and Michael Forrestal are all mentioned as government officials.[57] Chomsky does not point out that they were all CFR members and, as with Bundy and Rusk, he says nothing about their backgrounds or other private affiliations.

Throughout this book, in a pattern that is virtually identical to Lamont's writing on Cuba and Vietnam, Chomsky is totally silent on Wall Street, the Establishment, the upper class, and the CFR. Vietnam is Kennedy's war, and then it is LBJ's and Nixon's war. In at least three places the war is referred to simply as "Kennedy's war."[58] Those who created the policy are "Kennedy planners", "Kennedy and his circle," and "JFK and his advisors."[59] U.S. bombing missions in 1962 are "Kennedy's aggression" and the U.S. implemented "Kennedy's brutal strategic hamlet program."[60] Chomsky correctly notes that LBJ was a somewhat

---

[54.] Shoup and Minter, 1977, pp. 225-31.
[55.] Ibid., pp. 46-47.
[56.] Chomsky, 1993, pp. 49, 70-71, 89, 95-97, 130, 143.
[57.] Ibid., pp. 72-73, 87, 89.
[58.] Ibid., pp. 2, 61-63, 73.
[59.] Ibid., pp. 39, 59, 77.
[60.] Ibid., pp. 2, 52.

reluctant warrior in 1964, but he goes on to say that those who pressed for more aggressive action included "JFK's doves."[61] In fact, most of the people putting pressure on LBJ to expand the Vietnam intervention had had only a brief association with Kennedy and the important people pressuring LBJ were CFR, Establishment luminaries such as Rusk and Bundy.

Chomsky asserts that Kennedy intensified the U.S. involvement that began in 1954 thus "laying the groundwork for the huge expansion of the war in later years."[62] As Laurence Shoup and William Minter show in *Imperial Brain Trust*, formal discussion of the need to control Southeast Asia began at the CFR in 1940. In Chomsky's eyes, what Kennedy did in less than three years, under pressure from CFR-Establishment types, is what lays the groundwork, not over twenty years of Establishment activity.

Some of Chomsky's so-called evidence on what Kennedy intended to do is second hand, coming from sources that most informed people would find suspect. Proof of what Kennedy's intentions were is based on what Dean Rusk and Averill Harriman said Kennedy would do.[63] Rusk and Harriman, two upper level Establishment agents, are to be trusted, but Senator Mike Mansfield and long-time JFK advisor Kenneth O'Donnell are not.[64] Mansfield and O'Donnell, of course, said that Kennedy was deciding to severely limit or end our involvement in Vietnam. In the November 22, 1963, issue of *Life*, the editors of Time-Life-Fortune indicated that they shared O'Donnell's and Mansfield's perception that Kennedy was going to disengage from Vietnam, the difference being that they were against that decision.

In a few rare instances Chomsky himself is not so certain about Kennedy's intentions and thoughts. For example, on page 33 he says that Kennedy was "never fully willing to commit" to withdrawal proposals put forward by his advisors. What does that mean in a book that is otherwise committed to showing that Kennedy was an aggressor. Also, after blaming Kennedy for over two-thirds of the book, Chomsky (p. 116) says that the "internal record reveals that Kennedy left decisions in Vietnam largely in the hands of his advisors." I suspect that this was true for 1961 and, perhaps, much of 1962. If Chomsky believes what he said here, then the book as a whole makes no sense. It should have been

---

[61.] Ibid., p. 97.

[62.] Ibid., p. 23.

[63.] Ibid., pp. 73, 75.

[64.] Ibid., p. 116.

a book about the advisors, with plenty of discussion of Rusk's Rockefeller Foundation background and the blueblood ancestry of McGeorge Bundy. After analyzing the advisors to Kennedy, the Dulles brothers, the CFR, and the problem of neo-colonialism, Chomsky might have criticized Kennedy for going along with part of this policy for a period of time. That would have been a very different book and Chomsky apparently had no interest in such a book. I think Kennedy did go along for a period of time; he did so because he did not like communism.

There are unsubstantiated, and probably incorrect, accusations against Kennedy and there are instances where evidence cited by Chomsky does not support the point being made. Trying to prove that Kennedy's policy led to escalation, Chomsky quotes JFK's remarks from September 12, 1963, to show this. In fact , the remarks do not show this and quite likely imply something different. Kennedy said that "What helps to win the war we support; what interferes with the war effort, we oppose." He followed this with: "But we have a very simple policy in that area...we want the war to be won, the Communists to be contained, and the Americans to go home." Chomsky quotes these statements to demonstrate Kennedy's embrace of "extremist doctrines."[65] Kennedy's choice of words clearly suggests that Kennedy did not intend a full or major U.S. commitment. He didn't say we will win the war but that "we want the war to be won" and we will "support" "What helps to win the war." Taken at face value, these are hardly comments that represent what would have been extremist doctrine at the time. They are instead the kinds of comments that would lead the well informed editors of Time-Life-Fortune to warn the President against any plan of withdrawal.

Vietnam is not the only horror that Chomsky blames on Kennedy. Referring to the coup d'etat that overthrew Brazil's elected government in 1964, Chomsky says that Brazil's neo-Nazi Generals "took power with the help of the JFK-LBJ administrations."[66] Chomsky has no references or sources for this and he cites no evidence. There is no evidence that Kennedy had anything to do with the decision to overthrow that government. There is clear evidence to show that JFK's foreign policy opponent, John J. McCloy, supervised this operation, called Operation Brother Sam, about five months after Kennedy's death.[67]

[65.] Ibid., p. 93.
[66.] Ibid., pp. 11, 46.
[67.] Bird, 1992, pp. 552-53.

Similarly, Chomsky refers to "neo-Nazi National Security States" in Latin America "that had their roots in Kennedy Administration policies to prevent the Cuban rot from spreading."[68] Given the history of military and political intervention in South and Central America on behalf of such interests as United Fruit going back sixty years before Kennedy became President, this is clearly ludicrous. It is also ludicrous in light of the shift that Kennedy was enacting toward greater support for the rights and interests of the majority of people in Latin America. Chomsky knows better than this.

Chomsky refers to the Kennedy Administration's Alliance for Progress as "a statistical success and social catastrophe", except for foreign investors and domestic elites.[69] This comment is fundamentally bizarre on two counts. First, The Alliance was changed very soon after Kennedy's death. David Rockefeller pointed this out in his April, 1966, *Foreign Affairs* article. Rockefeller was almost gloating over the change. Second, the program under Kennedy only existed for a couple of years. With something on this scale, it is silly to evaluate it based on such a short period of time. If this were not a serious topic, we would have to suspect Chomsky of attempting to be humorous.

There are other strange stories in Chomsky's book. He charges Kennedy with introducing even more repression into Latin America, saying that:

> These improved modes of repression were a central component of Kennedy's Latin American policies, a companion to the Alliance for Progress, which required effective population control because of the dire impact of its development programs on much of the population. Related projects helped subvert democracy and bring on brutally repressive regimes in El Salvador, the Dominican Republic, Guatemala, British Guinea, Chile, Brazil, and elsewhere.[70]

Chomsky apparently decided here to just overwhelm the reader with charges against Kennedy. None of this is documented. The comments about the Alliance are absurd for reasons already stated. There is no evidence presented on the "brutally repressive regimes." We do know, for example, that Kennedy did defend democracy in the Dominican Republic while he was alive and that John J. McCloy and friends eliminated democracy in Brazil, not Kennedy.

[68.] Chomsky, 1993, pp. 16, 24-25.

[69.] Ibid., p. 25.

[70.] Ibid., p. 146.

There are other things. He describes the coup that overthrew Diem as "Kennedy inspired."[71] What does this mean? If he does not know that Kennedy ordered it, then this needs some explanation. If he knows that Kennedy ordered it, then the choice of words ("inspired") makes no sense. Chomsky is, after all, an expert on language, isn't he?

Chomsky refers to the program for manned exploration of the moon (a useful if not necessary step for further space exploration) as the "jingoist `man-on-the-moon' extravaganza." He criticizes Kennedy for implementing a huge increase in R&D funding. The Wall Street Journal said almost the same thing about this.[72]

Finally, Chomsky says that Kennedy posed no threat to "the business elite and the wealthy" citing info showing that Kennedy's tax breaks favored those groups. Chomsky went on to make the following comment:

> Note also that no policies relevant to the various theories about Kennedy-the-reformer were reversed under LBJ; those most opposed by the right were extended.[73]

There is of course no evidence for this statement of what did not happen. There is an abundant amount of evidence showing that most of Kennedy's basic economic policies, domestic and international, and his foreign policy were changed after his death. In the eighteen months following the assassination virtually all of the major pieces of Kennedy's program were abandoned.[74] Those policies related to the size and make-up of the federal budget, spending priorities, foreign aid, the Alliance, policy toward the Dominican Republic, Vietnam, and poor nations in general, interest rates, and other things. Chomsky apparently made this bold and unexamined assertion because that is the kind of book he was writing, a book to discredit and misrepresent Kennedy, a book to suppress the truth. Chomsky was the right man to deliver the first lectures commemorating Corliss Lamont's idol, Lord Bertrand Russell.

These three men together established a two fold strategy: first, discredit and misrepresent Kennedy and second, misdirect the investigation of his assassination. The misrepresentation of Kennedy's policies was also carried out

[71.] Ibid., p. 44.
[72.] Gibson, 1994, p. 66.
[73.] Chomsky, 1993, p 145.
[74.] Gibson, 1994, pp. 77-127.

by liberal and conservative writers.[75] We will look first at misleading work on the assassination in the next chapter and we will conclude with a discussion of the opposition to President Kennedy's policies.

[75.] Ibid., pp. 1-51.

Chapter Ten

THE INFORMATION AND
DISINFORMATION AGE

As we saw in the previous chapter, Corliss Lamont and Noam Chomsky have specialized in leading critics of U.S. policy into a general hatred of "the government." This diverts attention from the Establishment. Lamont's idol, Lord Russell, who hated Kennedy almost as much as he hated communism and nationalism, began just months after the assassination to promote the view that the power behind the assassination was either the United States government or local right-wingers, or both. He accused "American Authorities" and the "U. S. Government" of responsibility for the cover-up.

As we have also seen here, the initial cover story, and the one that became the official story, emerged during the afternoon and evening of November 22. In a dozen or so hours, or less, James Reston of the *New York Times* had already solved the case. Oswald did it because of a "strain of madness and violence" in the nation. Over the next few days the editors of the *New York Times*, the *New York Herald Tribune*, and the *Wall Street Journal* joined in this conclusion followed by *Time* magazine and, with a little less certainty, *Newsweek* and *U.S. News and World Report*.

Within a couple of days, Alan Belmont of the FBI was pushing the Oswald did it alone conclusion and shortly thereafter McCloy and Dulles were settling the dust with the same conclusion. The venue for the McCloy-Dulles work was the Commission created at the instigation of Rostow, Alsop, and Acheson. The cover-up was essentially an operation of private power based in the East Coast Establishment.

Eugene Rostow, Joseph Alsop, and, almost certainly, Dean Acheson were the men primarily responsible for pressuring LBJ into creating the Commission. None of the three held a government position at the time. All three had deep ties to the private Establishment. Their success prevented the emergence of Senate and House investigations. Those private individuals prevented more open investigations controlled by elected officials. Their success led to an investigation carried out in secret.

There is no evidence that the federal government was responsible for the initial promotion of the cover story, that is that Oswald did it alone and was probably a nut with leftist tendencies. Within a few hours of the President's death, Mayor Cabal of Dallas declared Oswald to be the lone assassin. The mayor, Earl Cabal, was the brother of General Charles Cabal, the former assistant at the CIA to Allen Dules. Kennedy had fired Charles Cabal and Allen Dulles in the aftermath of the Bay of Pigs fiasco. Around the same time, someone in the White House said something very similar to what Earl Cabal said. That person may have been quoting the wire services. Also someone provided, perhaps quite innocently, information about Oswald to the press within a couple of hours of the assassination. There was most likely a government source for that (Army intelligence, the FBI, CIA, or State Department).

By the night of the 22nd some of the most prestigious news organizations in the United States were declaring Oswald the lone assassin, an assassin with no real motive other than an irrational one born of mental instability. They were the first "authorities" to address the nation about the nature of the assassination. They were private authorities, not government.

The only acceptable explanation for the media's behavior would be that they knew with relative certainty that Oswald did it and did it alone. They had absolutely no way of knowing this. Given that, they must have had some reason to say what they could not know to say. There is no good reason for what they did. There was no visible unrest in the country. There were no riots, or lynchings, and no one was descending on the capital demanding that we attack Russia or Cuba or anyone else. No one was fomenting anything at this time. The only exception might have been some Senators and Representatives who were thinking that we should have an open investigation. To tell what amounted to lies at that time was in fact to create conditions of suspicion and unrest in the country. Those lies did lead later to all sorts of suspicions and mistrust.

None of the media that declared Oswald guilty needed to do that. Unlike the Dallas police they were under no direct pressure to provide answers to anything.

If they were worried about some future and imagined instability, they could have merely given great emphasis to the fact that the country's officials would pursue the truth and that there was absolutely no evidence that this was the act of a foreign government. Instead, they forcefully argued exactly the same point of view that would be set forth a couple of weeks later by Allen Dulles and John McCloy. This was a private cover-up.

McCloy and Dulles were the dominant people on the so-called Warren Commission. They frequently received support from Representative, later President, Gerald Ford. They were responsible for the appointment of J. Lee Rankin as General Counsel for the Commission. Dulles asserted the lone assassin theory from the beginning. They supported the magic bullet theory when other members of the Commission and key witnesses did not. They were present at, and often had significant influence on, the interrogations of many of the most important witnesses.

Was the Commission a government commission? Was it really the President's Commission or the Warren Commission? The critical roles played by McCloy and Dulles suggest that the Commission would be more accurately labeled the McCloy-Dulles Commission. Would it be correctly understood as a government commission? The answer to this is a slightly qualified but definite "no." A qualified no because the Commission was officially created by LBJ. It used government resources, particularly money and the FBI. It included a Chief Justice, two Senators, and two Representatives. Definitely no because McCloy and Dulles were first and foremost agents of the Establishment, not of the government. This is clearly true even though both men had previously held important government positions, although McCloy had not done so for over a decade prior to his brief work on arms control for Kennedy. Both of these men had always been the Establishment's men in the government; they were not the government's men in the Establishment.

Kai Bird, John J. McCloy's biographer, titled his book about McCloy *The Chairman: John J. McCloy & The Making of the American Establishment.* Mr. McCloy's character, values, beliefs, and politics were rooted in his private sector career and history, not in his career as a government official. Bird anoints McCloy the "Chairman" of the American Establishment (or Anglo-American Establishment) because of his service to the elite law firms of Cravath, Henderson & de Gersdorff and Milbank, Tweed, Hadley & McCloy, and because of his role as a leading figure at the Chase Manhattan Bank, Ford Foundation, and Council on Foreign Relations, and because he was lawyer to and representative of the big oil companies. As Bird indicates, being "Chairman" of the Establishment meant, in McCloy's case, being "servant to America's ruling elite."[1]

When McCloy served as a high commissioner in Germany or as president of the World Bank or as a member of the so-called Warren Commission, he did so as a servant of that ruling elite. His most extensive ties to that elite were to various Rockefeller family interests.[2] The other leading figure on that Commission, McCloy's longtime close friend Allen Dulles,[3] was also a man of that Establishment even though his name is almost always associated with the CIA.

Even in the case of Dulles' service with the CIA, what is significant about that history is not that he was a government bureaucrat, but that he headed an agency known to be dominated by private Wall Street and Establishment interests. His presence in that government agency was an expression of that dominance. The CIA was a replacement for the World War Two Office of Strategic Services (O.S.S.). The standing joke about the Office's initials was that they stood for Oh So Social, referring to the prominent roles played in the organization by upper class, Ivy League educated individuals.

The World War Two spy agency probably had a more diverse group of employees than its successor, but even the early version featured prominent members of the upper class in important positions. In addition to Allen Dulles himself, there were figures at the upper levels of the O.S.S. such as Andrew Mellon's son Paul and both sons of J. P. Morgan, Jr.[4]

Twenty-nine years before Dulles' service on the Warren Commission in 1964 and eighteen years before Dulles was appointed director of the CIA, he was a well known figure within the private, Morgan-Rockefeller led Council on Foreign Relations.[5] He was by ancestry, education, and association a member of that Establishment. He was one of those people whose work with the O.S.S. led to that Oh So Social joke. In 1935, 29 years before his service on the Warren Commission, Allen Dulles traveled to London as a representative of the Council on Foreign Relations to give one of the opening speeches at the meetings of the British Establishment's International Studies Conferences. Dulles served as

[1] Bird, 1992, p. 19.
[2] Ibid., pp. 19-20.
[3] Ibid., p. 485.
[4] Smith, 1972, pp. 15-16.
[5] Quigley, 1966, pp. 950-53; Shoup and Minter, 1977, pp. 85-114.

chairman of the study meetings.[6] Long before he held positions in intelligence or with the Warren Commission he was part of the private networks of power that bind together the upper classes of England and the United States. Long before he served as CIA director he was involved with those wealthy families looking to preserve the substance of the British Empire even as its form disappeared.

Seen against this backdrop, the so-called Warren Commission, or McCloy-Dulles Commission, was a creature of private power. What have the critics of the Warren Report said about this? What about the critics themselves?

CONFUSED AND NOT SO CONFUSED CRITICS, HONEST AND DISHONEST

Before the Warren Commission even issued its report, Lord Russell was forming his British Who Killed Kennedy? Committee and he was accusing the United States government and/or local right-wingers in Texas of the assassination. Russell's associate, Hugh Trevor-Roper, focused on the Dallas police in his introduction to Mark Lane's *Rush to Judgment* (1966). Since that time, with only a few exceptions, writers have blamed some part of the U.S. government and/or one or more of the following: organized crime, Cuban exiles, Conservative Texans or other right-wingers who don't live in the Northeast, unidentified rich guys, stock speculators, and/or the Israeli Mossad.

When the government is blamed, one or more of the following are accused: the Government, the executive branch, the CIA, elements within the CIA, the military or elements thereof, the military-intelligence complex, Army intelligence, elements of the FBI, elements of the Secret Service, and/or, by name, J. Edgar Hoover, LBJ, Nixon, and/or Clint Murchison. Taken quite literally not all of these accusations can be true. There probably were not enough people in Dealy Plaza that day to represent all those groups. The shooters would have been shooting each other.

A lot of this stuff is pathetic or absurd. Some of it is one step away from the fictional wanderings in the X-Files. Were it not for the significance of the events, some discussions would just be funny (like Bonar Menninger's 1992 book arguing that a Secret Service agent just happened to accidentally shoot Kennedy in the head while Oswald was coincidentally shooting at him, i.e., the only

[6.] Quigley, 1981, pp. 194-95.

accidental discharge of a Secret Service weapon around a President in one hundred years would by chance hit the President in the head and would by chance occur in the six or so seconds during which someone else was shooting at the President.). A few people have repeated or supported the Warren Report and have simply followed the lead of McCloy and Dulles and blamed Oswald. None of these people has seriously examined the cover-up. An early example of this would be Edward Jay Epstein's *Legend: The Secret World of Lee Harvey Oswald*, published in 1978. A later example is Gerald Posner's 1993 book *Case Closed*. Interestingly, one of the blurbs written for the book jacket of Posner's book came from Tom Wicker, who says that Posner has closed the case. Wicker's praise of Posner displays too much modesty since Wicker himself had substantially closed the case within hours of the shooting. It took Posner about thirty years to do it. Wicker may have followed the lead in 1963 of his superior at the *Times*, James Reston.

Among those who believe there was a conspiracy and who have focused on non-governmental forces, the favorite suspects are organized crime, anti-Castro Cubans, and various types of non-Establishment right-wingers. With one exception, none of these kinds of people appear in any significant role in the cover-up. The exception is Jack Ruby. Among the few certain things in the events surrounding the assassination is that Ruby shot Oswald. Ruby did have connections to organized crime. The problem is that no one knows why Ruby killed Oswald and we have no way of knowing what might have been the ultimate source of any pressure that might have been applied to Ruby to get him to shoot Oswald.

In Oswald's background there are a couple of indirect connections to organized crime figures. The most notable is Oswald's connection to David Ferrie who did some work for organized crime figure Carlos Marcello. The problem here is that Ferrie had many connections to other groups and there is no evidence that Oswald's association with Ferrie or Ferrie's association with Marcello had anything to do with the assassination. One can believe that organized crime killed the President, but the evidence for this is not much more substantial than the evidence for the existence of unicorns. Even if Marcello or Ferrie was a significant figure in the assassination we do not know that they acted on behalf of organized crime.

The only other possible connection to organized crime is Oswald's uncle Charles Murret. Murret's connection to Marcello was apparently in the area of gambling and bookmaking, not murder, and there is no evidence at all that this connection was of any significance. As we saw earlier, Charles Murret's daughter and Oswald's cousin, Marilyn Murret, had interesting connections to a variety of people other than organized crime figures.

The only substantial thing that we are left with out of this is that Ruby's history with crime types may have had something to do with his reasons for killing Oswald, but we do not know what that is. We do know that the cover-up was carried out by other kinds of people, people who definitely do not take orders from any Godfather. We must also suspect that killing a President would be viewed by organized crime figures as an enterprise that is just too dangerous. There certainly is absolutely no reason that they would expect or receive immediate help from the likes of a James Reston, Eugene Rostow, Dean Acheson, or John J. McCloy.

In spite of the mystery of Jack Ruby, all claims that organized crime assassinated the President of the United States are mere assertions, having no direct evidence related to the assassination and being contradicted by almost everything we know about events following the assassination. Nevertheless, organized crime or "the mob" or the Mafia is one of the favorite targets of many assassination books.[7]

Another favorite suspect is anti-Castro Cubans. They, of course, show up nowhere in the cover-up and there seems to be absolutely no direct evidence that they played any role in the assassination. Perhaps a few of those Cubans knowingly or unwittingly played some role in the orchestration of Oswald's activities prior to the assassination. Even if they did, there is no evidence that they as a group or an organization were in any sense a significant force in these events. Even so, they are frequently implicated.[8]

Right-wingers of several types have been identified as a or the force responsible for the assassination. One version of this is that the assassination was part of an attempt by wealthy Texans to seize power from Wall Street. The first version of this appeared in Thomas Buchanan's 1964 book *Who Killed Kennedy?*

---

[7] Anson, 1975, p. 344; Canfield and Weberman, 1975; Davis, 1989; Duffy, 1992, p. 235; Furiati, 1994, p. 125; Groden and Livingstone, 1989, p. 364; Marrs, 1989, p. 580; North, 1991; Oglesby, 1977, p. 324; Piper, 1993, pp. 8, 286, 288; Roberts, 1994, p. 188; Russell, 1992, p. 705; Scott, 1993; Summers, 1989, pp. 243-61.

[8] For examples see: Anson, 1975, p. 344; Duffy, 1992, p. 235; Furiati, 1994, p. 125; Groden and Livingstone, 1989, p. 364; Marrs, 1989, p. 580; Meagher, 1967, 384-86; Model and Groden, 1976, pp. 22-23; Oglesby, 1977, p. 324; Roberts, 1994, p. 188; Russell, 1992, p. 703; Summers, 1989, p. 227.

(There may be some connection between the title of this book and the name of Lord Russell's group, the British Who Killed Kennedy? Committee.) Buchanan implicated wealthy Texans based in Dallas, naming the Murchison family. A later version of this view was produced by Carl Oglesby in his 1977 *The Yankee and Cowboy War.*

According to Oglesby[9] "JFK was killed by a rightist conspiracy formed out of anti-Castro Cuban exiles, the Syndicate, and a Cowboy oligarchy supported by renegade CIA and FBI agents." The Cowboys were killing a Yankee President. Oglesby defined Yankee as Wall Street, the Council on Foreign Relations and Ivy League. Among the leading Yankees according to Oglesby were David Rockefeller and the Dulles brothers. This is a ludicrous idea. It is probably worse than that.

As we have seen, it was "Yankees" who carried out the cover-up, including Allen Dulles. As I briefly indicated in Chapter One and as I have shown elsewhere,[10] including in the final chapter of this book, Kennedy was at war with those "Yankees," including David Rockefeller. Kennedy was definitely, unmistakably at war with the same forces Oglesby claims that JFK represented. This may be simply a very big misunderstanding; it may be a big lie. There is no evidence that Texans organized the assassination. There is some evidence that the idea of a Yankee-Cowboy conflict is mostly or wholly a fiction. For example, according to Ferdinand Lundberg, Yankees were deeply involved in and owned much of the wealth of Texas[11] and, according to G. William Domhoff, the upper class of Texas intermingled with that of New York.[12] Oglesby has misrepresented everything he discusses.

Others have simply dumped various wealthy and/or conservative groups into the mix with no real evidence. Often this ends up being something like a laundry list of plausible or conceivable suspects (minus the New York-Boston upper-class Establishment). For example, Groden and Livingstone[13] blame CIA controlled Cuban exiles, organized crime, the "Ultra Right Wing" and "some politically well connected wealthy men." Mentioning "wealthy men" enhances the credibility of the list but it is too vague to lead anywhere.

---

[9] Oglesby, 1977, p. 324.
[10] Gibson, 1994.
[11] Lundberg, 1968, p. 55.
[12] Domhoff, 1974.
[13] Groden and Livingstone, 1989, p. 364.

Sometimes powerful and conservative private interests become part of a list of suspects that is so long that one winds up blaming everyone. Once you are blaming just about everyone, you might as well do what Henry Hurt did in his 1985 book *Reasonable Doubt*. That is, he ends up saying that there was a conspiracy but that he doesn't know who or why. It is not at all clear why Hurt would even care. Hurt sees little of value in Kennedy, saying that Kennedy's positive image is based on illusions. Hurt's opinion of the Warren Commission is more positive than his view of Kennedy.[14]

An example of someone who mixes "Cowboys" with a laundry list of suspects is James Hepburn's *Farewell America* (1968). Although the book contains some interesting political discussion, Hepburn ends up arguing that wealthy conservatives from Louisiana and Texas led an assassination group that included the far right, people in the CIA, the Dallas police, big oil, big business, the FBI, and others. Something similar is done by Harrison Livingstone who mixes in a couple of people who did contribute to the cover-up with a lengthy and loose list of others.

Livingstone[15] implicates the military, Texas oil people, the FBI, an unidentified "wealthy Establishment," the corporations Bell Helicopter and General Dynamics, the government, the Office of Naval Intelligence, and, by name, H. L. Hunt, Lyndon Johnson, Clint Murchison, General Charles Cabal, Mayor Earl Cabal, the CIA's David Atlee Phillips, Richard Nixon, and Dallas Chief of Police Jesse Curry. This is an assassination acid trip. There is no evidence at all for the smears against Johnson and Nixon, and Jesse Curry was one of a few officials to indicate that there had been a conspiracy. Curry wrote one of the few useful books about the assassination. Much of the rest of it is so vague and general that it could be neither proven nor disproven. Livingstone[16] also suggests that "New York banks and their owners" may have played some role because Kennedy was a fiscal conservative and the bankers hated this. In fact, bankers and parts of the media criticized Kennedy for almost the opposite reasons and government policies became decidedly more conservative shortly after Kennedy's death.[17]

---

[14] Hurt, 1985, pp. 4, 29, 43.
[15] Livingstone, 1993, pp. xxxiv, 542-51.
[16] Ibid., pp. 542, 547.
[17] Gibson, 1994, pp. 84-87.

Among others who present a long list of poorly defined or excessively general (e.g., "rich people") suspects are Jim Marrs, Craig Roberts, Dick Russell, and Peter Dale Scott. Marrs[18] implicates LBJ, organized crime, anti-Castro Cubans, the CIA, business and banking interests, the Southwestern oil interests, and the military. Marrs combines a dizzying array of forces and he does this without consistency. For example, near the end of his book, *Crossfire*, he says that the assassination involved "the highest level of the American business-banking-military-crime power structure." He goes on to pose the question "Who done it?" and then provides the following answer:

> A consensus of powerful men in the leadership of U.S. military, banking, government, intelligence, and organized crime circles ordered their faithful agents to manipulate Mafia-Cuban-Agency pawns to kill the chief. President Kennedy was killed in a military-style ambush orchestrated by organized crime with the active assistance of elements within the federal government of the United States. Pressure from the top thwarted any truthful investigation.[19]

This is much too vague. For example, who or what is "the leadership" of the U. S. government? Obviously it is not the President. Based on nothing, it is asserted that organized crime played a leading role. If they did, why was the ambush a military- style ambush instead of a mob hit?

Craig Roberts[20] has implicated anti-Castro Cubans, the CIA, the Mafia, the Military-Industrial-Banking complex, and LBJ and his Texas backers. Roberts says in his 1994 book *Kill Zone* that the primary force behind the assassination was an "international banking cabal" which wanted to prevent Kennedy from ending deficit spending, eliminating national debt, and putting the country back on the gold standard. No evidence or sources are offered for these Kennedy policies. They are essentially the opposite of or are irrelevant to Kennedy's primary economic goals and his policies. The idea of a banking cabal is not inconsistent with what we know about the cover-up. However, Roberts does not define it and so one is left to conjure up any imaginary group one wants. His completely unsupported and inaccurate listing of motives makes this an even bigger problem. It is very similar to what Livingstone did.

Dick Russell offers a lengthy list of suspects in his *The Man Who Knew Too Much* (the insider joke is that the 824 page book should have been titled the The

---

18. Marrs, 1989, pp. 580-90.
19. Ibid., p. 588.
20. Roberts, 1994, 188-89.

Man Who Wrote Too Much). Russell's list includes Cuban exiles, the Mob, Hoover's FBI, General Charles Willougby and associated far right groups, Army intelligence, and the CIA.

Peter Dale Scott has tried to give this kind of laundry list of bogeymen an aura of mystery by referring to them as the "deep political system."[21] This "system" includes "Texas oilmen, organized crime, the Dallas police, and army intelligence." Other than the Ruby connection to organized crime and the role of one or two high level military officers in influencing the autopsy, there is no evidence at all for this. We know that it is worse than absurd to overlook Establishment media and implicate the Dallas police. The Dallas police performance was stellar when compared to the *New York Times* and *Wall Street Journal*. There is no significant evidence against "army intelligence" or "Texas oilmen." In earlier work Scott implicated Clint Murchison and Richard Nixon.[22] Nixon may be guilty of saying nothing about his suspicions but there is no real evidence for this or anything else. While I find it interesting that Murchison was host to John J. McCloy during the summer of 1963,[23] something not discussed by Scott, there is no evidence linking Murchison to the assassination.

Scott offered an early defense of the Warren Commission saying that their failures could be attributed to a tight schedule and lack of investigators.[24] Scott praised the McCloy-Dulles-Warren Commission and the FBI saying that between them they

> meticulously demolished the prima facie case that Oswald and Ruby were agents of Castro and the Fair Play for Cuba Committee. Our criticisms of the Commission's performance should not lose sight of this achievement, which not only explains, but mitigates, their use of misinformation to achieve this end.[25]

In fact, the McCloy-Dulles-Warren Commission did not "meticulously" demolish any case or make any case. Their complete lack of interest in conspiracies of any kind is obvious. Their use of "misinformation" often had no connection to the issue raised by Scott. Sadly, Scott is not the only writer to

---

[21.] Scott, 1993, 299.

[22.] Scott, 1971, III 42-43, 10-17.

[23.] Bird, 1992, p. 542.

[24.] Scott, 1971, p. II-1.

[25.] Ibid., pp. 1-6, II-2.

exonerate McCloy and Dulles. For example, Robert Anson in his 1975 book and Lawrence and Kempton in 1967 have also given the Commission a clean bill of health.

In many of the arguments about the assassination some part of the federal government is implicated. Sometimes it is the whole government. As was noted at the beginning of this chapter, Lord Russell was very soon after the assassination accusing the United States government, which President Kennedy headed and loved, of killing JFK. This within months of the assassination and before the Warren Report was issued.

As we have just seen, many elements of the government have been named on various lists of so-called suspects. It does appear that individuals in the FBI (e.g., Alan Belmont), the military (perhaps a couple of high level officers at the autopsy), and the CIA (perhaps Richard Helms who oversaw the CIA's work with the Commission) joined the Establishment media and the Acheson and McCloy groups in carrying out the cover-up. They certainly were not "the government" and there is absolutely no evidence of any government involvement in the assassination itself.

"The government" did not hate the President. Most likely most of the government liked him. "The government" did not have men at the top of the Establishment media. "The government" did not order Alsop, Rostow, Acheson, McCloy, Dulles, and James Reston to do what they did. Groups within the Establishment did hate Kennedy. They did have their people at high levels of certain parts of the government. Those Establishment interests did close the case within hours of the assassination. Establishment people did create and control the so-called Warren Commission.

John Kennedy headed up the United States government, a government made up mostly of loyal, average Americans. The opposition within the government to Kennedy's policies did not come from those people. The opposition came from people whose primary loyalties were to various private interests, not the government or the country. To blame "the government" is in a sense to blame Kennedy, who was the government, who believed in the positive potential of government. To blame "the government" is, in a sense, to attack Kennedy a second time. I believe that this is why Lord Russell, who disliked Kennedy, came forward immediately to blame the government Kennedy loved for Kennedy's own murder.

As we have seen, various people have named various parts of the federal government as part of their list of suspects. Naming bureaucracies or agencies is usually the same as naming nobody while simultaneously creating mistrust of government organizations. It is a pointless exercise, unless the point is to discredit public institutions. Some writers have focused only or primarily on government agencies. Mark Lane has implicated a CIA faction.[26] Zirbel[27] and Brown[28] have accused the Vice-President of the United States, Lyndon Johnson. David Lifton blames the executive branch of the government.[29] He doesn't say who it would be. President Kennedy was in charge of the executive branch. Gaeton Fonzi[30] implicates people who did have ties to the Establishment (like CIA officers Richard Helms and David Phillips) but opts to think in terms of the upper echelons of the Federal Government. All of this is generally compatible with Lord Russell's argument. Some have simply continued his accusations against "the government."

In a 1996 book E. Martin Schotz implicates "the federal government" in the assassination and "the government" in the cover-up. The problem according to Schotz is in "the system."[31] Along the way he also implicates the CIA and the "warfare state."[32] Like Lord Russell, about the only thing that Schotz appreciates about Kennedy is Kennedy's interest in arms reduction. Schotz represents John J. McCloy as JFK's ally and collaborator.[33] Kennedy and McCloy were in fact at odds with each other on most major issues, particularly the general question of whether the United States should be a neo-colonial power in the mold of Great Britain. McCloy favored that and Kennedy opposed it.

Among some of the other outrageous things in Schotz's book is a suggestion that Katzenbach played a pivotal role in initiating the cover-up and that he acted on behalf of Robert Kennedy. Two years before this was written the public record showed that Katzenbach was not pivotal and there has never been any evidence that Robert Kennedy in any way initiated the cover-up. This unfounded accusation against Robert Kennedy suggests that Schotz shares still something else with Lord Russell - a distinct dislike for a Kennedy.

[26.] Lane, 1991.
[27.] Zirbel, 1991, p. 244.
[28.] Brown, 1995, p. 334.
[29.] Lifton, 1980, p. 697.
[30.] Fonzi, 1993, pp. 404-22.
[31.] Schotz, 1996, pp. 34, 284.
[32.] Ibid., pp. 15, 24.
[33.] Ibid., pp. 29-30, 255-60.

Vincent J. Salandria, a close associate of Schotz, has expressed the Russellite hatred of the United States government but did for a time hold a distinctly anti-Russell (and anti-Schotz) point of view and was one of the first people to implicate the Establishment. In fact, for a period of time in the 1970s Salandria did move somewhat toward the same conclusion that we will come to in the last chapter. Salandria has recently stated the Russell-Schotz view in a speech prepared for a conference of the Coalition on Political Assassinations held in Dallas in November of 1998.

In this speech Salandria referred briefly to the complicity of civilians and the media in the cover-up but the speech contains a multitude of references to "the government" or to national security and/or military elements of the government. The title of the speech referred to the assassination and the cover-up as "State Crimes." In the written version of the speech Salandria used a variety of terms including U.S. military-intelligence system and national security state. But the most commonly used image by a long shot is the "government." There are well over thirty references to the government plus some to the "state."

Without a shred of evidence Salandria asserts that the media chose "to serve the interests of the state." There is absolutely no reason to believe that James Reston and people at the other media institutions who decided within hours of the assassination that Oswald did it alone were acting for the state or government. Also, Salandria blames the Warren Report on the "government" rather than on McCloy, Dulles, Rankin, Belmont, and Ford. Earl Warren's failures are attributed by Salandria to "his dedication to our state" rather than to what we know happened, i.e., Warren allowed McCloy and Dulles to take control of the Commission

This inclination to blame "the government" and to ignore the Establishment has not been a constant in Salandria's work. In 1971, after he had focused for years on the Warren Commission's failures, Salandria began a discussion of the reasons for the assassination. That discussion led naturally to the question of who ordered it.

In the 1971 article, entitled "The Assassination of President John F. Kennedy: A Model for Explanation,"[34] Salandria began by referring to "the federal government" or just "the government" but then narrowed it to segments of the American government. Here Salandria settled on the "the American military" and "the CIA." The only direct evidence of military involvement

---

[34.] Salandria, 1971.

mentioned by Salandria was the apparent involvement of one or more high level officers in the direction, or misdirection, of the autopsy of the President. There is strong evidence that the autopsy was controlled in order to suppress evidence of conspiracy,[35] but there is absolutely no evidence that more than a couple of military people were involved. That is, to blame the entire United States military or its entire leadership for something a few officers were involved in is irrational. Those officers could have received direction form various sources. There is no evidence at all that any orders to distort the autopsy came through any normal chain of command. There is absolutely no evidence of involvement of the Joint Chiefs of Staff. There is no evidence of involvement of any one of the Chiefs. The officer or officers who interfered with the autopsy could have been responding to pressure from someone in the White House, the Defense Department, the CIA, military intelligence, or a private network. The officers may have responded to a request from important people that came through informal channels. We do not know, but we have absolutely no evidence that the ultimate source was military.

Salandria then examined "the question of whether the CIA was the specific federal agency which was the prime mover in the killing of President Kennedy." Salandria seemed unaware of or indifferent to the evidence that the CIA was created by and was heavily influenced by upper-class interests. He treats it simply as a government agency, even quoting Senator Eugene McCarthy's remark that the CIA had become "an important operating arm of the executive branch." That would suggest that on November 22 the CIA worked for President Kennedy. This is the tendency that once again dominates Salandria's thinking in recent years.

When Salandria moved to a discussion of particular events, however, he found himself talking about individuals who were either no longer officially part of the CIA at the time of the assassination or who had loyalties to groups other than that intelligence agency. Salandria focused on Allen Dulles and the Bundy brothers, William and McGeorge. None of the three men was officially part of the CIA in 1963. Dulles had been fired by JFK and McGeorge was an advisor to Presidents Kennedy and Johnson. William may have had a continuing relationship with the CIA. All three were part of the private Establishment.

[35.] Weisberg, 1995.

William Bundy was married to Dean Acheson's daughter. That wedding breakfast was hosted by John J. McCloy.[36]

Nevertheless, in his generalizations and conclusions Salandria continued to ignore the Establishment and to speak of "the CIA." There is not now nor has there ever been any evidence that the director of the CIA in 1963, John McCone, had anything to do with the assassination. He may have passively allowed others, such as Richard Helms, to control the CIA's activities after the assassination and contribute to the cover-up. In this area the number of CIA people who were involved would have been relatively small. As with the military, it makes no sense to talk as if the whole organization or even sizable parts of it had anything to do with the assassination or the cover-up.

Salandria's focus on the Bundys and Dulles could have led him in 1971 to specific forces within the Eastern Establishment. By 1977 he had almost gotten there. In an article titled "The Design of the Warren Report, to Fall to Pieces," Salandria again approached the question of who authored the assassination. This time Salandria posed the following question: who could get away with killing the President in a way that obviously involved a conspiracy and who could would benefit from killing him in an obviously conspiratorial way? While this line of thinking gave much too little attention to the Establishment's opposition to the Kennedy program, it did lead Salandria to that Establishment. Salandria:

> Then what was the purpose or purposes behind the killing of President Kennedy in a transparently conspiratorial way. The purpose for the transparent conspiracy to kill Kennedy, in my judgment was to attain for the Eastern establishment through the use of the intelligence community as its executive and executing arm, power over American politics and ultimately preeminent power over the minds of the American citizenry.

He referred to this as "The `Eastern Establishment' Model" of the assassination. Emphasizing that almost all elements of American politics and government were either blamed or discredited in the aftermath, Salandria continued with the following:

> So the transparent nature of the assassination in a very real sense framed us all; made us all feel guilty and served to paralyze us in a gripping sense of inadequacy. The transparent conspiracy paved the way for our despair and demoralization of the people. It eroded our trust in the nation states. But the

---

[36.] Isaacson and Thomas, 1986, p. 193.

alienation was deeper and more personal than the separation of people from confidence in their governments. The transparency of the assassination effectively destroyed politics. A counter culture was cultivated by the media and supported by the establishment which was to substitute for constitutional democracy and serve as an outlet for dissident energies.

And thus a post-Orwellian, Huxleyian world was ushered in by the new rulers. The drug culture was promoted. Individuality gave way to the abandonment of freedom, dignity and responsibility. The mind-expanding properties of drugs were to take us beyond human freedom and dignity. The embracing of our new servitude brought on by drug-induced pleasure and/or new charismatic mystical and religious movements moved people away from rationality.

The importance of education was downgraded. Only that was worth learning which was 'relevant.' Relevant was a catch word to describe that which gave us immediate sensory kicks. Nothing that required tough analysis and drudgery, therefore, was worth learning.

Although I do not concur with each and every element in Salandria's article, the overall direction of this particular analysis was consistent with what we now know about some of Oswald's connections, the behavior of the Establishment media after the assassination, the actions of Establishment figures such as Rostow, Alsop, and Acheson in creating the Warren Commission, and the role of Dulles and McCloy in directing that Commission. It is also consistent with the nature of the conflicts that arose around Kennedy's policies, something we will look at in the final chapter.

What happened with or to Salandria between 1977 and the 1990s, I do not know. What is clear is that in the late-1970s he was moving closer to the truth and was one of only a few people writing about the assassination who was getting to the truth. Sometime in the 1980s or early-1990s he became someone who blames "the government" for the assassination. This was a huge change. As shown in the quoted sections, Salandria believed in 1977 that one of the major negative results of and purposes of the assassination was the destruction of our belief in the potential good in politics and government. Salandria is now contributing to that destruction.

Instead of following up on Allen Dulles or McGeorge Bundy or pursuing the role of the "Eastern Establishment," he has concluded that the United States government is architect of the assassination. There really is no good reason for the accusations against the more than four million civilian and military employees of the federal government in 1963. Yet, that is in effect what Salandria and others are doing every time they say that "the government" killed

President Kennedy. It is an incorrect and absurd generalization. In today's world, a world in which the revenues of many giant transnational corporations and banks are larger than the revenues of most governments, it is worse.

A few other researchers or analysts of the assassination have, in varying degrees, implicated the New York-Boston centered financial elite, or Establishment. For example, L. Fletcher Prouty in his 1992 book, *JFK: The CIA, Vietnam, and the Plot to Assassinate John F. Kennedy,* alluded to a "High Cabal" and to the "great power centers of our society" and remarked that:[37]

> By now it has become clear that there was a plan to murder Kennedy in order to escalate the Vietnam war and decimate most of the less-developed countries through a form of banker-managed, predatory economic warfare.

Prouty has here implicated the forces that supported a policy of neo-colonialism. At the center of those forces is the web of Morgan-Rockefeller interests with which most of our principal characters were associated. It is that private Establishment that had (and has) the resources to activate people in a variety of private and public institutions, resources necessary in the cover-up.

Among the people who did the early work to expose the Warren Commission's fraudulent report was Harold Weisberg. Although various people contributed to this, including the aforementioned Vincent Salandria, probably no one matched Weisberg for both breadth and depth of critical analysis. Beginning in 1964 and continuing into the late-1990s, Weisberg has produced a series of books which destroy the credibility of the Warren Report.[38] Some of that work was referenced in Chapter One.

Although Weisberg has emphasized the military (and military-intelligence complex in conversations with the author) in his recent work,[39] he has had other suspicions over the years. Even in the more recent work, in the 1990s, Weisberg at times implies other things. For example, Weisberg indicates that the Commission intentionally suppressed evidence and he implies that this was not the fault of Senators Russell or Cooper or Representative Boggs.[40] That

[37.] Prouty, 1992, pp. 311, 334-35.
[38.] Weisberg, 1965; 1966; 1967; 1974; 1975; 1976; 1995.
[39.] Weisberg, 1995, pp. 133, 140, 148-49, 306, 310, 474.
[40.] Ibid., pp. 131, 221-26, 466.

implicates McCloy, Dulles, and Ford. Weisberg also implicates Rankin,[41] who was brought in by McCloy.

In this 1995 book, Weisberg[42] has charged that the media was complicit in and necessary for the cover-up. As I have shown, this may even understate their role since they are the first important source for the official cover story. Weisberg's recent work has also hinted at, probably not even intentionally, other economic and political motives for the assassination. Weisberg:

> The assassination of John Kennedy did turn this country around. It did turn the world around at the same time. From crime in the streets to the vast self-destructiveness of drugs; to the economy and the national debt and the loss, really the exportation of so many hundreds of thousands of our best jobs probably forever; and with this the simply enormous losses and increased costs and indebtedness from the loss of those industries and the loss of the profits from them, do we not see great change in our country in the wake of the assassination of President Kennedy.[43]

This is consistent with a broader reading of the motives for the assassination than what might come out of a focus on the role of military officers in the autopsy, the primary focus of the 1995 book.

Over the years Weisberg's research has led him to suspicions about other figures, some of them discussed in this book. For example, Weisberg earlier had concluded that John J. McCloy participated in the cover-up.[44]

The research and investigation done by Weisberg to assist District Attorney Jim Garrison's investigation led Weisberg to focus on the network of private and government intelligence operations that surrounded Oswald's time in New Orleans. This led Weisberg to identify connections between the CIA backed Cuban Revolutionary Council (CRC) and Edward S. Butler's INCA.[45] Weisberg found connections between David Ferrie and the CRC and between Bannister and the CIA.[46] Weisberg's investigation also led to strong suspicions about specific individuals within the FBI (e.g., Warren de Brueys) and the CIA (e.g., Tracy Barnes). Weisberg speculated that the CIA may have been involved in the

[41.] Ibid., p. 65.
[42.] Ibid., pp. 415, 466-67.
[43.] Ibid., p.423.
[44.] Weisberg, 1975, p. 626.
[45.] Weisberg, 1967, pp. 50-52, 255, 345.
[46.] Ibid., pp. 321-23, 329.

assassination and that foreign policy conflicts may have brought on the assassination.[47] Unfortunately, Weisberg did not pursue this and he did not attempt any analysis of the forces involved in foreign policy.

Garrison himself was never very sure about who ordered the assassination and he was either vague about it or produced a list of suspects that is too long and too general. In his 1970 book, *A Heritage of Stone*, Garrison implied that Kennedy was killed because of conflicts over Vietnam policy or the arms race. He did not explore the source of that Vietnam policy. In his later book, *On the Trail of the Assassins* (1988), he implicated "fanatical anti-Communists" within the intelligence community, the covert action arm of the CIA, and "extra-governmental collaborators."[48] These forces were assisted in the cover-up by "like-minded individuals in the FBI, Secret Service, and the Dallas police department, and the military." The purpose would be to prevent détente.

Neither Weisberg nor Garrison got around to the Eastern Establishment. The value of Weisberg's work is primarily in his devastating critique of the Warren Report and Garrison is significant because of his willingness to pursue an investigation of Clay Shaw and friends in spite of the pressures brought to bear on him and his investigation. Garrison's courage in this affair makes him an important figure.

There is one other person who has moved in the direction of attributing the assassination to the Eastern Establishment. In his 1992 book, *Destiny Betrayed*, James DiEugenio correctly emphasized the negative but important role played by McCloy and Dulles on the Warren Commission.[49] He concluded that those two, with help from Gerald Ford and Rankin, perpetrated a fraud. The evidence reviewed here supports that.

DiEugenio also noted that while the media was energetic in its attack on D.A. Jim Garrison while Garrison was trying to investigate the assassination, the media did not do its own investigation nor did most media question the Warren Report.[50] DiEugenio noted that the media's "gullibility in accepting the Warren Report was staggering."[51] As we have seen here, their role was far more active than that and apparently more sinister.

[47.] Ibid., pp. 9, 389, 394.
[48.] Garrison, 1988, pp. 277, 290.
[49.] DiEugenio, 1992, pp. 90-91, 276.
[50.] Ibid., pp. 167, 245-46.
[51.] Ibid., p. 245.

There were a number of other things discussed in his book which implicated or could lead to Establishment circles. For example, DiEugenio noted that Time-Life purchased the famous film of the assassination, the Zapruder film, and kept it from the public until Jim Garrison acquired it through subpoena in 1969. When *Life* magazine published some of the frames from that film, they presented them out of sequence in a way that lent support to the official story that all of the bullets were fired from the rear. This is made even more troublesome by the fact that much of the upper echelons of Time, Inc. were opposed to most of Kennedy's policies and/or were closely aligned with Kennedy's opponents.

DiEugenio also raised questions about Clay Shaw's connections to various upper-class people and to intelligence related operations. Clay Shaw's connections to the wealthy Stern family and to the operations of Alton Ochsner and INCA are noted as are Shaw's association with Permindex.[52] Establishment related figures operating in the intelligence world are also focused on in various parts of the book, including Richard Helms and Edward Lansdale.[53] This focus has developed in recent years into a conclusion that the assassination was an "Establishment-intelligence operation."[54]

Prouty, DiEugenio, Salandria in the late-1970s, and Weisberg at times have moved in the direction of identifying private Establishment interests as the force behind the assassination. That is the direction we have moved in this book. This suspicion is dictated by the evidence. James Reston, John Hay Whitney, the *Wall Street Journal*, *New York Times*, *New York Herald Tribune* and *Time* are all part of or are extensively connected to the higher circles of the Eastern Establishment. What Eugene Rostow, Dean Acheson, Joe Alsop, Allen Dulles, and John J. McCloy had in common was association with those same higher circles. So too did some of Oswald's friends in Dallas and his associates in New Orleans.

There is every reason to conclude that the cover-up was a highly coordinated project of that Establishment. Their authorship of the cover-up, apparent in four separate phases including connections to Oswald before the assassination, makes them the primes suspects in the assassination. Why would they kill the President? The problem is not one of finding a motive. The problem is to figure out which of the many apparent motives might have been decisive. In other words, the Establishment had so many reasons to eliminate the President, it is hard to know

---

[52.] Ibid., pp. 157, 206, 209-13, 215-16.
[53.] Ibid., pp. 220, 222, 238, 265, 337, 379.
[54.] Personal communication.

which one or ones actually triggered the decision. All reasons, however, are connected to President Kennedy's decision to be the enforcer of progress. We can access these matters through a figure who is by now familiar to us - John J. McCloy.

Chapter Eleven

THE BEGINNING

The truth about the assassination of President Kennedy is both forever obscure and also obvious. It is forever obscure because it is almost certain that only a few people know the names of those who were directly and criminally responsible for giving the order to murder the President. Those criminals, most or all of whom are probably dead, have escaped punishment. Unless there is a stunning revelation from a participant or a first-hand observer, that decision making process will never be exposed.

Nevertheless, the general nature of the assassination and the nature of the forces behind it are now obvious. This does not mean that this will become widely recognized. As Edgar Allen Poe indicated in his famous detective story, "The Purloined Letter," there are many people who will overlook or even reject the truth because it is obvious, preferring to view what is obvious as simply odd. What is obvious here is that the people who controlled the cover-up represented or were associated with people who had reason to kill Kennedy. In fact, the people who conducted the cover-up had reason to kill Kennedy.

The facts indicate that elements within and at the highest levels of the Establishment killed Kennedy because he was the popularly elected and increasingly successful enforcer of progress. JFK was elected power, the Establishment hereditary. He was public authority, they private power. He spoke for the nation, they for the empires of private wealth and property. He looked forward to continued use of governmental institutions to advance the interests of the people within and outside the United States. They looked to a world in which diminished state power would leave them to dominate a global corporate system free only in the sense of lacking interference from democratic authority. Kennedy sought peace through progress, the Establishment sought peace born of the submission of their opponents. Kennedy encouraged people to think of the United States as a Democratic Republic that needed alert and active citizens. The Establishment promotes a cynical withdrawal into a self-oriented passivity and indifference. Kennedy was the Establishment's nightmare. He was the "one," the President or Monarch whose first commitment was to the many, not the few. He was winning, democracy was working. They killed him.

This really is obvious in the sense that it is right in front of us. The Establishment's opposition to Kennedy and the Establishment's influence on the cover-up are embodied in people such as Acheson, Dulles, and McCloy. McCloy illustrates this as well as any of them.

John J. McCloy was probably the most important figure on the Warren Commission. If it wasn't him, it was his partner Allen Dulles. McCloy's actions led to the selection of the Commission's chief counsel. McCloy and Dulles dominated various phases of the process, introducing the lone-nut theory and controlling, often through their silence, the questioning of many key witnesses. McCloy also was someone who opposed almost everything that Kennedy tried to do.

Sounding a good bit like Lord Bertrand Russell,[1] McCloy said the following in his book *The Challenge to American Foreign Policy*:

> We all look with a certain nostalgia to the days when the world could be dominated by a single navy and the control of a relatively few trade passages and strategic centers.[2]

Most of the world felt no such nostalgia and certainly Kennedy's policies and goals represented something very different. Kennedy[3] attempted to reshape U.S. foreign policy, moving it away from the neo-colonialist or imperialist policies romanticized in McCloy's statement and expressed in McCloy's own actions over his entire career.

Kennedy did not want to use U.S. military power to support the upper class' international objectives (i.e., suppressing or limiting economic progress, controlling raw materials, opening up other countries' markets and companies for

---

[1] Russell, 1953, p. 108.
[2] McCloy, 1953, p. 26.
[3] Gibson, 1994, pp. 35-51; Kennedy, 1960, p. 260; 1961, p. 82.

take over) and he was interested in stimulating and supporting economic progress. The differences between Kennedy and the interests McCloy represented were profound and were reflected in subtle but clear ways in the thinking of the two men.

Whereas Kennedy thought in terms of changing and stimulating economies, McCloy thought in terms of maintaining "economic stability." Kennedy thought about cooperation and investment while McCloy spoke about trade and markets. Kennedy believed in the advancement of the nation through progress in science and technology and through education and opportunity. McCloy thought in terms of maximizing the freedom of personal interests.[4]

McCloy and the Establishment he represented embraced (and still embraces) a neo-Malthusian doctrine which is supported ideologically by gross distortions of the global population situation and which targets population growth as the source of global instability and backwardness.[5] Kennedy viewed the problems of poverty and backwardness as a challenge to be met through economic progress. He also was a proponent of the scientifically supported theory that economic development would eventually reduce population growth rates.[6] For Kennedy, the so-called population problem would be solved naturally through economic development. The Establishment was (and is) in no way committed to the progress and they viewed people as the problem

McCloy's protegee, Joseph Slater, became in 1969 the president of the Aspen Institute, an organization which promoted an extreme anti-modernist environmentalism beginning in the 1950s and continuing in the decades that followed. Slater was involved in helping Atlantic Richfield and Aspen Institute chairman Robert O. Anderson to plan the first Earth Day, which was celebrated in 1970.[7] James Reston, one of the originators of the Oswald-did-it-alone story and one of McCloy's closest friends,[8] was also involved in discussions of these issues at the Aspen Institute.[9]

In Kennedy's time the Establishment, including many people associated with McCloy, was preparing to launch a new effort to convince people that progress

---

[4] Gibson, 1994, pp. 19-34; McCloy, 1953, pp. 1, 7, 9.

[5] Bachrach and Bergman, 1973, pp. 43-48; Demerath, 1976, pp. 38-44; Gibson, 1994, p. 93.

[6] Gibson, 1994, pp. 96-97; Kennedy, 1961, pp. 265-67.

[7] Hyman, 1975, pp. 231-72.

[8] Bird, 1992, pp. 125, 313.

[9] Reston, 1970.

had become near impossible due to resource scarcity, overpopulation, and the destructive nature of large scale, modern industry. First called the new conservationism, it later became known as environmentalism. Kennedy was opposed to this sort of political, Malthusian environmentalism.[10] He showed no signs of accepting the pessimism associated with this movement and he was on record stating his optimism about the potentials of modern science and technology to overcome problems such as those related to resources.

Over the years McCloy supported various efforts to increase the Establishment's direct control over national policy. Writing in the early-1950s, McCloy expressed his support for a proposal made by Vannevar Bush, who was president of the Carnegie Institution and with whom McCloy and Acheson had worked after World War Two in an effort to control the spread of atomic energy.[11] The proposal was that the Joint Chiefs of Staff should be made to channel their communications with the President through the Secretary of Defense, a position usually filled by someone with Establishment connections. McCloy[12] said that "The influence of civilian Secretary of Defense should be increased by interposing him or his representative as a matter of custom between the military and the President."

Similarly, McCloy[13] criticized FDR for by-passing Secretary of War Henry Stimson and discussing war objectives directly with military officers. McCloy apparently felt no hesitation in trying to instruct the commander-in-chief that he is not permitted to speak with his subordinates. McCloy's later and more successful effort to instruct the Chief Justice of the United States about the selection of a chief counsel for the Commission was not that unusual an undertaking for McCloy.

McCloy attempted something like this again when he served in 1961 as disarmament advisor to President Kennedy. McCloy proposed that the director of the new disarmament agency should work directly for the Secretary of State, usually an Establishment figure, and communicate independently to the public through the United States Information Agency. McCloy also recommended a key role for unidentified private groups. Kennedy countered with his own plan and both were published by the New York Times. Kennedy's plan made no mention

---

[10] Gibson, 1994, pp. 20-26; 87-101; 120-27.
[11] Acheson, 1969, pp. 151-53, 166.
[12] McCloy, 1953, p. 47.
[13] McCloy, 1953, pp. 37-38.

of the Information Agency or the private groups and his plan had the disarmament agency director reporting directly to the President and merely keeping the Secretary of State informed.[14]

McCloy's biographer, Kai Bird, noted in reference to McCloy's view of President Kennedy that McCloy

> knew the young senator had made no effort to institute any connections to the Council on Foreign Relations or other Establishment institutions. All in all, the president-elect seemed to be a man of little experience or substance.[15]

In fact, Kennedy was a man of great substance and McCloy was merely an agent of powerful cliques based in inherited wealth. The rest of the comment is accurate.

Kennedy's differences with McCloy were part of his conflict with the Establishment forces that McCloy spoke and acted for. McCloy's long-term friendship with leaders of the anti-Kennedy Establishment, such as David Rockefeller,[16] should have disqualified him from service on the Warren Commission. His actions and his close associations with other participants in the cover-up, such as Dulles, Acheson, and Reston,[17] make him one of the pivotal figures in the events following the assassination. In the cover-up as well as his other activities, McCloy is important as an agent for Establishment interests. Kennedy was in something like continuous conflict with those interests, especially in the last eighteen months of his life.

KENNEDY AT WAR WITH THE ESTABLISHMENT

The breadth and depth of Establishment hostility toward Kennedy increased as the months of his presidency passed by. Some within the Establishment were opposed to him before he took office and others only came to that position after a year or so.[18] All of the differences between the Establishment and Kennedy related to his inclinations to use the powers of government to generate economic

---

[14.] Finney, 1961.
[15.] Bird, 1992, p. 496.
[16.] Bird, 1992, pp. 55, 395, 397, 456-57.
[17.] Bird, 1992, pp. 76-77, 99-100, 125, 313, 392-93; also see Chapter Five in this volume.
[18.] Gibson, 1994, pp. 53-76.

progress and his failure to use those powers in support of a neo-colonial foreign policy. In the simplest terms, JFK was doing too many things that the Establishment did not want done and he was reluctant to do some of the things they wanted him to do.

Spokesmen for the Establishment were clear about this; their views are part of the public record. For example, in June of 1961 *Fortune* magazine, part of the Luce-Morgan controlled Time Incorporated,[19] editorialized that Kennedy was much too inclined to interfere in the workings of the economy while too reluctant, as in the case of the Bay of Pigs, to use force in foreign affairs.[20]

John J. McCloy was a friend of Time, Inc.'s President, James A. Linen, and of Time director Paul Hoffman.[21] Another of the members of Time's board of directors and another of McCloy's friends was Maurice T. Moore. Moore was married to Henry Luce's sister and he was a member for decades of the law firm with which McCloy had spent fifteen years, the prestigious Cravath, Swaine & Moore (earlier known as Cravath, Henderson, Leffingwell and de Gersdorff).[22] Another member of that firm and a friend and mentor to McCloy was Russell C. Leffingwell,[23] who succeeded Thomas Lamont, Corliss Lamont's father, as chairman of J.P. Morgan in 1948.[24] Leffingwell served as a director of the Council on Foreign Relations for thirty years and was the Council's Chairman of the Board from 1946 to 1953. His successor in that position was McCloy, who served as Chairman for seventeen years, from 1953 to 1970. McCloy was followed by David Rockefeller who held the position until 1985. From 1953 to 1963 David Rockefeller, John J. McCloy, and Allen Dulles were among the CFR's twenty-one directors. At the time of the assassination, Dulles had been a director for thirty-six years.[25]

The 1961 Fortune editorial referred to above noted that Kennedy had promised to get America moving again and that he had sent about eighteen major messages to Congress and had done other things to fulfill that promise. The proposals sent to Congress and the other related actions were the things that JFK

[19.] Ibid., pp. 68-70.

[20.] Fortune, 1961.

[21.] Bird, 1992.

[22.] Bird, 1992, pp. 271-72, 294, 447, 605; Chernow, 1990, pp. 312-13, 480-85; Isaacson and Thomas, pp. 120-22; Kotz; Moody's Investors Service, 1963.

[23.] Bird, 1992, pp. 108, 283.

[24.] Chernow, 1990, pp. 312-13, 480-85.

[25.] Council on Foreign Relations, 1963; 1988.

was doing that disturbed McCloy and his superiors within the Establishment. As Chairman of the CFR and as head of one of the Morgan-Rockefeller network's most important banks, the Chase Manhattan, McCloy was one of the most visible and active representatives of the Establishment.

The contest between the Establishment and Kennedy played itself out in full public view, especially in 1962 and 1963. That 1961 *Fortune* editorial turned out to be only one of many shots fired across the bow of the Kennedy ship of state. In a series of vitriolic attacks on the President, *Fortune* clearly stated Time, Inc.'s strong opposition to Kennedy's efforts to use public authority and resources to support scientific and technological progress and to initiate or stimulate investments in production.

For example, John Davenport, one of Fortune's three Assistant Managing Editors and a member of the CFR, began an attack on Kennedy entitled "The Priority of Politics Over Economics" with the following statement:

> The trouble with the New Frontiersman is not that he is too radical but that he has missed the bus. In a literal sense he is reactionary; he belongs to a cult that is as old as Diocletian.[26]

The reference to Diocletian was apparently in relation to the Roman Emperor's efforts at price controls. Observing, correctly, that Kennedy was "doubtless an admirer of the *Federalist Papers*," most of which were written by Alexander Hamilton, Davenport chastised Kennedy for not giving greater attention to James Madison's emphasis in his part of that work on government's need to restrain itself.[27]

Davenport continued, saying that Kennedy's economic policies required "a positive and expansive role" for government leading to the domination of politics over economics (hence, the title of the article). What Davenport was really getting at here is that Kennedy was trying to shift some of the decision making power away from organized, private wealth to public institutions and elected authorities.

[26.] Davenport, 1962, p. 88.
[27.] Ibid., p. 89.

Davenport went on to refer to the view of Establishment journalist and McCloy associate Walter Lippmann that planning is bad. He also quoted David Rockefeller's admonition to Kennedy that he should limit government expenditures.[28]

The verbal assault on Kennedy in Time, Inc.'s publications intensified in 1963. Editorials in Time's *Life* magazine criticized Kennedy's budget and tax policies, complained about the administration's opposition to corporate mergers, and on the day Kennedy was killed, warned Kennedy against any early withdrawal of troops from Vietnam. More extreme views appeared in *Fortune*.

For example, Arthur Krock, who had earlier chosen James Reston to succeed him as the New York Times Washington bureau chief,[29] attacked Kennedy in March of 1963. Krock, a long-time friend of McCloy,[30] accused the Kennedy administration of the boldest and most cynical manipulation of news in the entire peace time history of the country. Attacking Kennedy for his failure to support the Dutch position in West New Guinea and for his foreign policy in general, Krock went on to accuse Kennedy himself of being the "most brilliant operator" behind the policy of coopting and manipulating reporters and broadcasters.[31]

A February 1962 *Fortune* article had warned that the Kennedy administration might be allying itself with nationalist and dirigistic forces in Latin America who were all too willing to use governmental powers to promote development.[32] In March of 1963, Fortune suggested that Kennedy was wrongly attempting similar things within the United States. Specifically, *Fortune* charged, with considerable accuracy, that Kennedy was using both taxation and spending policies to manage the economy and that he was embracing deficit spending for the same purpose.[33]

Earlier in 1963 *Fortune* had highlighted this issue with the following:

> It would be easy to make a counterlist of New Frontier words and deeds to which businessmen have taken justifiable exception. But the coolness of business toward the Administration arises out of something more than a list of specific grievances. There is some general characteristic of this

---

[28.] Ibid., pp. 90, 194.

[29.] Talese, 1971, p. 23.

[30.] Bird, 1992, pp. 176, 226, 575.

[31.] Krock, 1963, pp. 82, 199-202.

[32.] Fortune, 1962, pp. 79-82.

[33.] Fortune, 1963a, pp. 79-80; Gibson, 1994, pp. 19-34.

Administration that business suspects and opposes - but that business has not clearly formulated.

We suggest that the trouble can be found in the Administration's tendency to employ the vast discretionary powers of the federal government toward whatever ends the men in power consider desirable. An old way of expressing this tendency was to denounce it as `government of men, not of laws.' The opposite principle has been the most powerful idea in Western political progress. It began in Greece; it evoked the Magna Carta; it pervaded the American Declaration of Independence and the Constitution. But in recent decades the contrast between the rule of law and government by discretionary power has become blurred in the public mind.[34]

Although Kennedy clearly understood the Constitution differently than the author of this article and there is no evidence that most businessmen were seriously dissatisfied with Kennedy, the article does seem to accurately portray the attitudes of big business and old money toward Kennedy.

The above was followed up in March by a lengthy critique of Kennedy's program from *Fortune* editor Charles J. V. Murphy. Murphy attacked most if not all of Kennedy's policies. He implied that Kennedy should focus more on the problem of population growth than on increasing foreign aid. He also criticized the foreign aid program, which included aid and long-term, low interest loans, saying that it had no "unifying economic policy other than a wearied assumption that the U.S. must somehow satisfy the universal lust for industrialization and growth." He added that this process has "clearly got out of hand."[35]

The idea of stimulating general economic progress through government action, especially on a global scale, is of relatively recent origins. What Murphy was calling a "wearied assumption" was actually an energetic effort on Kennedy's part to break the United States away from a truly "wearied" and morally exhausted policy of suppressing economic progress elsewhere in the world in the interest of preserving global power for the Anglo-American Establishment.

Murphy made his position clear by suggesting that any economic assistance that might be provided should be accompanied by "a combined effort to organize the capacity of the underdeveloped countries to produce more and more primary

---

[34.] Fortune, 1963, p. 81.
[35.] Murphy, 1963, pp. 206, 210.

commodities for export, the only path for those countries toward 'self-sustaining' growth and social stability."[36]

This recommendation that countries would be best off in the long run if they concentrate their efforts on the production of "primary commodities" for export is absurd. No country seeking to develop itself would follow this advice. The United States did not behave this way in the nineteenth century. It amounts to a recommendation that underdeveloped countries voluntarily do to themselves what the British forced their colonies to do at gun point.

Murphy admonished the President for engaging in economic negotiations on a nation-to-nation basis, which bypassed the international financial community. Those financiers believe that they rather than elected representatives should organize the world's economic activities. Murphy also charged that the President was coopting U.S. businessmen by linking foreign aid to commitments to buy goods made in the United States.

There was also criticism of Kennedy's failure to attach tough conditions to foreign loans. Murphy wanted Kennedy to follow the lead of the International Monetary Fund (IMF) which demanded that borrowing countries adopt an austerity program and open up their economies to foreign takeover. John J. McCloy was involved in the planning and development of the IMF at the end of World War Two.[37] IMF demands, known as conditionalities (i.e., conditions to be met to qualify for further lending), generally include the following: abolition or liberalization of foreign exchange and import controls; currency devaluation; domestic anti-inflation measures (including limits on bank credit, higher interest rates, limits on government spending, higher taxes) elimination of government subsidies; elimination of price controls; and greater hospitality to foreign investment.[38] As the century draws to a close, IMF conditionalities are still a major source of conflict between indebted countries and the Anglo-American financial elite. Now those conflicts include even countries such as Russia. Those IMF policies are widely viewed as a substitute for colonial domination.

Murphy referred to some of this in the following criticism of Kennedy's development program for Latin America, the Alliance for Progress:[39]

---

[36] Ibid., p. 212.
[37] Bird, 1992, p. 228.
[38] Payer, 1976, p. 33.
[39] Murphy, 1963, pp. 211-12.

No 'self-sustained growth is going to come from the Alianza [Alliance for Progress] billions unless the client nations brace themselves for the most elementary fiscal disciplines. Some technicians suggest that without these the most salutary course for the U.S. might be to give no money at all. But because Kennedy has staked so much of his personal prestige on making the Alianza work, it is doubtful that Bell [administrator of the Agency for International Development, David Bell] could nerve himself for so drastic an action, even with governments as profligate as Brazil. Nevertheless, long second-thinking has prompted a basic question: Would it not have been wiser to seek a cure for Latin America's economic woes through an international apparatus that included the major European nations, long bankers to that region and its first market.

This suggestion that nation-to-nation loans and aid should be dropped in favor of arrangements that would achieve more "fiscal discipline" and greater involvement by European lenders accompanied other criticisms of the role that national considerations were playing in Kennedy's policies.

As noted above, the Kennedy administration was assisting projects in poorer nations based on an agreement that capital goods and technical services be purchased from U.S. producers. Murphy argued that this practice amounted to a "subsidy for U.S. business" and, because it enlisted business self-interest, often supported projects that were inappropriate.[40] Murphy buttressed his assertions by referring to the sources of these criticisms of Kennedy, saying that[41]

a new and formidable criticism is gathering strength in the American business community. That businessmen are critical is not so surprising as the nature of the new criticism; it puts industry itself in a culpable role in foreign aid. This line of attack comes principally from Eugene Black, who retired two months ago as president of the International Bank for Reconstruction and Finance, George Champion, chairman of the board of the Chase Manhattan Bank, and Herbert V. Prochnow, president of the First National Bank of Chicago, himself a former deputy Under Secretary of State for Economic Affairs in Eisenhower's Administration.

Black served as a director of the Morgan-Rockefeller controlled Chase Manhattan and Prochnow's First National Bank of Chicago was interconnected with those interests.[42] Champion, Black, and Prochnow were all members of the

---

[40.] Ibid., p. 212.

[41.] Ibid., p. 126.

[42.] Lundberg, 1975, p. 40; Collier and Horowitz, 1976, p. 416.

Council on Foreign Relations as were, of course, McCloy, Dulles, Rostow, Acheson, and Reston.[43]

McCloy and Black were good friends. McCloy played an important role in the selection of Black to head the World Bank.[44] McCloy, Black, and Dean Acheson served with David Rockefeller as members of a group formed to support an expanded U.S. involvement in Vietnam, the Committee for an Effective and Durable Peace in Asia.[45] McCloy was also close to George Champion, who succeeded McCloy and preceded David Rockefeller as Chairman of the Chase Manhattan. Champion reportedly acquired some of his anti-government orientations while combating the power of Governor Huey Long on behalf of the Chase bank's interests in Louisiana in the early-1930s.[46]

The point of view represented in Murphy's critique of Kennedy, and in other *Fortune* articles, was that of the international financial elite. They wanted a compliant president, one who would be aggressive in areas approved of by the Establishment and passive in areas viewed by them as off limits. Many of the same kinds of criticisms were stated in one of the Establishment's supposedly "liberal" publications, *Newsweek* magazine.[47] Unlike *Fortune*, *Newsweek*, owned by the Washington Post company, was not usually associated in people's minds with big international banking and business. Its views of Kennedy were, however, virtually indistinguishable from *Fortune's*.

The criticism of Kennedy's international economic policy was aimed at the purposes of aid and loans, the manner in which the policy was carried out, and the roles to be played by nations and private interests, particularly banks. The Luce-Morgan press stated clear preferences. Poorer nations should remain primarily exporters of raw materials and agricultural products. They should not "lust" after industrialization. Those nations should pursue very conservative government policy and keep their economies open to foreign penetration. Aid and trade should be left, as much as possible, to private enterprise under the guidance of international finance. These are roughly the same policies being promoted by the Anglo-American Establishment as the century draws to a close.

Kennedy's initiatives were significantly at odds with all of those Establishment preferences. His foreign aid program was supposed to further

---

[43.] Council on Foreign Relations, 1963.
[44.] Bird, 1992, pp. 285-86, 289, 295, 305, 448-52, 497-98.
[45.] Ibid., p. 581.
[46.] Ibid., pp. 396-98, 441, 454-56.
[47.] Hazlitt, 1962, p. 92; 1963, p. 70; 1963a, p. 78; 1963b, p. 84; 1963c, p. 90; 1963d, p. 97.

economic development and free Third World nations from the backwardness and inferiority which had been central to colonial and neo-colonial arrangements. He favored nation-to-nation agreements and was quite willing to bypass the private banks and the "free market." He showed no interest in aggressively demanding that recipients adhere to the other conditions that were required by the international banking community in exchange for loans or aid.[48] Kennedy showed no interest in supporting IMF policies.

The Establishment's criticisms of Kennedy's international policy were in many ways identical to their attacks on his domestic policy. In both cases he was condemned for intervening in the private economy with what the Establishment viewed as an excessive commitment to economic progress. This Establishment view of Kennedy was stated in other media and by leaders of the Establishment. In the media the criticisms of Kennedy were probably nowhere more extensive than in the *Wall Street Journal*. These criticisms were also much like those appearing in the Luce-Morgan press.

KENNEDY'S STOCK PLUMMETS ON WALL STREET

At least partial control of the *Journal* was in the hands of the Bancroft family. One of the Bancrofts, Mary, had an affair with Allen Dulles during the World War Two period.[49] The *Journal's* view of Kennedy was harsh from the beginning. It had already flunked Kennedy for his economic policy before he took office, and an unfriendly exchange occurred in January of 1961 between Kennedy and *Journal* Editor Vermont Royster.[50]

Weeks before the inauguration, the *Journal* editorialized that Kennedy should resist the inclination to create a "planned economy." It noted his comments about pursuing the spirit of the Employment Act of 1946, and advised him that the purposes of that act (i.e., maximizing employment, production, and purchasing power through government action) were purely a response to the depression and were not relevant to the 1960s. Finally, it warned him against big spending in either domestic or foreign policy.[51]

[48.] Gibson, 1994, pp. 35-51.
[49.] Mosely, 1978, pp. 189-202.
[50.] Wendt, 1982, pp. 360-64.
[51.] Wall Street Journal, 1961, p. 10; 1961a, p. 10; 1961b, p.10.

It is interesting in this context that John J. McCloy wrote an official memo during World War Two warning against any continuation of the economic planning implemented by FDR.[52] McCloy's warning was made in spite of, or because of, the huge success of government spending and lending during the war years. The program contributed to a revolution in many areas of the economy, including electronics, petrochemical synthetics, aircraft, and shipbuilding.[53] There were huge increases in output in goods such as locomotives, rails, steel and aluminum.[54]

One would have to go back to that World War Two period and its immediate aftermath to find a time when the productive capabilities of the nation improved as much as they did during and immediately after the Kennedy presidency.[55] The Establishment was not interested in the soundness of Kennedy's program or, since then, in its success. They were concerned that he was challenging their control over decision making.

The *Wall Street Journal's* criticisms of Kennedy, beginning before he took office, continued after he was dead. Near the end, the *Journal* was even more harsh in its condemnation of the President's policies than it had been at the outset. On October 15, 1963, it accused the Kennedy administration of giving mere "lip-service to economic freedom" while pursuing a foreign aid program that favored socialism and a domestic program that led to bureaucratic control of the economy. The paper charged that Kennedy's policies reflected a hostility to the "philosophy of freedom."[56] A couple of weeks later, it continued this assault, repeating what by that time had been almost continuous criticism of excessive spending, budget deficits, and easy money. There were reports that Kennedy was putting intense pressure on the Federal Reserve to keep interest rates down.[57]

The *Journal* characterized Kennedy's program as perhaps the "most restrictive and reactionary economic policy" in U.S. history. They claimed that government activity was crowding out private enterprise, that government was over-regulating the economy and interfering in private investment abroad. It concluded by claiming that Adam Smith's free-market economy was being replaced by the "corporate state," wherein the State directed everything without

[52] Bird, 1992, p. 131.
[53] Greider, 1987, p. 324.
[54] Department of Commerce, 1965; Greider; Taus; Tax Foundation.
[55] Kendrick, 1973, p. 51.
[56] Wall Street Journal, 1963n, p. 16.
[57] Nossiter, 1961, p. A4.

necessarily nationalizing the major organs of production and distribution. This, the *Journal* claimed, "smacks heartily" of eighteenth-century mercantilism.[58]

During the final week of Kennedy's life, the *Journal* acknowledged that there was general prosperity, but claimed that there was an uneasiness about Kennedy attributable to his attempts to control the economy, as well as to excessive spending and growth of government. In a separate article it said that Kennedy's foreign aid often fostered "statist and socialistic institutions."[59] Even after his death, the repudiation of his policies continued. The *Journal* noted its differences with Kennedy concerning the proper role of government and referred to Kennedy's spending policy as "economic nonsense." The paper praised Johnson for his apparent recognition that these policies were mistaken.[60]

Concerning foreign aid, the *Journal* had repeatedly accused Kennedy of encouraging state planning, statism, and socialism.[61] It criticized Kennedy for having increased the Eisenhower administration's practice of providing soft loans (long-term with little or no interest) and recommended that Kennedy follow more closely the policies of the World Bank.[62] The *Journal* was less enthusiastic than Time, Inc. about the use of military force, but, like the Luce-Morgan press it did take Kennedy to task for betraying European allies (e.g., Belgium and the Netherlands) in the interest of a rigid policy of opposing colonialism.[63]

There were numerous attacks on the Kennedy administration's tax, budget, and monetary policies. There was specific criticism of Kennedy's decision to engage in deficit spending in order to sustain growth, suggesting that Kennedy's policies would "make even Lord Keynes turn in his grave." The *Journal's* rhetoric suggested that the man in the White House was a dangerous radical, an incompetent, a madman, or all three. Kennedy was referred to as a "potential threat" to the national interest, as "living in a dream world," and indulging in "deep and damaging delusion," and as a failure on the "economic tests."[64]

[58.] 1963p, p. 16.

[59.] Wall Street Journal, 1963q, p. 18; 1963r, p. 18.

[60.] Wall Street Journal, 1963s, p. 8; 1963t, p.16; 1963u, p. 18.

[61.] Wall Street Journal, 1962d, p. 6; 1963b, p. 18; 1963j, p. 8.

[62.] Wall Street Journal, 1962g. p. 16.

[63.] Wall Street Journal, 1962e, p. 12.

[64.] Wall Street Journal, 1962b, p. 14; 1963a, p. 16; 1963d, p. 10; 1963e, p. 12; 1963h, p. 6; 1963l, p. 12; 1963m, p. 16.

All of this criticism was part of one overriding accusation leveled against Kennedy: the charge that he was attempting to use the powers of his office and of the federal government to influence and direct economic processes. This view was identical to that expressed in *Fortune*. The *Journal* complained that under Kennedy the government had become the "self-appointed enforcer of progress."[65] It was this tendency in Kennedy, more than any particular policy, that infuriated the Establishment. The *Journal* criticized many specific policies (e.g., Kennedy's actions against U.S. Steel, his proposal to put a tax on the purchase of foreign securities, and his proposal to tax the earnings of foreign subsidiaries of U.S. companies), but saved its most in-depth critique for Kennedy's overall attempt to "enforce progress."

In October of 1962 it suggested that Kennedy and his advisors were moving toward a "managed economy." This, they said, was "a flop in the days of Diocletian and of the mercantilists" as well as in various communist and socialist programs. John Davenport of *Fortune*, as noted earlier, had also associated Kennedy's policies with Diocletian. Elsewhere the *Journal* expressed misgivings about the "effect of the totality of all the Administration's economic and social programs" and claimed that many "can see in the unchecked expansion of Government and its controls the very specter of compulsion that our political institutions were designed to prevent." In the *Journal's* view, Kennedy's actions were leading toward "all-encompassing Government," a violation of eighteenth-century principles which limited the government's role to national defense, maintenance of order, and preservation of personal liberty. The attempt by Kennedy to shift decision-making power to government was an encroachment on the "grand design of liberty itself."[66] The fact is that the only "liberty" endangered by JFK was the elite's freedom to dominate the country.

Other than highly qualified approval of certain tax breaks for business, there was very little abut Kennedy's economic policies that *Journal* did approve. Even Kennedy's commitment to supporting research and development came under fire. The *Journal* criticized its size and cost ($14 billion, accounting as of 1963 for two-thirds of all R &D), the rate of increase (a speed that is staggering"), and its

[65] Wall Street Journal, 1963c, p. 12.
[66] Wall Street Journal, 1962, p. 10; 1962a, p. 10; 1962c, p. 8; 1962f, p. 18; 1962h, p. 14; 1962i, p. 18; 1962j, p. 14; 1963, p. 16; 1963c, p. 12; 1963f, p. 3; 1963g, p.6.

impact on university programs (making them "top-heavy on science at the expense of other disciplines").[67]

There was no appreciation for Kennedy's commitment to the principles of competition and the free market when his brother's Justice Department aggressively opposed mergers in its 1963 actions against Continental Can Co., ALCOA, and Colonial Pipeline Company.[68] This lack of appreciation for these efforts does make sense, It was not interference with the decentralized, competitive sectors of the economy that was ever at issue; it was Kennedy's effort to shift decision-making away from large-scale, concentrated private power to the federal government that aroused the ire of opinion shapers at places like *Fortune* and the *Wall Street Journal*.

The *Journal* did report occasionally on the conflicts between Kennedy and the financial establishment for which the *Journal* spoke. For example, in October of 1963 the Journal reported that there was an ongoing shift within the Kennedy administration on global monetary policy. According to the *Journal*, the shift began late in 1962 as the "activists" in the administration supplanted the "conservatives." The conservatives were identified as Secretary of the Treasury C. Douglas Dillon, Under-Secretary Robert V. Roosa, and the members of the Federal Reserve Board. Dillon, like Allen Dulles and McCloy, was a close friend of David Rockefeller.[69] The Chairman of the Federal Reserve at that time, William McChesney Martin, would later become a supervisor of the Rockefeller family's trust fund.[70] The activists, also described as "Kennedy lieutenants" and "the professors," were led by Council of Economic Advisors Chairman Walter Heller, former Kennedy assistant Carl Kaysen, Under-Secretary of Commerce Franklin D. Roosevelt, Jr., and Under-Secretary of State George Ball.[71]

The *Journal* suggested that the conservatives wanted to deal with U.S. balance-of-payments problems by reducing the amount of money available in the economy and cutting government spending. The activists rejected this, arguing that it was counterproductive for the United States or any other nation to adopt such policies to deal with transitory balance-of-payments problems. This suggests that the "activists" would not support IMF conditionalities. Around these kinds of issues the battle to see who would determine policy was being

---

[67] Wall Street Journal, 1963i, p. 14.

[68] Mathewson ,1963, pp. 1, 10.

[69] Collier and Horowitz, 1976, p. 412.

[70] Chernow; Collier and Horowitz, 1976; Greider; Hoffman.

[71] Geyelin, 1963, p. 16.

waged. According to the *Journal*, the activists didn't "entirely trust bankers," and Kennedy had come to the same view. Rightly or wrongly, the article concluded, "Mr. Kennedy has come increasingly to believe that large and global banking problems are too important to be left to bankers."

Around this time, the Bank for International Settlements, one of the most influential of international financial institutions, recommended that the Kennedy administration allow all interest rates to rise.[72] The Bank represented the collective goals of the central banks of the leading non-communist economies of the world, including the U.S. Federal Reserve Bank. While Kennedy thought that banking was too important to be left entirely to bankers, the members of the Bank for International Settlements thought that financial policy could not be left to nations and their politicians.[73] The Wall Street Journal was in agreement with that view.

One of those bankers, McCloy's close friend David Rockefeller, tried to determine Presidential policy in economic affairs. Rockefeller, of course, was also involved in pressuring President Johnson to escalate the war in Vietnam. In July of 1962, *Life* magazine, part of Time, Inc., featured an exchange of letters between David Rockefeller and President Kennedy. In this public and somewhat polite airing of differences, Rockefeller offered praise for some of Kennedy's actions, but he ultimately located the source of the country's economic problems in the president's policies. Claiming to represent the concerns of bankers in the U.S. and abroad, Rockefeller advised the president to make a "vigorous effort" to control government spending and to balance the budget. He also suggested to Kennedy that interest rates were being kept too low and too much money was being injected into the economy. In his reply, Kennedy either rejected or ignored these arguments.[74]

Rockefeller's concern for what he called "fiscal responsibility" was also expressed in a report issued around this time by the Committee for Economic Development (CED). The CED was created in the early 1940s and its membership was largely leaders of the largest non-financial corporations, including two of the directors of Time, Inc. In 1958 the CED created a Commission on Money and Credit, which included David Rockefeller, to do a study on national economic policy with a focus on money and credit. Although

---

[72] Rowen, 1964, p. 179.

[73] Epstein, 1983.

[74] Life, 1962, pp. 30-34.

the report, issued in 1961, contained a multitude of diverse recommendations, probably reflecting input from a large staff, there was some continuity in theme. The report claimed that the government's spending, taxation, and monetary policies should be geared to stabilization of the economy. In this view, actions such as tax reductions and increases in money supply were only appropriate during downturns in the economy.[75] In these basic areas, the recommendations were in direct conflict with the course Kennedy would take as President.

There was also a difference in emphasis in the area of international economic relations. The CED wanted the government to make free trade and private activity central to U.S. foreign policy.[76] This and related issues brought Rockefeller into conflict with Kennedy over the Alliance for Progress.

Rockefeller was opposed to Kennedy's foreign policy from the beginning, critical of what he viewed as too much government involvement and too little emphasis on the creation of the right kind of investment climate. These views were expressed in personal statements and in a report issued in 1963 by Chase Manhattan.[77]

In 1966 Rockefeller reacted to criticism of U.S. activity in Latin America in an article he wrote for *Foreign Affairs*, the official publication of the Council on Foreign Relations. In defending the contribution to Latin American economies by U.S. business, Rockefeller noted the investment figures for 1964 and said that the main reason for alleged recent success was a change of the "policy which prevailed in the early years of the Alliance of placing too much emphasis on rapid and revolutionary social change and on strictly government-to-government assistance." He later referred to the "overly ambitious concepts of revolutionary social change which typified the thinking of many who played an important part in the Alliance in its early years."[78] The "early years" were when Kennedy was alive. The more acceptable program appeared after he was dead.

---

[75] Commission on Money and Credit, 1961, pp. viii-x, 64-67, 126-30, 255-58.
[76] Commission on Money and Credit, 1961, pp. 227-28, 236-41.
[77] Collier and Horowitz, 1976, pp. 413-14.
[78] Rockefeller, 1966, pp. 408, 416.

CONCLUSION AND BEGINNING

JFK acting as President of the United States and John J. MCloy acting as executive secretary for the Establishment represented two different and conflicting views of government. Kennedy's view was descendent from Alexander Hamilton and Supreme Court Chief Justice John Marshall. That view was also expressed in the policies and goals of John Quincey Adams, Abraham Lincoln, and Franklin D. Roosevelt. In a very slightly populist form, it also appeared in the politics of Huey Long.

McCloy, Acheson, Dulles, Rostow, Alsop, and Reston all spoke and acted for a different concept of government. They represented an Eastern Establishment or Anglo-American Establishment view that has its origins in the political philosophy of John Locke. Locke's amalgamation of feudalist and early capitalist values assigns to government the task of maintaining and defending the privileges of the dominant propertied interests. In this very wearied tradition, government is to be generally passive except in its police and defense functions. Above all else, and at times in conflict with its police and defense responsibilities, government is assigned the duty of actively protecting those property interests. The disaster of the 1930s had led to a resurrection of some of the traditions and policies of Hamiltonianism and its successors. Kennedy sought to maintain and deepen that trend. McCloy's masters were heading in a different direction.

Kennedy's foreign policy and his opposition to the Anglo-American Establishment's neo-colonialism were based on his general commitment to progress and on his sense of justice. He related to his own Irish ancestry partly in terms of this issue. In January of 1962 President Kennedy said the following to Prime Minister Jawaharlal Nehru of India:[79]

> I grew up in a community where the people were hardly a generation away from colonial rule. And I can claim the company of many historians in saying that the colonialism to which my immediate ancestors were subject was more sterile, oppressive and even cruel than that of India.[79]

Kennedy's opposition to colonialism and all similar policies was part of the public record throughout most of his political career.[80]

[79.] Mahoney, 1983, Chapter 1.
[80.] Gibson, 1994, pp. 35-51; Mahoney, 1983, pp. 15-19.

His economic policy was derived from his own reasoning and it appears to be based at least partly on his appreciation of the early Hamilton Federalists and later like-minded ideas. His sense of government may well have been reinforced by his understanding of Christianity.

In 1967, Pope Paul VI, who had assumed his position the year that Kennedy was assassinated, issued an encyclical letter entitled "On the Development of Peoples." Perhaps addressing Kennedy's opponents, the Pope offered the following observations on industrialization and "liberal" capitalism. The reader should keep in mind that Paul VI used the term "liberalism" in its traditional European usage, referring to the philosophy of people such as John Locke plus the ideas of free market economics. What the Pope called "liberal" we in the United States in the post-World War Two era would call free market or free enterprise conservatism. Pope Paul VI:

> The introduction of industry is a necessity for economic growth and human progress; it is also a sign of development and contributes to it. By persistent work and use of his intelligence man gradually wrests nature's secrets from her and finds a better application for her riches. As his self-mastery increases, he develops a taste for research and discovery, an ability to take a calculated risk, boldness in enterprises, generosity in what he does and a sense of responsibility.
>
> But it is unfortunate that on these new conditions of society a system has been constructed which considers profit as the key motive for economic progress, competition as the supreme law of economics, and private ownership of the means of production as an absolute right that has no limits and carries no corresponding social obligation. This unchecked liberalism leads to dictatorship rightly denounced by Pius XI as producing 'the international imperialism of money.' One cannot condemn such abuses too strongly by solemnly recalling once again that the economy is at the service of man. But if it is true that a type of capitalism has been the source of excessive suffering , injustices and fratricidal conflicts whose effects still persist, it would also be wrong to attribute to industrialisation itself evils that belong to the woeful system which accompanied it. On the contrary one must recognise in all justice the irreplaceable contribution made by the organisation of labour and of industry to what development as accomplished.[81]

To mark the twentieth anniversary of the publication of Paul VI's letter, John Paul II published his letter entitled "On Social Concern." Therein, the Pope

---

[81.] Paul VI, 1967, pp. 16-17.

criticized both Marxist collectivism and "liberal" capitalism, saying that both are "imperfect and in need of radical correction."[82]

In order to prevent and offset the problems of ownership as "absolute right" and the "dictatorship" and "imperialism of money," JFK attempted to implement a program of "radical correction." JFK's program was based on neither collectivism nor the "liberal" capitalism which leads quickly to political, social, and economic dictatorship by the super-rich.

These expressions by the leaders of Kennedy's church are completely consistent with what he was doing. Both are consistent with the tradition we have referred to with the names of Hamilton,[83] Lincoln,[84] and Roosevelt. The suppression of this tradition, in policy terms, in political debate, and in the media, since Kennedy's death has facilitated the current near dictatorship of the super-rich.

John Kennedy was committed to developing and using his own abilities. He was just as committed to the development and well-being of other people. Pope Paul VI referred to the obligation for self-development in the following:

> In the design of God, every man is called upon to develop and fulfill himself, for every life is a vocation. At birth, everyone is granted , in germ, a set of aptitudes and qualities for him to bring to fruition. Their coming to maturity , which will be the result of education received from the environment and personal efforts, will allow each man to direct himself toward the destiny intended for him by his Creator. Endowed with intelligence and freedom, he is responsible for his fulfillment as he is for his salvation. He is aided or sometimes impeded, by those who educate him and those with whom he lives, but each one remains, whatever be these influences affecting him, the principle agent of his own success or failure. By the unaided effort of his own intelligence and his will, each man can grow in humanity, can enhance his personal worth, can become more a person.[85]

The commitment to others is then emphasized:

> But each man is a member of society. He is part of the whole of mankind. It is not just certain individuals, but all men who are called to this fullness of development. Civilisations are born, develop and die. But humanity is

---

[82] John Paul II, 1987, p. 35.

[83] McDonald, 1982.

[84] Boritt, 1978.

[85] Paul VI, 1967, p. 11.

advancing along the path of history like the waves of a rising tide encroaching gradually on the shore. We have inherited from past generations, and we have benefited from the work of our contemporaries: for this reason we have obligations towards all, and we cannot refuse to interest ourselves in those who will come after us to enlarge the human family. The reality of human solidarity, which is a benefit for us, also imposes a duty.[86]

President Kennedy's conception of his obligations as a President was that he had to energetically defend and promote the general welfare. He apparently saw his duties as a Christian in the same way. President Kennedy demonstrated his intention to fulfill those obligations and duties in the face of extreme opposition. He behaved with courage as he himself defined it. He offered the following meaning of the word courage:

A man does what he must - in spite of personal consequences, in spite of obstacles and dangers and pressures - and that is the basis of all human morality.[87]

It is probably not possible now to bring the murderers to justice. What is important now, and always, is that the truth be served. In the process we will serve ourselves and our descendents. John Kennedy embodied an idea of government, nation, and humanity that is necessary for the future.

---

[86] Ibid., p. 12.

[87] Kennedy, 1964a, p. 216.

BIBLIOGRAPHY

Acheson, Dean. 1959. *Sketches From Life*. New York: Harper & Brothers.

--. 1969. *Present At The Creation: My Years In The State* Department. New York: W. W. Norton & Co.

Air Force One Transcripts. 1995. Transcribed by Kathleen Cunningham. Sherman Oaks, CA: Citizens for Truth about the Kennedy Assassination.

Almquist, Leann Grabavoy. 1993. *Joseph Alsop and American Foreign Policy: The Journalist as Advocate*. New York: University Press of America.

A. N. Marquis. 1926. *Who's Who In America*. Chicago, IL: A. N. Marquis.

--. 1940. *Who's Who In America*. Chicago, IL: A. N. Marquis.

Anson, Robert Sam. 1975. *"They've Killed the President!" The Search for the Murderers of John F. Kennedy*. New York: Bantam Books.

Archer, Jules. 1973. *The Plot to Seize the White House*. New York: Hawthorn Books, Inc.

Bachrach, Peter and Elihu Bergman. 1973. *Power and Choice: The Formulation of American Population Policy*. Lexington, MA: Lexington Books/D.C. Heath.

Basso, Hamilton. 1946. "The Huey Long Legend." *Life* (December 9): 106-21.

Beals, Carleton. 1971 (1935). *The Story of Huey P. Long*. Westport, CT: Greenwood Press.

Bedford, Sybille. 1973. *Aldous Huxley*. New York: Alfred A. Knopf/Harper & Row.

Bernstein, Irving. 1991. *Promises Kept: John F. Kennedy's New Frontier*. New York: Oxford University Press.

Beschloss, Michael R. 1997. *Taking Charge: The Johnson White House Tapes, 1963-1964*. New York: Simon & Schuster.

Bird, Kai. 1992. *The Chairman: John J. McCloy and the Making of the American Establishment*. New York: Simon & Schuster.

Birmingham, Stephen. 1987. *America's Secret Aristocracy*. Boston, MA: Little, Brown and Co.

Bishop, Jim. 1968. *The Day Kennedy Was Shot*. Toronto: HarperCollins.

Blair, John M. 1976. *The Control of Oil*. New York: Vintage Books/Random House.

Boritt, G. S. 1978. *Lincoln and The Economics of The American Dream*. Memphis, TN: Memphis State University Press.

Brinkley, Alan. 1983. "Minister Without Portfolio." *Harper's* (February): 31-46.

Brinkley, Douglas. 1992. *Dean Acheson: The Cold War Years, 1953-71*. New Haven, CT: Yale University Press.

Brown, Walt. 1995. *Treachery In Dallas*. New York: Carroll & Graf.

Buchanan, Thomas G. 1964. *Who Killed Kennedy?* New York: G. P. Putnam's Sons.

Bundy, McGeorge. 1988. *Danger and Survival*. New York: Random House.

Burch, Philip H., Jr. 1980. *Elites in American History: The New Deal to the Carter Administration*. New York: Holmes & Meier.

Burns, James MacGregor. 1961. *John Kennedy: A Political Profile*. New York: Avon Book Division/Hearst Corporation.

Caldwell, Guy A. 1965. *Early History of the Ochsner Medical Center*. Springfield, IL: Charles C. Thomas, Publisher.

Canfield, Michael and Alan Weberman. 1975. *Coup d'etat In America*. New York: Third Press/Joseph Okpaku.

Carpenter, Arthur E. 1987 (1993). "Gateway to the Americas: New Orleans's Quest For Latin American Trade, 1900-1970." Ph.D. Dissertation. Ann Arbor, MI: U.M.I. Dissertation Services.

--. 1989. "Social Origins of Anticommunism: The Information Council of the Americas." *Louisiana History*, Vol. xxx (Spring): 117-43.

Chace, James. 1998. *Acheson: The Secretary of State Who Created the American World*. New York: Simon & Schuster.

Chernow, Ron. 1990. *The House of Morgan*. New York: Touchstone/Simon & Schuster.

Chomsky, Noam. 1993. *Rethinking Camelot: JFK, the Vietnam War, and US Political Culture*. Boston, MA: South End Press.

The Christchurch Star. 1963. "Arrested Man Lived In Russia." *The Christchurch Star* (November 23): 1.

Clark, Ronald W. 1968. *The Huxleys*. New York: McGraw-Hill.

--. 1975. *The Life of Bertrand Russell*. London: Jonathan Cape and Weidenfeld & Nicolson.

Cohen, Warren I. 1978. *The Chinese Connection*. New York: Columbia University Press.

Collier, Peter and David Horowitz. 1976. *The Rockefellers: An American Dynasty*. New York: Signet/New American Library.

Commission on Money and Credit. 1961. *Money and Credit: Their Influence on Jobs, Prices, and Growth*. Englewood Cliffs, NJ: Prentice-Hall, Inc.

Cooke, Blanche Wiesen. 1981. *The Declassified Eisenhower*. Garden City, NY: Doubleday & Company.

Corey, Lewis. 1930. *The House of Morgan: A Social Biography of the Masters of Money*. New York: G. Howard Watt.

Costello, John. 1988. *Mask of Treachery*. New York: Warner Books.

Council on Foreign Relations. 1963. *Annual Report, Council on Foreign Relations*. New York: Harold Pratt House.

--. 1988. *Annual Report, Council on Foreign Relations*. New York: Council on Foreign Relations, Inc.

Curry, Jesse. 1969. *JFK Assassination File*. Dallas, TX: American Poster and Printing Company, Inc.

The Dallas Morning News. 1963. "Cabell Says Dallas Shocked by Slaying" *The Dallas Morning News* (November 23): 14.

Daniell, F. Raymond. 1935. "Throngs Pass Long's Bier As Friends Discuss Plot" New York Times (September 12): 1, 18.

Davenport, John. 1962. "The Priority of Politics over Economics." *Fortune* (October): 88-91, 188-200.

Davis, Deborah. 1991 (1979). *Katharine the Great: Katharine Graham and Her Washington Post Empire*. New York: Sheridan Square Press.

Davis John H. 1989. *Mafia Kingfish: Carlos Marcello and the Assassination of John F. Kennedy*. New York: Signet/New American Library.

Deakin, F. W. and G. R. Storry. 1966. *The Case of Richard Sorge*. New York: Harper & Row.

Demerath, Nicholas J. 1976. *Birth Control and Foreign Policy: The Alternatives to Family Planning*. New York: Harper and Row.

Department of Commerce. 1965. *The Statistical History of the United States*. Stamford, CT: Fairfield Publishers.

Dickson, Paul. 1971. *Think Tanks*. New York: Atheneum.

DiEugenio, James. 1992. *Destiny Betrayed: JFK, Cuba and the Garrison Case*. New York: Sheridan Square Press.

--. 1999. "Dodd and Dulles vs. Kennedy in Africa." *Probe* (January- February): 18-25.

Domhoff, G. William. 1971. *Higher Circles: The Governing Class in America*. New York: Vintage Books/Random House.

--. 1974. *The Bohemian Grove and Other Retreats*. New York: Harper Torchbooks/Harper & Row.

--. 1983. *Who Rules America Now? A View for the '80s*. Englewood Cliffs, NJ: Prentice-Hall, Inc.

Donovan, John C. 1974. *The Cold Warriors: A Policy-Making Elite*. Lexington, MA: D.C. Heath and Co.

Donovan, Robert J. 1952. *The Assassins*. New York: Harper & Brothers.

Dooley, Peter C. 1969. "The Interlocking Directorate." *The American Economic Review* LIX: 314-23.

Duffy, James R. 1992. *Conspiracy: Who Killed JFK?* New York: S.P.I./Shapolsky.

Eddy, Sherewood. 1944. *A Century With Youth: A History of the Y.M.C.A. from 1844 to 1944*. New York: Association Press.

Epstein, Edward Jay. 1966. *Inquest: The Warren Commission and the Establishment of Truth*. New York: Bantam Books/Viking Press.

--. 1978. *Legend: The Secret World of Lee Harvey Oswald*. London: Arrow Books.

--. 1983. "Ruling the World of Money." *Harper's* (November): 43-48.

Evans, Rowland and Robert Novak. 1966. *Lyndon Johnson: The Exercise of Power*. New York: The New American Library.

Federal Bureau of Investigations. 1963. Memorandum for Mr. Johnson. November 22. Lyndon Baines Johnson Library, Austin, Texas.

Feinberg, Barry and Ronald Kasrils. 1983. *Bertrand Russell's America, 1945-1970*. Boston, MA: South End Press.

Finney, John W. 1961. "Kennedy Urges Congress To Set Up Peace Agency." *New York Times* (June 30): 1, 4.

Fischer, Erika J. and Heinz D. Fischer. 1994. *John J. McCloy: An American Architect of Postwar Germany*. New York: Peter Lang.

Flynn, John T. 1953. *The Lattimore Story*. New York: Devin-Adair Company.

Fonzi, Gaeton. 1966. "The Warren Commission, The Truth, and Arlen Specter." *Philadelphia Magazine* (August):38-45, 79-88.

--. 1993. *The Last Investigation*. New York: Thunder's Mouth Press.

Forbes, John Douglas. 1974. *Stettinius, Sr.: Portrait of a Morgan Partner*. Charlottesville, VA: University Press of Virginia.

Ford, Gerald R. and John R. Stiles. 1965. *Portrait of the Assassin*. New York: Simon and Schuster.

Fortune. 1952. "The Internationalists of New Orleans" *Fortune* (June): 126-40.

--. 1961. "Activism in the White House." *Fortune* (June): 117-18.

--. 1962. "The Quality of Foreign Aid." *Fortune* (February): 79-82.

--. 1963. "What the Hell Do Those Fellows Want." *Fortune* (February): 81-82.

--. 1963a. "How to save the Tax Cut." *Fortune* (March): 79-80.

--. 1964. "Jock Whitney: Unclassified Capitalist." *Fortune* (October): 114-19, 184-96.

Frewin, Anthony. 1994. Late-Breaking News on Clay Shaw's United Kingdom Contacts. Williamsport, PA: Last Hurrah Bookshop.

Furiati, Claudia. 1994. *ZR Rifle: The Plot to Kill Kennedy and Castro*. Trans. Maxine Shaw. Melbourne, Australia: Ocean Press.

Garrison, Jim. 1970. *A Heritage Of Stone*. New York: Berkley Publishing Corporation.

--. 1988. *On The Trail Of The Assassins*. New York: Sheridan Square Press.

Geyelin, Philip. 1963. "U.S. Support for a World Monetary Study Is Victory for Administration 'Activists.'" *Wall Street Journal* (October 3): 16.

Gibson, Donald. 1994. *Battling Wall Street: The Kennedy Presidency*. New York: Sheridan Square Press.

--. 1996. "Clay Shaw, Freeport Sulphur, and the Eastern Establishment." *Probe* (November-December): 16-20.

--. 1997. "The Creation of the Warren Commission." *Mid-America: An Historical Review* 79: 203-54.

Greider, William. 1987. *The Secrets of the Temple*. New York: Touchstone/Simon & Schuster.

Groden, Robert J. & Harrison Edward Livingstone. 1989. *High Treason: The Assassination of President John F. Kennedy - What Really Happened*. New York: The Conservatory Press.

Grose, Peter. 1994. *Gentleman Spy: The Life of Allen Dulles*. New York: Houghton Mifflin Company.

Hailey, Foster. 1963. "Lone Assassin the Rule in U.S.; Plotting More Prevalent Abroad." *New York Times* (November 25): 9.

Hair, William Ivy. 1991. *The Kingfish and His Realm*. Baton Rouge, LA: Louisiana State University Press.

Halifax, Lord (Edward Wood). 1957. *Fullness of Days*. New York: Dodd, Mead & company.

Hazlitt, Henry. 1962. "To Restore Confidence." *Newsweek* (May 14): 92.

--. 1963. "Sham Tax Cut." *Newsweek* (September 2): 70.

--. 1963a. "Exporting Inflation." *Newsweek* (September 9): 78.

--. 1963b. "A Shortsighted Tariff." *Newsweek* (October 28): 84.

--. 1963c. "Tax Cut in Wonderland." *Newsweek* (November 4): 90.

--. 1963d. "Does Foreign Aid Aid?" *Newsweek* (November 25): 97.

Healy, George W., Jr. 1946. "The Deep South." *New York Times* (November 17): Sec. IV, 6.

Hearings Before the President's Commission on the Assassination of President Kennedy, Volumes I through XXVI. 1964. Washington, DC: United States Government Printing Office.

Hearings Before the Select Committee on Assassinations of the United States House of Representatives. 1979. Vols. III and XI. *Investigation of the Assassination of President John F. Kennedy*. Washington, DC: United States Government Printing Office.

Heller, Walter W. 1966. *New Dimensions of Political Economy*. Cambridge, MA: Harvard University Press.

Hennelly, Robert and Jerry Policoff. 1992. "JFK: How the Media Assassinated the Real Story." *The Village Voice* (March 31): 33- 38.

Hepburn, James. 1968. *Farewell America*. Vaduz, Liechtenstein: Frontiers Publishing Co.

Hersh, Burton. 1992. *The Old Boys: The American Elite and the Origins of the CIA*. New York: Charles Scribner & Sons.

Hewett, Carol. 1997. "The Paines Know." *Probe* (November-December): 11-18.

Hewett, Carol, Steve Jones, and Barbara LaMonica. 1996. "The Paines: Suspicious Characters." *Probe* (May-June): 14-16.

Hill, Gladwin. 1963. "Leftist Accused" *New York Times* (November 23): 1, 4.

--1963a. "Evidence Against Oswald Described As Conclusive." *New York Times* (November 24): 1.

Hoffman, William. 1971. *David*. New York: Lyle Stuart.

Hoover, J. Edgar. 1963. Memorandum from J. Edgar Hoover to Clyde Tolson, Alan Belmont, et al. November 22, 2:21 P.M. (Sent at 5:00 P.M.)

--. 1963a. Memorandum from J. Edgar Hoover to Clyde Tolson, Alan Belmont, et al. November 22, 4:01 P. M. (Sent at 5:00 P.M.)

--. 1963b. Memorandum from J. Edgar Hoover to Clyde Tolson, Alan Belmont, et al. November 22, 5:15 P.M.

--. 1963c. Memorandum from J. Edgar Hoover to Clyde Tolson, Alan Belmont, et al. November 22, 5:42 P.M.

--. 1963d. Telephone call from J Edgar Hoover to President Johnson. November 23, 10:01 A.M. Transcript provided by Lyndon Baines Johnson Library, Austin, Texas.

Hopkins, Howard. 1951. *History of the Y.M.C.A. in North America*. New York: Association Press.

Howard, Perry H. 1957. *Political Tendencies in Louisiana, 1812- 1952*. Baton Rouge, LA: Louisiana State University Press.

Hoyt, Edwin P., Jr. 1966. *The House of Morgan*. New York: Dodd, Mead & Company.

Hurt, Henry. 1985. *Reasonable Doubt*. New York: Henry Holt and Company.

Hyde, H. Montgomery. 1962. *Room 3603*. New York: Farrar, Straus & Company.

Hyman, Sidney. 1975. *The Aspen Idea*. Norman, OK: University of Oklahoma Press.

Isaacson, Walter and Evan Thomas. 1986. *The Wise Men*. New York: Touchstone Book/Simon and Schuster.

Jeansonne, Glen. 1993. *Messiah of the Masses: Huey P. Long and the Great Depression*. New York: Harper Collins College Publishers.

John Paul II. 1987. *On Social Concern* (Encyclical Letter). Boston, MA: St. Paul Books & Media.

Johnson, Lyndon Baines. 1971. *The Vantage Point: Perspectives of the Presidency, 1963-1969*. New York: Holt, Rinehart and Winston.

Jones, Brendan M. 1958. "Visitors Major In U.S. Business." *New York Times* (June 10): 47, 56.

Josephson, Matthew. 1934. *The Robber Barons*. New York: Harcourt Brace Jovanovich.

Kahn, E. J., Jr. 1981. *Jock: The Life and Times of John Hay Whitney*. Garden City, NY: Doubleday & Company.

Kane, Harvett T. 1941. *Louisiana Hayride*. New York: William Morrow & Co.

Kantor, Seth. 1978. *The Ruby Cover-Up*. New York: Zebra Books/Kensington Publishing Corporation.

Karp, Walter. 1979. *The Politics of War*. New York: Harper & Row.

Kendrick, John W. 1973. *Postwar Productivity Trends in the United States, 1948-1969*. New York: National Bureau of Economic Research/Columbia University Press.

Kennedy, John F. 1940 (1962). *Why England Slept*. Garden City, NY: Dolphin Books/Doubleday & Co.

--. 1961. *The Strategy of Peace*. Edited and introduction by Allan Nevins. New York: Popular Library.

--. 1961a. "Program to Restore Momentum to the American Economy." *House Documents, 87th Congress, 1st Session, Doc. No. 81*. Washington, DC: Government Printing Office.

--. 1961b. "Natural Resources." *House Documents, 87th Congress, 1st Session, Doc. No. 94*. Washington, DC: Government Printing Office.

--. 1961c. "Foreign Aid." *House Documents, 87th Congress, 1st Session, Doc. No. 117*. Washington, DC: Government Printing Office.

--. 1961d. "Our Federal Tax System." *House Documents, 87th Congress, 1st Session, Doc. No. 140*. Washington, DC: Government Printing Office.

--. 1962 (1988). "Economic Report of the President." In James Tobin and Murray Weidenbaum, eds., *Two Revolutions in Economic Policy*. Cambridge, MA: The MIT Press. 87-113.

--. 1962a. "Our Conservation Program." *House Documents, 87th Congress, 2nd Session, Doc. No. 348*. Washington, DC: Government Printing Office.

--. 1962b. News Conference, April 11. *New York Times* (April 12): 20.

--. 1962c. News Conference, April 18. *New York Times* (April 19): 16.

--. 1963a. "State of the Union Address." *House Documents, 88th Congress, 1st Session, Doc. No. 2*. Washington, DC: Government Printing Office.

--. 1963b. "Revision of Our Tax Structure." *House Documents, 88th Congress, 1st Session, Doc. No. 43*. Washington, DC: Government Printing Office.

--. 1963c. "Program for Education." *House Documents, 88th Congress, 1st Session, Doc. No. 54*. Washington, DC: Government Printing Office.

--. 1963d. "Our Foreign Assistance Act." *House Documents, 88th Congress, 1st Session, Doc. No. 94*. Washington, DC: Government Printing Office.

--. 1964. *The Burden and the Glory*. Allen Nevins, ed. New York: Harper & Row.

--. 1964a (1955). *Profiles In Courage*. New York: Harper & Row.

Kennedy, Joseph P. 1936. *I'm for Roosevelt*. New York: Reynal & Hitchcock.

Kevles, Daniel J. 1985. *In the Name of Eugenics*. Los Angeles, CA: University of California Press.

Knowles, Clayton. 1968. "Humphrey Gets An Offer of Aid" *New York Times* (October 17): 39.

Kohlberg, Alfred. 1953. "Evaluating the I.P.R." *New York Times* (May 17): Sec. IV, 10.

Kotz, David. 1978. *Bank Control of Large Corporations in the United States*. Los Angeles: University of California Press.

Krock, Arthur. 1963. "Mr. Kennedy's Management of the News." *Fortune* (March): 82, 199-202.

LaMonica, Barbara. 1998. "Michael Paine and His $300,000 Trust Fund." *Probe* (July-August): 6-7.

Lamont, Corliss. 1940. "Cooperation With Russia" *New York Times* (December 17): 24.

--. 1962. "Vietnam Aid Protested" *New York Times* (February 26): 26.

--. 1963. "To Pursue a Policy of Peace." *New York Times* (July 10): 34.

--. 1974. *Voices in the Wilderness*. Buffalo, NY: Prometheus Books.

Landry, Stuart O. 1938. *History of the Boston Club*. New Orleans, LA: Pelican Publishing Company.

Lane, Mark. 1966. *Rush To Judgment*. Greenwich, CT: Fawcett.

--. 1991. *Plausible Denial: Was the CIA Involved in the Assassination of JFK*. New York: Thunder's Mouth Press.

Lawrence, Lincoln and Kenn Thomas Kempton. 1987. *Mind Control, Oswald & JFK: Were We Controlled?* Kempton, IL: Adventures Unlimited Press.

Liebling, A.J. 1960. "The Great State" *The New Yorker* (May 28): 41- 91.

Life. 1963. "How to Rescue the Tax Cut." *Life* (March 1): 4.

--. 1963a. Why Kennedy's Tax Cut Trouble Gets Deeper." *Life* (March 29): 4.

--. 1963b. "Unblock That Merger Track!" *Life* (April 5): 4.

--. 1963c. "Press the War in Vietnam." *Life* (November 22): 4.

Lifton, David S. 1968. *Document Addendum to the Warren Report*. El Segundo, CA: Sightext Publications.

--. 1980. *Best Evidence: Disguise and Deception in the Assassination of John F. Kennedy*. New York: Carroll & Graf.

Livingstone, Harrison Edward. 1993. *Killing the Truth: Deceit and Deception in the JFK Case*. New York: Carroll & Graf.

Lonergan, Bernard J. F. 1970, *Insight: A Study of Human Understanding*. New York: Philosophical Library.

Long, Huey P. 1933 (1964). *Every Man A King: The Autobiography of Huey P. Long*. Chicago, IL: Quadrangle.

--. 1935. My First Days in the White House. Harrisburg, PA: The Telegraph Press.

--. 1985. *Kingfish to America: Share Our Wealth*. Intro. by Henry M. Christman. New York: Schocken Books.

Lukas, J. Anthony. 1971. "The Council on Foreign Relations - Is It a Club? Seminar? Presidium? `Invisible Government'?" *New York Times Magazine* (November 21): 34, 123-42.

Lundberg, Ferdinand. 1937. *America's 60 Families*. New York: The Vanguard Press.

--. 1968. *The Rich and the Super-Rich*. New York: Bantam Books.

--. 1975. *The Rockefeller Syndrome*. Secaucus, NJ: Lyle Stuart.

Mahl, Thomas E. 1998. *Desperate Deception: British Covert Operations in the United States, 1939-44*. Washington, DC: Brassey's.

Mahoney, Richard D. 1983. *JFK: Ordeal in Africa*. New York: Oxford University Press.

Mahoney, William P., Jr. 1968. Nkrumah in Retrospect." *The Review of Politics* XXX: 246-50.

Manchester, William. 1967. *The Death of a President*. New York: Harper & Row.

Marquis Who's Who. 1962-63. *Who's Who in America*. Chicago: Marquis Who's Who.

--. 1964-65. *Who's Who in America*. Chicago: Marquis Who's Who.

--. 1978-79. *Who's Who in America*. Chicago: Marquis Who's Who.

Marrs, Jim. 1989. *Crossfire*. New York: Carroll & Graf.

Mathewson, Joseph D. 1963. "U.S. Seeks High Court Rulings to Upset Some Business Combinations." *Wall Street Journal* (July 22): 1, 10.

May, Stacy and Galo Plaza. 1958. *The United Fruit Company In Latin America*. New York: National Planning Association.

McCloy, John J. 1953. *The Challenge to American Foreign Policy*. Cambridge, MA: Harvard University Press.

McDonald, Forrest. 1982. *Alexander Hamilton, A Biography*. New York: W.W. Norton & Co.

McLellan, David S. 1976. *Dean Acheson: The State Department Years*. New York: Dodd, Mead & Co.

Meagher, Sylvia. 1967. *Accessories After the Fact: The Warren Commission, The Authorities & The Report*. New York: Vintage Books/Random House.

Medvin, Norman. 1974. *The Energy Cartel: Who Runs the American Oil Industry*. New York: Vintage Books/Random House.

Menninger, Bonar. 1992. *Mortal Error: The Shot That Killed JFK*. New York: St. Martin's Press.

Merry, Robert W. 1996. *Taking On The World: Joseph and Stewart Alsop-Guardians of the American Century*. New York: Viking/Penguin Books.

Model, F. Peter and Robert J. Groden. 1976. *JFK: The Case For Conspiracy*. New York: Manor Books Inc.

Moody's Investors Service. 1963. *Moody's Industrial Manual*. New York: Moody's Investors Service, Inc.

Morris, John D. 1963. "Johnson Names A 7-Man Panel To Investigate Assassination; Chief Justice Warren Heads It." *New York Times* (November 30): 1, 12.

Morse, Richard C. 1919. *History of the North American Young Men's Christian Associations*. New York: Association Press.

Mosley, Leonard. 1978. *Dulles: A Biography of Eleanor, Allen, and John Foster Dulles and Their Family Network*. New York: Dell Book.

Murphy, Bruce Allen. 1988. *Fortas: The Rise and Ruin of a Supreme Court Justice*. New York: William Morrow and Company.

Murphy, Charles J.V. 1963. "Foreign Aid: Billions in Search of a Good Reason." *Fortune* (March): 126-30, 205-12.

Myers, Gustavus. 1917. *History of the Great American Fortunes*, Vol. II. Chicago: Charles H. Kerr & Company.

Newman, John M. 1992. *JFK and Vietnam: Deception, Intrigue, and the Struggle For Power*. New York: Warner Books/Time Warner.

Newman, Robert P. 1992. *Owen Lattimore and the `Loss of China'*. Los Angeles, CA: university of California Press.

Newsweek. 1963. "The Marxist Marine." *Newsweek* (December 2): 27.

New York Herald Tribune. 1963. "Shame of a Nation - History of Assassinations." *New York Herald Tribune* (November 23): 4.

--. 1963a. "A Day of Grief and Shame." *New York Herald Tribune* (November 23): 14. New York Times. 1925. "J.D. Rockefeller Jr. Gift." *New York Times* (April 28): 10.

--. 1925a. "Peace Maneuvers Planned In Pacific." *New York Times* (May 25): 19.

--. 1925b. "Plan of Conference on Pacific Relations." *New York Times* (June 22): 27.

--. 1925c. "Impossible, But a Fact." *New York Times* (June 23): 18.

--. 1925d. "Pacific Conference To Begin on July 1." *New York Times* (June 28): 16.

--. 1925e. "New Orleans Will Exhibit World Trade." *New York Times* (July 12): Sec VIII, 9.

--. 1925f. "Debate On World Court." *New York Times* (November 12): 18.

--. 1925g. "Debate On World Court." *New York Times* (November 13): 14.

--1925h. "Favor the World Court." *New York Times* (November 14): 14.

--. 1927. Tea For Rockefellers." *New York Times* (April 28): 23.

--. 1927a. "Delegates Gather For Pacific Parley." *New York Times* (July 15): 6.

--. 1929. "East and West To Meet In Council at Kyoto." *New York Times* (October 27): Sec. X, 7.

--. 1932. "Students of Many Races In Plea For Peace Here." *New York Times* (January 18): 17.

--. 1932a. "Assails Colleges For Radical Trend." *New York Times* (October 2): 9.

--. 1932b. "Chicago Receives Rockefeller House." *New York Times* (October 6): 25.

--. 1932c. Hails Security of Soviet." *New York Times* (December 14): 16.

--. 1933. "Inquiry On Soviet Begun By Notables." *New York Times* (July 3): 3.

--. 1934. Corliss Lamont Seized as Picket." *New York Times* (June 28): 3.

--. 1934a. "Lamont Opposes Delay In Trial." *New York Times* (July 6): 9.

--.1935. "Long Asks Road Program" *New York Times (February 24)*: 2.

--. 1936. "Classrooms and Campus." *New York Times* (May 10)): Sec. X, 10.

--. 1936a. "World's Students Gather Tomorrow." *New York Times* (June 14): Sec. II, 8.

--. 1936b. "Stimson Heads Trustees." *New York Times* (June 16): 27.

--. 1937. "Student Club In Geneva." *New York Times* (May 9): Sec. II, 8.

--. 1937a. "Rockefeller Bids World Have Faith." *New York Times* (November 20): 19.

--. 1937b. "A House of Many Nations." *New York Times* (November 22): 18.

--. 1942. "Full Unity Urged With The Russians." *New York Times* (November 8): 36.

--. 1944. Heads International House." *New York Times* (April 8): 21.

--. 1946. "Corliss Lamont Accused By House." *New York Times* (June 27): 4.

--. 1946. "Dewey Picks Board For Trade Center." *New York Times* (July 7): 1, 27.

--. 1946a. "Bipartisan Policy On Trade Is Urged." *New York Times* (November 12): 46, 49.

--. 1946b. "New Orleans Sets `Free-Port' Trade." *New York Times* (November 17): 58.

--. 1947. "Acheson Confirms Choice of Osborn." *New York Times* (March 6): 21.

--. 1947a. "New Orleans' Rise In Trade Reviewed." *New York Times* (June 14): 29.

--. 1947b. "World Trade Body Ready To Function." *New York Times* (September 24): 35.

--. 1947c. "World-Wide Groups Set Up For Peace." *New York Times* (November 17): 23.

--. 1947d. "International House." *New York Times* (November 26): 22.

--. 1949. "Murals a Puzzle, Davies' Art To Go'." *New York Times* (August 3): 13.

--. 1950. "Dulles Asks Unity To Win `Cold War'." *New York Times* (May 17): 2.

--. 1950a. "General Wood Wins Cunningham Award." *New York Times* (October 15): 1.

--. 1951. "International House." *New York Times* (March 18): Sec. II, 17.

--. 1951a. "Soviet Knew Ahead of Tokyo War Plan" *New York Times* (August 10): 1, 3.

--. 1951b. "Lamont Charges `Smear' Attempt." *New York Times* (September 17): 12.

--. 1953. "No Red Grip Found On Foundation Aid." *New York Times* (January 3): 5.

--. 1953a. "Corliss Lamont Defies McCarthy; Senator to ask Contempt Citation." *New York Times* (September 24) 1, 10.

--. 1953b. "The Limits of Inquiry." *New York Times* (September 25): 20.

--. 1953c. "Lamont Declares He Disputes Reds." *New York Times* (September 28): 14.

--. 1954. "Press Parley On Today." *New York Times* (November 8): 41.

--. 1954a. "Friends of Japan Meet" *New York Times* (November 9): 13.

--. 1955. "U.S. Official New Head Of International House." *New York Times* (September 13): 25.

--. 1955a. "Institute Loses Tax Exemption," *New York Times* (October 14).

--. 1956. "2 Elected by International House ." *New York Times* (May 16): 12.

--. 1957. "Censorship Bar Noted." *New York Times* (May 10): 2.

--. 1957a. "Attorney Nears China." *New York Times* (December): 2.

--. 1959. "Pacific Institute Loses 2 Tax Tests." *New York Times* (April 28): 29.

--. 1960. "Pacific Institute Leaving Country." *New York Times* (December 7): 8.

--. 1961. "In The Post-McCarthy Era." *New York Times* (July 20): 26.

--. 1961a. "Eisenhower Named." *New York Times* (September 30): 23.

--. 1963. "European Ports Deeply Impress Visiting U.S. Trade Mission." *New York Times* (September 9): 37, 39.

--. 1963a. "Eyewitnesses Describe Scene of Assassination." *New York Times* (November 23) 5.

--. 1964. "Rockefeller Hits U.S. Latin Policy." *New York Times* (April 22): 37.

--. 1964a. "New Williams College Trustee." *New York Times* (November 15): 59.

--. 1965. "International House Forms Worldwide Alumni Council." *New York Times* (August 30). --.1965a. "FBI Chief Names Possible Successor To a Key Position." *New York Times* (December 3): 26.

--. 1967. "Yelling Match Disrupts Rights Forum." *New York Times* (December 10): 1, 40.

--. 1968. Leaders of Peace Groups Term President's Decision a Victory." *New York Times* (April 1): 28.

--. 1974. "Global Communications." *New York Times* (June 19): 44.

--. 1974a. "Students' Haven Marks 50 Years." *New York Times* (July 21): 19.

--. 1975. "Ball to Head Board Of International House." *New York Times* (January 15): 16.

--. 1977. "A New Orleans Club Bars Talk By Young." *New York Times* (February 11): 7.

--. 1977a. "Club's Decision Not to Invite Young Stirs Controversy in New Orleans." *New York Times* (February 12): 46.

--. 1977b. "Club in New Orleans Apologizes to Young" *New York Times* (February 13): 26.

North, Mark. 1991. *Act of Treason*. New York: Carroll & Graf.

Nossiter, Bernard D. 1961. "Kennedy and Fed Clash Again." *Washington Post* (March 24): A4.

Oglesby, Carl. 1977. *The Yankee and Cowboy War: Conspiracies from Dallas to Watergate and Beyond*. New York: Berkley Publishing.

O'Donnell, Kenneth P. and David F. Powers. 1973. *Johnny, We Hardly Knew Ye*. New York: Pocket Books.

O'Neill, William L. 1993. *A Democracy At War*. New York: Free Press/Macmillan.

Paul VI. 1967. *On The Development of Peoples* (Encyclical Letter). Boston, MA: Pauline Books and Media.

Payer, Cheryl. 1974. *The Debt Trap: The International Monetary Fund and the Third World*. New York: Monthly Review Press.

Pease, Lisa. 1996. "David Atlee Phillips, Clay Shaw & Freeport Sulphur." *Probe* (March-April).

--. 1996a. "Indonesia, President Kennedy & Freeport Sulphur." *Probe* (May-June): 18-26, 30-31.

--. 1998. "Sirhan and the RFK Assassination, Part II: Rubrick's Cube." *Probe* (May-June): 4-9, 27-36.

Piper, Michael Collins. 1993. *Final Judgment: The Missing Link in the JFK Assassination Conspiracy*. Washington, DC: The Wolfe Press.

Popham, John N. 1948. "Trade Leadership By U.S. Advocated." *New York Times* (November 30): 41.

--. 1948. "Port Is Dedicated To World Trade." *New York Times* (December 1): 43.

Posner, Gerald. 1993. *Case Closed: Lee Harvey Oswald and the Assassination of JFK*. New York: Random House.

Powers, Thomas. 1979. *The Man Who Kept the Secrets: Richard Helms and the CIA*. New York: Washington Square Press/Pocket Books.

Prange, Gordon W. 1984. *Target Tokyo: The Story of the Sorge Spy Ring*. New York: McGraw Hill.

President's Commission on the Assassination of President Kennedy. 1963-64. Executive Sessions(Transcripts). Washington, DC: National Archives.

President's Commission on the Assassination of President Kennedy. 1964. *The Warren Commission Report on the Assassination of John F. Kennedy*. Intro. by Robert J. Donovan. Toronto: Popular Library.

President's Commission on the Assassination of President John F. Kennedy. 1993. *The Warren Commission Report*. Stamford, CT: Longmeadow Press.

Prouty, L. Fletcher. 1992. *JFK: The CIA, Vietnam and the Plot to Assassinate John F. Kennedy*. New York: Birch Lane/Carol Publishing.

Quigley, Carroll. 1966. *Tragedy and Hope: A History of the World in Our Time*. New York: Macmillan Co.

--. 1981. *The Anglo-American Establishment*. New York: Books in Focus.

Raffeto, Francis. 1963. "'Act of Maniac' Not Tied to City: Cabell." *The Dallas Morning News* (November 23): 4.

Reisman, Judith A. 1998. *Kinsey: Crimes and Consequences*. Arlington, VA: Institute for Media Education.

Reston, James. 1963. "Why America Weeps." *New York Times* (November 23): 1.

--. 1970. "Aspen Colo.: Human Rights vs. Property Rights." *New York Times* (August 30): IV, p. 12.

--. 1991. *Deadline: A Memoir*. New York: Random House.

Roberts, Craig. 1994. *Kill Zone: A Sniper Looks At Dealey Plaza*. Tulsa, OK: Typhoon Press/Christian Patriot Press.

Rockefeller, David. 1966. "What Private Enterprise Means to Latin America." *Foreign Affairs* 44 (April): 403-16.

Roffman, Howard. 1975. *Presumed Guilty*. Rutherford, NJ: Fairleigh Dickinson University Press.

Rostow, Eugene V. 1972. *Peace in the Balance: The Future of U.S. Foreign Policy*. New York: Simon & Schuster.

Rowen, Hobart. 1964. *The Free Enterprisers: Kennedy , Johnson and the Business Establishment*. New York: G.P. Putnam's Sons.

Russell, Bertrand. 1924. *Icarus, or The Future of Science*. New York: E.P. Dutton & Co.

--. 1953. *The Impact of Science on Society*. New York: Simon & Schuster.

--. 1969. *The Autobiography if Bertrand Russell, 1944-1967*. London: George Allen and Unwin Ltd.

Russell, Dick. 1992. *The Man Who Knew Too Much*. New York: Carroll & Graf.

Salandria, Vincent. 1965. "The Warren Report-?" *Liberation* (March): 16-22.

--. 1971. "The Assassination of President John F. Kennedy: A Model for Explanation." *Computers and Automation* (December).

--. 1977. "The Design of the Warren Report, to Fall to Pieces." *People and the Pursuit of Truth* (April).

--. 1998. "The JFK Assassination - A False Mystery Concealing State Crimes." Speech presented at 1998 conference of Coalition on Political Assassinations, Dallas, Texas.

Salinger, Pierre. 1966. *With Kennedy*. Garden City, NY: Doubleday & Company.

Samuels, Gertrude. 1960. "A House of Brotherhood." *New York Times* (May 1): Sec. VI, 30-31.

Schlesinger, Arthur M., Jr. 1960. *The Age of Roosevelt: The Politics of Upheaval*. Cambridge, MA: Riverside Press/Houghton Mifflin.

Schlesinger, Arthur M., Jr. 1965. *A Thousand Days: John F. Kennedy in the White House*. Boston, MA: Houghton Mifflin Company.

Schlesinger, Stephen and Stephen Kinzer. 1982. *Bitter Fruit: The Untold Story of the American Coup in Guatemala*. Garden City, NY: Doubleday & Company.

Schotz, E. Martin. 1996. *History Will Not Absolve Us*. Brookline, MA: Kurtz, Ulmer & DeLuca.

Scott, Peter Dale. 1971. *The Dallas Conspiracy*. Aptos, CA: Tom Davis Books.

--. 1993. *Deep Politics and the Death of JFK*. Los Angeles, CA: University of California Press.

Scott, Peter Dale and Jonathan Marshall. 1991. *Cocaine Politics: Drugs, Armies, and the CIA in Central America*. Los Angeles, CA: University of California Press.

Seldes, George. 1947. *One Thousand Americans*. New York: Boni & Gaer.

Sherrill, Robert. 1983. *The Oil Follies of 1970-1980*. Garden City, NY: Anchor Press/Doubleday.

Shoup, Laurence H., and William Minter. 1977. *Imperial Brain Trust: The Council on Foreign Relations and United States Foreign Policy*. New York: Monthly Review Press.

Sindler, Allan P. 1956. *Huey Long's Louisiana: State Politics, 1920-1952*. Baltimore: The Johns Hopkins Press.

Smith, R. Harris. 1972. *OSS: The Secret History of America's First Central Intelligence Agency*. New York: Delta Books/Dell Publishing.

Smith, Robert M. 1969. "International House: A World In Miniature." *New York Times* (May 23): 49.

Sorensen, Theodore C. 1965. *Kennedy*. New York: Bantam Books.

Sprague, Richard E. 1974. *The Taking of America, 1-2-3*. Aptos, CA: Tom Davis Books.

Stelle, Charles Clarkson. 1981. *Americans and the China Opium Trade in the Nineteenth Century*. New York: Arno Press/New York Times Co.

Stevenson, William. 1976. *A Man Called Intrepid*. New York: Ballantine Books.

Stone, Oliver and Zachary Sklar. 1992. *JFK: The Book of the Film*. New York: Applause Books.

Strober, Gerald S. and Deborah H. Strober. 1993. *"Let Us Begin Anew:" An Oral History of the Kennedy Presidency*. New York: HarperCollins.

Summers, Anthony. 1989. *Conspiracy*. New York: Paragon House.

Talese, Gay. 1971. *The Kingdom and the Power*. New York: Ivy Books.

Tarbell, Ida. 1925. *History of the Standard Oil Company*, 2 vols. New York: Macmillan Company.

Taus, Esther R. 1981. *The Role of the Treasury in Stabilizing the Economy, 1941-1946*. Washington, DC: University Press of America.

Tax Foundation. 1979. *Facts and Figures on Government Finance*. Washington, DC: Tax Foundation.

Thomas, John N. 1974. *The Institute of Pacific Relations*. Seattle, WA: University of Washington press.

Time. 1935. "Share-the-Wealth Wave" *Time* (April 1): 15-17.

--. 1963. "The Early Assassins." Time (November 29): 28.

Trevor-Roper, Hugh. 1966. "Introduction," pp. 9-20 in Mark Lane *Rush To Judgment*. Greenwich, CT: Fawcett.

Trussell, C. P. 1954. "Trust Funds Said To Drift To Left." *New York Times* (June 9): 18.

Tucker, William. 1977. "Environmentalism and the Leisure Class." *Harper's* (December): 47-56, 73-80.

U.S. News and World Report. 1963. "The Moment of Tragedy." *U.S. News and World Report* (December 2): 6, 32, 35.

Valentine, Douglas. 1990. *The Phoenix Program*. New York: Avon Books.

Waggoner, Walter H. 1961. "Corliss Lamont." *New York Times* (September 26): 10.

Wall Street Journal. 1961. "Depression Baby." *Wall Street Journal* (January 4): 10.

--. 1961a. "Foreign Aid-Fact and Fancy." Wall Street Journal (January 4): 10.

--. 1961b. "Fading Dreams." *Wall Street Journal* (January 4): 10.

--. 1962. "Those Cantankerous Congressmen." *Wall Street Journal* (July 2): 10.

--. 1962a. "A Self-Defeating Strategy." *Wall Street Journal* (July 2): 10.

--. 1962b. "Flunking an Economic Test." *Wall Street Journal* (July 17): 14.

--. 1962c. "An Impractical Pragmatism." *Wall Street Journal* (July 30): 8.

--. 1962d. "No Cause for Celebration." *Wall Street Journal* (August 6): 6.

--. 1962e. "A Short-Sighted Long View." *Wall Street Journal* (September 4): 12.

--. 1962f. "The President and the Planners." *Wall Street Journal* (October 3): 18.

--. 1962g. "The World Bank's Way." *Wall Street Journal* (October 23): 16.

--. 1962h. "The Uses of Presidential Power." *Wall Street Journal* (November 6): 14.

--. 1962i. "A Compliment from Russia." *Wall Street Journal* (November 20): 18.

--. 1962j. "The Professor's Tough Course." *Wall Street Journal* (December 7): 14.

--. 1963. "Passing Debate and Abiding Questions." *Wall Street Journal* (January 14): 16.

--. 1963a. "Message From the Land of Dreams." *Wall Street Journal* (January 18): 16.

--. 1963b. "Too Much Money, Too Little Thought." *Wall Street Journal* (March 26): 18.

--. 1963c. "Enforcer of Progress." *Wall Street Journal* (May 10): 12.

--. 1963d. "Too Much for Keynes." *Wall Street Journal* (July 10): 10.

--. 1963e. "Umbrellas for the Dollar." *Wall Street Journal* (July 18): 12.

--. 1963f. "Kennedy Asks Tax on Foreign Tax Buying And on Long-Term Lending to Foreigners." *Wall Street Journal* (July 19): 3.

--. 1963g. "Dramatizing the Dollar's Distress." *Wall Street Journal* (July 22): 6.

--. 1963h. "The New Dogmatists." *Wall Street Journal* (August 2): 6.

--. 1963i. "Trapped in a Maze." *Wall Street Journal* (August 6): 14.

--. 1963j. "When Friends Become Foes." *Wall Street Journal* (August 15): 8.

--. 1963k. "Non-Answers to Non-Critics." *Wall Street Journal* (August 27): 12.

--. 1963l. "Those Foolish Businessmen." *Wall Street Journal* (September 19): 12.

--. 1963m. "Government by Rationalization." *Wall Street Journal* (October 3): 16.

--. 1963n. "Search for a Purpose." *Wall Street Journal* (October 15): 16.

--. 1963o. "Wavelets into Waves." *Wall Street Journal* (October 21): 12.

--. 1963p. "Mercantilists in Liberal Clothing." *Wall Street Journal* (October 31): 16.

--. 1963q. ""The Anti-Business Image." *Wall Street Journal* (November 19): 18.

--. 1963r. "Blunt Talk on a Blunt Tool." *Wall Street Journal* (November 19): 18.

--. 1963s. "President Kennedy." *Wall Street Journal* (November 25): 8.

--. 1963t. "A Time for Stock-Taking." *Wall Street Journal* (November 26): 16.

--. 1963u. "Standards of Responsibility." *Wall Street Journal* (December 4): 18.

Wechsberg, Joseph. 1968. *The Merchant Bankers*. New York: Pocket Books.

Wecht, Cyril H. 1972. "Pathologist's View of JFK Autopsy: An Unsolved Case." *Modern Medicine* (November 27): 28-32.

Wecht, Cyril H. and Robert P. Smith. 1974. "The Medical Evidence In The Assassination of President John F. Kennedy" *Forensic Science*, Vol. 3: 105-128.

Weisberg, Harold. 1965. *Whitewash: The Report on the Warren Report*. Hyattstown, MD: Self-published. (Published by Dell, 1966)

--.1966. *Whitewash II: The FBI-Secret Service Cover-up*. Hyattstown, MD: self-published.

--. 1967. *Oswald in New Orleans*. New York: Canyon Books.

--. 1974. *Whitewash IV: Top Secret JFK Assassination Transcript*. Frederick, MD: self-published.

--. 1975. *Post Mortem*. Frederick, MD: Self-published.

--. 1976. *Photographic Whitewash: Suppressed Kennedy Assassination Pictures*. Frederick, MD: self-published.

--. 1995. *Never Again!* New York: Carroll & Graf.

Welles, Chris. 1975. *The Last Days of the Club*. New York: E.P. Dutton & Co.

Wendt, Lloyd. 1982. *The Wall Street Journal*. New York: Rand McNally & Co.

Whalen, Richard J. 1964. *The Founding Father: The Story of Joseph P. Kennedy*. New York: Signet Books/New American Library.

White, Theodore H. 1965. *The Making of the President, 1964*. New York: Signet Book/New American Library.

Whitworth, William. 1970. *Naive Questions About War and Peace*. New York: W. W. Norton & Co.

Wicker, Tom. 1963. "Gov. Connally Shot; Mrs. Kennedy Safe." *New York Times* (November 23): 1,2.

Wilds, John. 1976. *After-noon Story: A Century of the New Orleans States-Item*. Baton Rouge, LA: Louisiana State University press.

Wilds, John and Ira Harkey. 1990. *Alton Ochsner: Surgeon of the South*. Baton Rouge, LA: Louisiana State University Press.

Williams, T. Harry. 1969. *Huey Long*. New York: Bantam Books.

Willougby, Charles A. 1952. *Shanghai Conspiracy*. Boston, MA: The Americanist Library/Western Islands.

Wise, David and Thomas B. Ross. 1967. *The Espionage Establishment*. New York: Bantam Books.

Yoder, Edwin M., Jr. 1995. *Joe Alsop's Cold War: A Study of Journalistic Influence and Intrigue*. Chapel Hill, NC: University of North Carolina Press.

Zilg, Gerard Colby. 1974. *DuPont: Behind the Nylon Curtain*. Englewood Cliffs, NJ: Prentice-Hall.

Zinman, David H. *The Day Huey Long Was Shot*. Jackson, MI: University Press of Mississippi.

Zirbel, Craig I. 1991. *The Texas Connection*. New York: Warner Books/Time
    Warner.

INDEX

A

Acheson, Dean Gooderham, 60, 61, 63, 64, 66, 67, 70, 72, 75, 84, 85, 87, 88, 89, 96, 97, 126, 128, 129, 130, 131, 132, 133, 134, 135, 136, 170, 185, 189, 193, 199, 204, 205, 215, 217, 225, 226, 231, 236, 240, 241, 245, 248, 250, 251, 258, 266
Adams, Francis W. H., 95, 96
aggression, 193, 218
agriculture, 146
Air Force One, 24, 26
Allen, O. K., 141
Alliance for Progress, 3, 118, 140, 183, 221, 256, 257, 265
Alsop, Joseph, 58, 59, 66, 67, 68, 69, 70, 72, 75, 81, 82, 85, 86, 87, 88, 126, 128, 129, 130, 132, 133, 134, 136, 168, 189, 199, 200, 215, 225, 226, 236, 241, 245, 266
Alsop, Stewart, 131
alternative, 46
Anderson, Robert O., 249
Anson, Robert, 231, 236
anti-Castro Cubans, 137, 230, 231, 234
anti-Establishment, 163
anxiety, 147
Archer, Jules, 171, 176, 185
Arends, Les, 80
aristocrats, 174, 198, 211, 212

Armour, J. Ogden, 188
arms race, 213, 244
army intelligence, 226, 229, 235
Asia, 258
Associated Press, 28, 37, 166, 168
Astor, W. W., 189
attitudes, 29, 255
attribution, 27
Australia, 169
autopsy, 6, 8, 19, 113, 114, 115, 116, 121, 136, 235, 236, 239, 243

B

Baker, Marion, 9, 10
balance-of-payments problems, 263
Ball, Edward W., 163
Ball, George W., 185, 218, 263
Ball, Joseph A., 96, 104
Bancroft, Mary, 177, 259
bank credit, 256
bankers, 127, 134, 145, 149, 171, 207, 233, 257, 264
banks, 163
Bannister, Guy, 12, 172, 178, 179, 204, 243
Barnes, C. Tracey, 134, 177, 243
Bay of Pigs, 121, 162, 166, 206, 209, 210, 226, 252
Beebe, James, 167

Beebe, Lucius Morris, 167
Belgium, 261
Belin, David W., 35, 97, 104
Bell Helicopter, 233
Bell, Jack, 28, 233, 257
Belmont, Alan Harnden, vii, 29, 34, 35, 36,
    37, 39, 41, 42, 43, 44, 51, 52, 55, 68, 77,
    78, 93, 99, 102, 103, 112, 119, 122, 123,
    126, 132, 135, 136, 199, 200, 201, 215,
    225, 236, 238, 277
Belmont, Sr., August, 174
Benjamin, Judah P., 174
Bernays, Edward, 164
Beruch, Bernard, 188
Beschloss, Michael R., 68, 86, 272
Birch Society, 163
Bird, Kai, 86, 87, 99, 130, 131, 132, 133,
    135, 165, 170, 177, 184, 217, 220, 227,
    228, 235, 249, 251, 252, 254, 256, 258,
    260, 272
Birmingham, Stephen, 129
Black, Eugene, 135, 257
Black, Peter, 170
Blunt, Anthony, 194, 216, 217, 289
Boggs, Hale, 7, 73, 75, 83, 84, 89, 91, 92,
    94, 104, 112, 120, 242
Boston Club, 150, 160, 162, 163, 166, 167,
    173, 174, 175, 279
Boswell, J. Thornton, 113, 115, 116
Bourgeois, Ernest, 152
Bozeman, Harry, 155
Bradford, Amory H., 135
Bradford, Carol Warburg Rothschild, 135
Brazil, 118, 220, 221, 257
Brennan, Howard Leslie, 22
Brent, Theodore, 164, 165, 168
Brinkley, Douglas, 67, 68, 75, 131, 170,
    200, 272
Britain, 206
Brock, Herman C., 167, 168, 183
Brockman, Fletcher S., 188
Brooks Club, 129
Broussard, Edwin S., 149, 175
Brown Brothers, 169
Brown, Adele, 169

Brown, Governor Pat, 55
Brownell, Herbert, 192
Buchanan, James, 174
Bundy, McGeorge, 26, 89, 97, 131, 218,
    220, 241
Bundy, William, 131, 240
bureaucracy, 209
Burgess, Guy, 194
Burnham, Lamont, 176
Bush, George H.W., 133, 169
Bush, Prescott, 169
Bush, Vannevar, 250
business community, 149, 257
Butler, Edward S., 161, 162, 166, 168, 173,
    175, 243
Butler, General Smedley, 145

C

Cabell, Charles P., 32, 166
Cabell, Mayor Earle, 24, 32, 100, 121, 133,
    162, 166, 179
Cabot, John Moors, 177
Cabot, Thomas Dudley, 177
Calder, Sir John, 216
Campbell, Wesley Glenn, 35, 215
Canada, 140
cancer, 33
capitalism, 267, 268
Carpenter, Arthur, 162, 163, 164, 165, 166,
    167, 168, 172, 175, 272
Carr, Attorney General Waggoner, 21, 49,
    94, 104, 109, 118, 119
Carter, Edward C., 187, 272
Cason, B. W., 153
Castro, Fidel, 42, 51, 54, 77, 80, 112, 201,
    235, 275
Catledge, Turner, 165
Central America, 145, 149, 150, 221, 287
Century Club, 129
Chace, James, 132, 133, 272
Champion, George, 175, 257, 258
Chayes, Abram, 119
Chennault, General Claire Lee, 128, 200
Chile, 221

China, 128, 190, 191, 206
Chomsky, Noam, viii, 203, 217, 218, 219, 220, 221, 222, 225, 272
Christenberry, Earle, 153, 157
Christenberry, Herbert, 153, 156, 157, 158, 159
Christianity, 188, 267
Christmas, Lee, 149
CIA, 9, 24, 32, 54, 79, 80, 81, 85, 120, 121, 128, 130, 131, 132, 134, 136, 166, 177, 178, 195, 209, 216, 226, 228, 229, 232, 233, 234, 235, 236, 237, 238, 239, 240, 242, 243, 244, 276, 279, 285, 287
citizenship, 24, 37
civil liberties, 63, 65
Civil War, 31, 173, 174
Clark, Tom, 96, 211, 213, 214, 273
Clayton, Will, 59, 279
Clements, Manning C., 39
Clifton, Chester V., 26
Cold War, 272, 274, 283, 290
Colegrove, Kenneth, 190
Coleman, Jr., William T., 96
Collier, Peter, 127, 133, 135, 182, 184, 187, 206, 257, 263, 265, 273
colonialism, 191, 261, 266
communism, 102, 109, 123, 139, 172, 187, 205, 214, 220, 225
communist conspiracy, 68, 70
Communist Party, 37, 58, 197
community, 185
concession, 95
conflicts, xi, 30, 45, 90, 98, 143, 194, 241, 244, 256, 263, 267
Congressional hearings, 69
Connally, Governor John, 4, 5, 6, 7, 8, 78, 112, 114, 115, 119, 120, 290
conservatism, 139, 163, 267
conservatives, 189, 190, 191, 200, 204, 207, 233, 263
constitution, 188
consumption, 140, 142
Coolidge, Jr., T. Jefferson, 176
Cooper, John Sherman, 7, 75, 80, 83, 84, 89, 92, 94, 104, 109, 110, 111, 112, 120, 242

cooperation, 70, 83, 119, 249
Cordell Hull Foundation, 164
Corey, Lewis, 167, 273
Corliss, Florence Haskell, 204
corruption, 159
cotton, 143
Council on Foreign Relations, 31, 127, 128, 130, 133, 134, 170, 176, 177, 184, 185, 187, 189, 206, 209, 218, 227, 228, 232, 251, 252, 258, 265, 273, 280, 287
Couzens, James, 129
cover-up, 12, 13, 15, 34, 36, 44, 54, 88, 93, 107, 113, 123, 125, 126, 128, 130, 132, 135, 136, 154, 181, 194, 195, 199, 203, 215, 216, 225, 227, 230, 231, 232, 233, 234, 236, 237, 238, 240, 242, 243, 244, 245, 247, 248, 251
Cox, Archibald, 49, 74
Cravath, 127, 227, 252
critical analysis, 242
Cuba, 25, 36, 37, 38, 39, 68, 77, 109, 110, 117, 171, 204, 218, 226, 235, 274
Curry, Police Chief Jesse, 10, 16, 17, 18, 19, 20, 21, 24, 29, 41, 104, 105, 106, 107, 108, 109, 216, 233, 273
Curtis, Lionel, 189
Czechoslovakia, 193

D

Dallas authorities, 15, 16, 41
Dallas police, 9, 12, 17, 18, 19, 23, 24, 35, 39, 41, 55, 68, 69, 102, 107, 217, 226, 229, 233, 235, 244
Davenport, John, 253, 254, 262, 273
Davies, Joseph, 207, 283
Davis, John W., 128, 135, 174, 176, 185, 231, 273, 287
Davison, Harry P., 171
De Armond, John, 153
de Brueys, Warren, 243
de Gaulle, Charles, 131, 185
de Gersdorff, 127, 227, 252
Deakin, F. W., 195, 197, 198, 273
Dealy Plaza, 28, 105, 113, 120, 229

Dean, Arthur, 190
Declaration of Independence, 255
DeLoach, Cartha D., 52, 66
DeMenil, Jean, 185
democracy, 153, 202, 221, 241, 248
DeMohrenschildt, George, 185
devaluation, 256
Dewey, John, 205
DiEugenio, James, xiii, 12, 128, 130, 159,
    164, 165, 166, 167, 172, 179, 185, 188,
    192, 209, 244, 245, 274
Dinwiddie, George, 167
Dirksen, Senator Everett M., 48, 73
Dodd, Thomas, 82, 274, 276, 277, 281
Dodge, Cleveland H., 184
Dodge, Phelps, 127, 171
Dodge, William E., 188
domestic economy, 140
Domhoff, William, 130, 136, 232, 274
Dominican Republic, 118, 221, 222
Donovan, Robert J., 30, 100, 285
Donovan, William J., 134, 193
drug trade, 175, 176
drug trafficking, 175
Duff, Sir Michael, 193, 217
Dulles, Allen W., 7, 30, 35, 49, 75, 80, 83,
    86, 87, 88, 89, 100, 103, 105, 121, 122,
    126, 127, 130, 131, 132, 171, 177, 193,
    215, 218, 226, 227, 228, 232, 239, 241,
    245, 248, 252, 259, 263, 275
Dulles, John Foster, 185, 208, 281

E

Easley, Ralph M., 186
Eastern Establishment, 200, 240, 241, 244,
    245, 266, 275
Eastland, James O., 70, 71, 74, 75, 79, 82
economic development, 173, 191, 213, 249,
    259
economic growth, 267
economic policy, 141, 144, 255, 258, 259,
    260, 264, 267
economic system, 205
Edmonds, Harry, 182

education, 71, 133, 140, 141, 146, 188, 228,
    241, 249, 268, 278, 286
educational institutions, 3
educational programs, 2
Eisenberg, Melvin A., 97, 105
Eisenhower, Milton, 94, 172, 192, 206, 208,
    209, 257, 261, 273, 284
El Salvador, 221
elections, 145, 148, 153, 154
Ellender, Allen, 148
Ellis, Crawford, 165, 167, 168, 175
emergence, 15, 68, 226
Emerson, Ralph Waldo, 177
employment, 259
England, 129, 173, 174, 196, 197, 210, 211,
    216, 229, 278
Epstein, Edward, 7, 90, 91, 96, 97, 103, 230,
    264, 274
Establishment, viii, ix, 58, 88, 90, 125, 126,
    127, 131, 135, 136, 137, 162, 166, 168,
    169, 173, 175, 176, 179, 187, 189, 191,
    193, 194, 196, 198, 200, 202, 203, 204,
    205, 207, 208, 209, 210, 216, 218, 219,
    225, 226, 227, 228, 232, 233, 235, 236,
    237, 238, 239, 240, 241, 242, 245, 247,
    248, 249, 250, 251, 252, 253, 254, 255,
    258, 259, 260, 262, 266, 272, 274, 285,
    286, 290
Establishment media, 162, 216, 235, 236,
    241
Europe, 140, 204
Evans, Rowland, 86, 274
excuse, 31
executive branch, 229, 237, 239
exercise, 188, 203, 237
exploitation, 3

F

fact-finding, 46
failure, 12, 15, 121, 166, 252, 254, 256, 261,
    268
Fair Play for Cuba Committee, 37, 38, 77,
    109, 110, 235

family, 91, 121, 127, 128, 129, 133, 135,
    155, 163, 166, 167, 169, 171, 172, 176,
    177, 179, 188, 192, 194, 195, 206, 207,
    211, 228, 232, 245, 259, 263, 269
Far East, 178
Farley, James A., 151, 158
FBI, 3, 6, 8, 9, 11, 12, 13, 15, 16, 19, 21, 22,
    23, 24, 25, 29, 33, 34, 35, 36, 37, 38, 39,
    41, 42, 43, 44, 47, 48, 50, 51, 52, 55, 58,
    59, 60, 61, 62, 64, 65, 66, 67, 68, 69, 71,
    76, 77, 78, 80, 81, 91, 93, 95, 98, 99, 102,
    103, 107, 108, 111, 112, 114, 120, 121,
    122, 123, 132, 135, 162, 199, 200, 201,
    215, 216, 225, 226, 227, 229, 232, 233,
    235, 236, 243, 244, 284
FBI agents, 6, 232
federal budget, 2, 222
federal reserve, 2, 144, 172, 191, 260, 263,
    264
Federal Reserve Board, 172, 263
Federal Reserve System, 2
Ferrie, David, 12, 137, 159, 178, 185, 230,
    243
Field, Frederick Vanderbilt, 186, 189
financial support, 150, 165, 167, 205
Finck, Lt. Col. Pierre, 113, 115, 116
Fisher, Joe, 151
Fletcher, Horace, xiii, 24, 174, 188, 216,
    242, 285
flexibility, 142
Florida, 163
Fonzi, Gaeton, 4, 6, 7, 8, 113, 178, 237, 275
Forbes, Elise Cabot, 177
Forbes, W. Cameron, 177, 188, 194
Ford, Gerald R., 7, 35, 75, 80, 81, 83, 89, 91,
    92, 93, 96, 102, 103, 104, 107, 112, 122,
    123, 126, 127, 130, 165, 183, 201, 227,
    238, 243, 244, 275
foreign economic interests, 3
foreign exchange, 256
foreign investment, 256
foreign policy, 3, 51, 117, 118, 127, 140,
    190, 207, 220, 222, 244, 248, 252, 254,
    259, 265, 266

Foreign Policy Association, 167, 186, 189,
    206, 209
foreign trade, 192
Forrestal, James V., 200
Forrestal, Michael, 218
Fortas, Abe, 45, 49, 67, 73, 74, 75, 76, 85,
    86, 89, 281
Fosdick, Dr. Harry Emerson, 206
Fosdick, Dr. Raymond B., 184, 185
France, 174
Frankfurt, 197
Franklin, George S., 185
Free Cuba Movement, 109
free market, 259, 263, 267
Freeport Sulphur, viii, 168, 170, 171, 275,
    285
Friendly, Alfred, 61, 64, 66, 67, 70, 85
Fritz, Captain Will, 16, 23, 24, 29, 104, 107,
    108, 109

G

Garrison, Jim, 10, 11, 12, 159, 162, 166,
    167, 170, 178, 179, 180, 192, 217, 243,
    244, 245, 274, 275
Garwood, John, 59
Gates, Thomas S., 206, 209
Gaudet, William G., 164, 178
Gayn, Mark Julius, 194
General Dynamics, 233
General Motors, 208
Germany, 127, 131, 195, 196, 197, 198, 217,
    228, 274
Ghana, 128
global economy, 186, 191, 202
Goldberg, Alfred, 97, 109
Goodell, Charles E., 48
government, 29, 30, 76, 117, 158, 190, 202,
    215, 225, 229, 237, 262, 276, 278, 280,
    288, 289
government intervention, 172
government policy, 207, 209, 258
government spending, 256, 260, 263, 264
Grace, J. Peter, 172
Graham, Dale, 175

Graham, Katherine Meyer, 67, 70, 85, 150
Great Britain, 31, 117, 131, 195, 237
Greece, 255
Greene, Jerome D., 188, 189
Griffin, Burt W., 97
Grose, Peter, 87, 89, 130, 177, 275
Guatemala, 130, 177, 221, 287
Guzma, Jacobo Arbenz, 177

H

Halifax, Lord, 193, 204, 217, 276
Halleck, Charles, 79, 81
Hamilton, Alexander, v, 139, 253, 266, 267,
    268, 271, 280
handwriting evidence, 16
Harriman, Averill, 127, 170, 218, 219
Harriman, E. H., 169
Harriman, W. A., 134
hate, 18, 31, 65, 74, 80, 163, 210, 236
Haushofer, Karl, 197
Hawaii, 26, 181
Hecht, Rudolph, 164, 165, 168
Heidel, A., 40
Heller, Walter, 2, 263, 276
Helms, Richard, 128, 236, 237, 240, 245,
    285
Hepburn, James, 233, 276
Hidell, Alek J., 23
Hills, Robert Chadwick, 169, 170
Hoffman, Paul, 166, 252, 263, 276
Hong Kong, 178
Hoover, J. Edgar, vii, 22, 23, 34, 35, 36, 37,
    38, 39, 40, 41, 42, 47, 51, 52, 53, 56, 57,
    58, 70, 75, 76, 77, 78, 84, 85, 87, 93, 95,
    96, 102, 112, 120, 123, 151, 184, 199,
    200, 201, 215, 229, 235, 277
Horowitz, David, 127, 133, 135, 182, 184,
    187, 206, 257, 263, 265, 273
House of Representatives, 41, 47, 48, 50, 56,
    69, 79, 93, 105, 276
Hubert, Jr., Leon D., 96
Hubert, Leon, 105, 121
Hull, Cordell, 182
human rights, 286

Humes, James J., 6, 113, 114, 115, 116
Humphrey, Hubert, 208, 279
Hunt, H.L., 195, 233
Hurt, Henry, 87, 233, 277
Huxley, Aldous, 214, 271

I

Ickes, Harold, 151
impeachment, 155
imperialism, 267, 268
independence, 62, 191
India, 178, 266
industrialization, 255, 258, 267
Information Council of the Americas
    (INCA), 162, 166, 167, 178, 243, 245,
    272
infrastructure, 141, 143, 145
Institute of Pacific Relations (IPR), viii, 181,
    182, 184, 186, 187, 188, 189, 190, 191,
    192, 194, 195, 196, 197, 198, 199, 200,
    201, 202, 204, 206, 207, 288
integrity, 60, 91
intelligence, 10, 12, 35, 42, 100, 112, 120,
    128, 132, 137, 182, 188, 193, 197, 216,
    226, 229, 234, 235, 239, 240, 243, 244,
    245, 267, 268
interest rates, 140, 222, 256, 260, 264
Internal Security, 199, 207
International House (IH), viii, 160, 163, 164,
    165, 166, 167, 168, 172, 173, 175, 180,
    181, 182, 183, 184, 185, 186, 187, 192,
    194, 195, 197, 201, 202, 204, 282, 283,
    284, 287
International Monetary Fund, 129, 140, 256,
    259, 263, 285
international policy, 3, 129, 259
International Trade Exhibition, 181, 192
International Trade Mart (ITM), viii, 157,
    160, 163, 164, 165, 166, 167, 168, 171,
    172, 173, 180, 181, 183, 192, 194, 202,
    204, 209
International Trade Zone, 192
intervention, 130, 177, 209, 218, 219, 221

interview, 16, 17, 35, 39, 42, 109, 121, 122, 201
investment, 2, 3, 140, 249, 260, 265
investment tax credit, 3, 140
irrigation, 144
Isaacs, Harold, 195, 196, 197, 198, 199
Israeli Mossad, 229
Italy, 185

J

J. P. Morgan & Co., 127, 134, 145, 150, 171, 185, 200, 204, 206, 210
Jackson, C. D., 60, 163, 177, 290
Japan, 30, 131, 182, 195, 196, 197, 283
Jaworski, Leon, 49, 59, 92
Jefferson, Thomas, 174, 176
Jenkins, Walter, 40, 41, 47, 49, 53, 56, 57, 76
Jerusalem, 31, 133
Johnson, Alexis, 53, 118
Johnson, President Lyndon B., 3, 5, 26, 35, 39, 40, 41, 44, 45, 46, 47, 48, 49, 50, 53, 54, 55, 56, 57, 58, 59, 60, 61, 62, 63, 64, 65, 66, 67, 70, 71, 72, 73, 74, 75, 76, 77, 78, 79, 80, 81, 82, 83, 84, 85, 86, 87, 89, 91, 125, 130, 170, 171, 199, 208, 209, 210, 218, 222, 226, 227, 229, 233, 234, 237, 264, 274, 277
Josephson, Matthew, 142, 277
Judd, Orin C., 192

K

Kaiser, Edgar, 171
Kai-shek, Chiang, 191
Katzenbach, General Nicholas, 41, 42, 43, 44, 45, 47, 48, 49, 50, 51, 52, 53, 54, 55, 56, 57, 58, 63, 64, 66, 67, 68, 69, 70, 71, 72, 74, 76, 84, 85, 87, 93, 94, 97, 103, 119, 122, 123, 237
Kaysen, Carl, 263
Keedick, Lee, 167, 209
Keith, Minor, 176

Kennedy, Joseph, 129, 156
Kennedy, President John F., v, xi, xii, 1, 2, 3, 4, 5, 6, 9, 12, 16, 18, 19, 20, 21, 22, 23, 25, 26, 27, 28, 30, 31, 32, 33, 35, 39, 43, 45, 54, 58, 68, 78, 79, 82, 89, 91, 94, 96, 99, 100, 101, 103, 105, 107, 108, 109, 112, 113, 114, 116, 117, 118, 119, 121, 122, 128, 129, 131, 137, 147, 153, 156, 159, 160, 166, 170, 172, 176, 178, 179, 181, 194, 204, 208, 209, 210, 213, 217, 218, 219, 220, 223, 232, 234, 236, 237, 238, 239, 240, 242, 243, 246, 247, 250, 251, 252, 262, 264, 266, 268, 269
Kennedy, Robert, v, 23, 36, 38, 48, 49, 86, 237
Kerr, W. P. (Lord Lothian), 189, 281
Kissinger, Henry, 185
Klausen, Max, 198
Klu Klux Klan, 36
knowledge, 6, 9, 17, 18, 27, 33, 35, 77, 91, 104, 106, 116, 119, 125, 209
Kohlberg, Alfred, 190, 201, 279
Konoye, Prince Fumimaro, 197, 198
Kornfeder, Joseph, 201
Krock, Arthur, 254, 279

L

Lamont, Corliss, 171, 182, 193, 203, 204, 205, 206, 208, 209, 210, 213, 222, 225, 252, 282, 283, 288
Lamont, Thomas S., 171, 206
Lamont, Thomas W., 134, 150, 171, 184, 185, 189, 193, 204, 213
Lane, Mark, 215, 217, 229, 237, 279, 285, 288
Lansdale, Edward, 128, 245
Latin America, 3, 163, 164, 166, 172, 173, 179, 182, 183, 221, 254, 256, 257, 265, 272, 280, 286
Lattimore, Owen, 199, 200, 201, 275, 281
Lawson, Winston G., 19, 105, 107, 109
LBJ Library, 26, 47, 55, 57, 59, 70, 72, 73, 74, 75, 76, 79, 81, 82, 84, 85

lead, 42, 44, 49, 84, 87, 92, 102, 123, 154,
    159, 201, 203, 210, 213, 220, 226, 230,
    232, 240, 245, 256
leadership, 80, 117, 118, 141, 163, 187, 218,
    234, 239
Leche, Governor, 155, 157
Leffingwell, Russell C., 252
legislation, 3, 143, 146, 154
liberalism, 139, 176, 267
liberalization, 256
liberals, 200
Liebler, Wesley J., 97
Lincoln, Abraham, v, 30, 33, 100, 101, 139,
    202, 266, 268, 272, 279
Linen, James A., 252
Links, 129, 134
loans, 140, 255, 256, 257, 258, 259, 261
Locke, John, 176, 266, 267
Lockwood, John E., 193
Lodge, Henry Cabot, 177
Loeb, John L., 171
Long, Augustus, 168
Long, Huey Pierce, v, viii, 137, 141, 142,
    147, 152, 153, 156, 158, 159, 160, 161,
    163, 164, 166, 173, 175, 179, 258, 266,
    271, 287, 290
Long, Senator Russell, 160
Loomis, Charles F., 187
Lothian, Lord, 189
Louisiana, 137, 141, 142, 143, 144, 145,
    146, 148, 149, 150, 151, 152, 153, 154,
    155, 157, 158, 159, 166, 173, 174, 175,
    178, 180, 233, 258
Lovett, Robert Abercrombie, 127, 169, 170,
    184
Lovett, Robert S., 169, 175
loyalty, 146
Lucas, Oliver, 130, 170, 175
Luce, Henry, 170, 172, 189, 191
Luce-Morgan, 252, 258, 259, 261
Lukas, J. Anthony, 200, 280
Lundberg, Ferdinand, 136, 168, 232

M

MacArthur, General Douglas, 190, 195, 196,
    198
Mackenzie, Sir Compton, 216
Maclean, Donald, 194
Macmillan, Harold, 213
Madison, James, 253
Mafia, 231, 234, 273
Mahl, Thomas, 189, 280
Mallet-Prevost, 171, 193
Maloney, Guy, 149, 151
managed economy, 262
Mann, Thomas, 118
Mansfield, Mike, 71, 72, 73, 219
Mao Zedong, 191
Marcello, Carlos, 230, 273
marriage, 127, 134
Marrs, Jim, 2, 23, 231, 234, 280
Marshall, John, 175, 266, 287
Martin, William McChesney, 172, 263
Marxism, 102
Massachusetts, 79
Matsumoto, Shigeharu, 182, 195, 197
Mauze, Jean, 168
McCarran Committee, 199
McCarran, Senator Patrick A., 199
McCarthy, Joe, 162, 187, 199, 200, 201,
    205, 239, 283
McCloy, John J., vii, 13, 29, 35, 36, 43, 44,
    74, 75, 77, 80, 82, 83, 86, 88, 89, 90, 91,
    92, 93, 94, 95, 96, 98, 99, 100, 103, 104,
    105, 107, 113, 114, 115, 116, 117, 118,
    119, 120, 121, 122, 123, 126, 127, 128,
    129, 130, 131, 132, 133, 134, 135, 136,
    165, 170, 175, 177, 183, 184, 193, 194,
    200, 204, 208, 215, 217, 218, 220, 221,
    225, 227, 228, 229, 230, 231, 235, 236,
    237, 238, 240, 241, 243, 244, 245, 246,
    248, 249, 250, 251, 252, 253, 254, 256,
    258, 260, 263, 264, 266, 272, 274, 280
McCloy-Dulles Commission, vii, 13, 89, 90,
    227, 229
McCloy-Dulles-Warren Commission, 235
McCone, John, 240

McCormack, John, 79
McCormack, Mike, 79
McCormick, Cyrus, 188
McCoy, John, 74, 178
media, 13, 16, 19, 22, 24, 27, 30, 39, 55,
    100, 102, 103, 107, 111, 123, 125, 126,
    130, 133, 134, 135, 136, 153, 189, 215,
    226, 233, 238, 241, 243, 244, 259, 268
Mellon, Paul, 134, 228
Metropolitan Club, 129, 134, 135
Mexico, 36, 38, 43, 51, 77, 84, 109, 112,
    118, 164, 178
Meyer, Eugene, 150
Meyers, Gustavus, 142
MI5, 216
Michigan, 129
military, 3, 26, 43, 49, 91, 117, 118, 136,
    145, 164, 179, 195, 196, 221, 229, 233,
    234, 235, 236, 238, 240, 241, 242, 243,
    244, 250, 261
military force, 145, 261
military intelligence, 23, 24, 26, 239
military power, 3, 140, 164, 248
Milner, Lord, 188, 206
Minter, William, 167, 176, 206, 208, 218,
    219, 228, 287
Mississippi, 60, 70, 164, 167, 290
Mohr, John P., 66
monetary policy, 263
money, 2, 112, 127, 134, 136, 141, 142, 145,
    147, 151, 157, 163, 182, 183, 187, 189,
    190, 198, 211, 215, 227, 255, 257, 260,
    263, 264, 267, 268
money supply, 65, 265
Monroe, J. Blanc, 165, 166
Montgomery, Joseph W., 149, 164, 166,
    167, 175
Montgomery, Peter, 193, 217
Moody, Dwight L., 135, 188, 252, 281
Moore, Maurice T., 252
morality, 269
Morgan, J.P., 127, 129, 133, 134, 140, 145,
    150, 151, 153, 167, 171, 174, 175, 176,
    182, 183, 184, 188, 189, 190, 194, 209,
    228, 252, 272, 273, 275, 277

Morgan, Jr., J. P., 175, 228
Morgan, Junius Spenser, 167
Morgenthau, Henry, 151
Morse, Wayne, 70, 188, 281
Moscow, 168, 198
motivation, 68
Mott, John, 182, 187
Mott, Stewart Rawlings, 208
Moyers, William, 48, 50, 53, 54, 55, 56, 57,
    61, 64, 66, 67, 68, 70
Murchison, Clint, 165, 229, 232, 233, 235
Murphy, Bruce, 75
Murphy, Grayson M-P, 134, 185
Murret, Charles, 137, 230
Murret, Dorothy, 195, 199
Murret, Marilyn, 231

N

Nagy, Ferenc, 185
nation states, 240
National Civic Federation, 187
national interest, 261
national policy, 250
national power, 163, 164
national security, 26, 97, 131, 169, 209, 221,
    238
nationalism, 172, 186, 191, 213, 225
Nebraska, 94, 156, 192
negotiation, 79
Nehru, Jawaharlal, 266
neo-colonialism, 3, 220, 242, 266
Netherlands, 117, 261
New Deal, 147, 176, 200, 272
New England Society, 173
New Jersey, 166, 176
New Orleans, xiii, 12, 37, 137, 146, 148,
    149, 151, 153, 158, 160, 161, 162, 164,
    165, 166, 167, 168, 172, 173, 175, 176,
    178, 179, 180, 181, 182, 183, 186, 192,
    193, 194, 243, 245
New Zealand, 24
Nicaragua, 163
Nicholson, Leonard, 175
Nietzsche, Friedrich, 197

Nixon, Richard, 49, 55, 208, 210, 218, 229, 233, 235
Nkrumah, President Kwame, 128, 280
Norris, Senator George, 145, 150, 156
Norstad, Gen. Lauris, 74, 77
North Carolina, 28
Novak, Robert, 86, 274
nuclear energy, 2
Nutter, Charles P., 166, 168

O

Ochsner, Alton, viii, 161, 162, 163, 164, 165, 166, 167, 168, 172, 173, 174, 175, 179, 183, 245, 272, 290
Oglesby, Carl, 231, 232, 284
Olney, Warren, 44, 91, 92, 93, 95, 99, 122
Oregon, 70
organized crime, 35, 137, 229, 230, 231, 232, 234, 235
Osborn, Frederick, 184
Osborn, Henry Fairfield, 184
Oswald, Lee Harvey, viii, 3, 4, 5, 6, 7, 8, 9, 10, 11, 12, 13, 15, 16, 17, 19, 20, 21, 22, 23, 24, 25, 26, 28, 29, 30, 32, 33, 34, 35, 36, 37, 38, 39, 40, 41, 42, 43, 44, 46, 47, 48, 51, 52, 54, 55, 56, 57, 58, 66, 67, 68, 69, 70, 77, 78, 84, 87, 88, 99, 101, 102, 103, 104, 105, 107, 108, 109, 110, 111, 112, 114, 118, 119, 120, 122, 125, 126, 130, 133, 135, 136, 137, 159, 161, 162, 163, 164, 167, 171, 177, 178, 179, 180, 181, 185, 188, 193, 194, 197, 198, 199, 201, 202, 204, 206, 207, 209, 210, 225, 226, 229, 230, 231, 235, 238, 241, 243, 245, 274, 276, 279, 285, 290
Oswald, Marina, 177
Oswald-Ruby connection, 20, 112
output, 260
Ozaki, Hotzumi, 182, 195, 196, 197, 198

P

Pacific, viii, 127, 150, 169, 181, 182, 184, 186, 187, 194, 195, 201, 202, 204, 206, 207, 282, 284, 288
Paine, Michael, 177, 188, 194, 279
Paine, Ruth, 177
Paley, William, 134
Parker, John M., 134, 150, 155, 175
Parker, Jr., Samuel C., 134
Parkland Memorial Hospital, 8, 23, 113
particulate matter, 99
Pawley, William, 178
Payne, Oliver, 133, 194
Payson, Charles, 134
Pearl Harbor, 59, 81
Pearson, Drew, 200
perceptions, 7, 104
Perry, Commodore, 31, 174, 277
personal relations, 128, 130, 132, 180, 211
personal worth, 268
pessimism, 250
Phelps, Ashton, 166, 167
Phelps, Esmond, 149, 166, 175
Philby, Kim, 194, 216
Phillips, David Atlee, 204, 233, 237, 285
planned economy, 259
Poe, Edgar Allen, 247
police, 9, 12, 17, 18, 19, 22, 23, 24, 26, 33, 35, 37, 39, 40, 41, 55, 68, 69, 95, 100, 102, 107, 109, 155, 184, 217, 226, 229, 233, 235, 244, 266
policy making, 130
political culture, 218, 272
political groups, 29, 78
political movement, 191
political process, 136
Pope John Paul II, 267, 268, 277
population growth, 213, 249, 255
population growth rate, 249
Posner, Gerald, 87, 230, 285
poverty, 140, 173, 249
Preston, Andrew, 176
price controls, 253, 256
private enterprise, 172, 258, 260

private interests, 1, 139, 148, 149, 153, 159,
    164, 195, 215, 218, 233, 236, 258
private power, 127, 209, 225, 229, 247, 263
private wealth, 142, 247, 253
propaganda, 128, 163, 178, 210
Prouty, Fletcher, xiii, 10, 12, 24, 216, 242,
    245, 285
public good, 1, 2
public image, 77
public interest, 1, 46
public ownership, 143
public speculation, 48, 69

Q

Queen Victoria, 211
Quigley, Carroll, 127, 128, 133, 135, 136,
    187, 188, 189, 190, 192, 193, 194, 196,
    198, 217, 228, 229, 285

R

racism, 182
racists, viii, 174
Raigorodsky, Paul, 185
Rankin, J. Lee, 35, 42, 90, 93, 94, 95, 96, 97,
    98, 103, 104, 105, 106, 107, 108, 109,
    110, 111, 112, 113, 116, 117, 118, 119,
    120, 121, 122, 123, 126, 130, 136, 169,
    192, 227, 238, 243, 244
Ransdell, Joseph E., 149, 150
Rathbone, Monroe J., 166
rationality, 241
raw materials, 139, 172, 248, 258
reasoning, 6, 267
reconstruction, 257
Redlich, Norman, 35, 97, 105, 109
Reid, Mrs. Ogden, 189
Reid, Whitelaw, 134
Reily, H. Eustis, 167
Reily, William B., 167
reproduction, 185
research and development, 3, 262

Reston, James, 27, 28, 40, 66, 99, 122, 133,
    136, 179, 210, 225, 230, 231, 236, 238,
    245, 249, 251, 254, 258, 266, 286
rhetoric, 261
right-wingers, 162, 215, 225, 229, 230
Robbins, Stanton, 168
Roberts, Craig, 59, 231, 234, 286
Rockefeller 3d, John D., 183, 184, 185
Rockefeller Sr., John D., 188
Rockefeller, Abby, 168
Rockefeller, David, 165, 169, 175, 183, 218,
    221, 232, 251, 252, 254, 258, 263, 264
Rockefeller, Godfrey, 169
Rockefeller, James Stillman, 169
Rockefeller, John D., 135, 169, 182, 183,
    184, 185, 187, 188
Rockefeller, Jr., John D., 182, 187, 188
Rockefeller, Nelson, 168, 183
Rockefeller, William, 133, 169, 175, 184
Roosa, Robert V., 263
Roosevelt, Franklin D., 263, 266
Roosevelt, Theodore, 129, 188
Rosenwald, Julius, 188, 194
Rostow Commission, 13
Rostow, Eugene, 13, 45, 54, 55, 56, 57, 58,
    66, 68, 69, 70, 72, 85, 86, 87, 88, 97, 126,
    128, 132, 134, 135, 136, 199, 215, 225,
    226, 231, 236, 241, 245, 258, 266, 286
Rowe, L.S., 192
Rowley, James J., 36
Royster, Vermont, 259
Ruby, Jack, 33, 34, 36, 37, 38, 46, 77, 98,
    109, 110, 111, 112, 121, 122, 230, 231,
    235, 278
ruling elite, 228
Runciman, Sir Steven, 193, 217
Runciman, Viscount, 193
Rusk, Dean, 53, 54, 71, 72, 73, 79, 82, 85,
    86, 88, 89, 116, 117, 118, 119, 123, 131,
    170, 218, 219, 220
Russell, Dick, 80, 195, 234
Russell, Lord Bertrand, 194, 203, 210, 211,
    217, 222, 248, 273, 274, 286
Russell, Prime Minister John, 203
Russell, Richard B., 75, 83, 84

Russia, 23, 25, 30, 37, 43, 51, 109, 195, 196,
    197, 198, 212, 226, 256, 273, 279, 288
Ryan, Frank T., 193

S

Sage, Mrs. Russell, 188
Saionji, Prince Kinkazu, 196, 197
Salandria, Vincent J., 6, 7, 238, 239, 240,
    241, 242, 245, 286
Sanders, Barefoot, 109, 119
Sanders, Jared Y., 149, 155
Sanders, Jr., Jared Y., 148, 152
Schlel, Norbert A., 37
Schlesinger, Arthur, 2, 150, 151, 154, 164,
    177, 178, 286, 287
Schmidt, Benno C., 169
Schoenmann, Ralph, 217
Schroder, Henry, 131
science and technology, 212, 249, 250
Scott, Peter Dale, 234, 235
Secret Service, 6, 19, 35, 36, 39, 59, 65, 91,
    98, 105, 107, 120, 229, 244
security, xiii, 10, 15, 18, 19, 35, 105, 106,
    107, 123, 215, 216, 238
select committee, vii, 41, 47, 48, 49, 50, 51,
    56, 69, 79, 93, 105, 276
self-interest, 257
Seligman, Hans, 185
Shanghai, 178, 195, 197, 198, 290
Shaw, Clay, viii, 12, 31, 120, 149, 159, 160,
    161, 163, 164, 165, 166, 167, 168, 170,
    171, 172, 173, 175, 179, 180, 181, 183,
    185, 188, 192, 193, 194, 204, 209, 217,
    244, 245, 275, 285
Shaw, Dr. Robert, 120
Shepardson, Whitney H., 130
Sherman B., 80, 83, 271
Shoup, Laurence, 167, 176, 206, 208, 218,
    219, 228, 287
sincerity, 186
Sirhan Sirhan, 207
Skull and Bones, 133, 169
Slater, Joseph, 249
Slawson, W. David, 97

Slidell, John, 174
Sloane, William, 188
small business, 142
Smedley, Agnes, 195, 196, 197, 198, 199
Smith, Gerald K., 148
Smith, Sergio Aracha, 178
social change, 265
social justice, 141
social progress, 139
socialism, 205, 260, 261
soft loans, 261
Songy, Sidney, 152, 158
Sorge, Richard, 182, 195, 196, 197, 198,
    199, 200, 273, 285
South Carolina, 176
Southeast Asia, 178, 208, 218, 219
sovereignty, 65
Soviet Union, 25, 42, 51, 81, 117, 119, 120,
    190, 196, 205, 211
space program, 3, 140
Speaker of the House, 79
Specter, Arlen, 97, 113, 114, 116, 123, 275
spending policy, 261
standard of living, 213
Standard Oil, 133, 143, 145, 147, 149, 150,
    151, 152, 155, 158, 159, 166, 167, 189,
    194, 288
State Department, 24, 25, 51, 119, 128, 170,
    201, 226, 271, 281
state planning, 261
statism, 261
Stein, Guenther, 196, 198, 199
Stephenson, Sir William, 193
Stern, Edgar B. and Edith Rosenwald, 165
Stern, Edith, 188, 194
Stern, Percival and Edgar B., 167
Stern, Samuel A., 35, 97
Stettinius, Edward R., 171, 193, 275
Stevenson, Chief, 109, 216, 287
Stillman, Chauncey Devereux, 169
Stillman, Elizabeth Goodrich, 169
Stillman, James A., 169, 175
Stimson, Henry L., 184, 250, 282
Storry, G. R., 195, 197, 198, 273
Story, Bill, 55

Straight, Michael, 194
Straight, Willard, 194
Sullivan & Cromwell, 127
Sullivan, John P., 149
Sullivan, William, 42
Sulzberger, Arthur Hays, 135, 189
Supreme Court, 3, 55, 59, 63, 71, 73, 81, 90,
    176, 266, 281
Swaine, 127, 252
Switzerland, 182, 185
Symington, Senator Stuart, 129, 134

T

Tarbell, Ida, 142, 288
tax evasion, 151
tax laws, 2
tax system, 140
taxes, 140, 143, 256
Taylor, E.P., 193
Texas oilmen, 235
Texas School Book Depository, 4, 6, 8, 9,
    19, 23, 25, 28, 78, 105, 115, 177
Texas Theater, 23
Thayer, Walter N., 134
Thomas, J. Parnell, 205
Tippit, J. D., 10, 22, 24, 30, 103
Tolson, Clyde, 36, 37, 41, 43, 51, 52, 93,
    277
transportation, 144
Trevor-Roper, Hugh Redwald, 216, 217,
    229, 288
troops, 149, 150, 254
Truly, Roy, 23
Truman, Harry S, 170

U

U.S. military power, 140, 248
United Fruit, viii, 127, 145, 149, 150, 151,
    164, 165, 166, 167, 168, 175, 176, 177,
    179, 186, 188, 221, 280
United Kingdom, 275
United Nations, 183, 185

United States, 1, 3, 29, 30, 41, 47, 48, 50,
    56, 58, 68, 69, 78, 82, 93, 98, 99, 105,
    117, 119, 128, 129, 130, 132, 136, 140,
    149, 159, 172, 173, 176, 179, 180, 187,
    189, 193, 195, 196, 197, 199, 206, 209,
    212, 213, 215, 225, 226, 229, 231, 234,
    236, 237, 238, 239, 241, 247, 250, 254,
    255, 256, 263, 266, 267, 274, 276, 278,
    279, 280, 287

V

Vanderbilt, Cornelius, 188, 189
Vanderlip, Frank A., 175
Venezuela, 168
Vermilye, Peter H., 183
Vermont, 259
Vidrine, Dr. Arthur, 154
Vietnam, xiii, 128, 131, 170, 207, 208, 209,
    210, 218, 219, 220, 222, 242, 244, 254,
    258, 264, 272, 279, 281, 285
violence, 28, 102, 152, 212, 214, 215, 225
voting, 142

W

Wade, Henry, 16, 20, 21, 29, 108, 109, 110,
    111
Walmsley, Mayor T. Semmes, 148, 151,
    175
Warfield, 96
Warren Commission, vii, 3, 4, 5, 6, 10, 11,
    13, 16, 19, 21, 30, 35, 41, 42, 43, 45, 47,
    50, 52, 54, 78, 79, 85, 86, 87, 88, 90, 101,
    104, 117, 121, 125, 126, 130, 132, 134,
    160, 170, 177, 179, 183, 193, 199, 204,
    207, 209, 215, 217, 227, 228, 229, 233,
    235, 236, 238, 241, 242, 244, 248, 251,
    274, 275, 281, 285
Warren Report, vii, xiii, 1, 4, 28, 128, 217,
    229, 230, 236, 238, 240, 242, 244, 279,
    286, 290

Warren, Chief Justice Earl, 3, 35, 44, 49, 52,
    73, 74, 75, 80, 82, 89, 90, 91, 93, 98, 119,
    126, 238, 281
water power, 144
Weisberg, Harold, xiii, 4, 5, 6, 7, 8, 9, 10,
    11, 12, 16, 19, 21, 22, 23, 33, 66, 84, 108,
    113, 114, 116, 119, 120, 121, 130, 178,
    239, 242, 243, 244, 245, 290
Weiss, Dr. Carl, 154, 155, 157
Weiss, Seymour, 148, 151, 153, 157, 158,
    163, 165
Western Europe, 205
Whitney, Cornelius Vanderbilt, 133
Whitney, Dorothy Payne, 194
Whitney, Harry Payne, 133
Whitney, John Hay (Jock), 31, 32, 40, 133,
    134, 168, 169, 245, 275, 277
Wicker, Tom, 27, 28, 230, 290
Wiggins, James Russell, 66, 70, 85
Wight, Charles A., 170, 171
Wilkie, Wendell, 189
Willens, Howard P., 97, 103
Williams, Kemper, 175
Williams, Langbourne, 169, 170
Williams, Sir George, 187
Williams, T. Harry, 147, 157
Williamson, Norris C., 150
Willoughby, General Charles, 195
Wingfield, Edmund Duane, 170, 172
win-win situation, 210
Wirin, Abraham, 206
Wisner, Frank, 128, 134

Wood, Edward Frederick Lindley, 193
Wood, Knight, 169
Wood, Robert E., 185
World Bank, 127, 135, 140, 228, 258, 261,
    288
world economy, 191
world peace, 186
world trade, 193
World War Two, xi, 127, 128, 129, 131,
    134, 144, 170, 178, 184, 185, 189, 191,
    193, 197, 216, 228, 250, 256, 259, 260
Wriston, Henry M., 218

Y

Young Men's Christian Associations
    (Y.M.C.A.), 182, 281
Young, Ruth Forbes Paine, 177, 182, 183,
    281, 284

Z

Zapruder film, 11, 120, 163, 177, 245
Zapruder, Abraham, 9, 11 120
Zemurray, Sam, 149, 151, 164, 165, 168,
    176
Zetzmann, William, 167, 168
Zinsser, John S., 127